BOICHI

Nothing makes me happier than the rough drafts I receive from Inagaki Sensei each week. Getting to draw all these nature scenes is such a joy.

Every week I think about the giant trees, vines and mosses. I think about Senku, living amongst all that. He's a man striking out on his own in the grandeur of this world. As someone trying to make his way in the big bad world of Japanese manga, I have an inkling of what he must be going through.

Senku!! Life is all about that trade-off! Loneliness for grandeur!

RIICHIRO INAGAKI

A writer is different than a mangaka in that he or she has no staff. The stalwart author sits silently in the office, always toiling alone.

How lonely! Solo work all day every day would get lonely as heck!

Working themselves to the bone just like Senku, alone in the world... If it ever comes to that for me, I don't think I could stand it. You're one impressive guy, Senku!

Boichi is a Korean-born artist currently living and working in Japan. His previous works include *Sun-Ken Rock* and *Terra Formars Asimov*.

Riichiro Inagaki is a Japanese manga writer from Tokyo. He is the writer for the sports manga series *Eyeshield 21*, which was serialized in *Weekly Shonen Jump*.

Dr.STONE

2

SHONEN JUMP Manga Edition

Story **RIICHIRO INAGAKI**
Art **BOICHI**

Translation/**CALEB COOK**
Touch-Up Art & Lettering/**STEPHEN DUTRO**
Design/**JULIAN [JR] ROBINSON**
Editor/**JOHN BAE**
Science Consultant/**KURARE**

Consulted Works:
• Asari, Yoshito, *Uchu e Ikitakute Ekitainenryo Rocket wo DIY Shite Mita (Gakken Rigaku Sensho), Gakken Plus*, 2013
• Dartnell, Lewis, *The Knowledge: How to Rebuild Civilization in the Aftermath of a Cataclysm*, translated by Erika Togo, Kawade Shobo Shinsha, 2015
• Davies, Barry, *The Complete SAS Survival Manual*, translated by Yoshito Takigawa, Toyo Shorin, 2001
• Kazama, Rinpei, *Shinboken Techo (Definitive Edition)*, Shufu to Seikatsu Sha, 2016
• McNab, Chris, *Special Forces Survival Guide*, translated by Atsuko Sumi, Hara Shobo, 2016
• Olsen, Larry Dean, *Outdoor Survival Skills*, translated by Katsuji Tani, A&F, 2014
• Weisman, Alan, *The World Without Us*, translated by Shinobu Onizawa, Hayakawa Publishing, 2009
• Wiseman, John, *SAS Survival Handbook, Revised Edition*, translated by Kazuhiro Takahashi and Hitoshi Tomokiyo, Namiki Shobo, 2009

Dr. STONE © 2017 by Riichiro Inagaki, Boichi
All rights reserved.
First published in Japan in 2017 by SHUEISHA Inc., Tokyo.
English translation rights arranged by SHUEISHA Inc.

Printed in the U.S.A.

Published by VIZ Media, LLC
P.O. Box 77010
San Francisco, CA 94107

10 9 8 7 6 5 4 3 2 1
First printing, November 2018

viz.com shonenjump.com

PARENTAL ADVISORY
DR. STONE is rated T for Teen and is
recommended for ages 13 and up. This
volume contains fantasy violence.

Dr.STONE

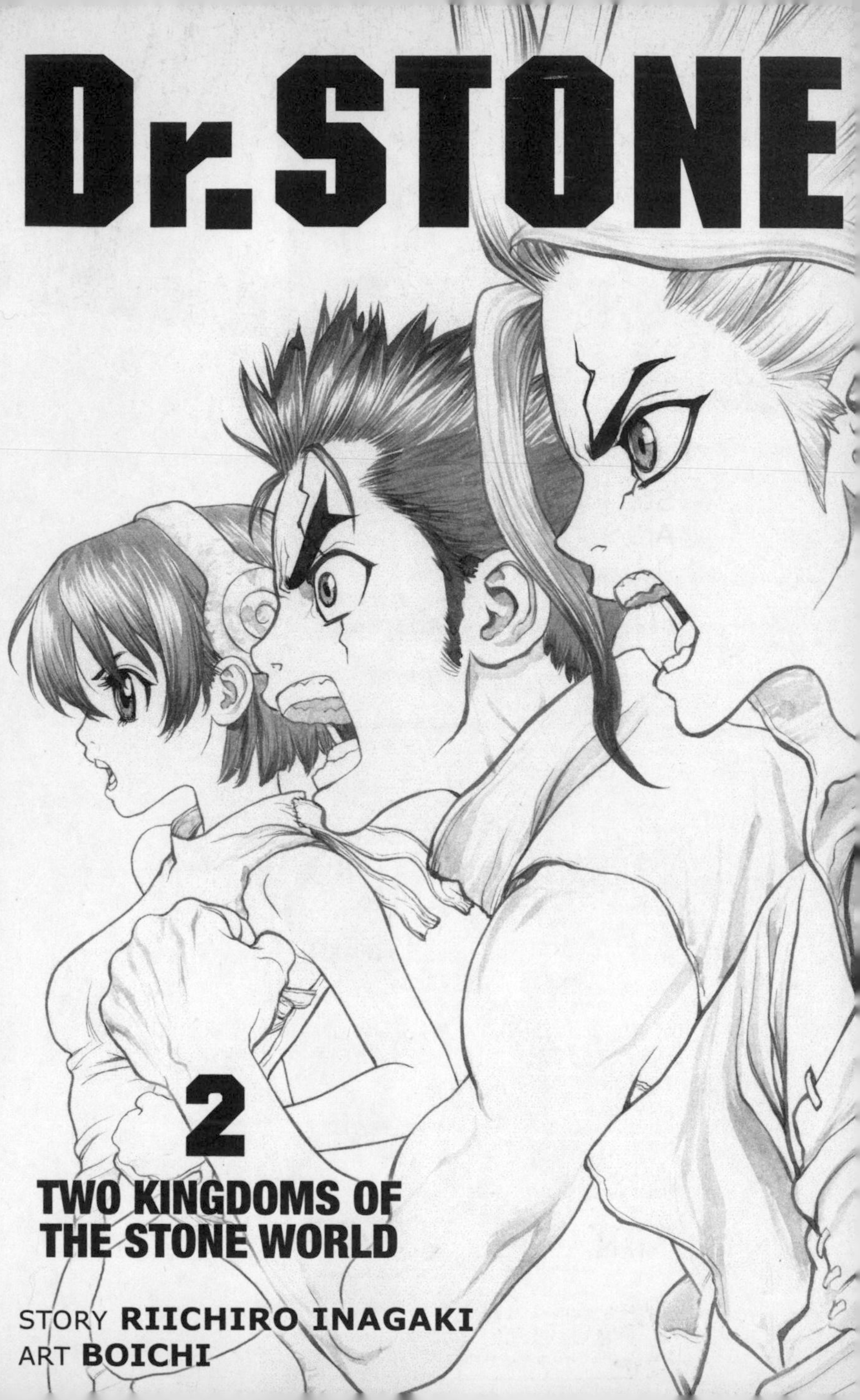

2

TWO KINGDOMS OF THE STONE WORLD

STORY **RIICHIRO INAGAKI**
ART **BOICHI**

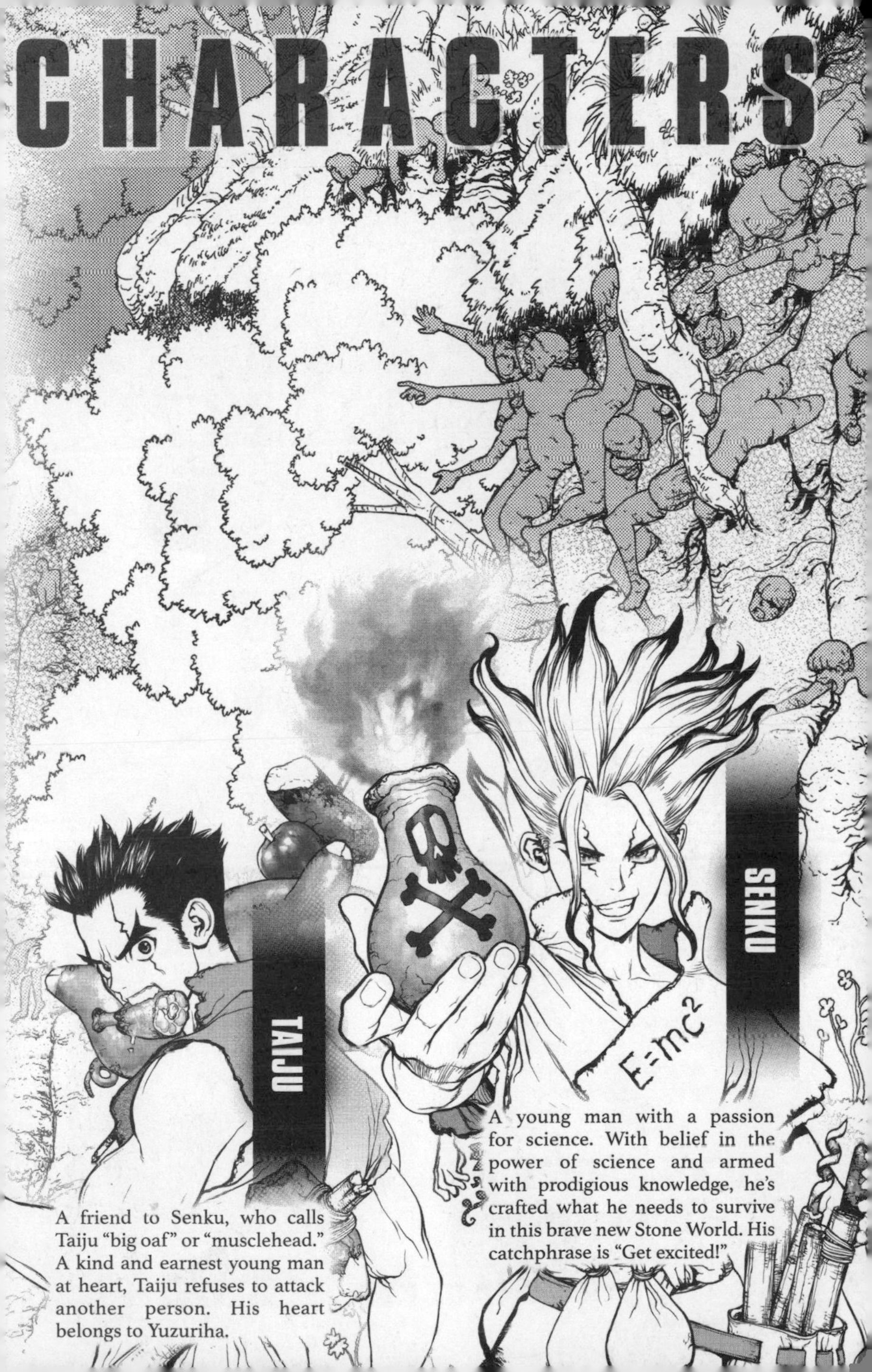
CHARACTERS
SENKU
E=mc²
A young man with a passion for science. With belief in the power of science and armed with prodigious knowledge, he's crafted what he needs to survive in this brave new Stone World. His catchphrase is "Get excited!"
TAIJU
A friend to Senku, who calls Taiju "big oaf" or "musclehead." A kind and earnest young man at heart, Taiju refuses to attack another person. His heart belongs to Yuzuriha.

STORY

Every human on Earth is turned to stone by a mysterious phenomenon, including high school student Taiju. Nearly 3,700 years later, Taiju awakens and finds his friend Senku, who revived a bit earlier. Together, they vow to restore civilization!

It's been a year since Taiju freed himself from petrification, and he and Senku have finally perfected the revival formula! With this potion, they manage to revive a battle-ready ally named Tsukasa. However, their new friend has other plans in mind and starts smashing petrified people in an effort to cleanse humanity. After reviving an old classmate, Yuzuriha, our heroes have charted a course for Hakone, where they hope to make the one thing that might possibly stop Tsukasa—gunpowder!

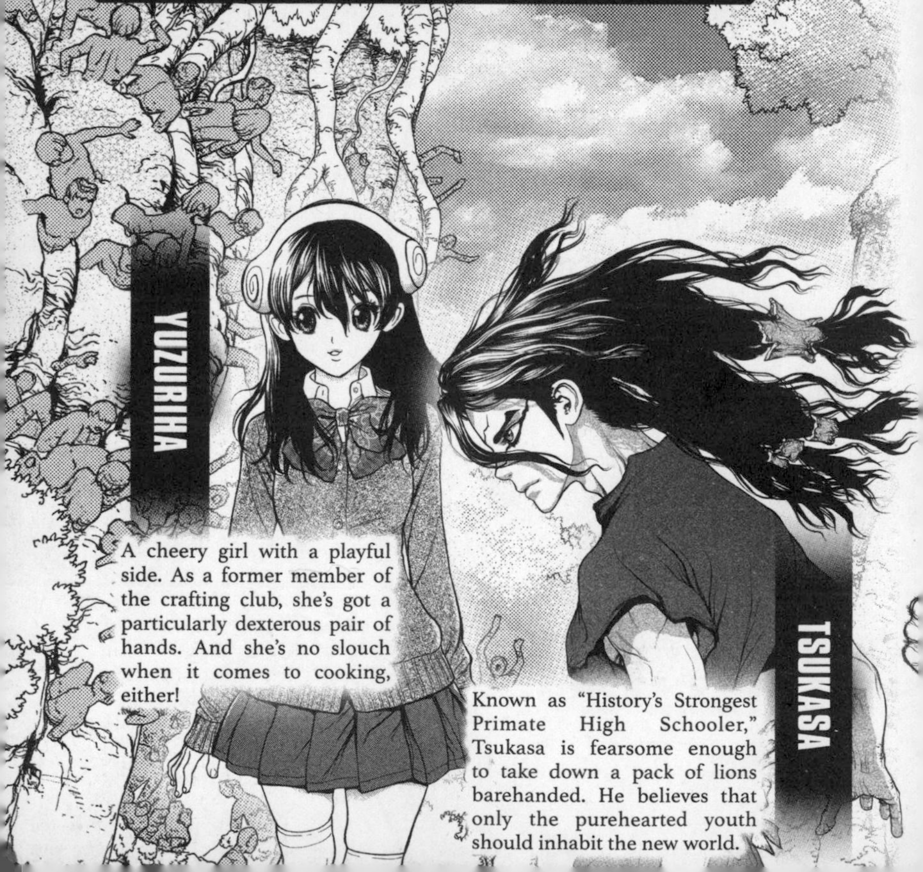
YUZURIHA
A cheery girl with a playful side. As a former member of the crafting club, she's got a particularly dexterous pair of hands. And she's no slouch when it comes to cooking, either!
TSUKASA
Known as "History's Strongest Primate High Schooler," Tsukasa is fearsome enough to take down a pack of lions barehanded. He believes that only the purehearted youth should inhabit the new world.

CONTENTS

2
WO KINGDOMS OF
THE STONE WORLD

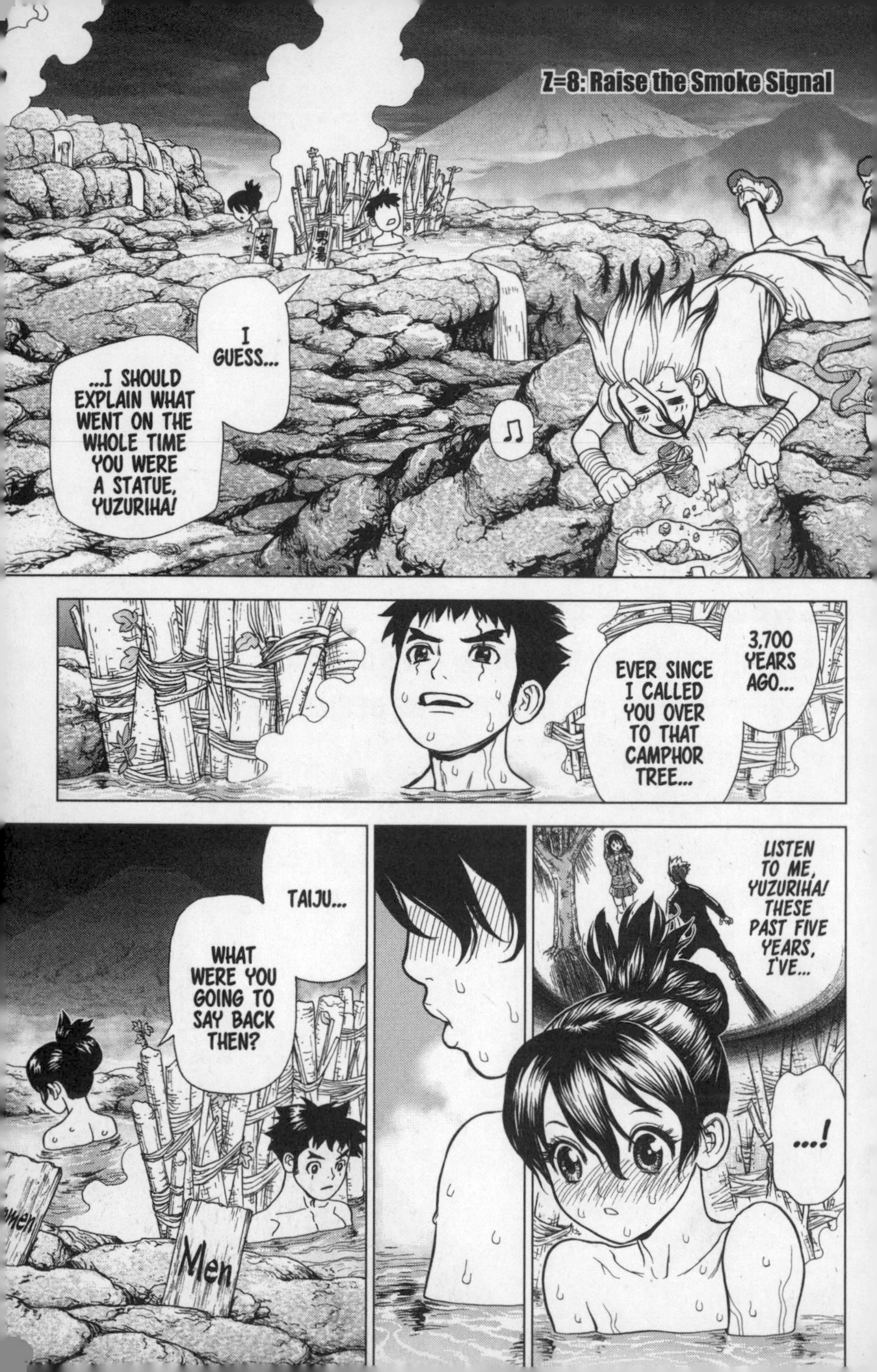
Z=8: Raise the Smoke Signal
♫
I GUESS...
...I SHOULD EXPLAIN WHAT WENT ON THE WHOLE TIME YOU WERE A STATUE, YUZURIHA!
3,700 YEARS AGO...
EVER SINCE I CALLED YOU OVER TO THAT CAMPHOR TREE...
LISTEN TO ME, YUZURIHA! THESE PAST FIVE YEARS, I'VE...
...!
TAIJU...
WHAT WERE YOU GOING TO SAY BACK THEN?
Men

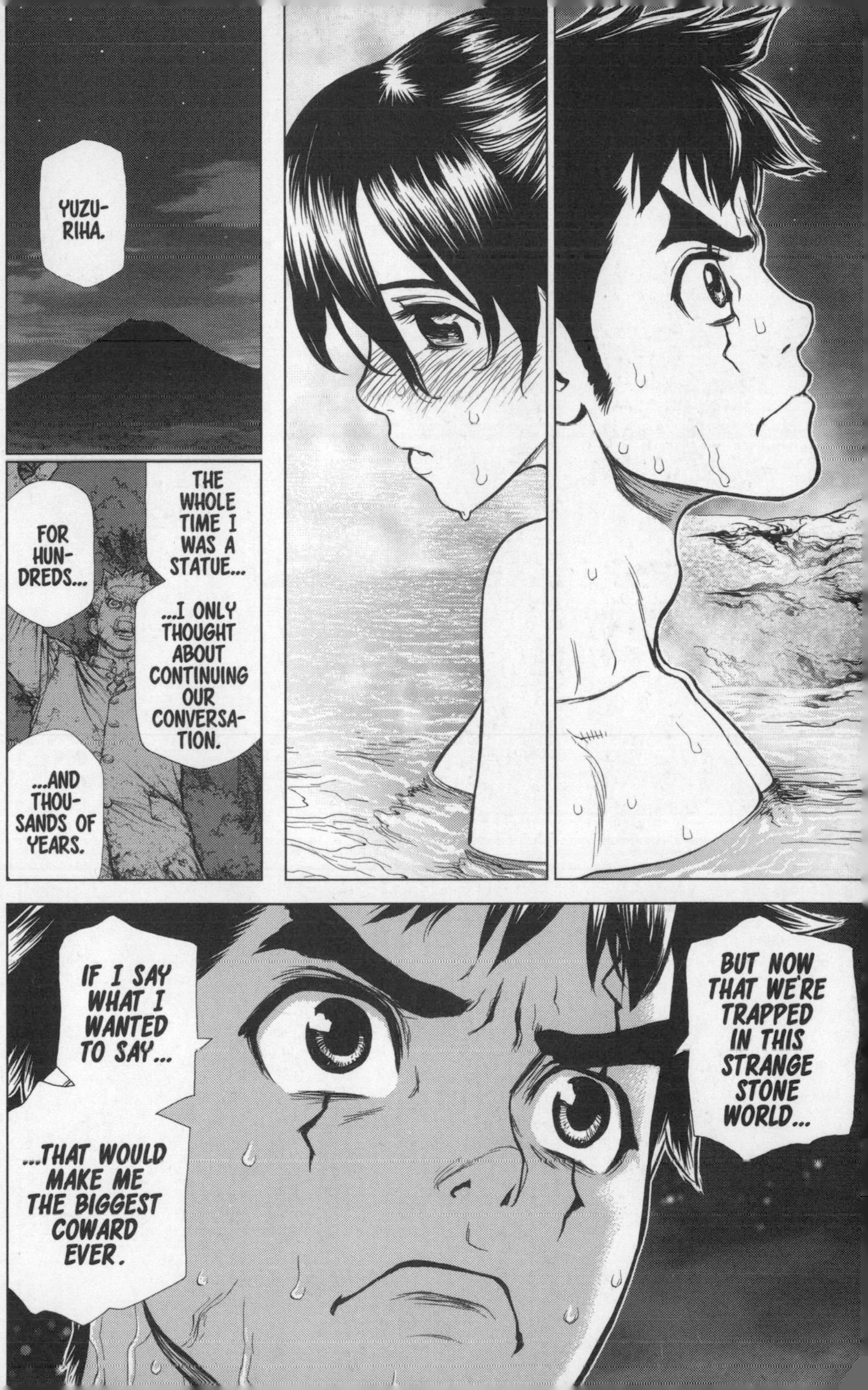
YUZU-RIHA.
THE WHOLE TIME I WAS A STATUE...
FOR HUNDREDS...
...AND THOUSANDS OF YEARS.
...I ONLY THOUGHT ABOUT CONTINUING OUR CONVERSATION.
BUT NOW THAT WE'RE TRAPPED IN THIS STRANGE STONE WORLD...
IF I SAY WHAT I WANTED TO SAY...
...THAT WOULD MAKE ME THE BIGGEST COWARD EVER.

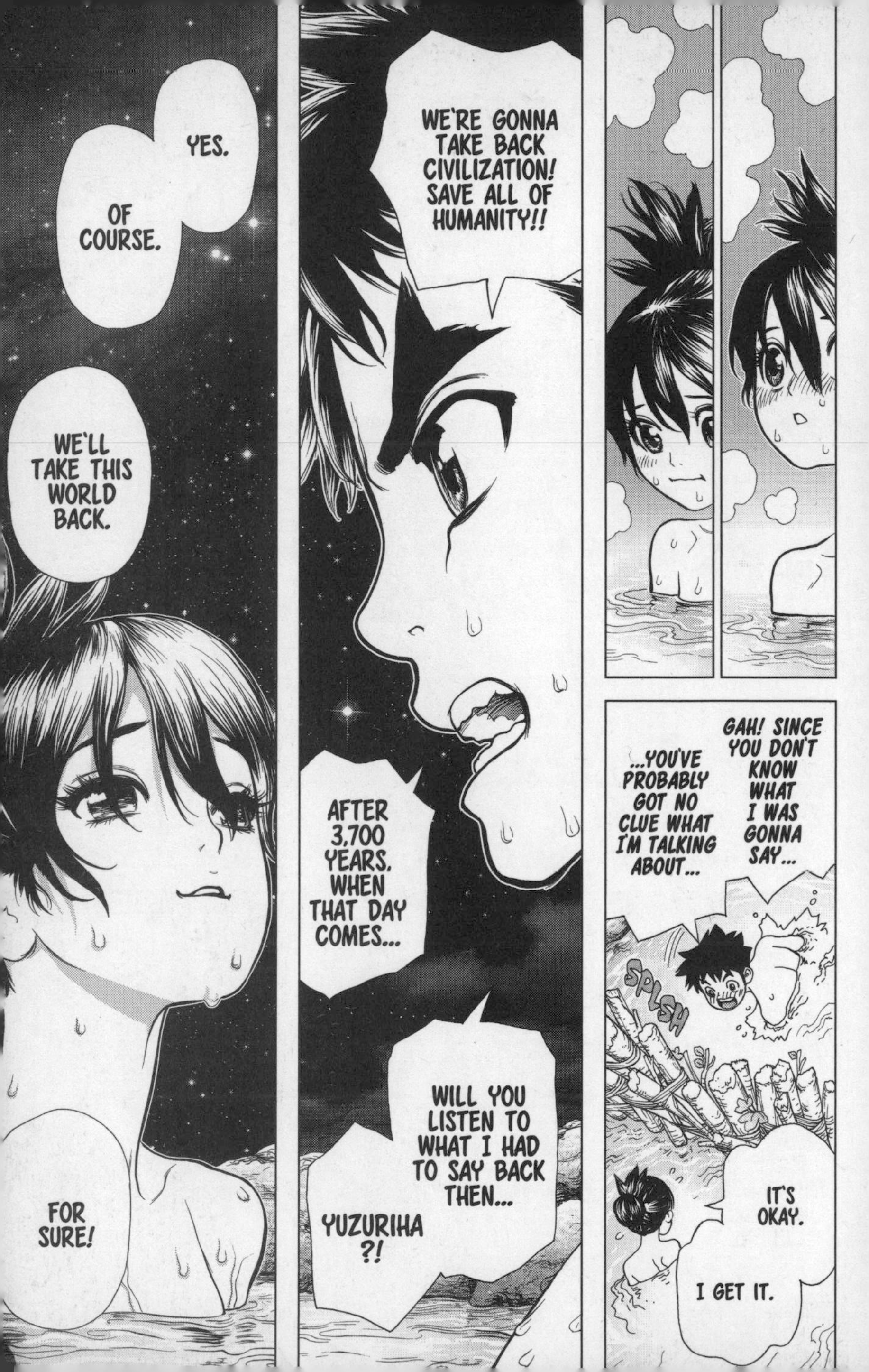
GAH! SINCE YOU DON'T KNOW WHAT I WAS GONNA SAY...
...YOU'VE PROBABLY GOT NO CLUE WHAT I'M TALKING ABOUT...
SPLSH
IT'S OKAY.
I GET IT.
WE'RE GONNA TAKE BACK CIVILIZATION! SAVE ALL OF HUMANITY!!
AFTER 3,700 YEARS. WHEN THAT DAY COMES...
WILL YOU LISTEN TO WHAT I HAD TO SAY BACK THEN...
YUZURIHA ?!
YES.
OF COURSE.
WE'LL TAKE THIS WORLD BACK.
FOR SURE!

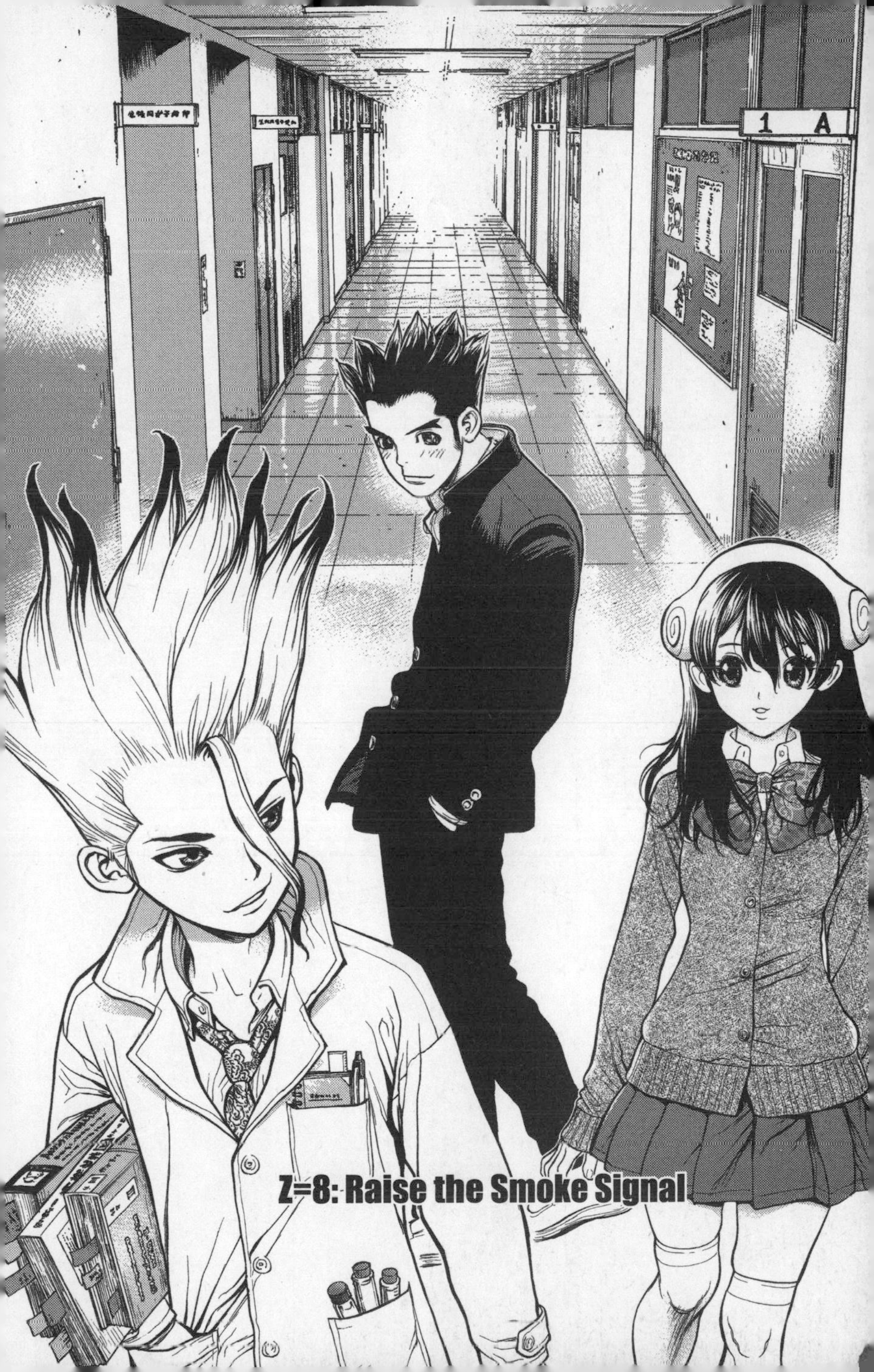
1 A
Z=8: Raise the Smoke Signal

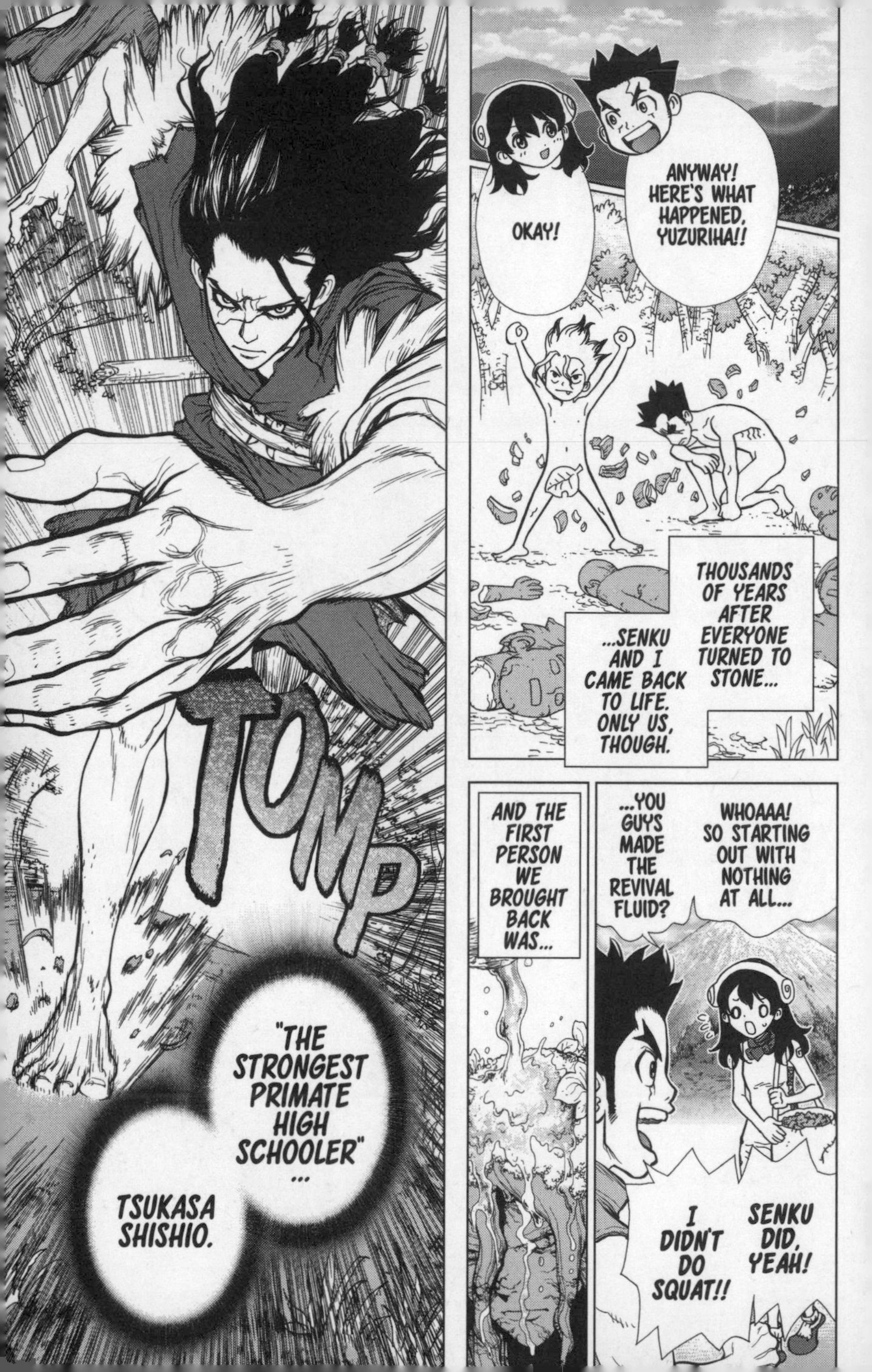
ANYWAY! HERE'S WHAT HAPPENED, YUZURIHA!!
OKAY!
THOUSANDS OF YEARS AFTER EVERYONE TURNED TO STONE...
...SENKU AND I CAME BACK TO LIFE. ONLY US, THOUGH.
WHOAAA! SO STARTING OUT WITH NOTHING AT ALL...
...YOU GUYS MADE THE REVIVAL FLUID?
SENKU DID, YEAH!
I DIDN'T DO SQUAT!!
AND THE FIRST PERSON WE BROUGHT BACK WAS...
TOMP
"THE STRONGEST PRIMATE HIGH SCHOOLER"...
TSUKASA SHISHIO.

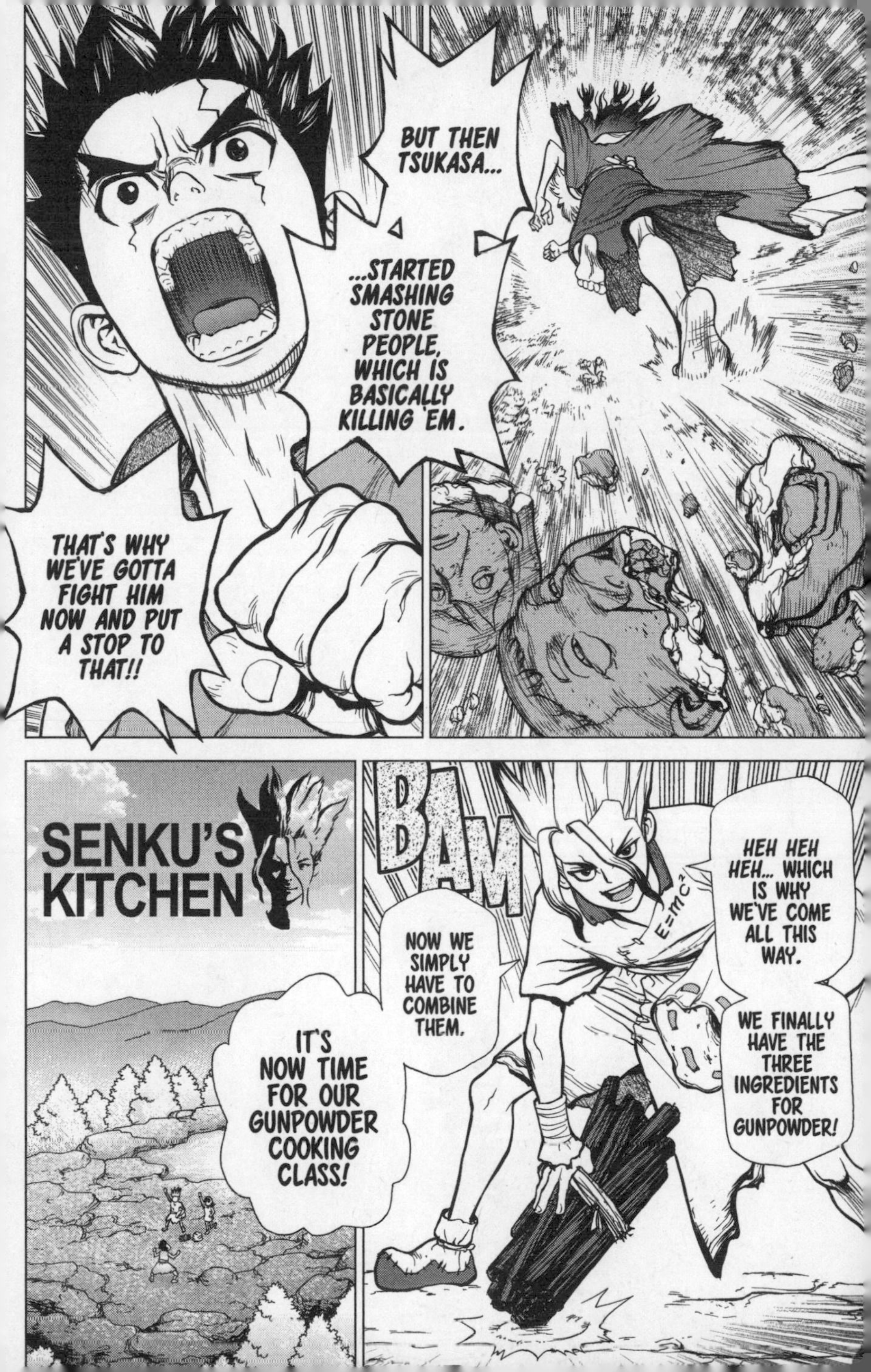
BUT THEN TSUKASA...
...STARTED SMASHING STONE PEOPLE, WHICH IS BASICALLY KILLING 'EM.
THAT'S WHY WE'VE GOTTA FIGHT HIM NOW AND PUT A STOP TO THAT!!
BAM
$E=MC^2$
HEH HEH HEH... WHICH IS WHY WE'VE COME ALL THIS WAY.
WE FINALLY HAVE THE THREE INGREDIENTS FOR GUNPOWDER!
NOW WE SIMPLY HAVE TO COMBINE THEM.
IT'S NOW TIME FOR OUR GUNPOWDER COOKING CLASS!
SENKU'S KITCHEN

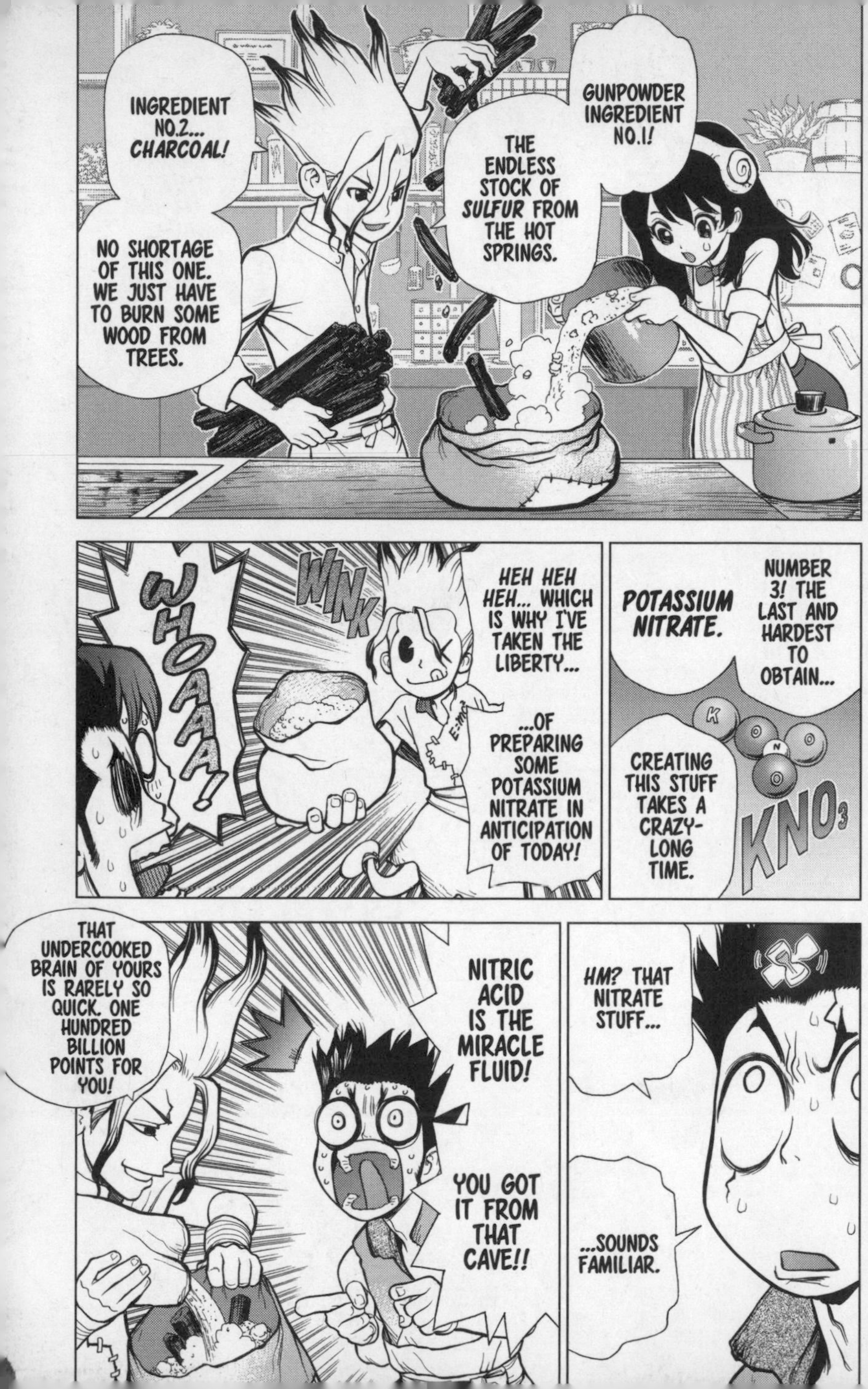
GUNPOWDER INGREDIENT NO.1!
THE ENDLESS STOCK OF *SULFUR* FROM THE HOT SPRINGS.
INGREDIENT NO.2... *CHARCOAL!*
NO SHORTAGE OF THIS ONE. WE JUST HAVE TO BURN SOME WOOD FROM TREES.
NUMBER 3! THE LAST AND HARDEST TO OBTAIN...
POTASSIUM NITRATE.
CREATING THIS STUFF TAKES A CRAZY-LONG TIME.
KNO_3
WINK
HEH HEH HEH... WHICH IS WHY I'VE TAKEN THE LIBERTY...
...OF PREPARING SOME POTASSIUM NITRATE IN ANTICIPATION OF TODAY!
WHOAAAA!
HM? THAT NITRATE STUFF...
...SOUNDS FAMILIAR.
NITRIC ACID IS THE MIRACLE FLUID!
YOU GOT IT FROM THAT CAVE!!
THAT UNDERCOOKED BRAIN OF YOURS IS RARELY SO QUICK. ONE HUNDRED BILLION POINTS FOR YOU!

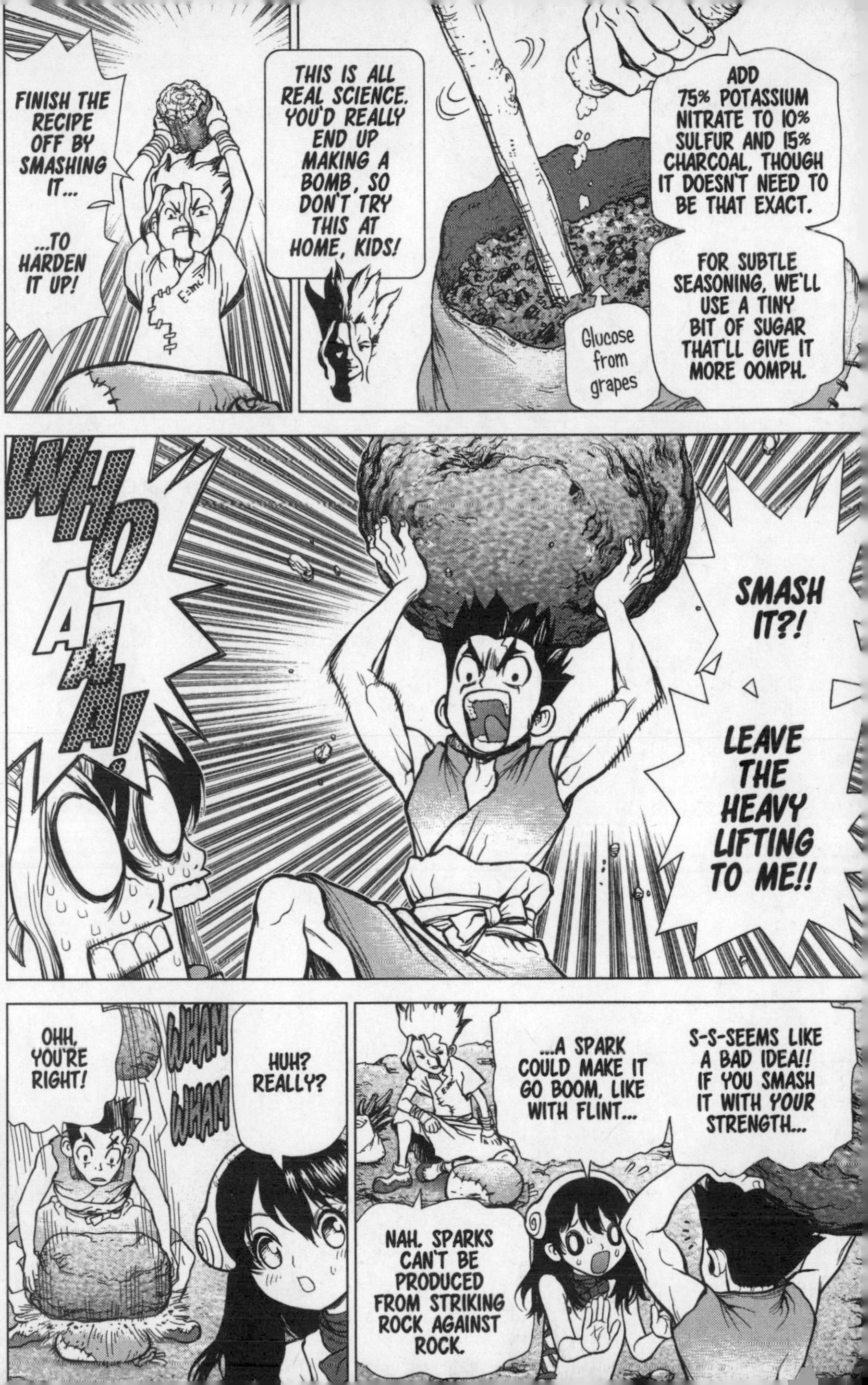
ADD 75% POTASSIUM NITRATE TO 10% SULFUR AND 15% CHARCOAL, THOUGH IT DOESN'T NEED TO BE THAT EXACT.
FOR SUBTLE SEASONING, WE'LL USE A TINY BIT OF SUGAR THAT'LL GIVE IT MORE OOMPH.
Glucose from grapes
THIS IS ALL REAL SCIENCE. YOU'D REALLY END UP MAKING A BOMB, SO DON'T TRY THIS AT HOME, KIDS!
FINISH THE RECIPE OFF BY SMASHING IT...
...TO HARDEN IT UP!
SMASH IT?!
LEAVE THE HEAVY LIFTING TO ME!!
WHOAAA!
S-S-SEEMS LIKE A BAD IDEA!! IF YOU SMASH IT WITH YOUR STRENGTH...
...A SPARK COULD MAKE IT GO BOOM, LIKE WITH FLINT...
NAH. SPARKS CAN'T BE PRODUCED FROM STRIKING ROCK AGAINST ROCK.
HUH? REALLY?
WHAM
WHAM
OHH, YOU'RE RIGHT!

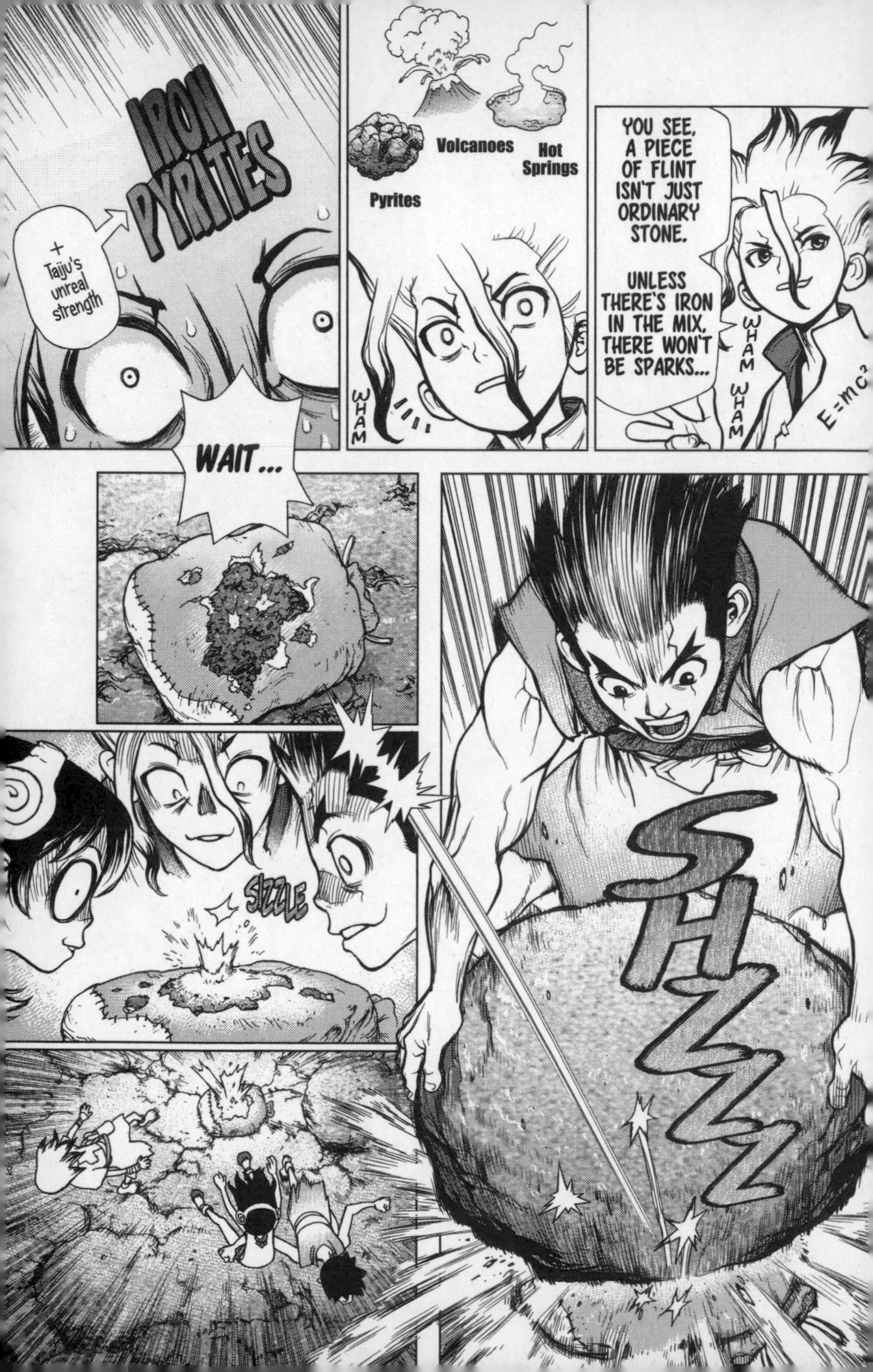

YOU SEE, A PIECE OF FLINT ISN'T JUST ORDINARY STONE.
UNLESS THERE'S IRON IN THE MIX, THERE WON'T BE SPARKS...
WHAM WHAM
E=mc²
Volcanoes
Hot Springs
Pyrites
WHAM
IRON PYRITES
+ Taiju's unreal strength
WAIT...
SHZZZ
SIZZLE

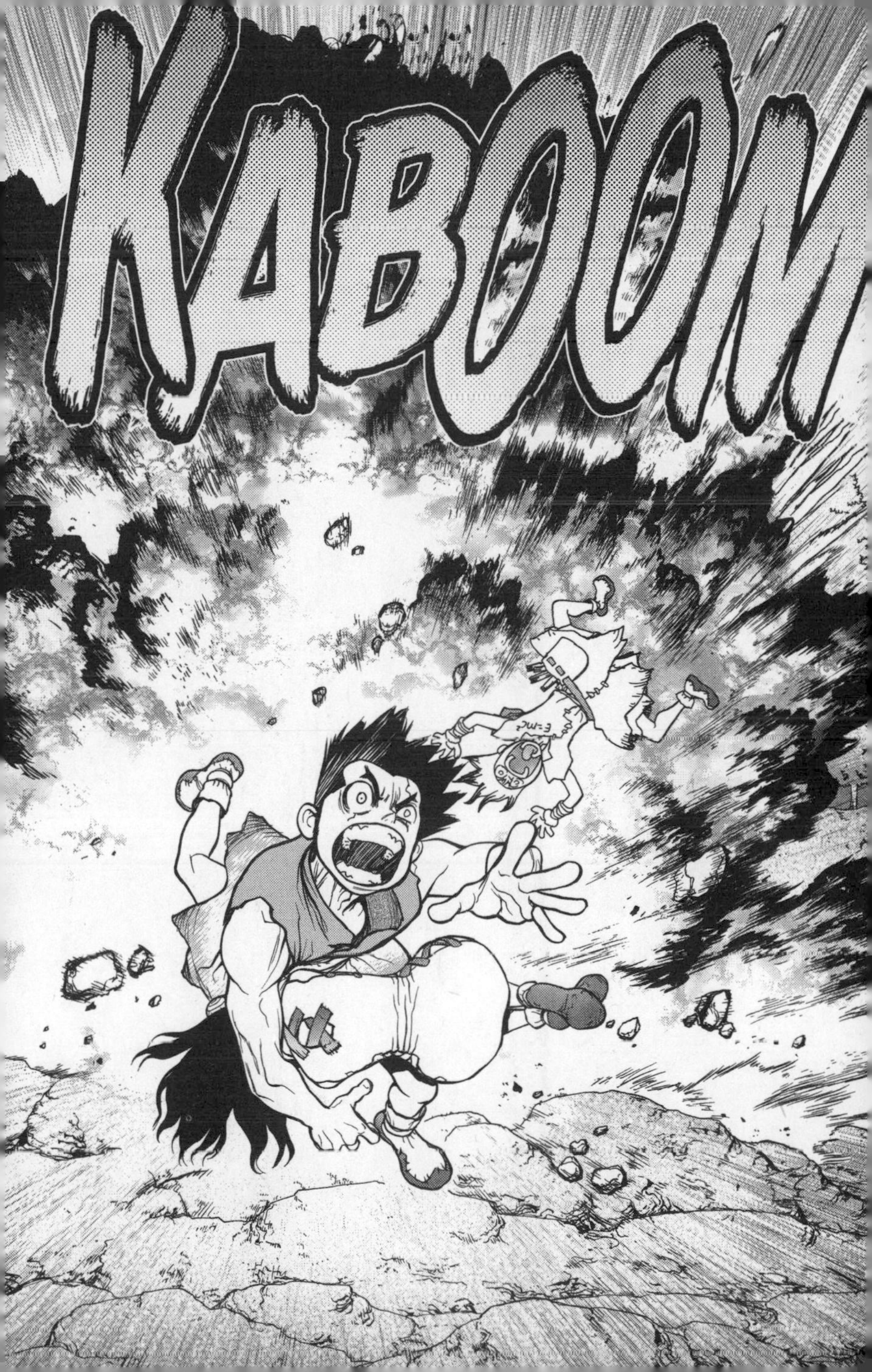
KABOOM

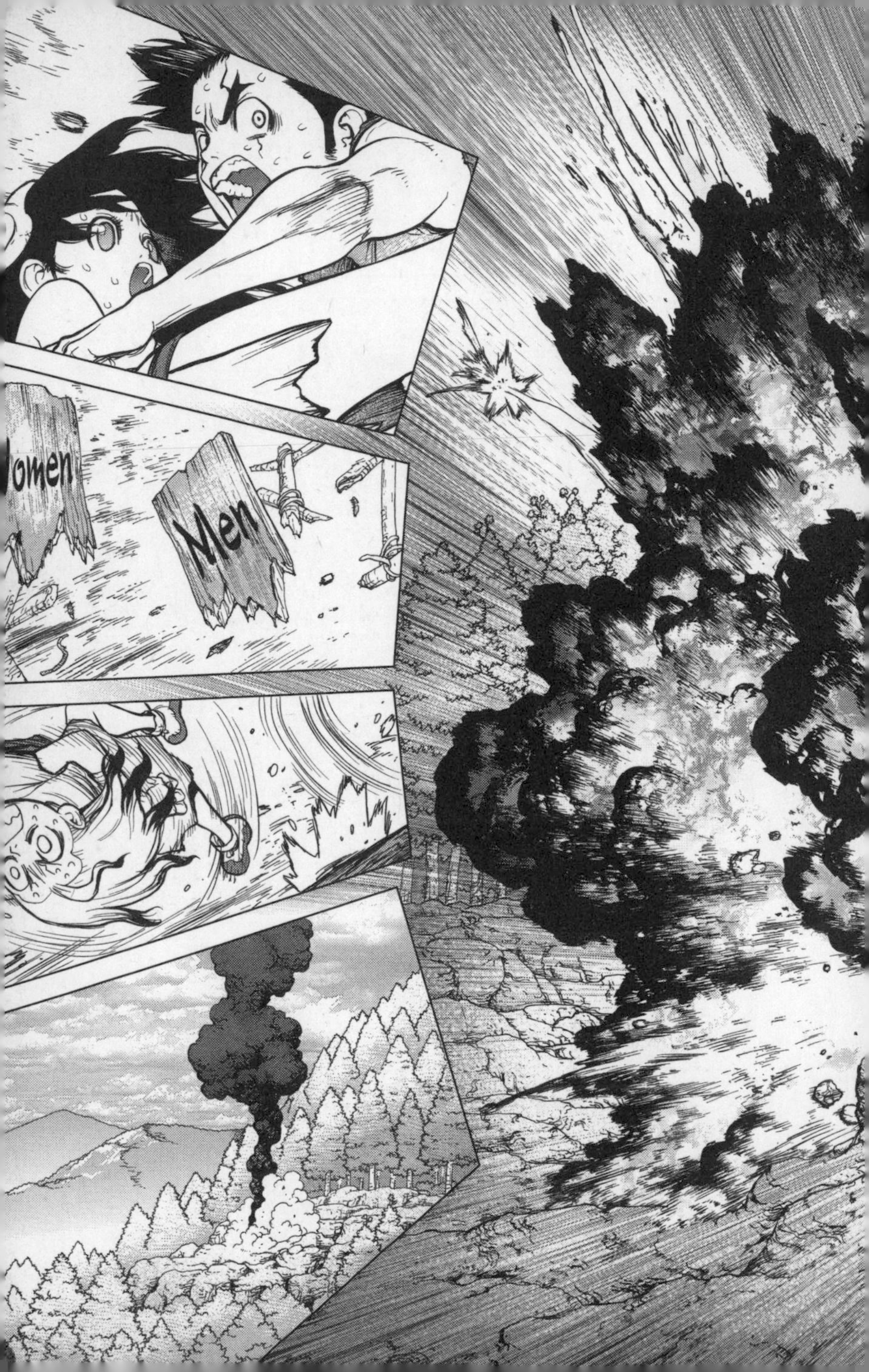
Men
omen

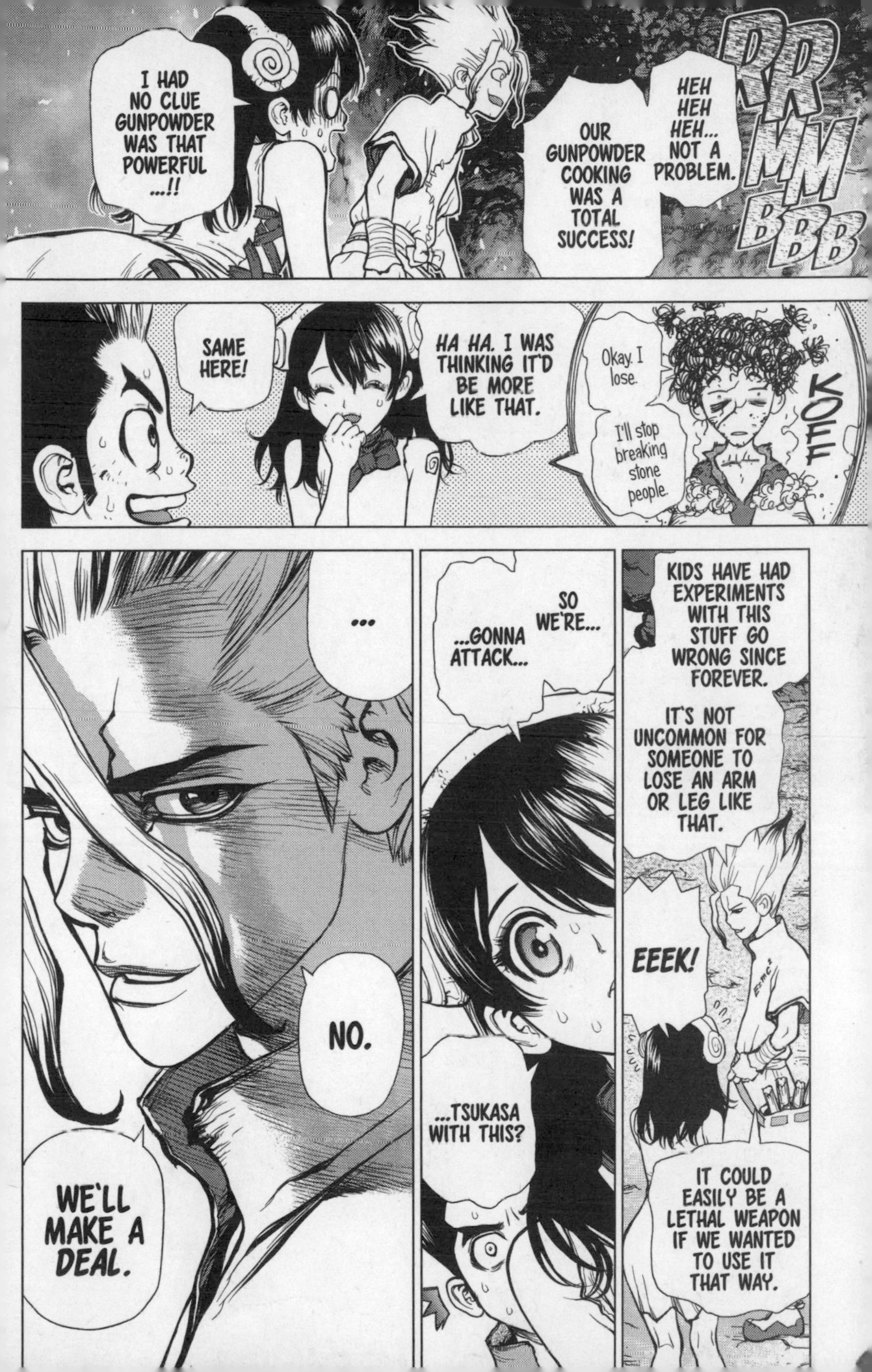
RRMMBBB
HEH HEH HEH... NOT A PROBLEM.
OUR GUNPOWDER COOKING WAS A TOTAL SUCCESS!
I HAD NO CLUE GUNPOWDER WAS THAT POWERFUL ...!!
KOFF
Okay. I lose.
I'll stop breaking stone people.
HA HA. I WAS THINKING IT'D BE MORE LIKE THAT.
SAME HERE!
KIDS HAVE HAD EXPERIMENTS WITH THIS STUFF GO WRONG SINCE FOREVER.
IT'S NOT UNCOMMON FOR SOMEONE TO LOSE AN ARM OR LEG LIKE THAT.
EEEK!
IT COULD EASILY BE A LETHAL WEAPON IF WE WANTED TO USE IT THAT WAY.
SO WE'RE...
...GONNA ATTACK...
...TSUKASA WITH THIS?
...
NO.
WE'LL MAKE A DEAL.

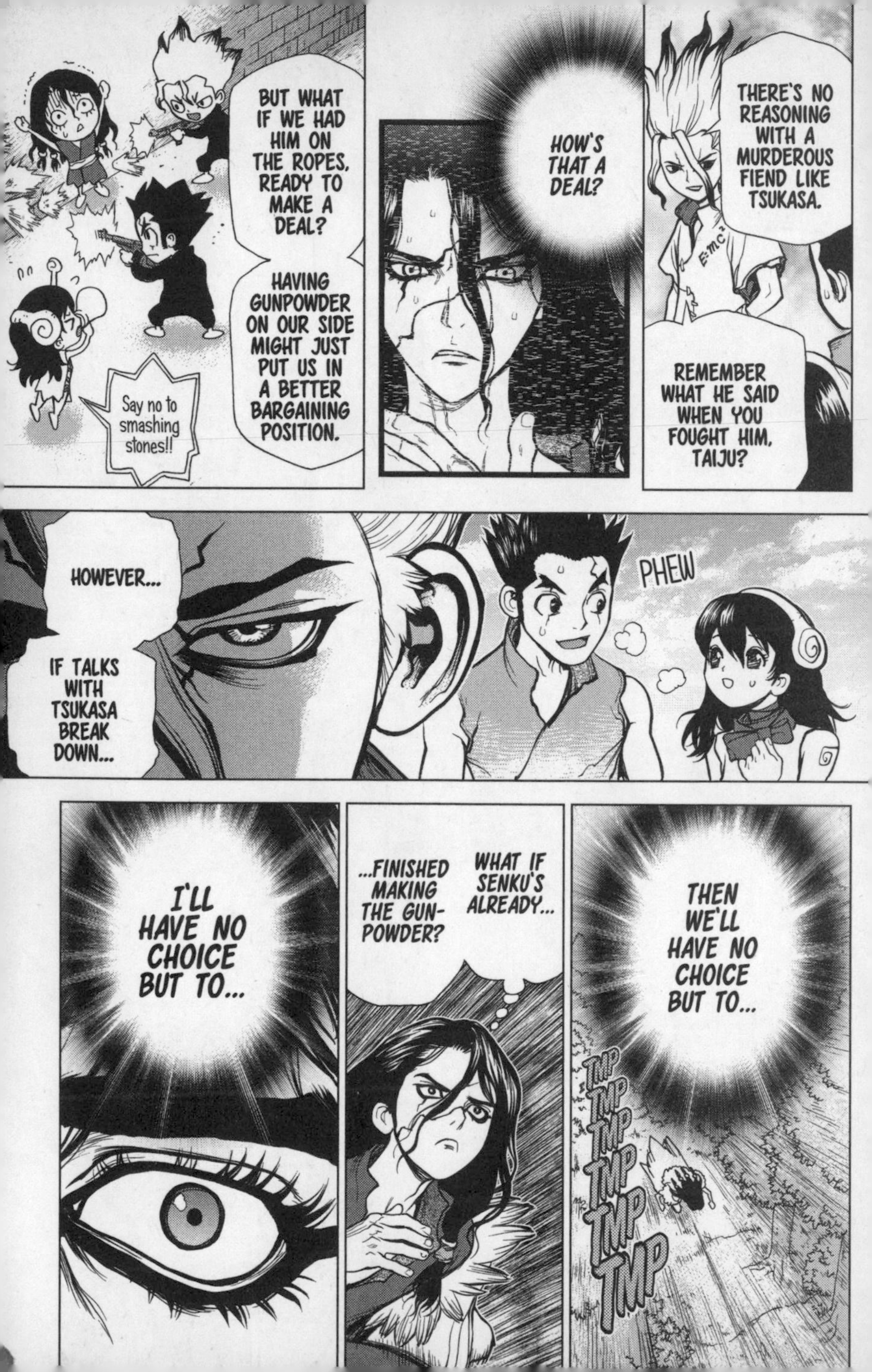
THERE'S NO REASONING WITH A MURDEROUS FIEND LIKE TSUKASA.
REMEMBER WHAT HE SAID WHEN YOU FOUGHT HIM, TAIJU?
HOW'S THAT A DEAL?
BUT WHAT IF WE HAD HIM ON THE ROPES, READY TO MAKE A DEAL?
HAVING GUNPOWDER ON OUR SIDE MIGHT JUST PUT US IN A BETTER BARGAINING POSITION.
Say no to smashing stones!!
PHEW
HOWEVER...
IF TALKS WITH TSUKASA BREAK DOWN...
THEN WE'LL HAVE NO CHOICE BUT TO...
TMP TMP TMP TMP TMP TMP TMP
WHAT IF SENKU'S ALREADY...
...FINISHED MAKING THE GUN-POWDER?
I'LL HAVE NO CHOICE BUT TO...

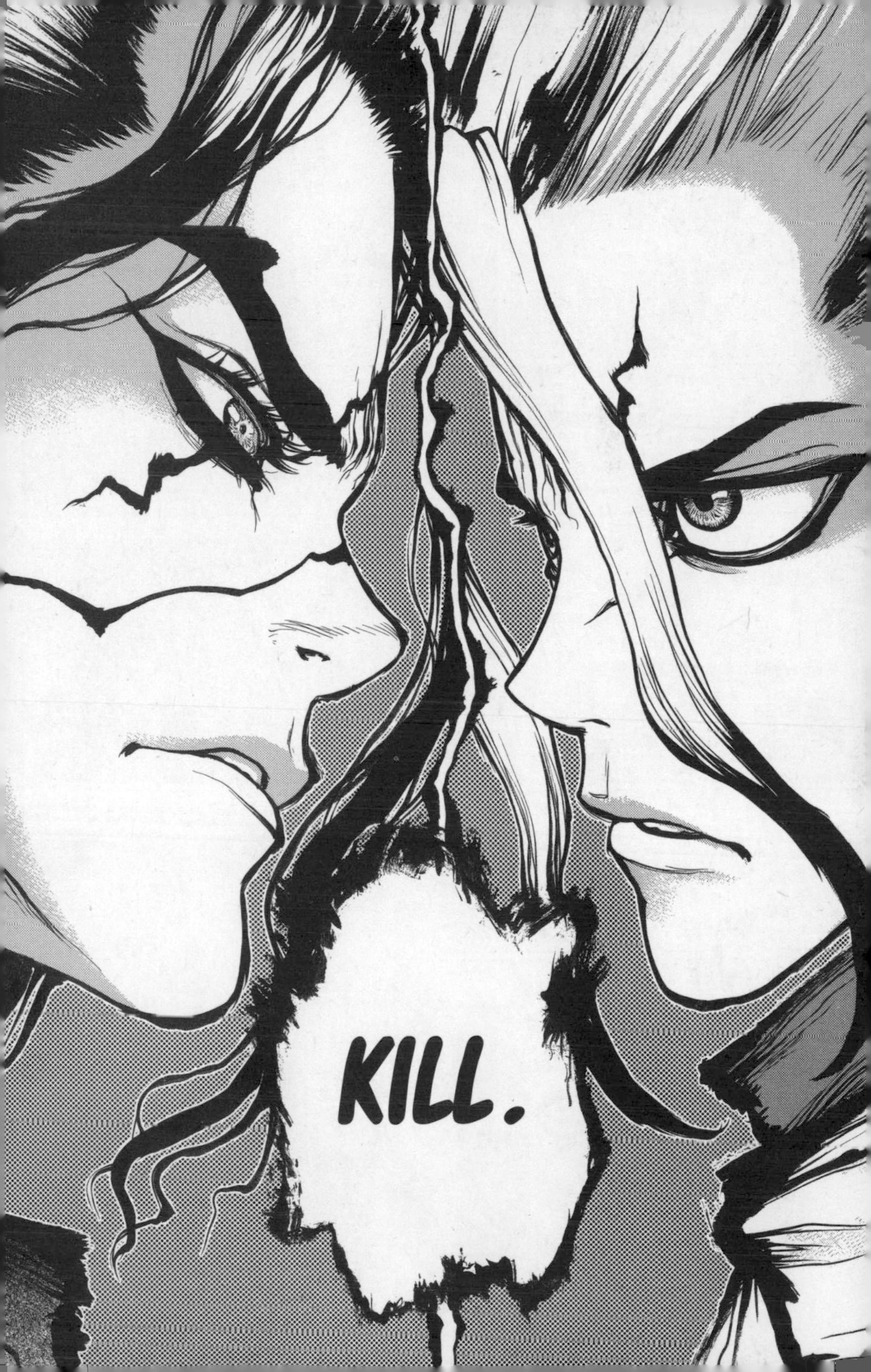
KILL.

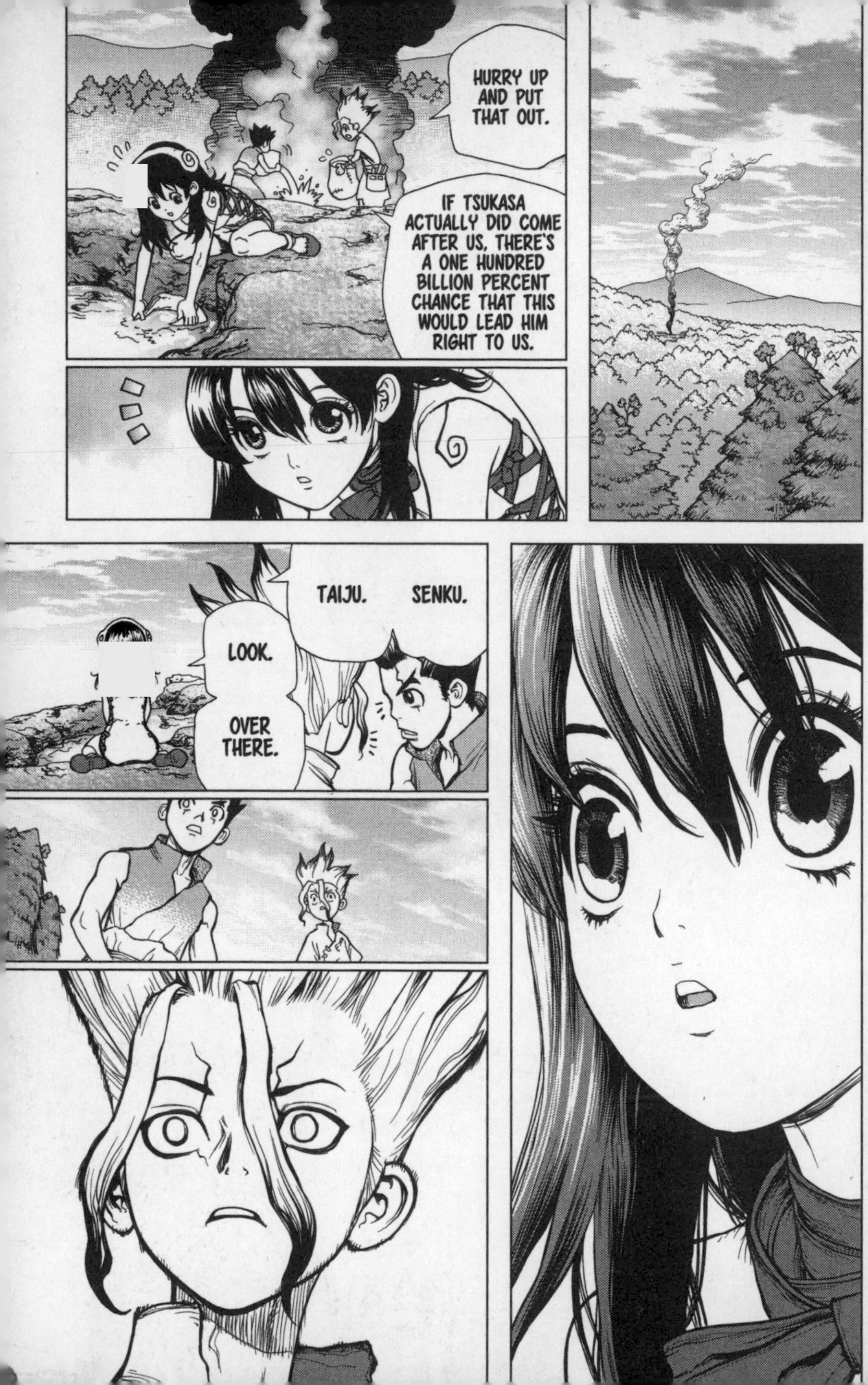
HURRY UP AND PUT THAT OUT.
IF TSUKASA ACTUALLY DID COME AFTER US, THERE'S A ONE HUNDRED BILLION PERCENT CHANCE THAT THIS WOULD LEAD HIM RIGHT TO US.
TAIJU. SENKU.
LOOK.
OVER THERE.

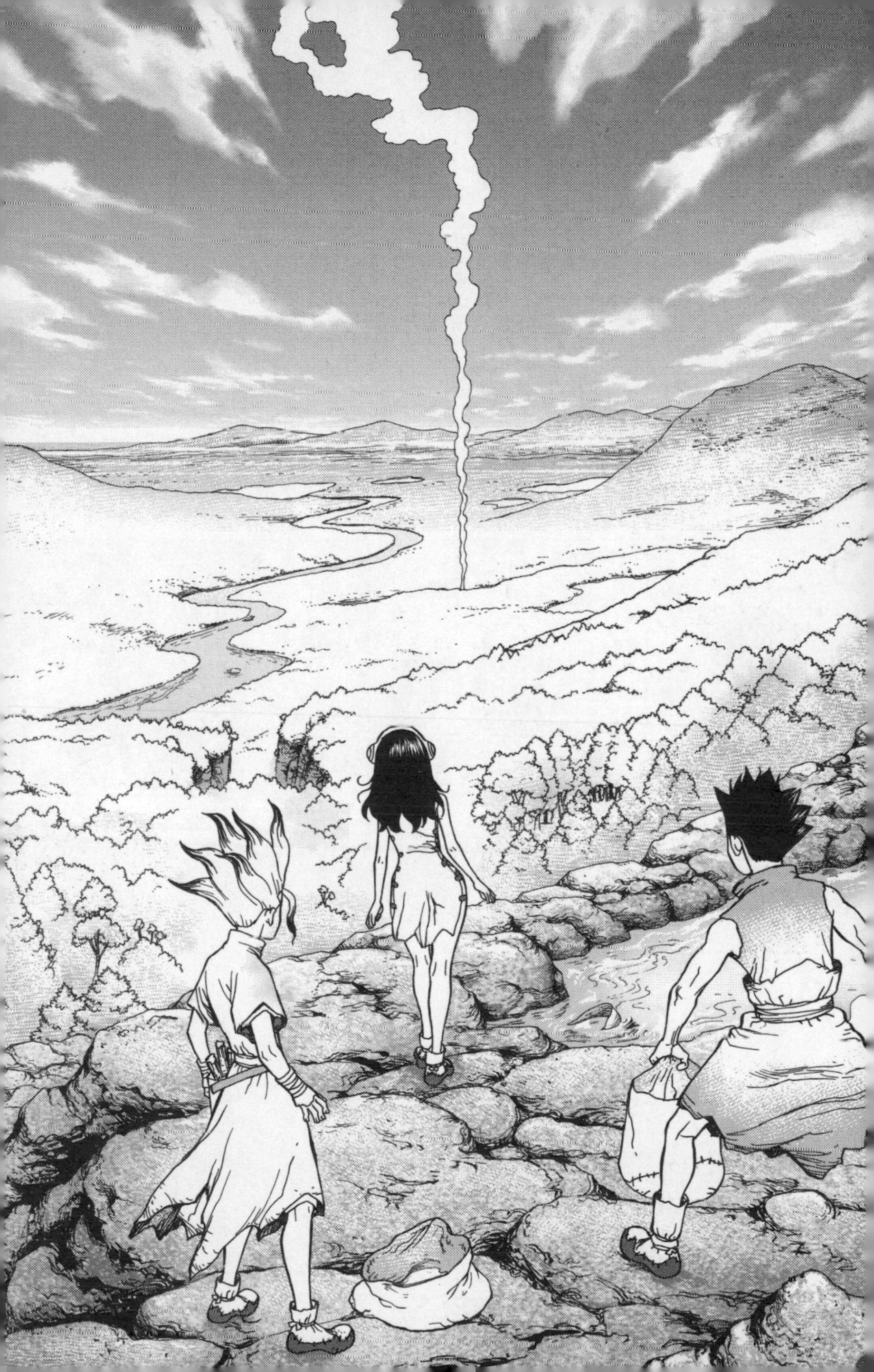

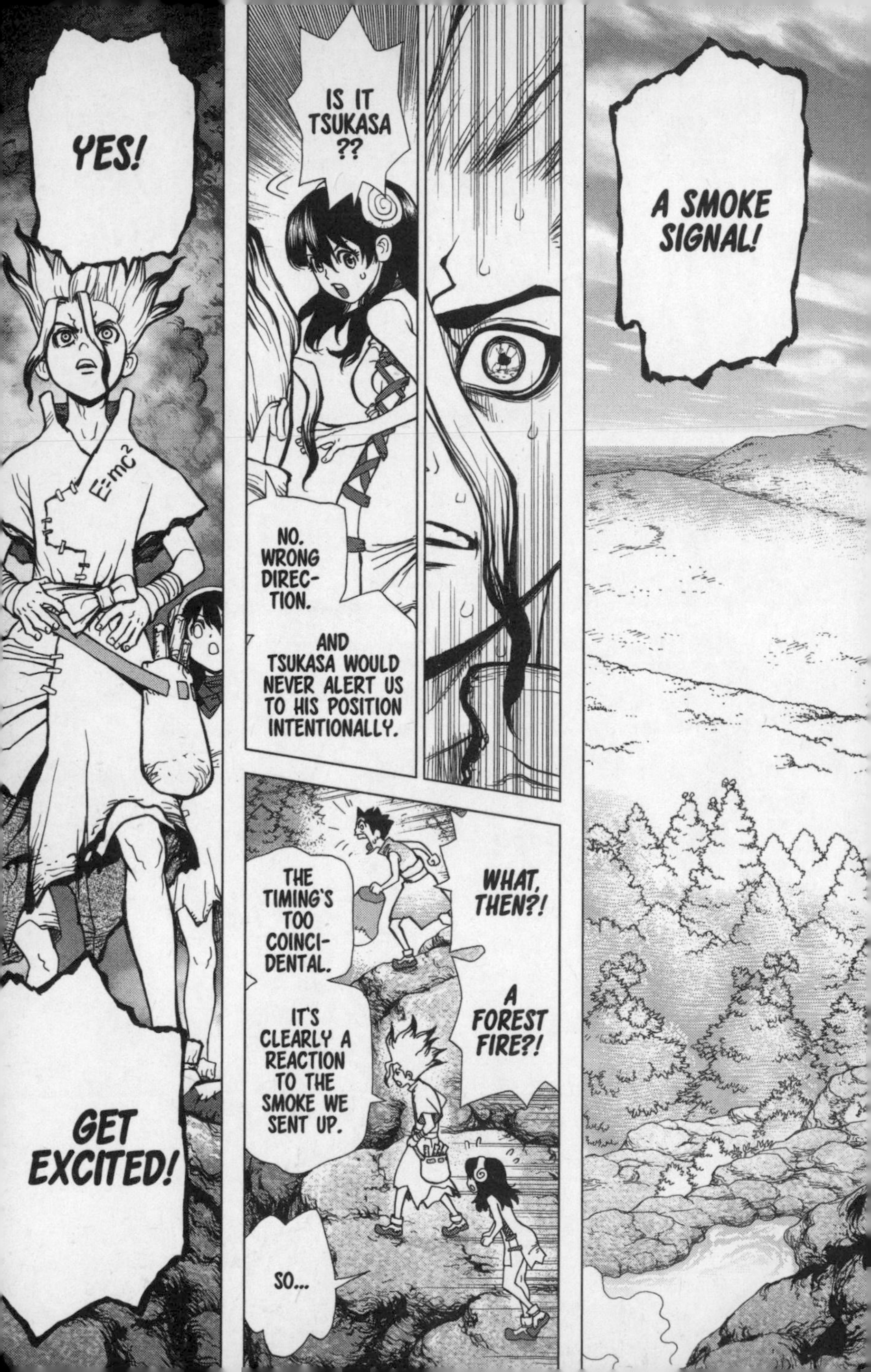
A SMOKE SIGNAL!
IS IT TSUKASA??
NO. WRONG DIRECTION.
AND TSUKASA WOULD NEVER ALERT US TO HIS POSITION INTENTIONALLY.
WHAT, THEN?!
A FOREST FIRE?!
THE TIMING'S TOO COINCIDENTAL.
IT'S CLEARLY A REACTION TO THE SMOKE WE SENT UP.
SO...
YES!
GET EXCITED!
E=mc²

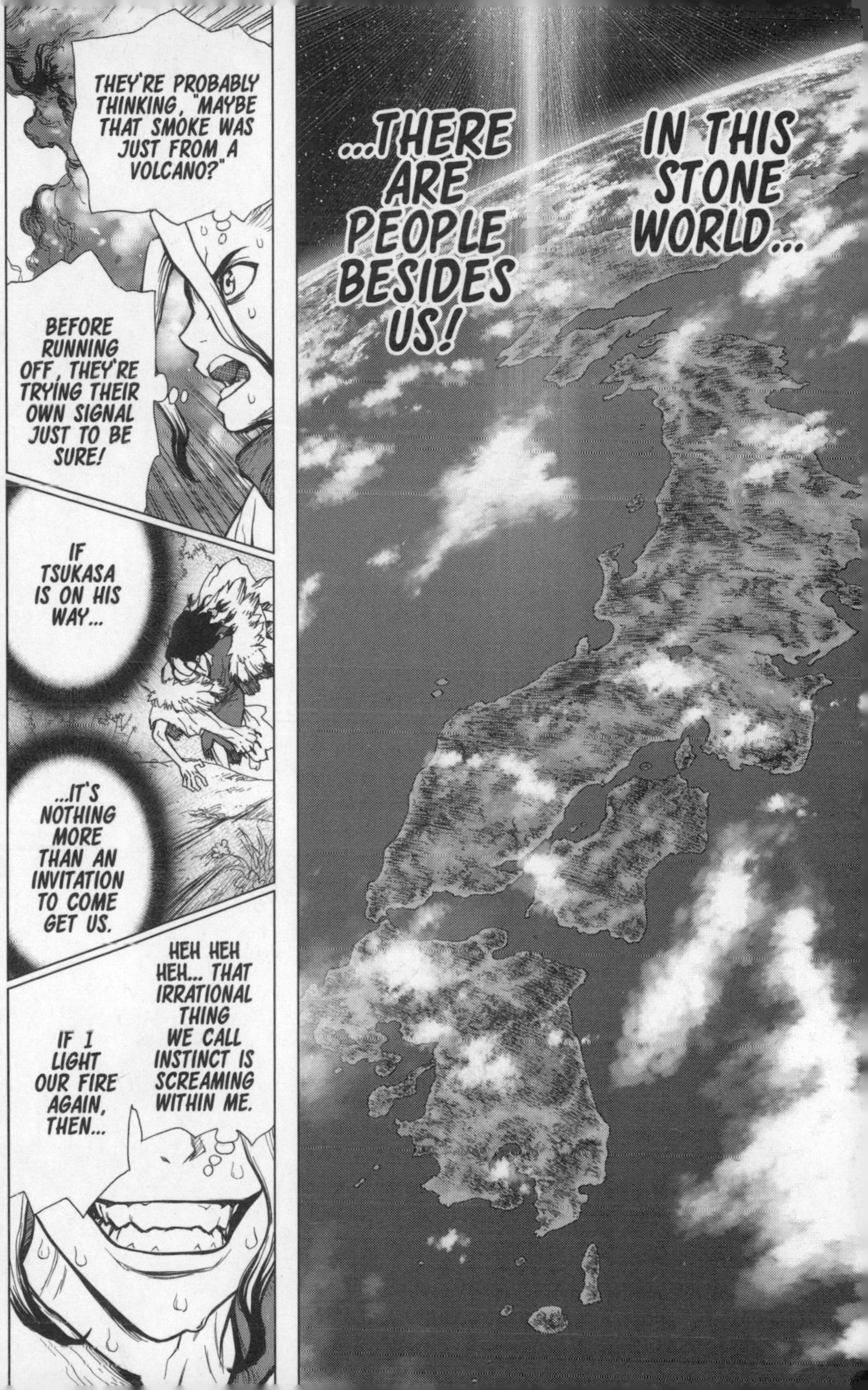
IN THIS STONE WORLD...
...THERE ARE PEOPLE BESIDES US!
THEY'RE PROBABLY THINKING, "MAYBE THAT SMOKE WAS JUST FROM A VOLCANO?"
BEFORE RUNNING OFF, THEY'RE TRYING THEIR OWN SIGNAL JUST TO BE SURE!
IF TSUKASA IS ON HIS WAY...
...IT'S NOTHING MORE THAN AN INVITATION TO COME GET US.
HEH HEH HEH... THAT IRRATIONAL THING WE CALL INSTINCT IS SCREAMING WITHIN ME.
IF I LIGHT OUR FIRE AGAIN, THEN...

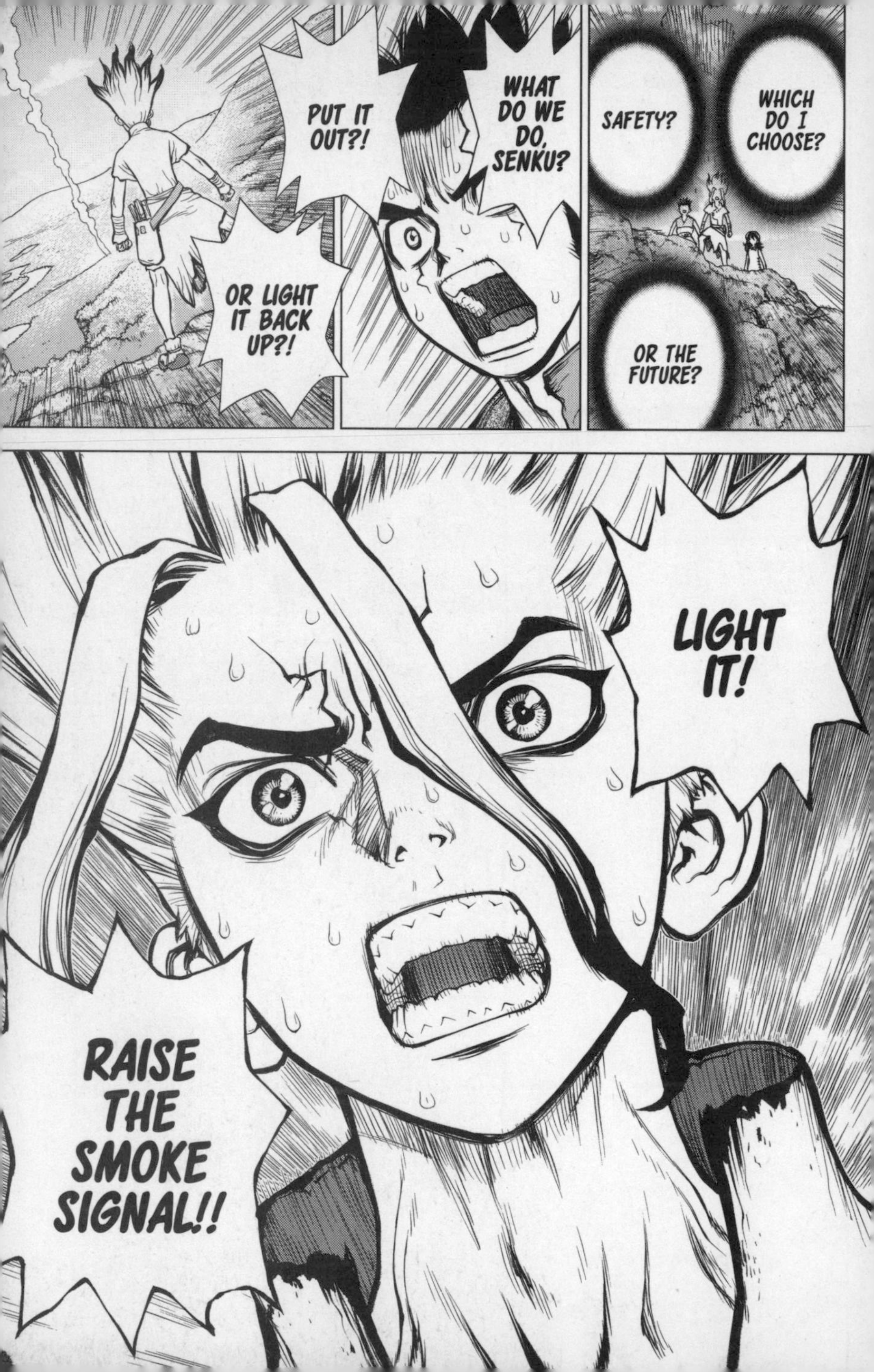
WHICH DO I CHOOSE?
SAFETY?
OR THE FUTURE?
WHAT DO WE DO, SENKU?
PUT IT OUT?!
OR LIGHT IT BACK UP?!
LIGHT IT!
RAISE THE SMOKE SIGNAL!!

Senku's Early Days

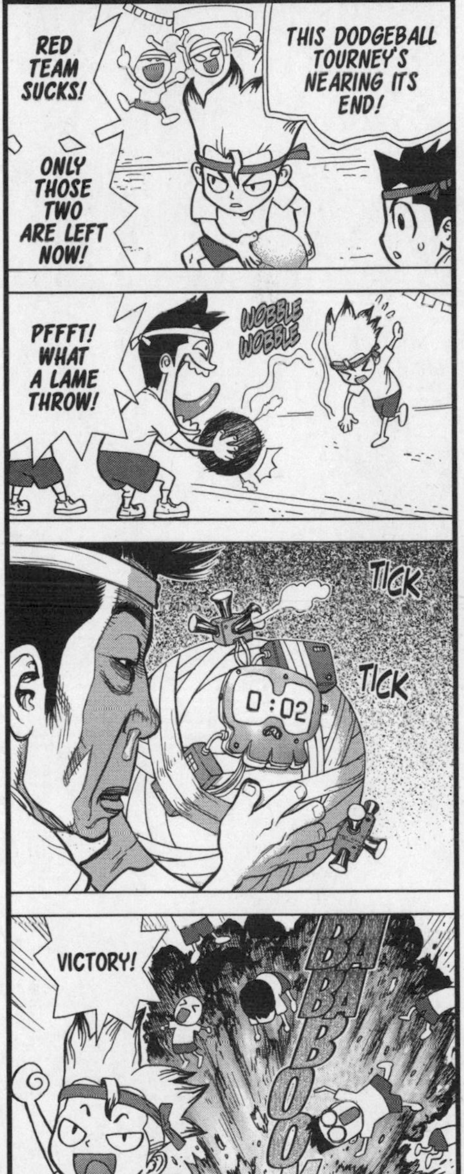

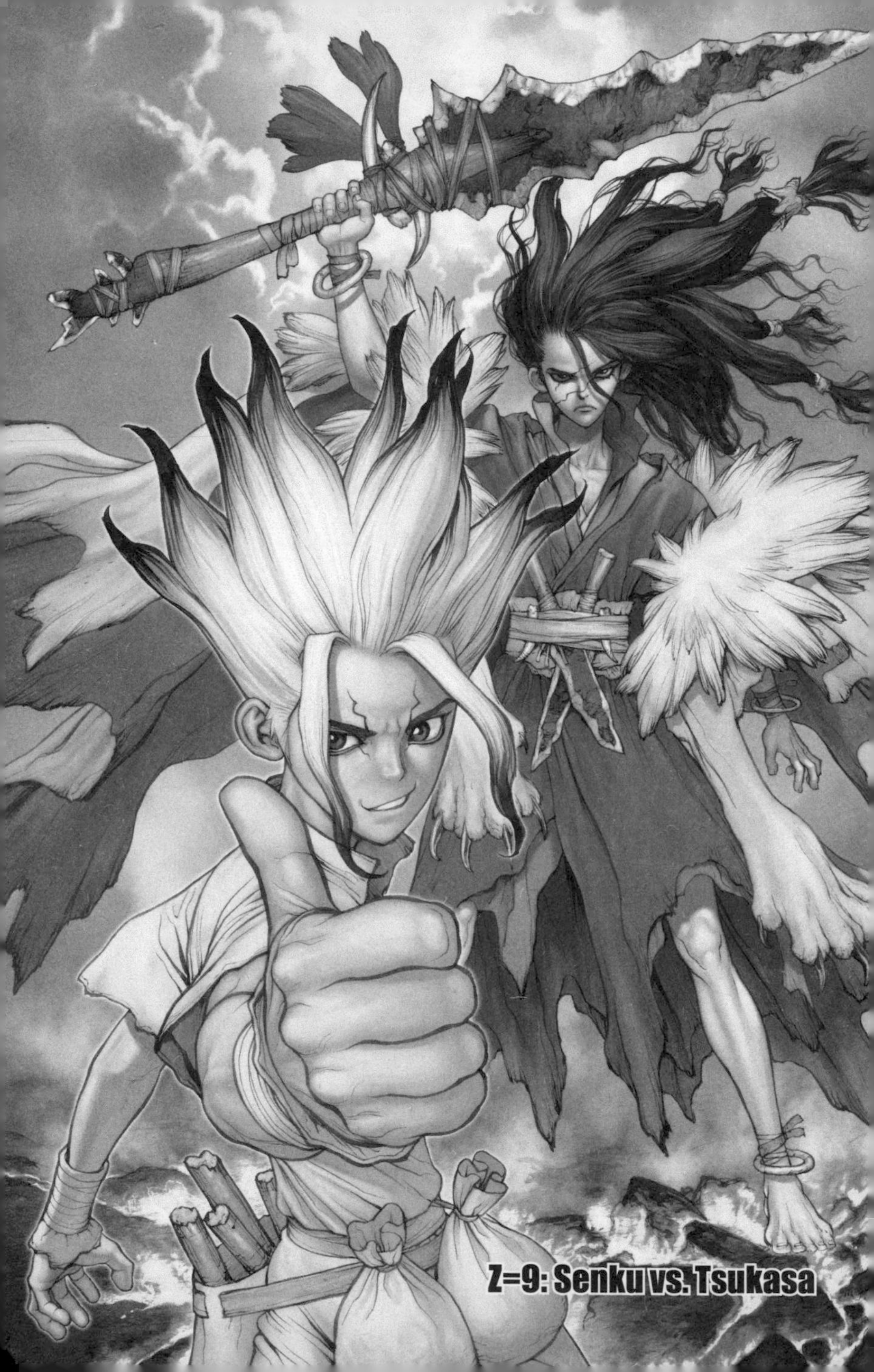
Z=9: Senku vs. Tsukasa

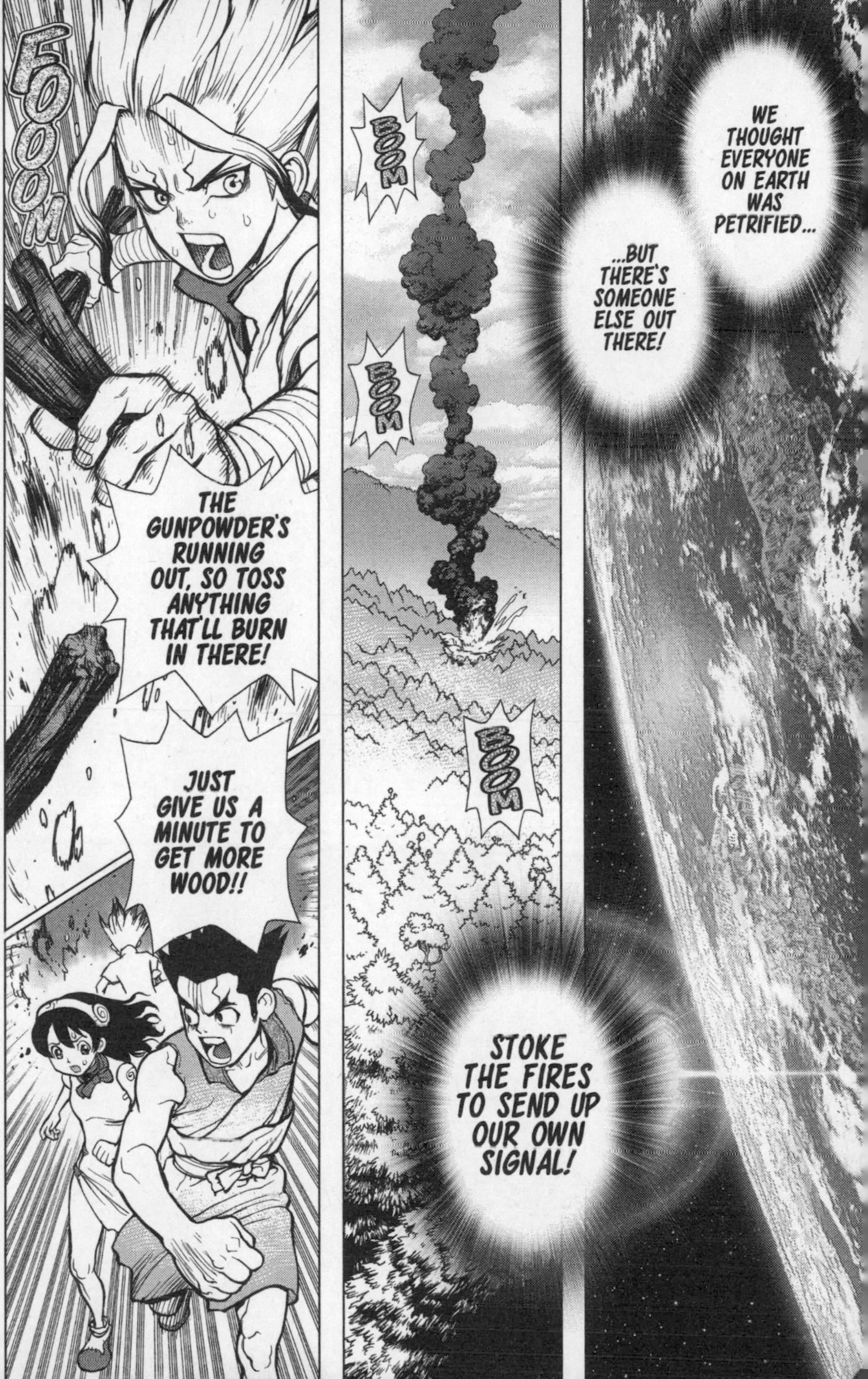
WE THOUGHT EVERYONE ON EARTH WAS PETRIFIED...
...BUT THERE'S SOMEONE ELSE OUT THERE!
BOOM
BOOM
BOOM
STOKE THE FIRES TO SEND UP OUR OWN SIGNAL!
FOOOM
THE GUNPOWDER'S RUNNING OUT, SO TOSS ANYTHING THAT'LL BURN IN THERE!
JUST GIVE US A MINUTE TO GET MORE WOOD!!

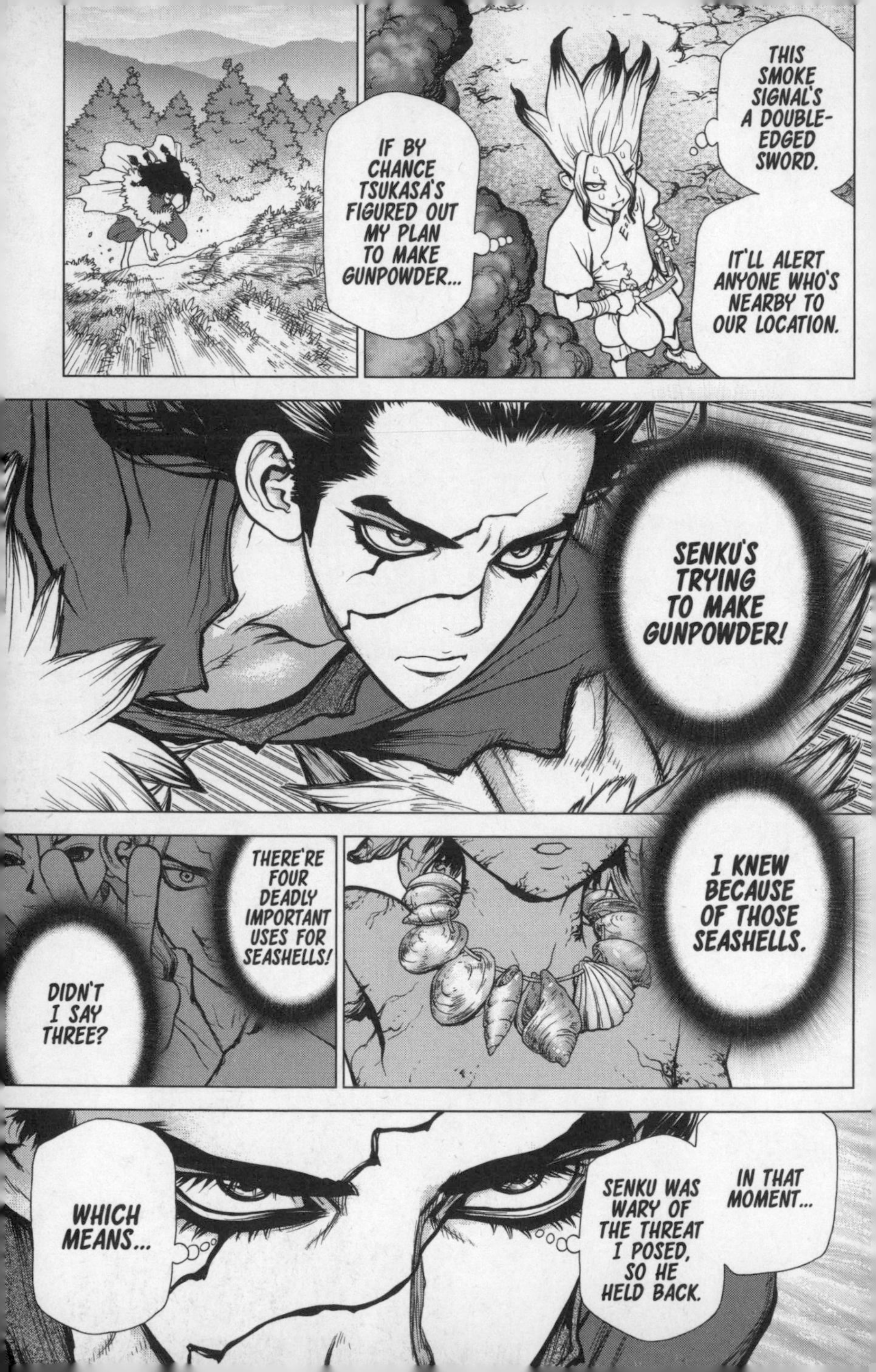
THIS SMOKE SIGNAL'S A DOUBLE-EDGED SWORD.
IT'LL ALERT ANYONE WHO'S NEARBY TO OUR LOCATION.
IF BY CHANCE TSUKASA'S FIGURED OUT MY PLAN TO MAKE GUNPOWDER...
SENKU'S TRYING TO MAKE GUNPOWDER!
I KNEW BECAUSE OF THOSE SEASHELLS.
THERE'RE FOUR DEADLY IMPORTANT USES FOR SEASHELLS!
DIDN'T I SAY THREE?
IN THAT MOMENT...
SENKU WAS WARY OF THE THREAT I POSED, SO HE HELD BACK.
WHICH MEANS...

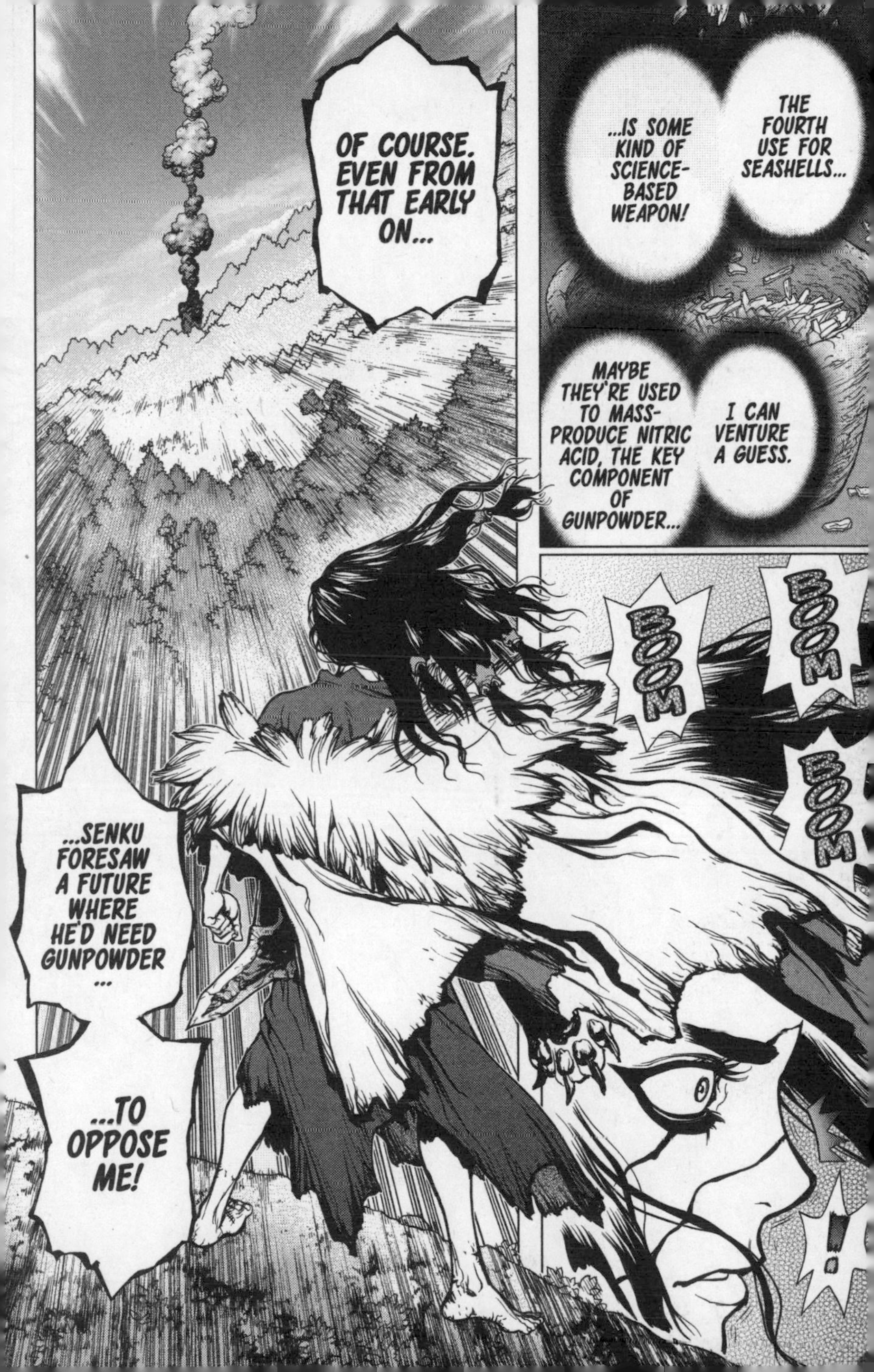
THE FOURTH USE FOR SEASHELLS...
...IS SOME KIND OF SCIENCE-BASED WEAPON!
I CAN VENTURE A GUESS.
MAYBE THEY'RE USED TO MASS-PRODUCE NITRIC ACID, THE KEY COMPONENT OF GUNPOWDER...
BOOM
BOOM
BOOM
!
OF COURSE. EVEN FROM THAT EARLY ON...
...SENKU FORESAW A FUTURE WHERE HE'D NEED GUNPOWDER...
...TO OPPOSE ME!

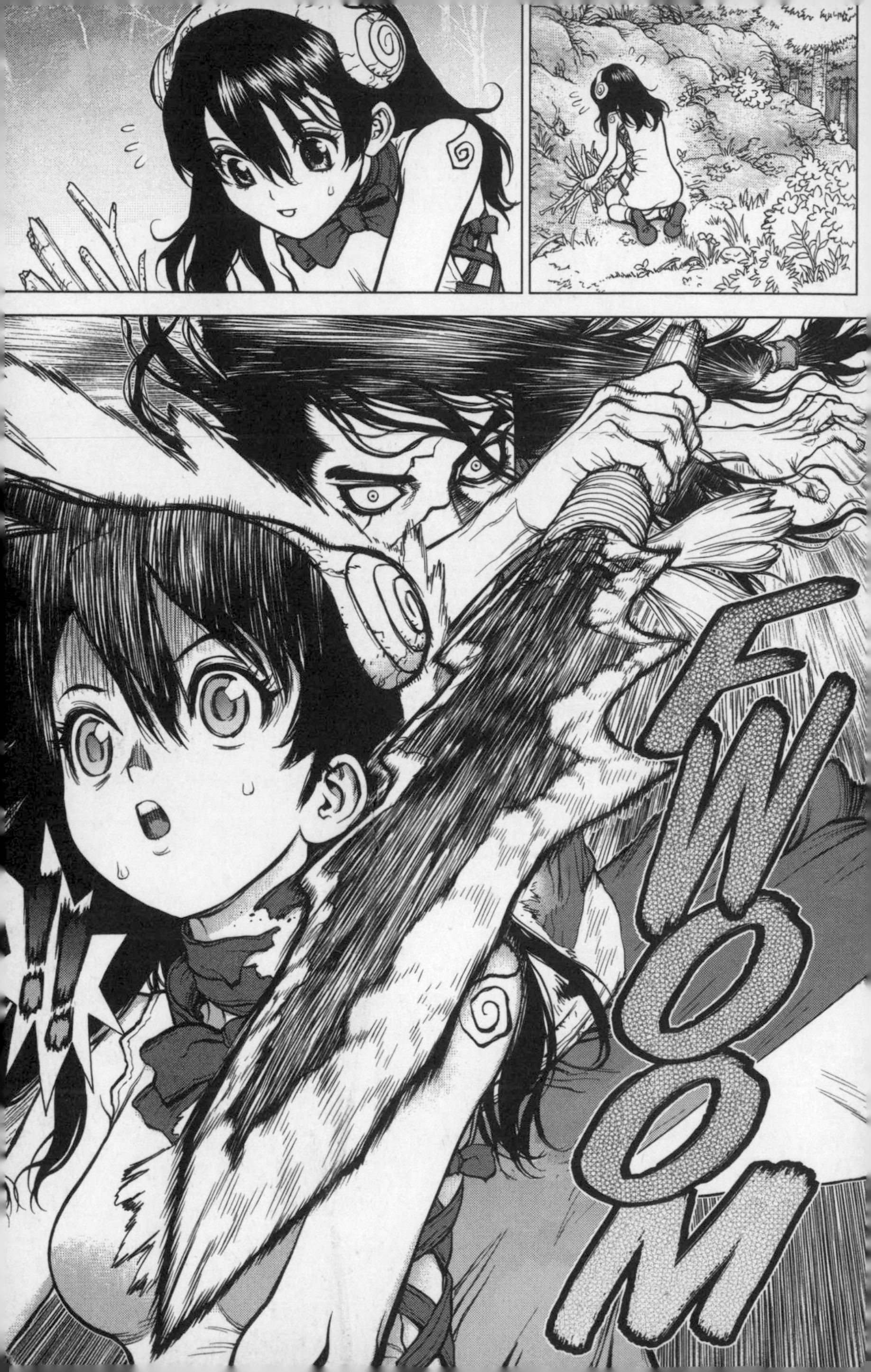
FWOOM

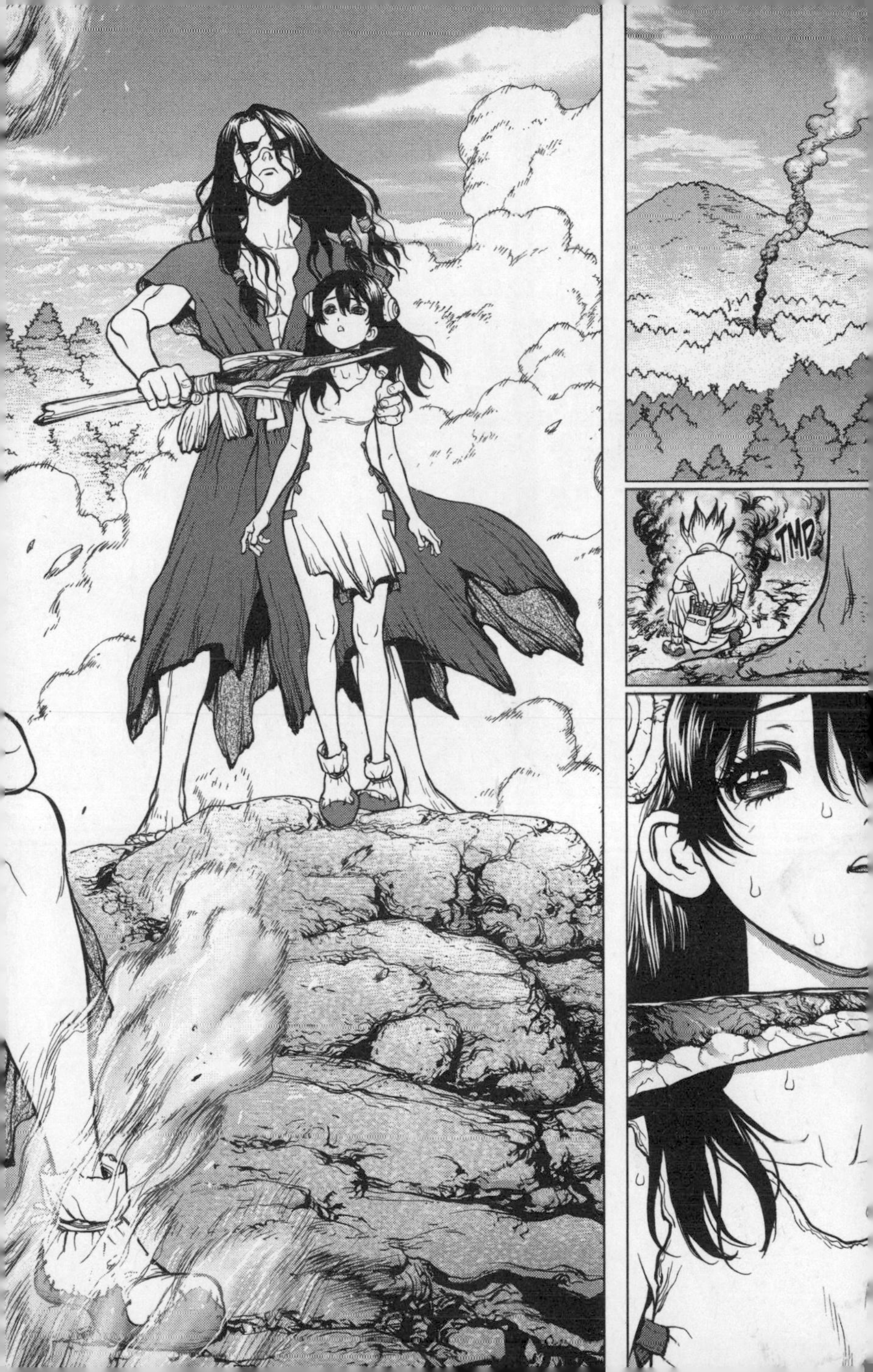
TMP

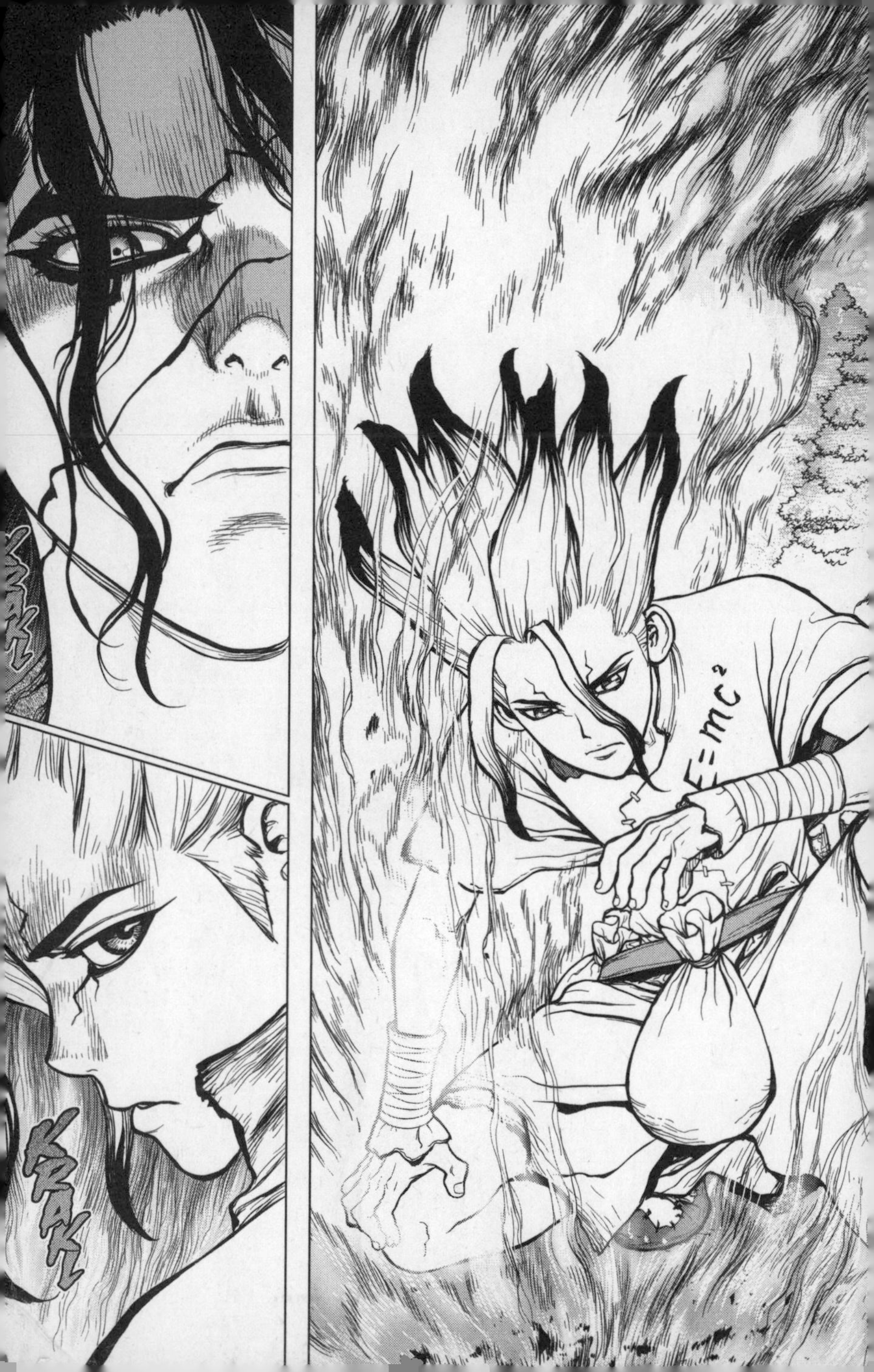
E=mc²
KRAK!

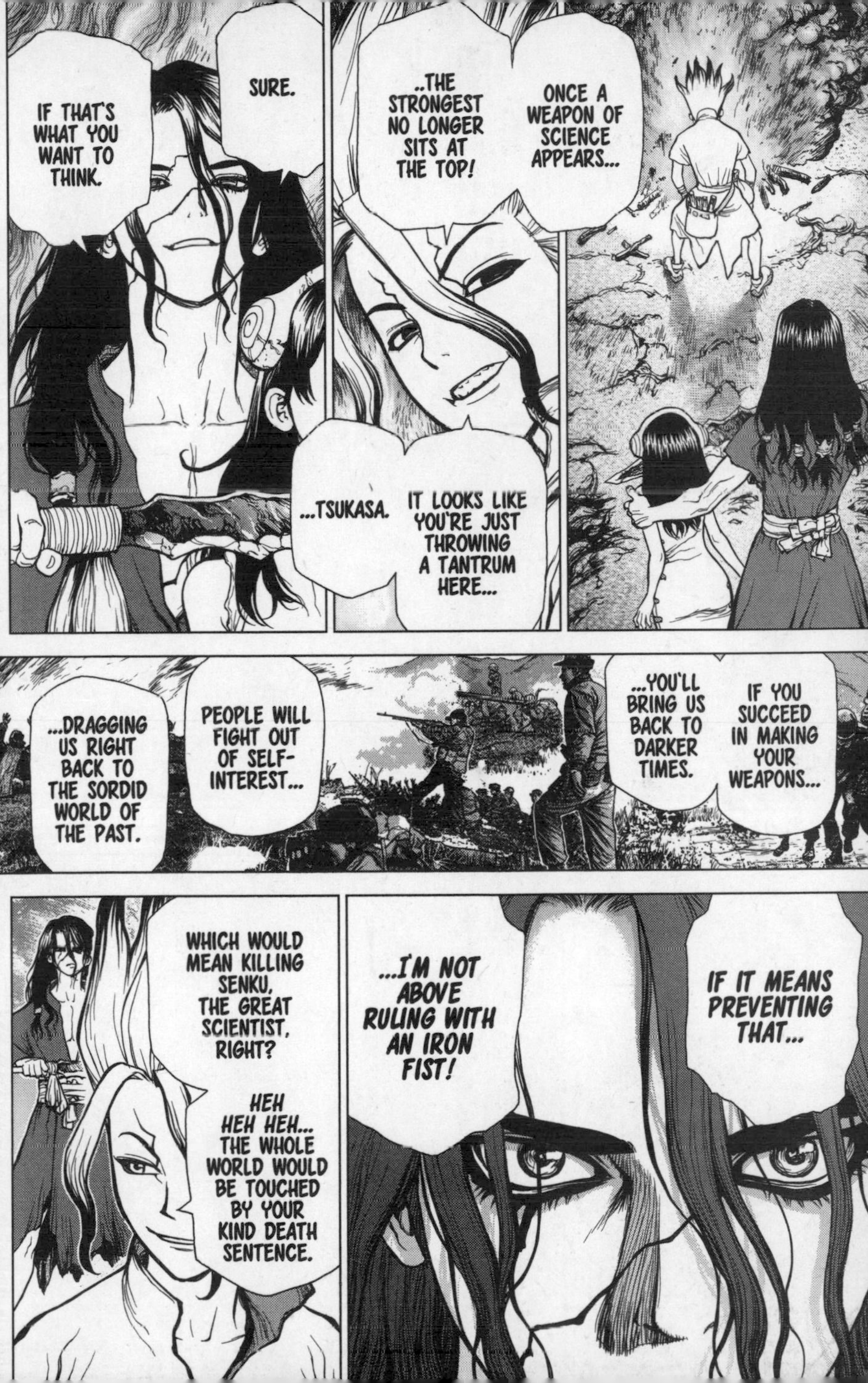
ONCE A WEAPON OF SCIENCE APPEARS...
..THE STRONGEST NO LONGER SITS AT THE TOP!
IT LOOKS LIKE YOU'RE JUST THROWING A TANTRUM HERE...
...TSUKASA.
SURE.
IF THAT'S WHAT YOU WANT TO THINK.
IF YOU SUCCEED IN MAKING YOUR WEAPONS...
...YOU'LL BRING US BACK TO DARKER TIMES.
PEOPLE WILL FIGHT OUT OF SELF-INTEREST...
...DRAGGING US RIGHT BACK TO THE SORDID WORLD OF THE PAST.
IF IT MEANS PREVENTING THAT...
...I'M NOT ABOVE RULING WITH AN IRON FIST!
WHICH WOULD MEAN KILLING SENKU, THE GREAT SCIENTIST, RIGHT?
HEH HEH HEH... THE WHOLE WORLD WOULD BE TOUCHED BY YOUR KIND DEATH SENTENCE.

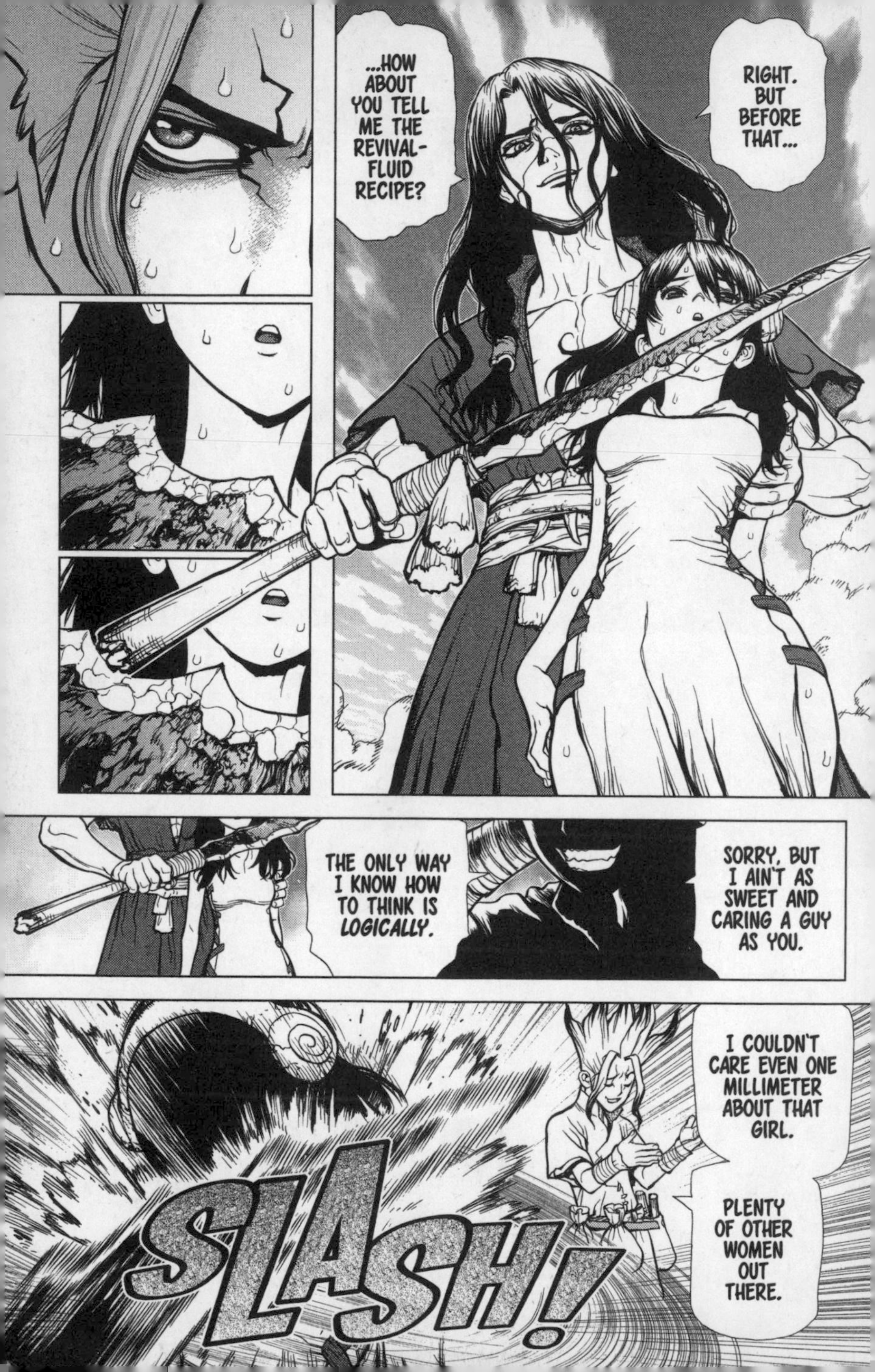
RIGHT. BUT BEFORE THAT...
...HOW ABOUT YOU TELL ME THE REVIVAL-FLUID RECIPE?
SORRY, BUT I AIN'T AS SWEET AND CARING A GUY AS YOU.
THE ONLY WAY I KNOW HOW TO THINK IS *LOGICALLY.*
I COULDN'T CARE EVEN ONE MILLIMETER ABOUT THAT GIRL.
PLENTY OF OTHER WOMEN OUT THERE.
SLASH!

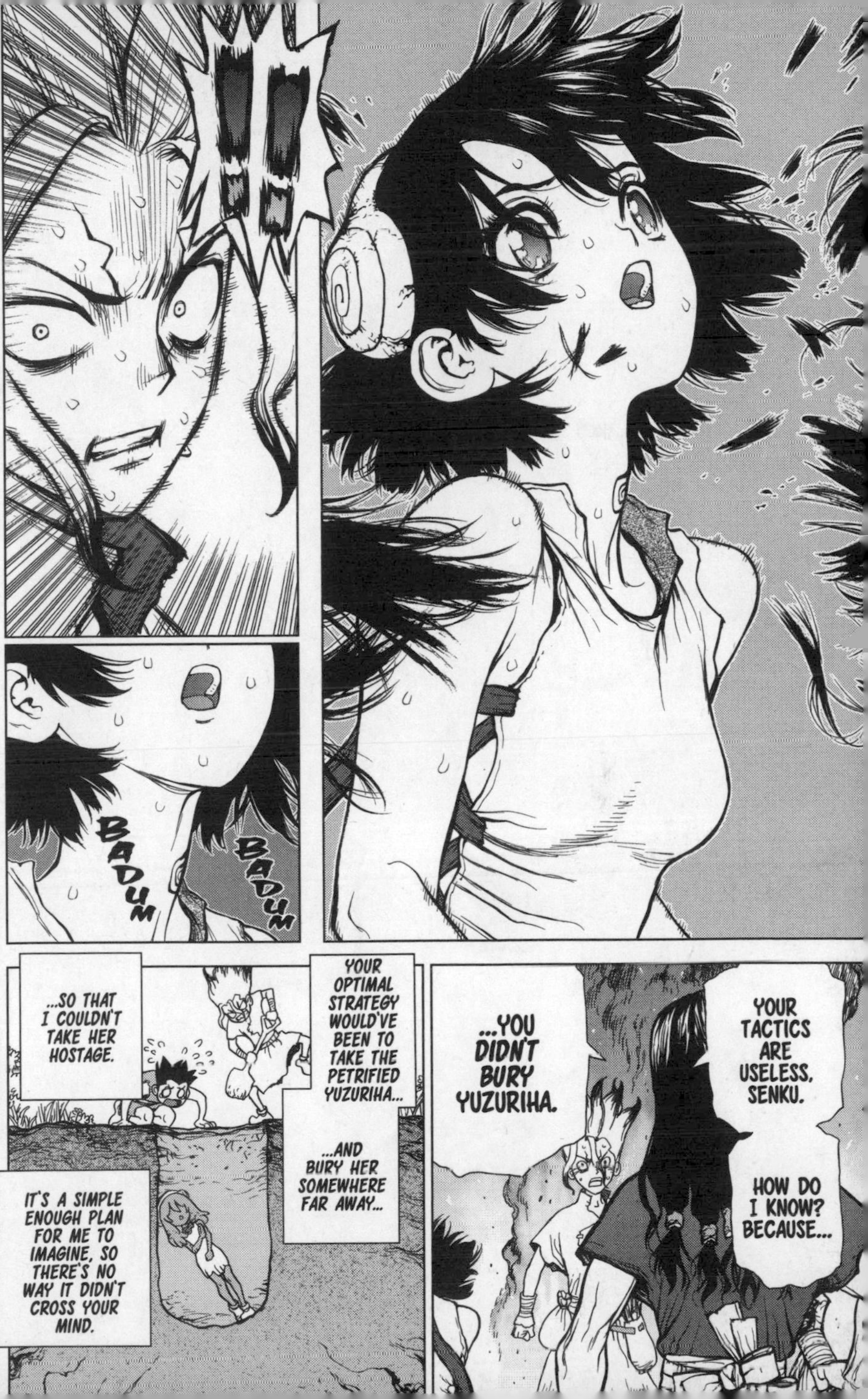
!!
BADUM
BADUM
YOUR TACTICS ARE USELESS, SENKU.
HOW DO I KNOW? BECAUSE...
...YOU DIDN'T BURY YUZURIHA.
YOUR OPTIMAL STRATEGY WOULD'VE BEEN TO TAKE THE PETRIFIED YUZURIHA...
...AND BURY HER SOMEWHERE FAR AWAY...
...SO THAT I COULDN'T TAKE HER HOSTAGE.
IT'S A SIMPLE ENOUGH PLAN FOR ME TO IMAGINE, SO THERE'S NO WAY IT DIDN'T CROSS YOUR MIND.

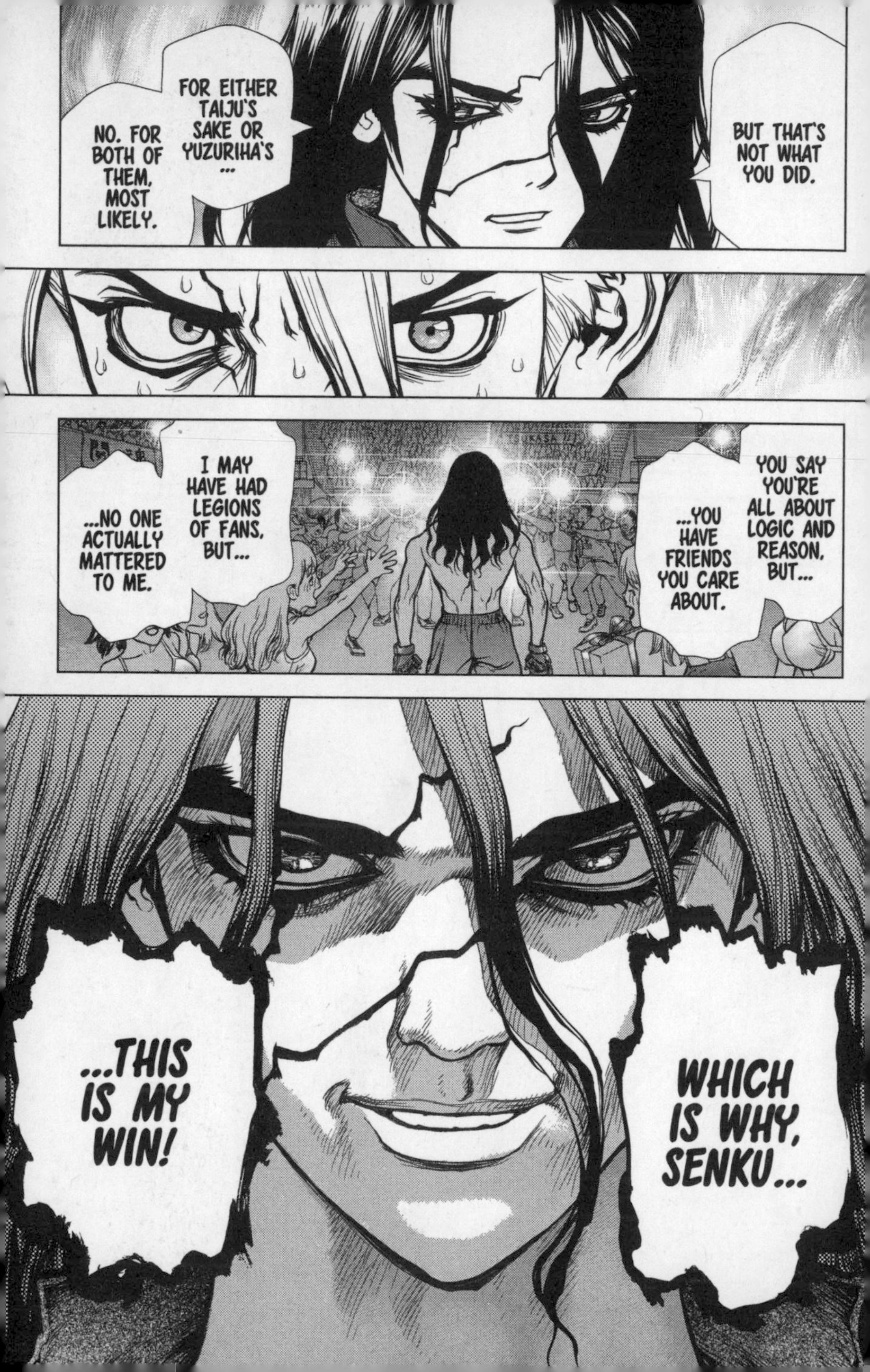
BUT THAT'S NOT WHAT YOU DID.
FOR EITHER TAIJU'S SAKE OR YUZURIHA'S ...
NO. FOR BOTH OF THEM, MOST LIKELY.
YOU SAY YOU'RE ALL ABOUT LOGIC AND REASON, BUT...
...YOU HAVE FRIENDS YOU CARE ABOUT.
I MAY HAVE HAD LEGIONS OF FANS, BUT...
...NO ONE ACTUALLY MATTERED TO ME.
WHICH IS WHY, SENKU...
...THIS IS MY WIN!

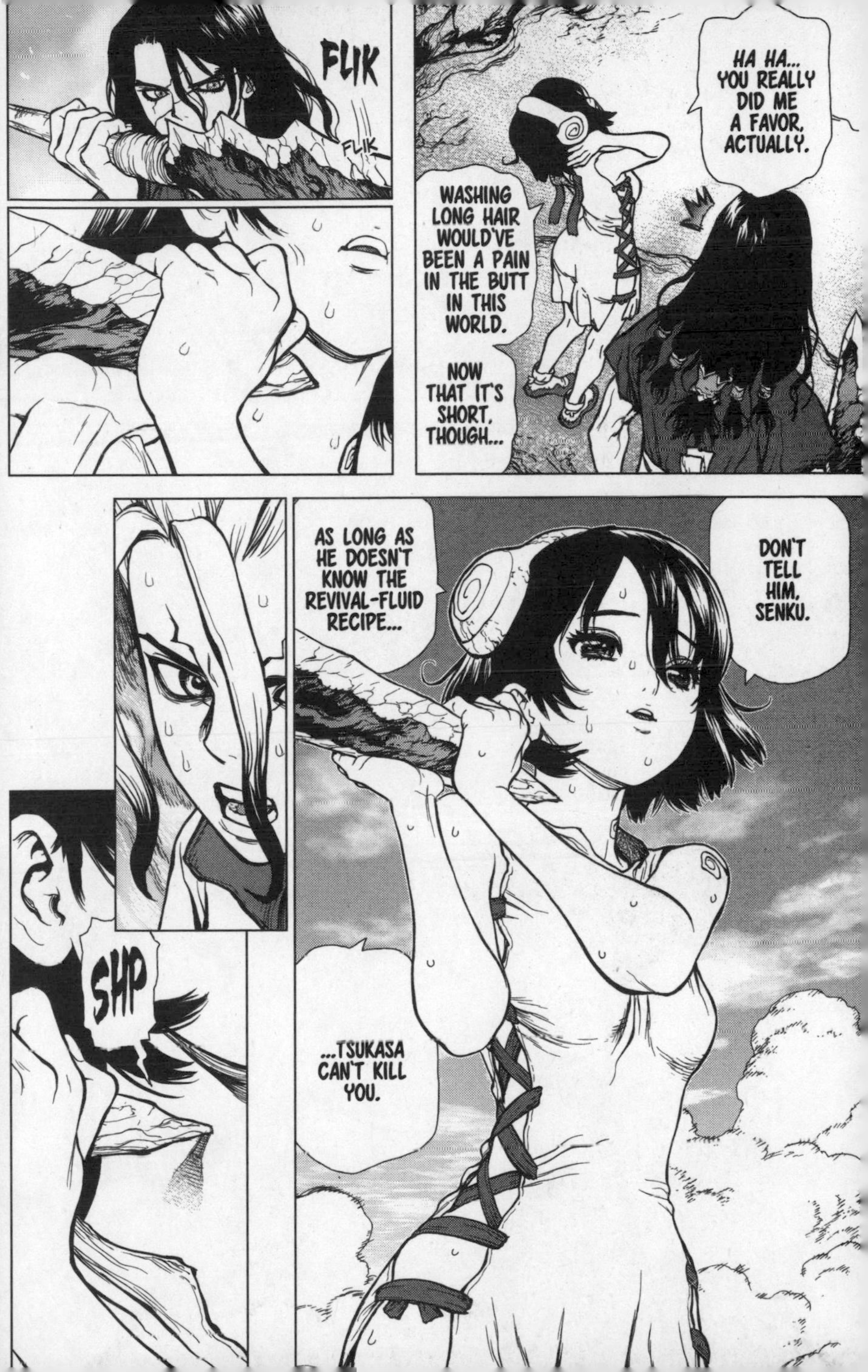
HA HA... YOU REALLY DID ME A FAVOR, ACTUALLY.
WASHING LONG HAIR WOULD'VE BEEN A PAIN IN THE BUTT IN THIS WORLD.
NOW THAT IT'S SHORT, THOUGH...
FLIK
FLIK
DON'T TELL HIM, SENKU.
AS LONG AS HE DOESN'T KNOW THE REVIVAL-FLUID RECIPE...
...TSUKASA CAN'T KILL YOU.
SHP

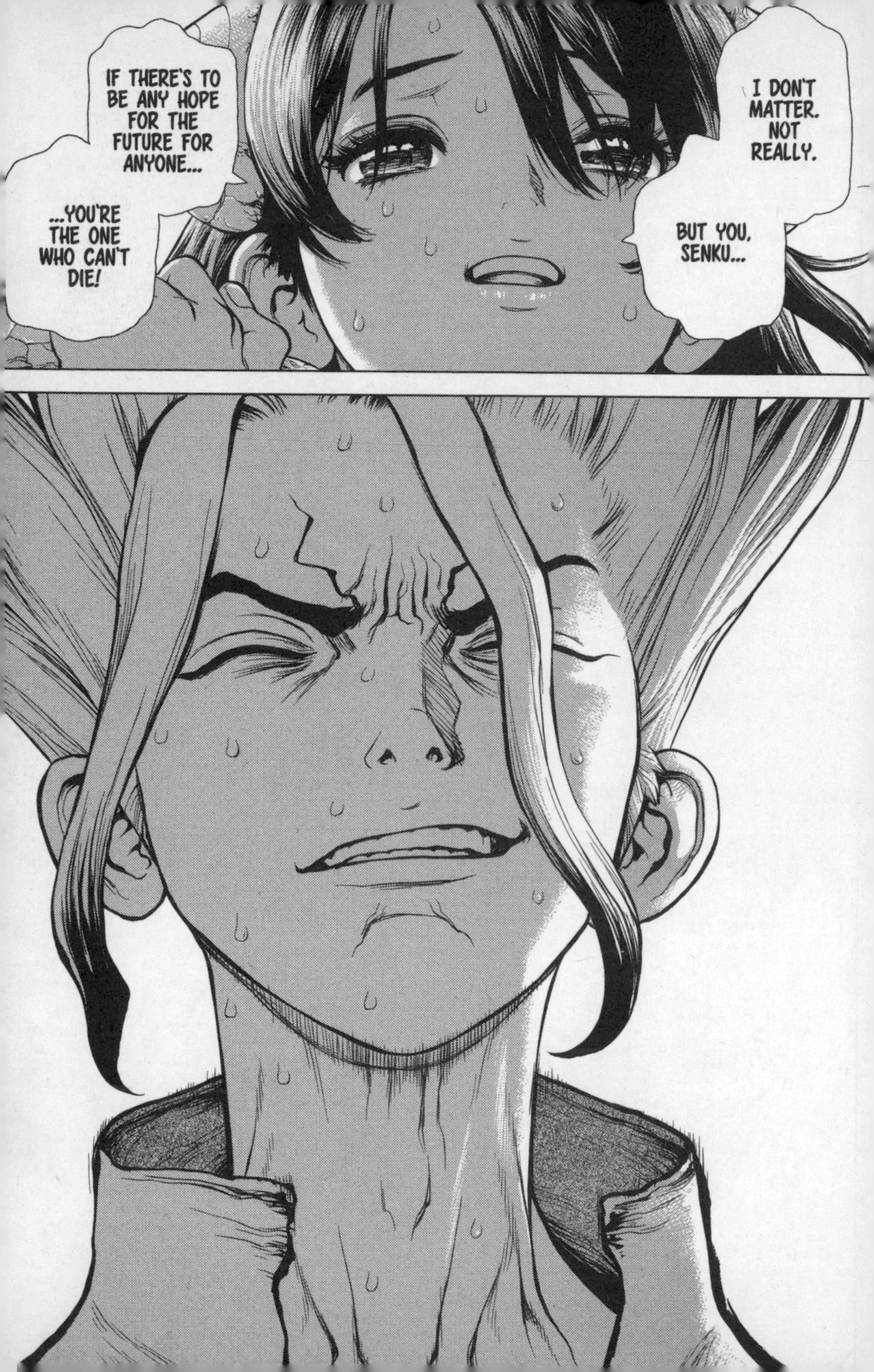
I DON'T MATTER. NOT REALLY.
BUT YOU, SENKU...
IF THERE'S TO BE ANY HOPE FOR THE FUTURE FOR ANYONE...
...YOU'RE THE ONE WHO CAN'T DIE!

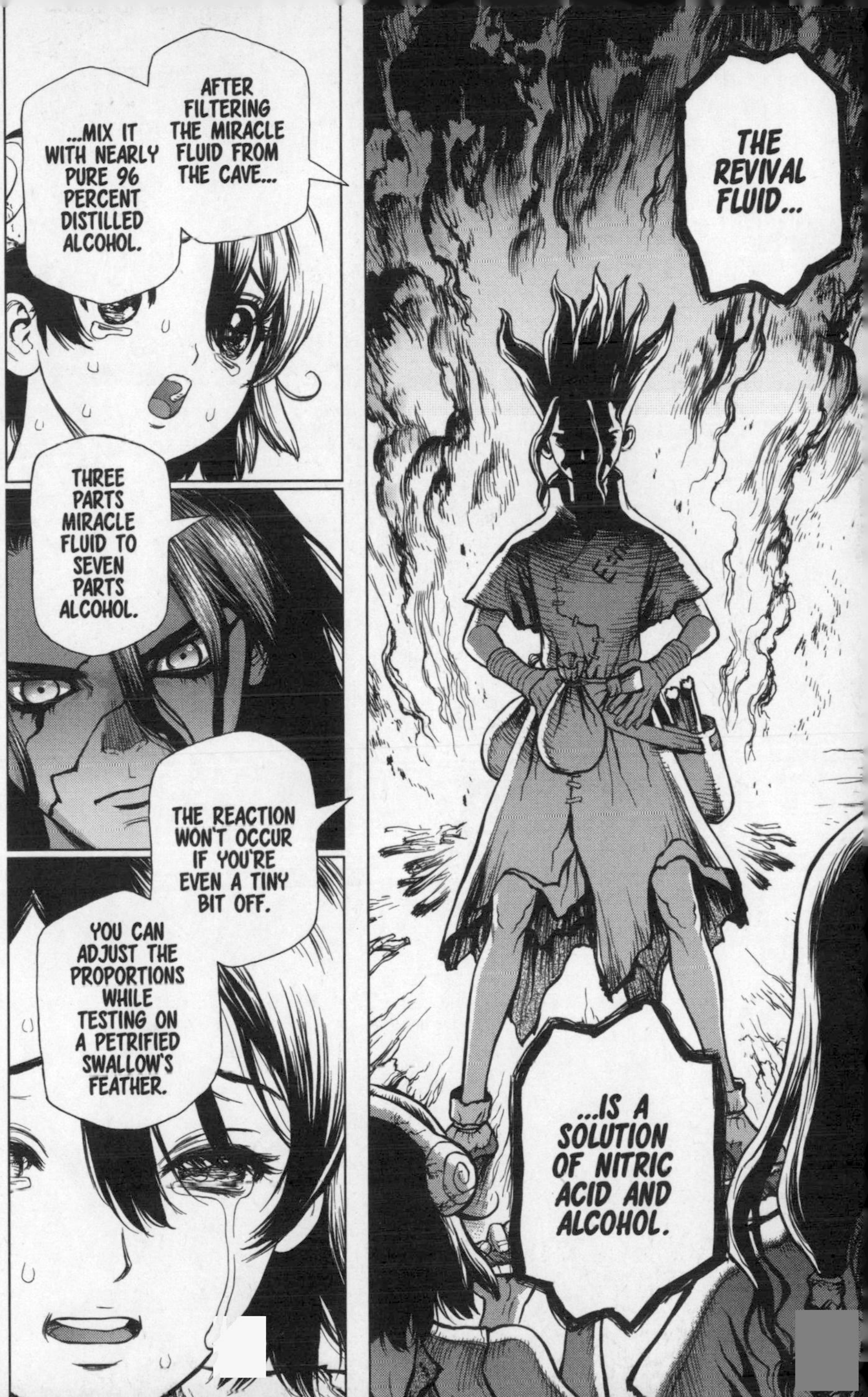
THE REVIVAL FLUID...
...IS A SOLUTION OF NITRIC ACID AND ALCOHOL.
AFTER FILTERING THE MIRACLE FLUID FROM THE CAVE...
...MIX IT WITH NEARLY PURE 96 PERCENT DISTILLED ALCOHOL.
THREE PARTS MIRACLE FLUID TO SEVEN PARTS ALCOHOL.
THE REACTION WON'T OCCUR IF YOU'RE EVEN A TINY BIT OFF.
YOU CAN ADJUST THE PROPORTIONS WHILE TESTING ON A PETRIFIED SWALLOW'S FEATHER.

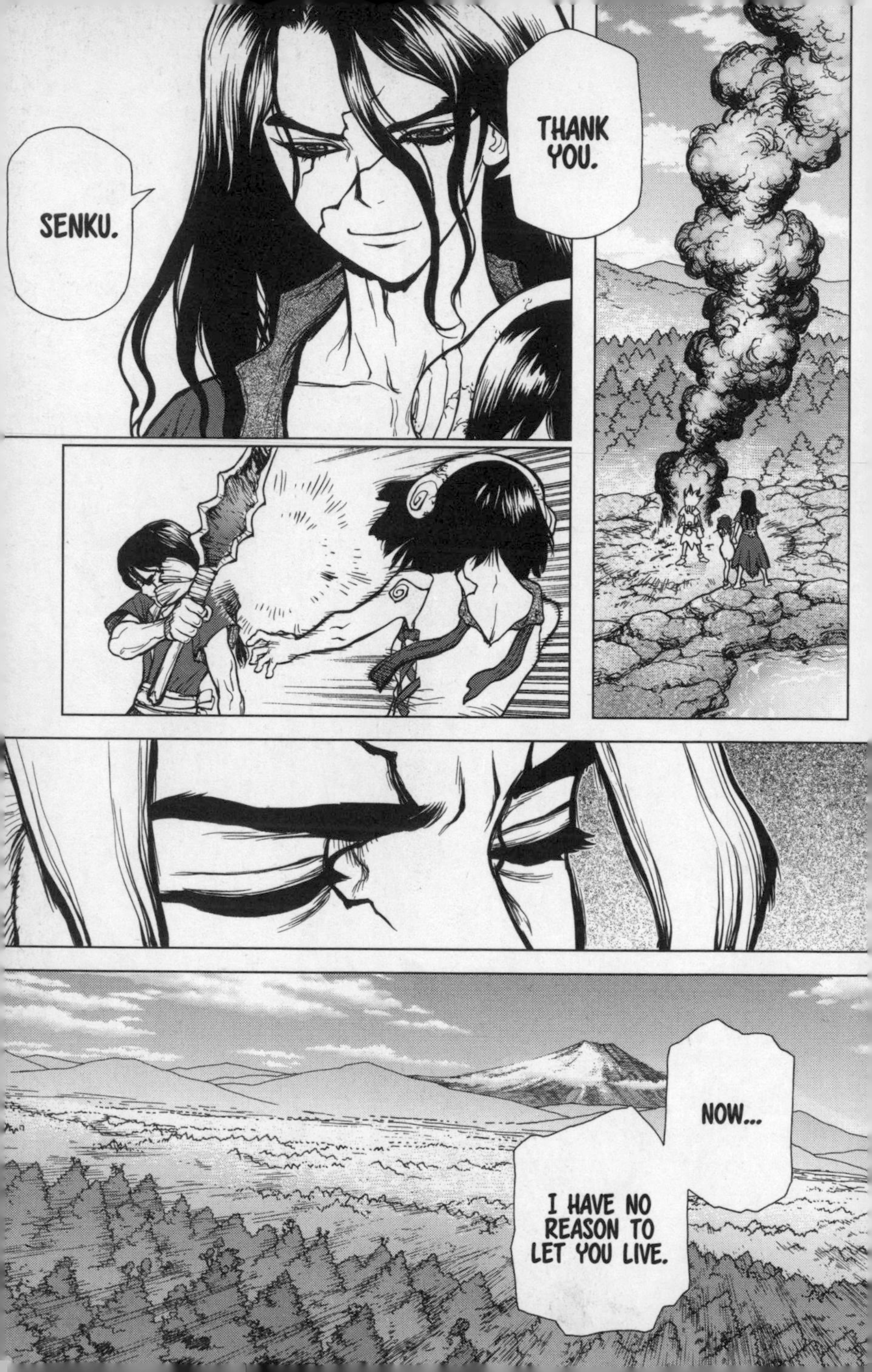
THANK YOU.
SENKU.
NOW...
I HAVE NO REASON TO LET YOU LIVE.

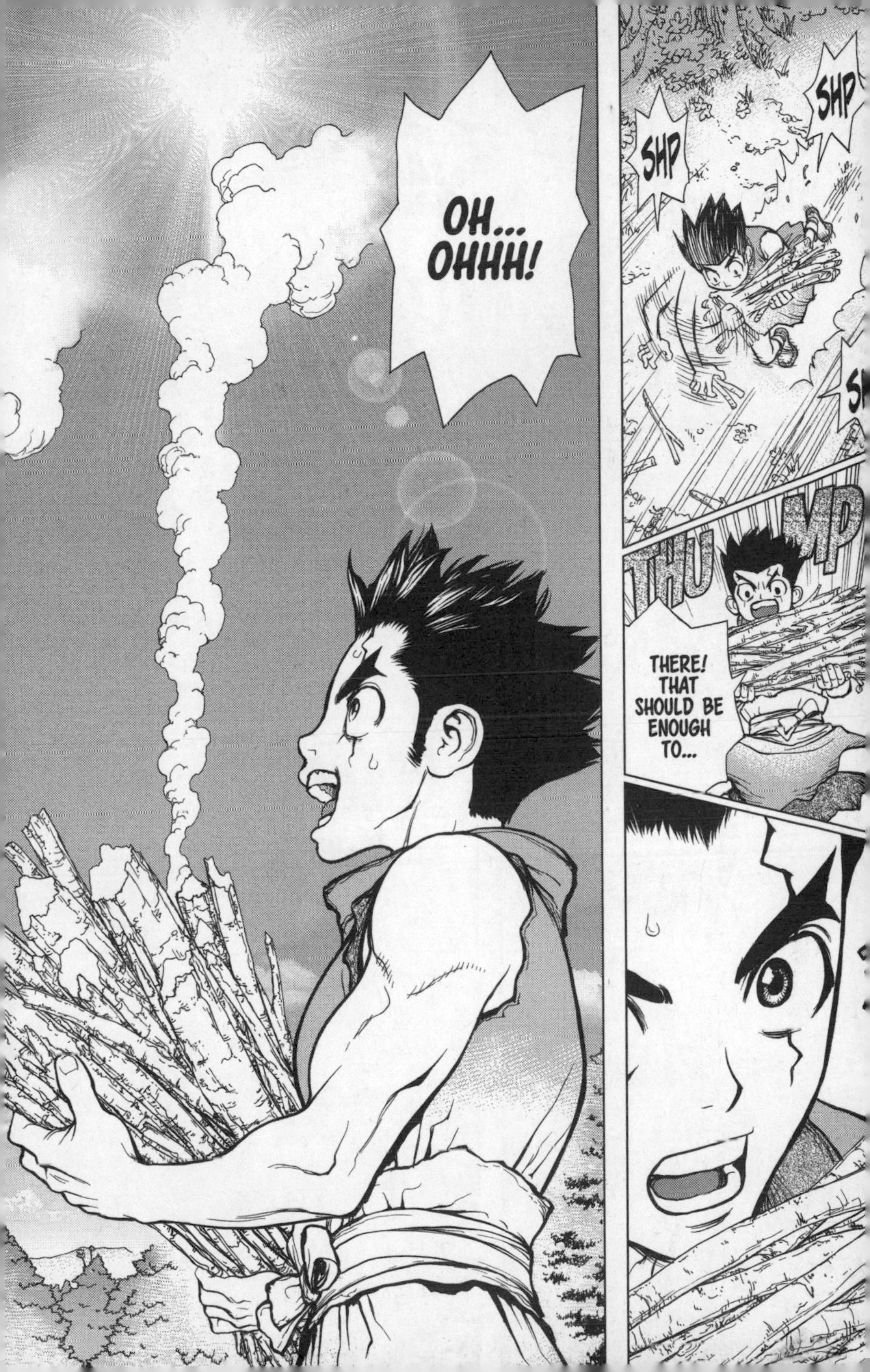
SHP
SHP
THUMP
THERE! THAT SHOULD BE ENOUGH TO...
OH... OHHH!

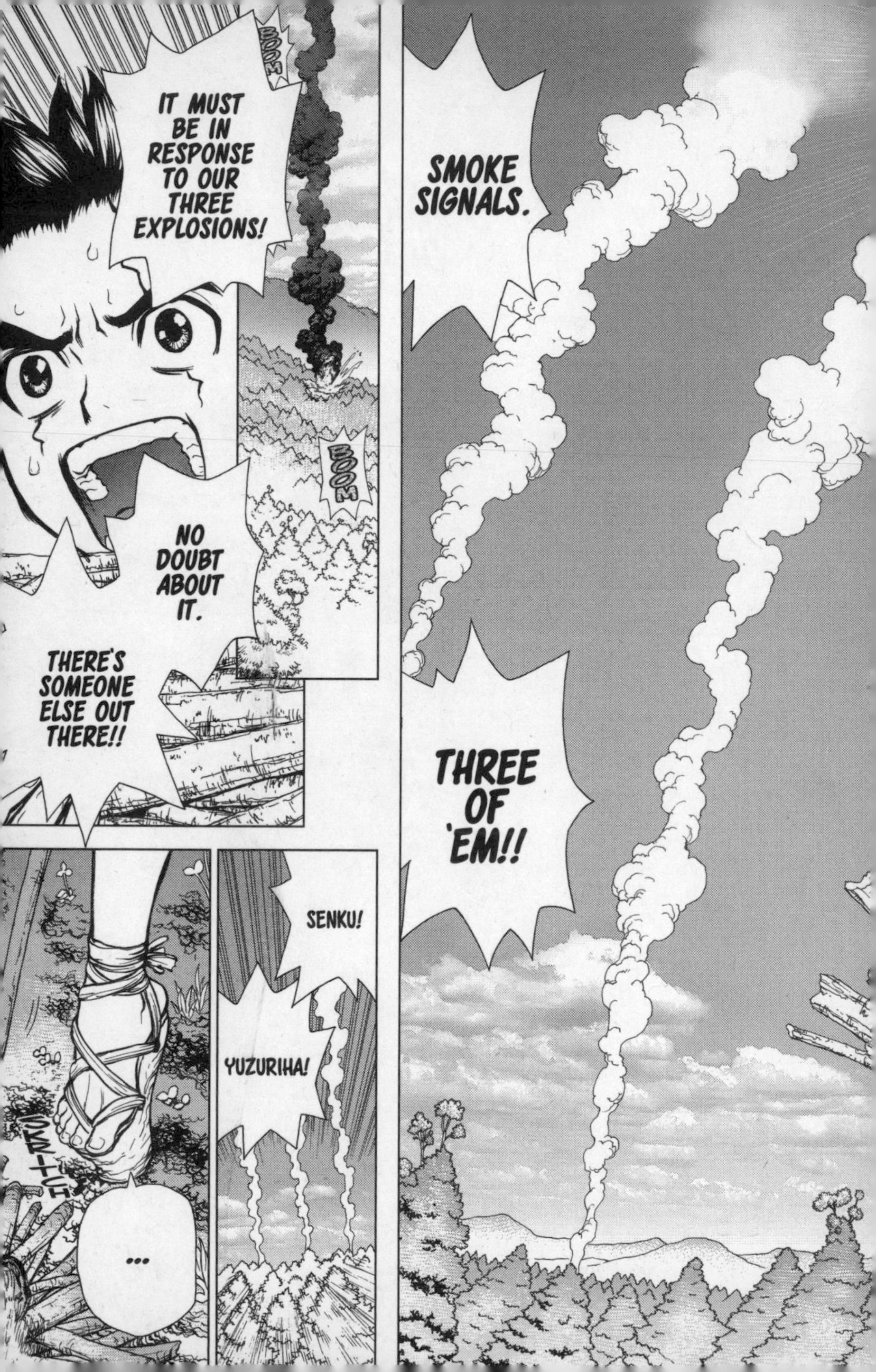
SMOKE SIGNALS.
THREE OF 'EM!!
BOOM
IT MUST BE IN RESPONSE TO OUR THREE EXPLOSIONS!
BOOM
NO DOUBT ABOUT IT.
THERE'S SOMEONE ELSE OUT THERE!!
SENKU!
YUZURIHA!
SKRITCH
...

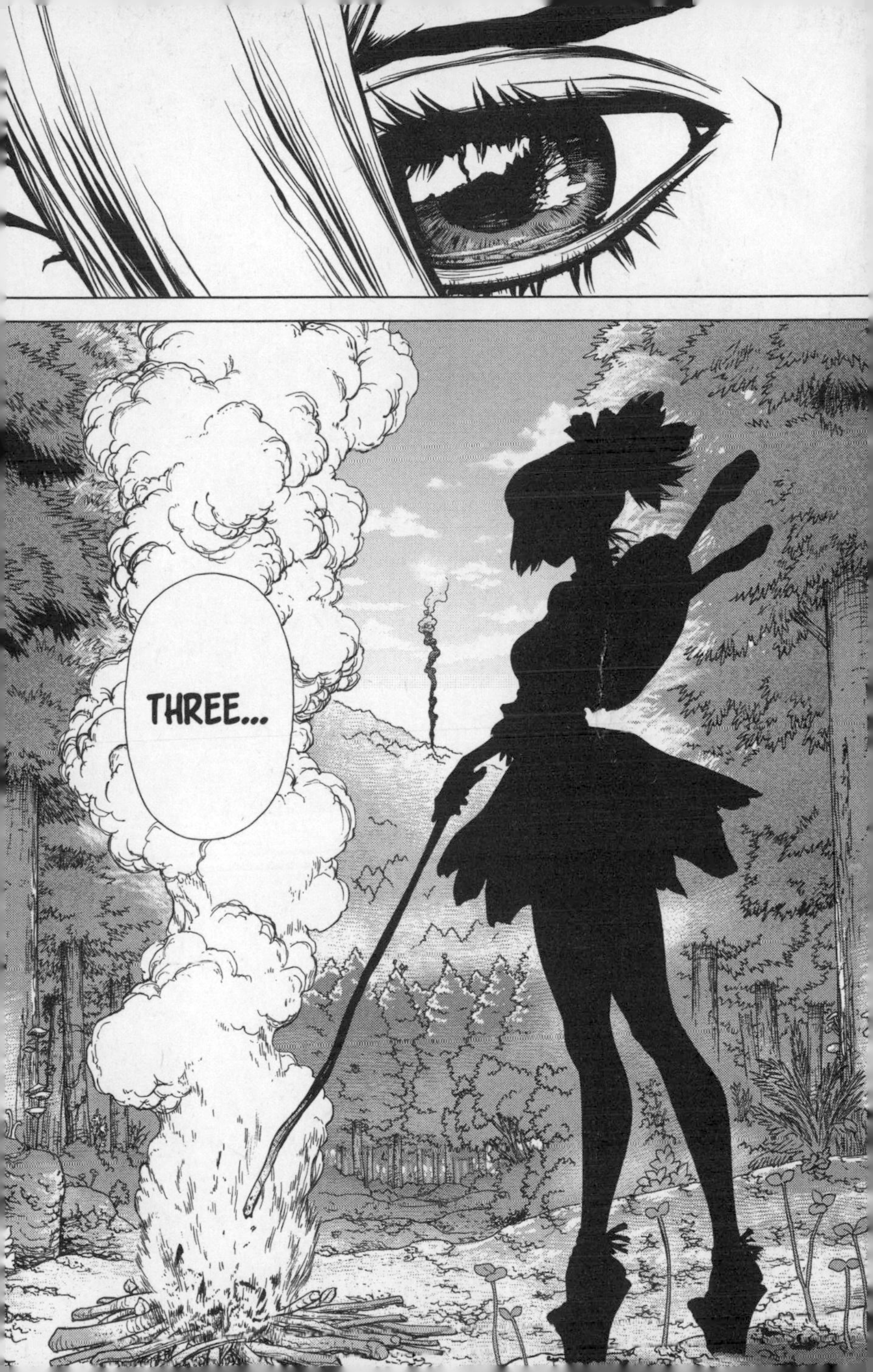
THREE...

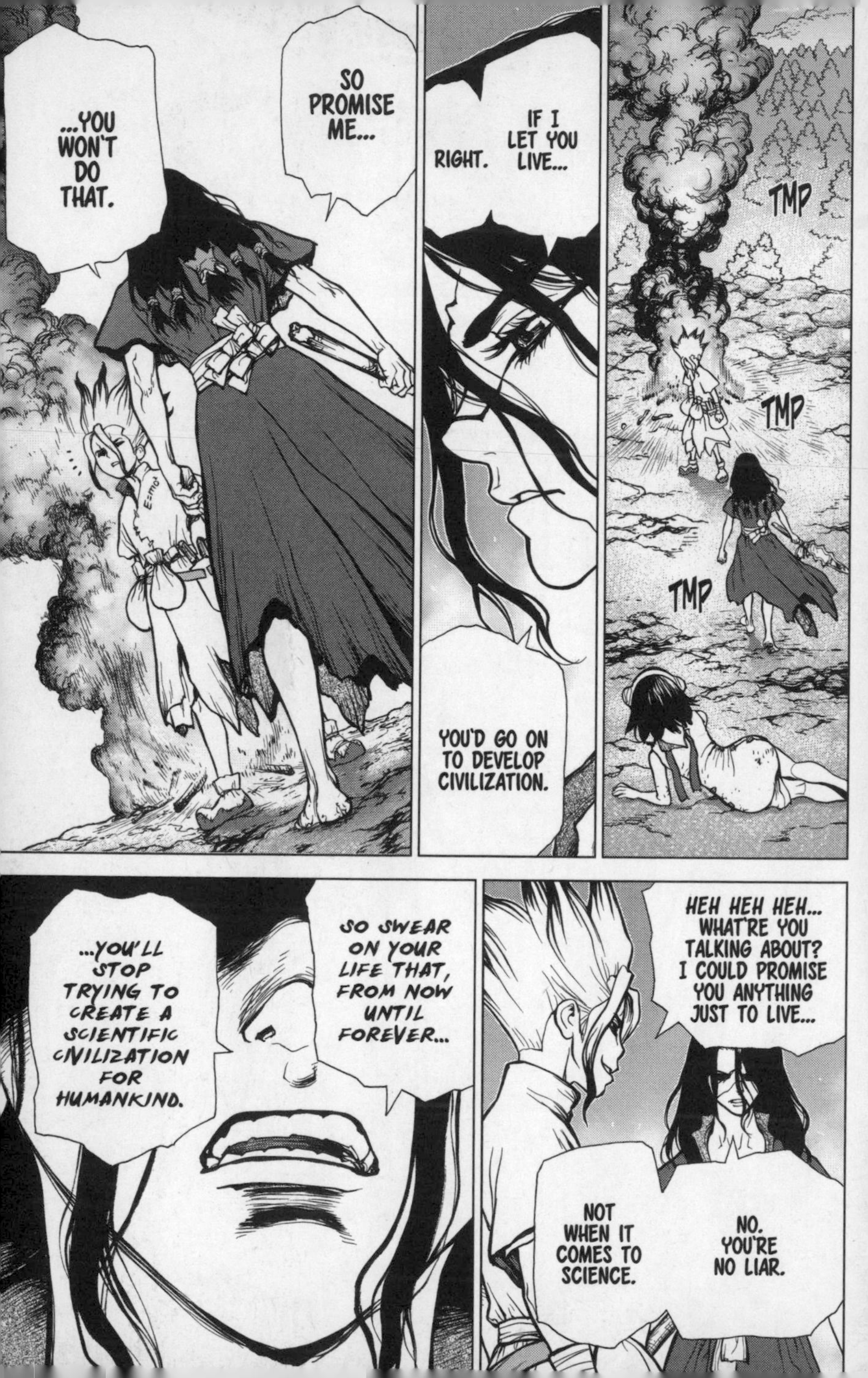
TMP
TMP
TMP
IF I LET YOU LIVE...
RIGHT.
YOU'D GO ON TO DEVELOP CIVILIZATION.
SO PROMISE ME...
...YOU WON'T DO THAT.
HEH HEH HEH... WHAT'RE YOU TALKING ABOUT? I COULD PROMISE YOU ANYTHING JUST TO LIVE...
NO. YOU'RE NO LIAR.
NOT WHEN IT COMES TO SCIENCE.
SO SWEAR ON YOUR LIFE THAT, FROM NOW UNTIL FOREVER...
...YOU'LL STOP TRYING TO CREATE A SCIENTIFIC CIVILIZATION FOR HUMANKIND.

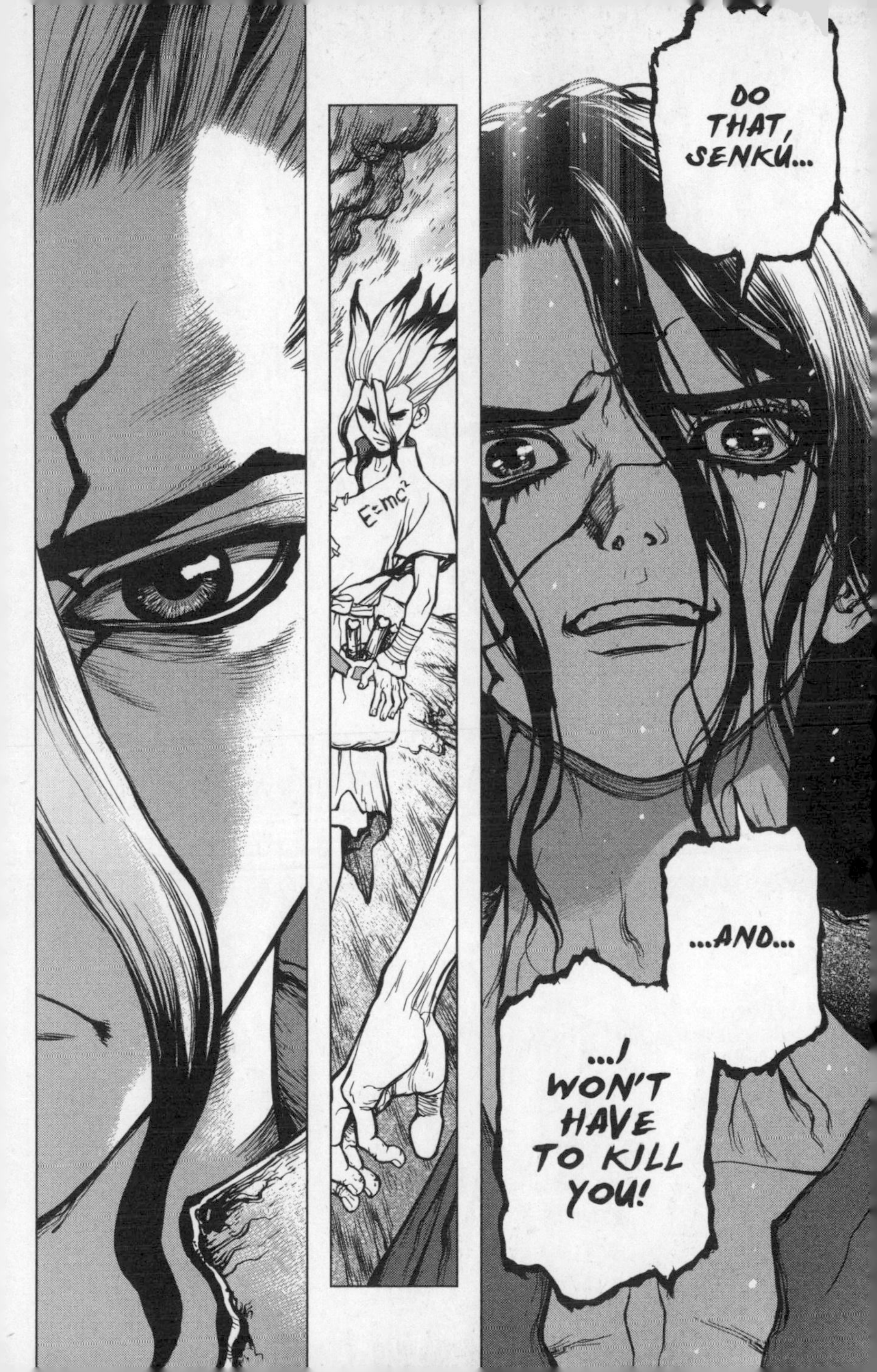
DO THAT, SENKU...
...AND...
...I WON'T HAVE TO KILL YOU!
$E=mc^2$

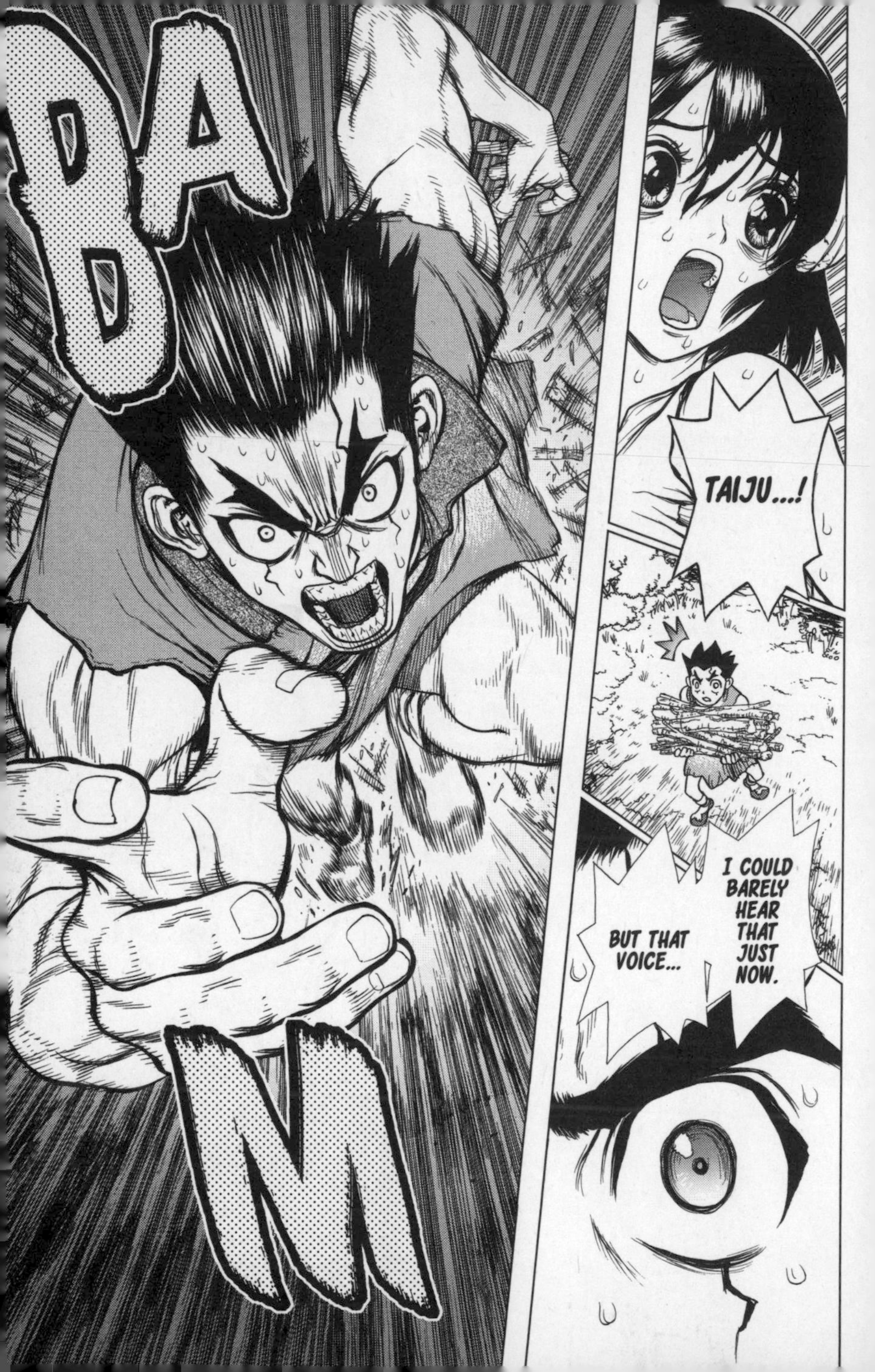
TAIJU...!
I COULD BARELY HEAR THAT JUST NOW.
BUT THAT VOICE...
DA
D
M

Taiju's Early Days

FOR SOME REASON, BREAKING THE RULES LIKE THAT GOT YOU KICKED OUTTA THE GAME, SENKU!
SOME REASON?! THAT WAS AN EXTREME VIOLATION!
BUT I'LL GET REVENGE FOR YOU!
HERE I GO!
KRIK KRIK
RAHHHHHHH
HHHHHHH!
KRIK
WHAT'S THIS? THE OTHER TEAM'S SURRENDERING!
VICTORY!

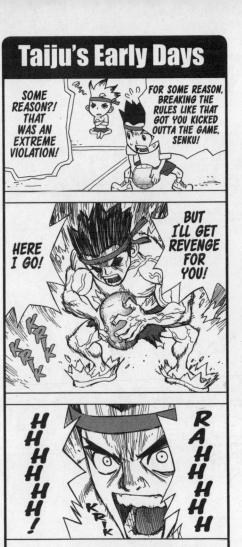

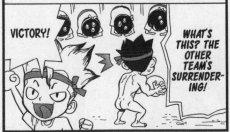

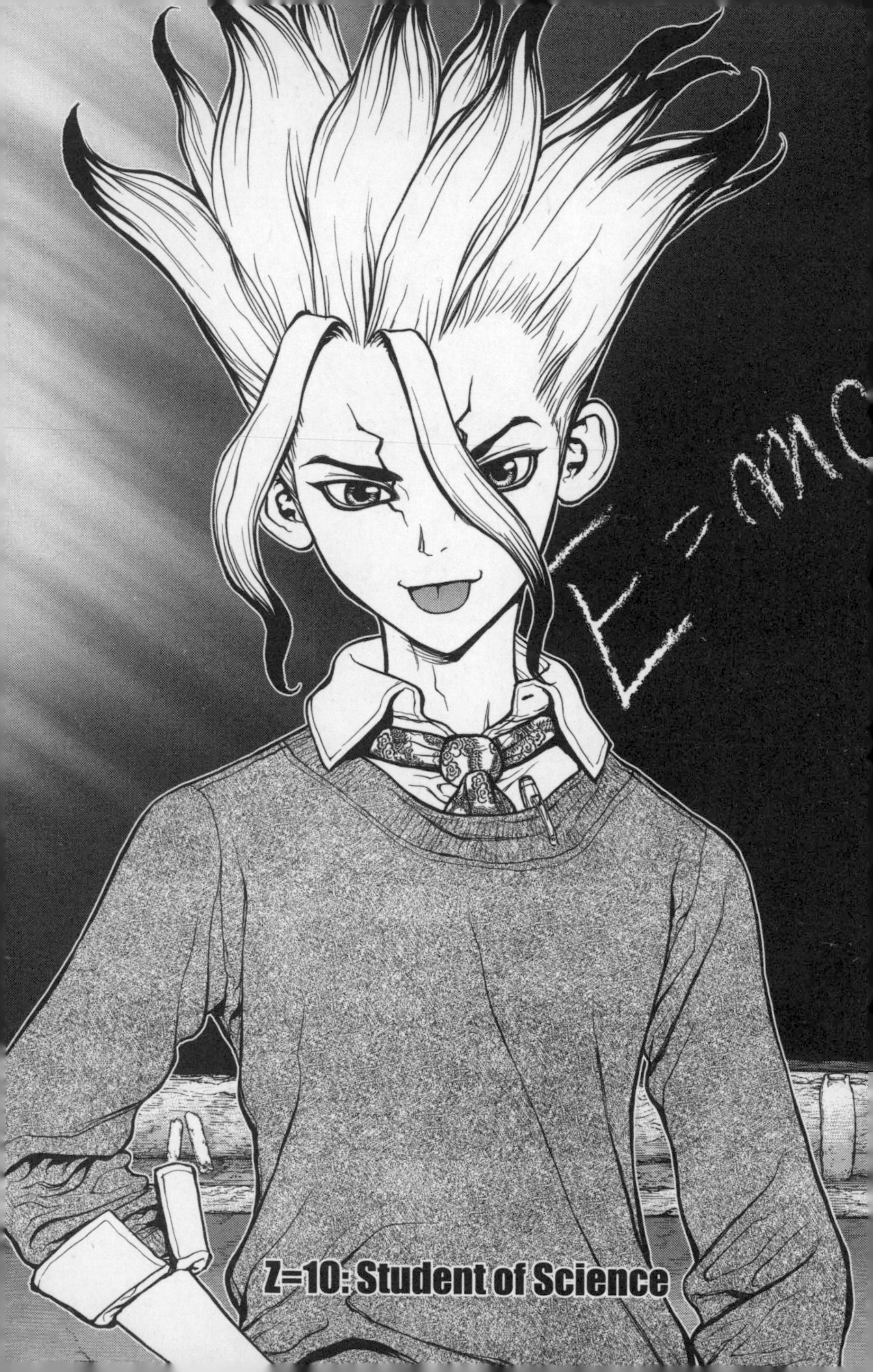
E = mc

Z=10: Student of Science

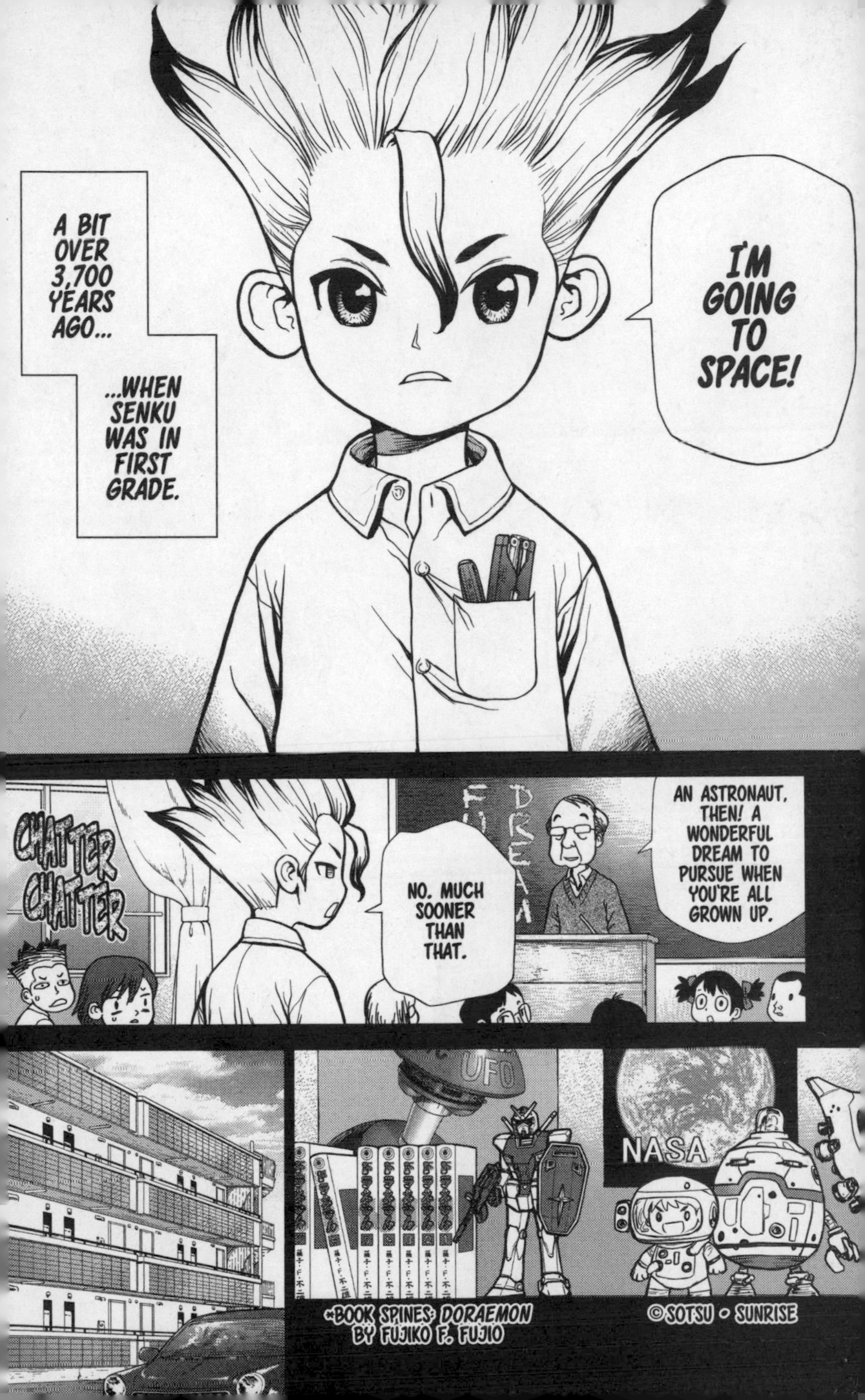
I'M GOING TO SPACE!
A BIT OVER 3,700 YEARS AGO...
...WHEN SENKU WAS IN FIRST GRADE.
AN ASTRONAUT, THEN! A WONDERFUL DREAM TO PURSUE WHEN YOU'RE ALL GROWN UP.
NO. MUCH SOONER THAN THAT.
CHATTER CHATTER
NASA
©SOTSU • SUNRISE
UFO
*BOOK SPINES: DORAEMON BY FUJIKO F. FUJIO

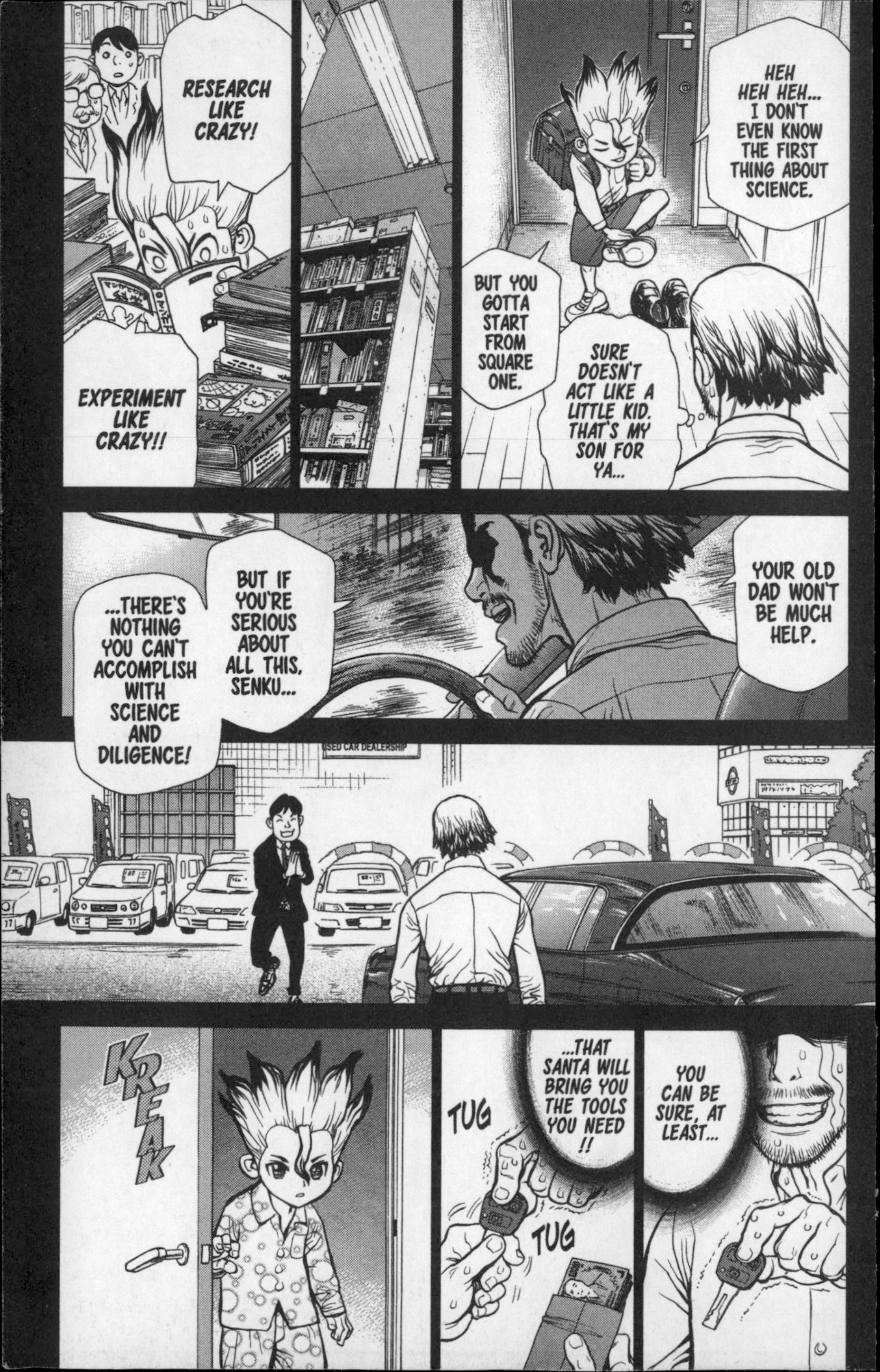
HEH HEH HEH... I DON'T EVEN KNOW THE FIRST THING ABOUT SCIENCE.
BUT YOU GOTTA START FROM SQUARE ONE.
SURE DOESN'T ACT LIKE A LITTLE KID. THAT'S MY SON FOR YA...
RESEARCH LIKE CRAZY!
EXPERIMENT LIKE CRAZY!!
YOUR OLD DAD WON'T BE MUCH HELP.
BUT IF YOU'RE SERIOUS ABOUT ALL THIS, SENKU...
...THERE'S NOTHING YOU CAN'T ACCOMPLISH WITH SCIENCE AND DILIGENCE!
SED CAR DEALERSHIP
YOU CAN BE SURE, AT LEAST...
...THAT SANTA WILL BRING YOU THE TOOLS YOU NEED !!
TUG
TUG
KREAK

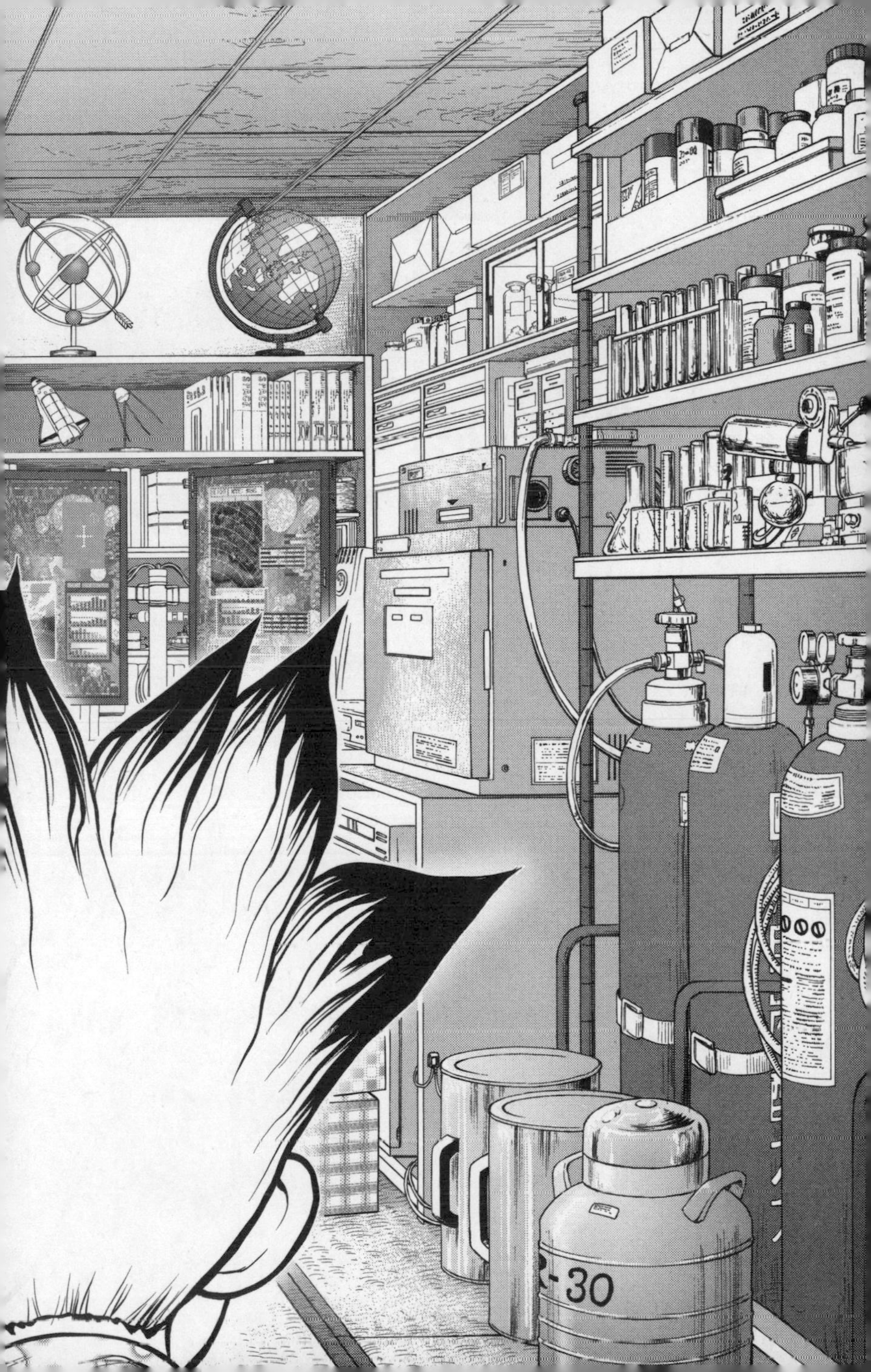
SPACE
SPACE
IV
III
II
I
-30

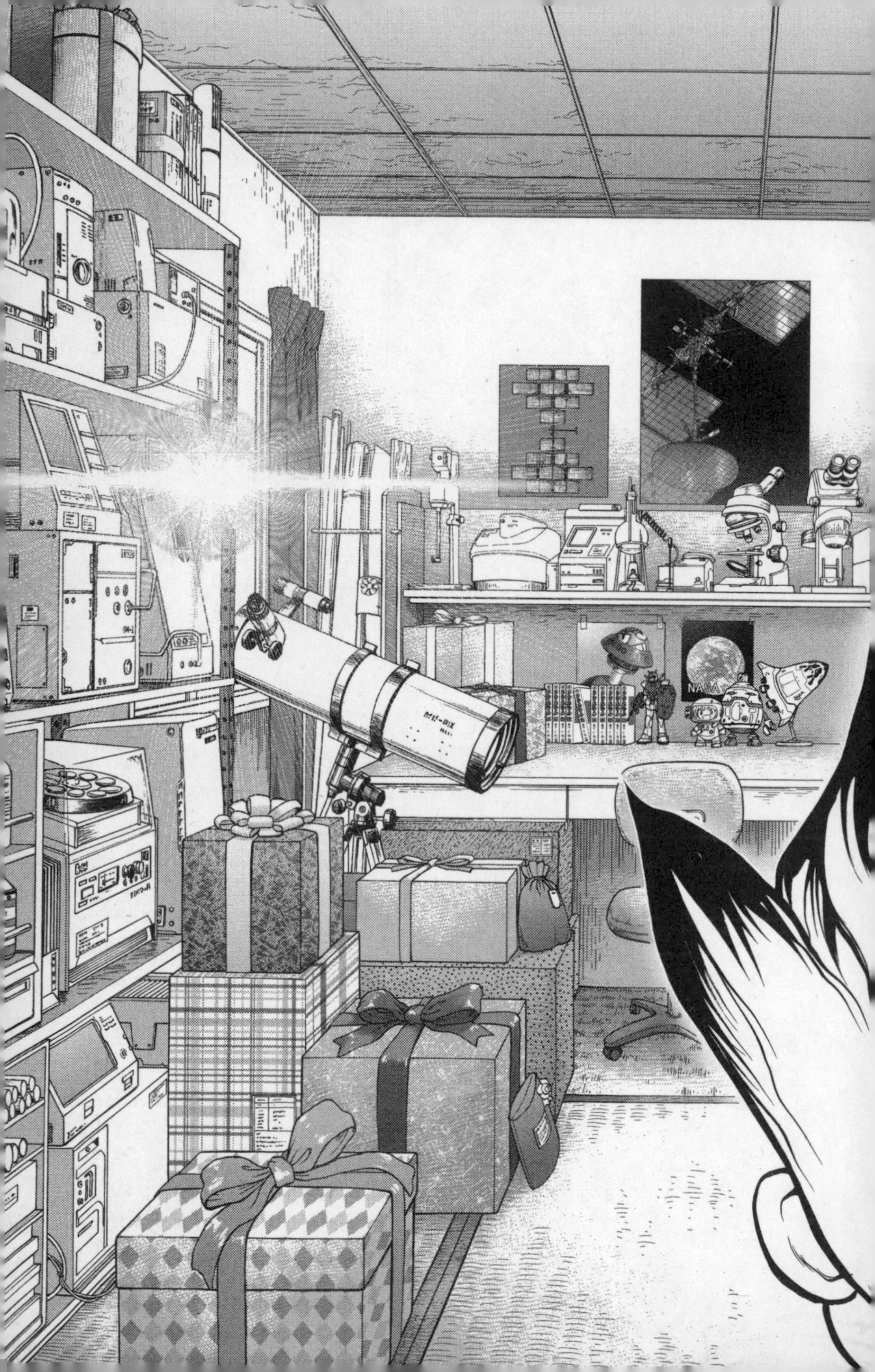
NASA

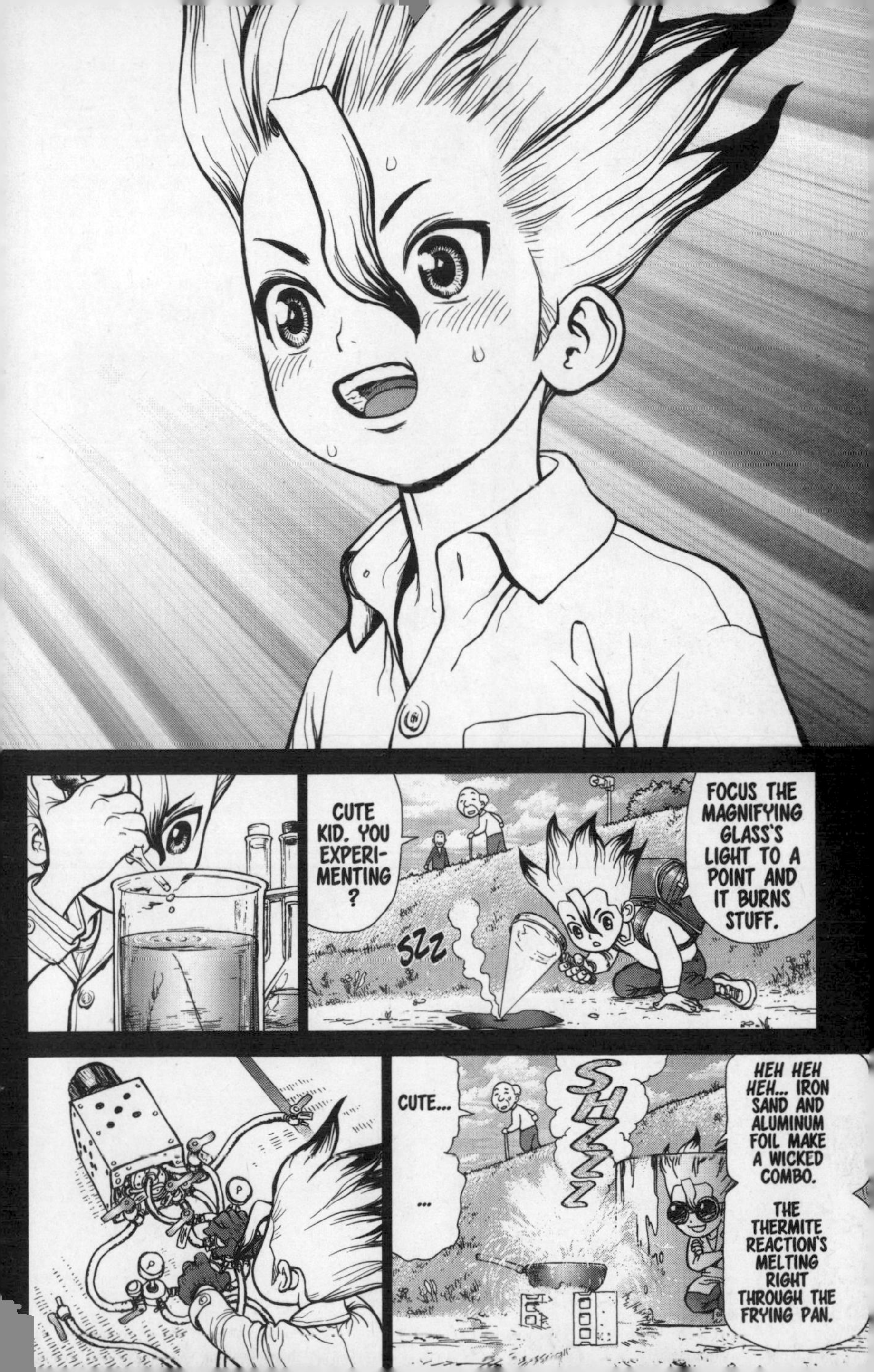
FOCUS THE MAGNIFYING GLASS'S LIGHT TO A POINT AND IT BURNS STUFF.
CUTE KID. YOU EXPERI-MENTING?
SZZ
HEH HEH HEH... IRON SAND AND ALUMINUM FOIL MAKE A WICKED COMBO.
THE THERMITE REACTION'S MELTING RIGHT THROUGH THE FRYING PAN.
SHZZZZ
CUTE...
...

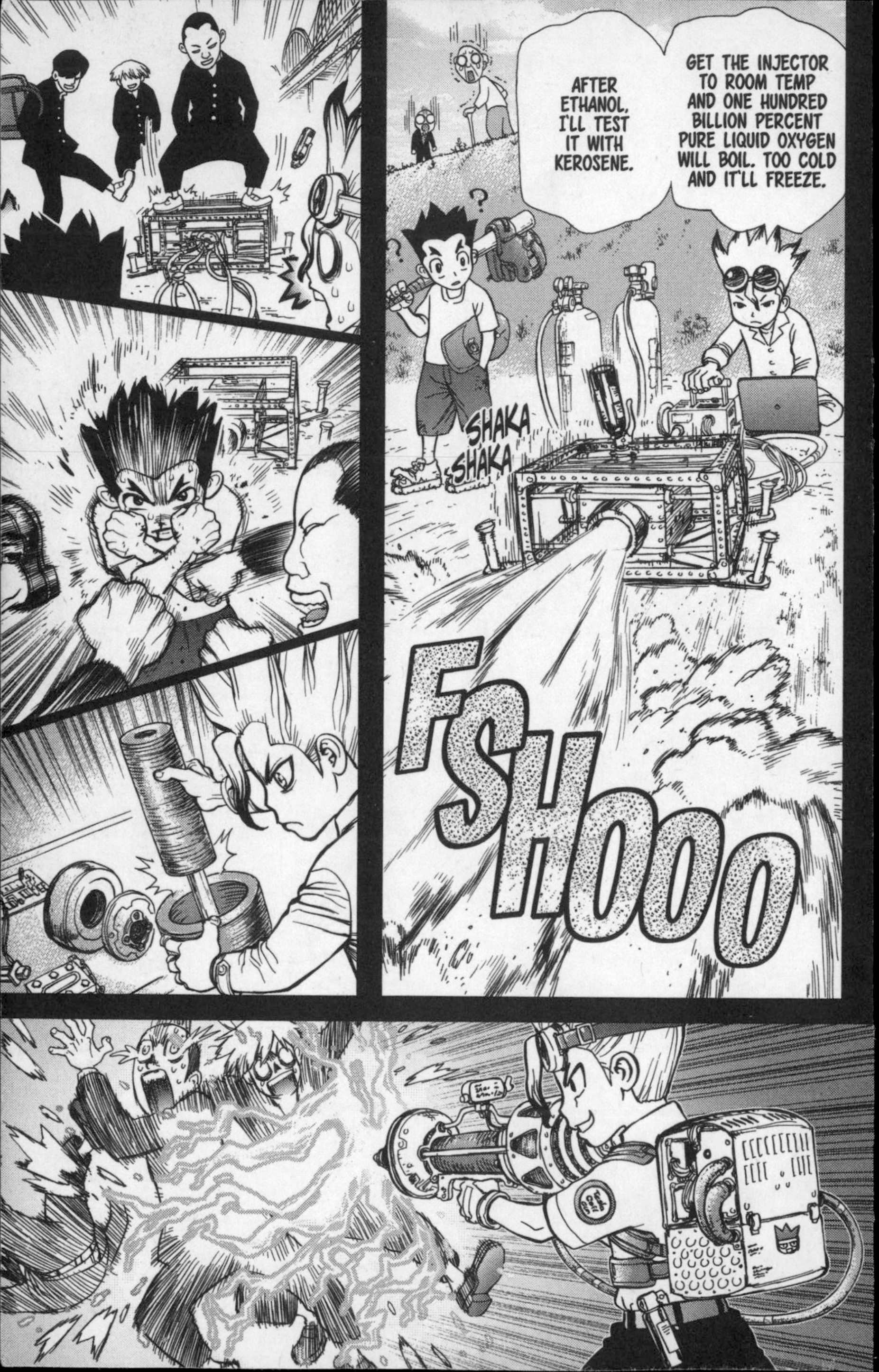
GET THE INJECTOR TO ROOM TEMP AND ONE HUNDRED BILLION PERCENT PURE LIQUID OXYGEN WILL BOIL. TOO COLD AND IT'LL FREEZE.
AFTER ETHANOL, I'LL TEST IT WITH KEROSENE.
SHAKA SHAKA
FSHOOO

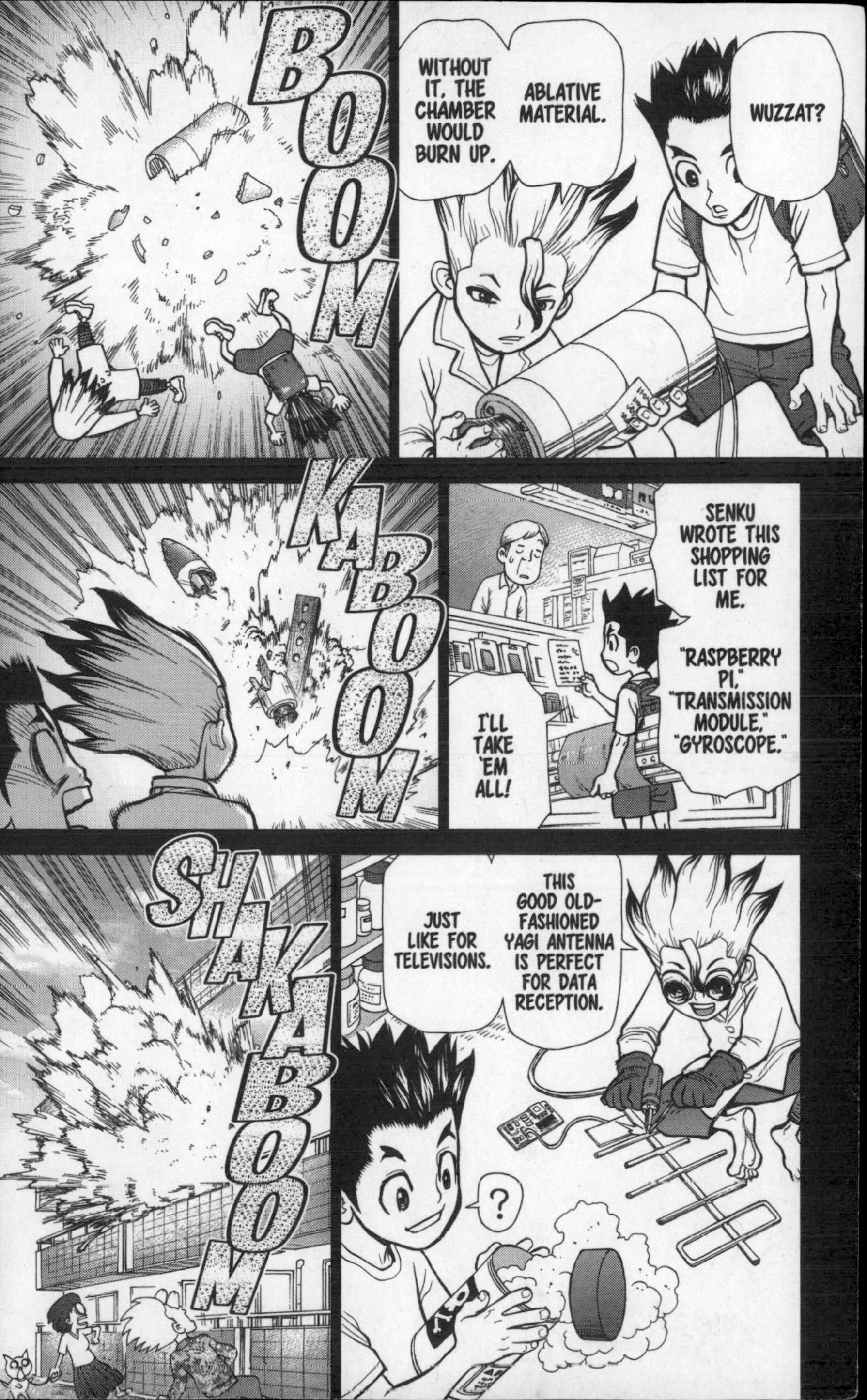
WUZZAT?
ABLATIVE MATERIAL.
WITHOUT IT, THE CHAMBER WOULD BURN UP.
BOOOM
SENKU WROTE THIS SHOPPING LIST FOR ME.
"RASPBERRY PI," "TRANSMISSION MODULE," "GYROSCOPE."
I'LL TAKE 'EM ALL!
KABOOOM
THIS GOOD OLD-FASHIONED YAGI ANTENNA IS PERFECT FOR DATA RECEPTION.
JUST LIKE FOR TELEVISIONS.
?
SHAKABOOOM

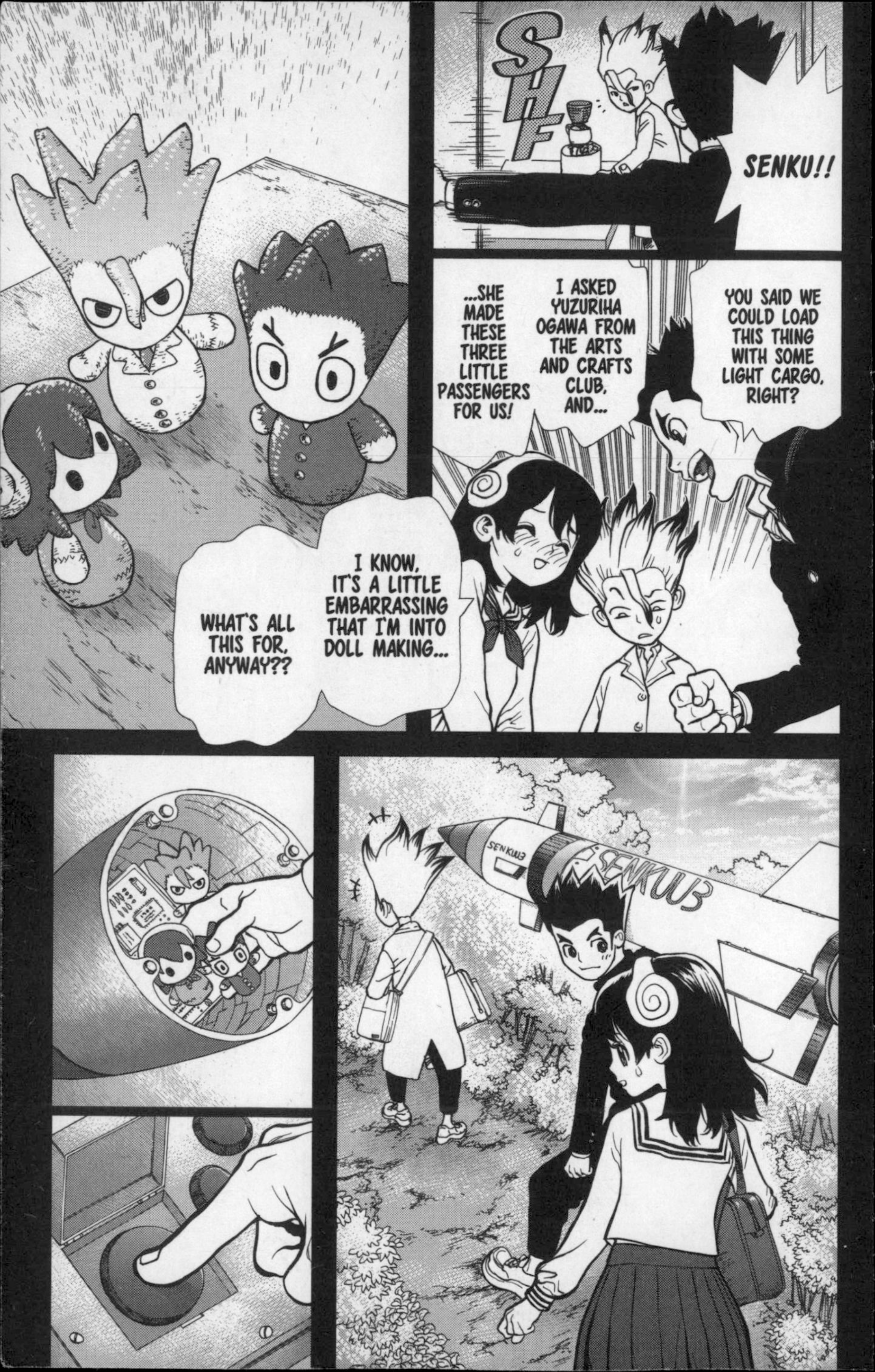
SHF
SENKU!!
YOU SAID WE COULD LOAD THIS THING WITH SOME LIGHT CARGO, RIGHT?
I ASKED YUZURIHA OGAWA FROM THE ARTS AND CRAFTS CLUB, AND...
...SHE MADE THESE THREE LITTLE PASSENGERS FOR US!
I KNOW, IT'S A LITTLE EMBARRASSING THAT I'M INTO DOLL MAKING...
WHAT'S ALL THIS FOR, ANYWAY??

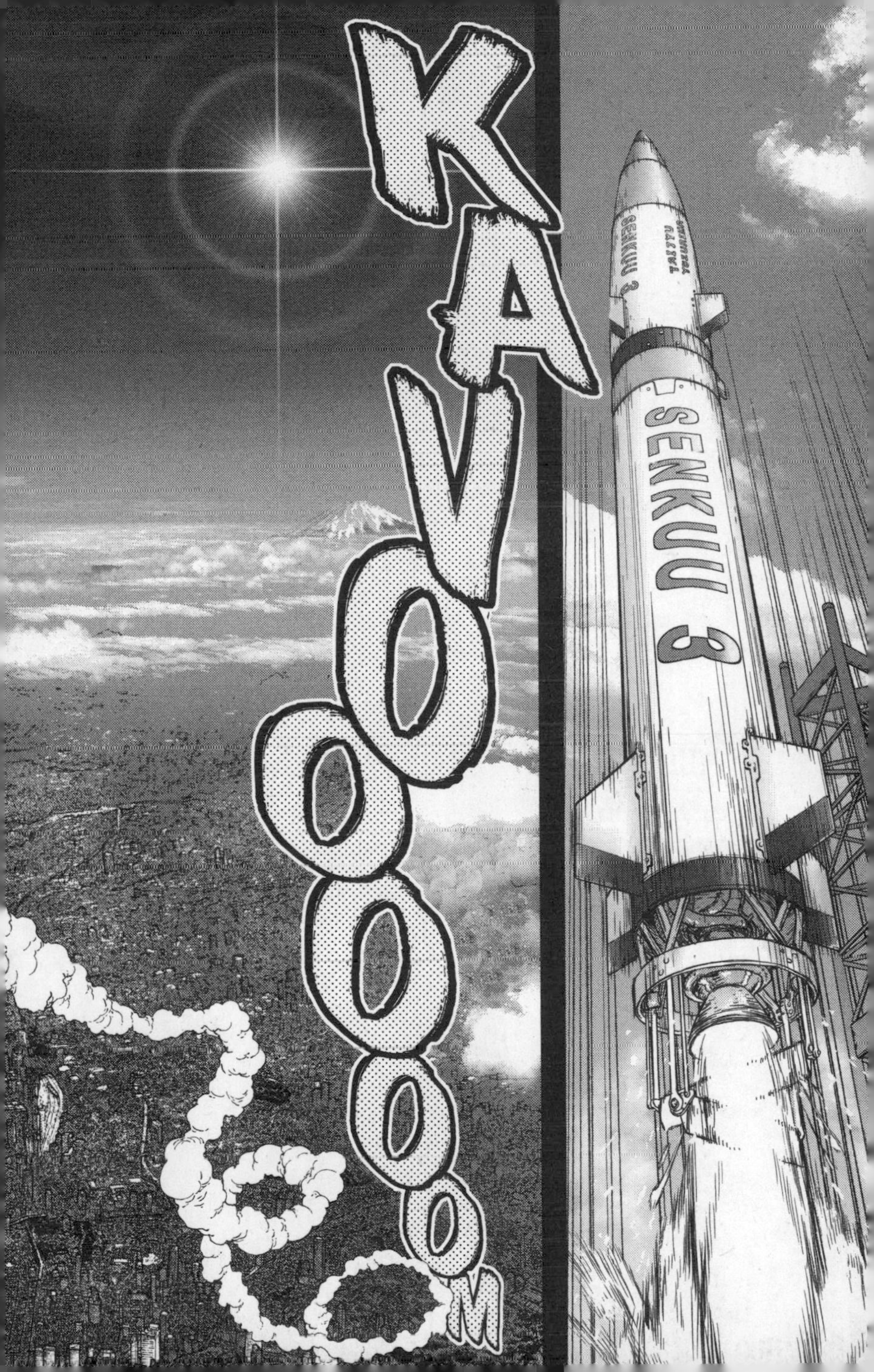
SENKUU 3
SENKUU 3
KAVOOOOOM

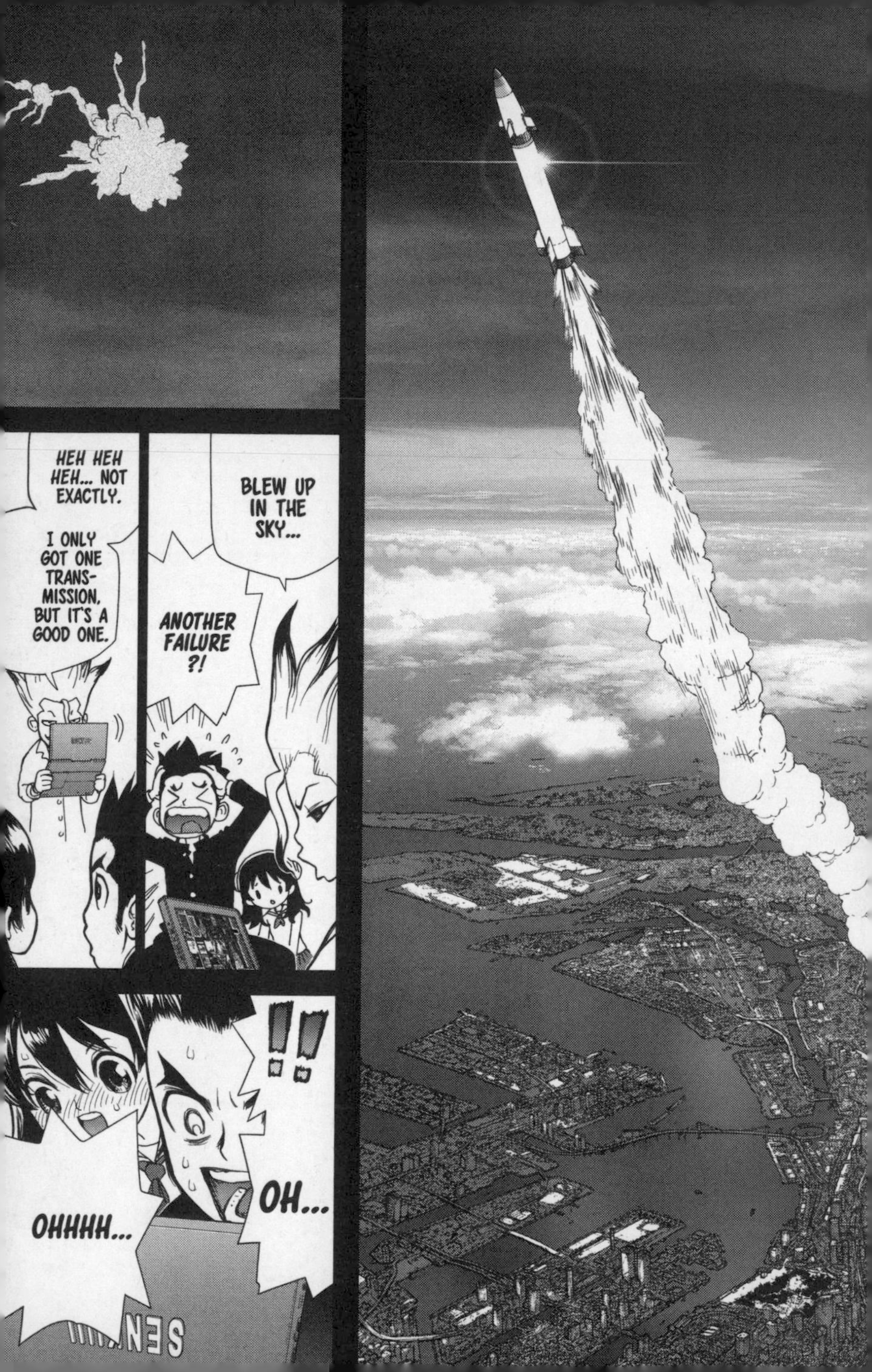
BLEW UP IN THE SKY...
ANOTHER FAILURE ?!
HEH HEH HEH... NOT EXACTLY.
I ONLY GOT ONE TRANSMISSION, BUT IT'S A GOOD ONE.
!!
OH...
OHHHH...

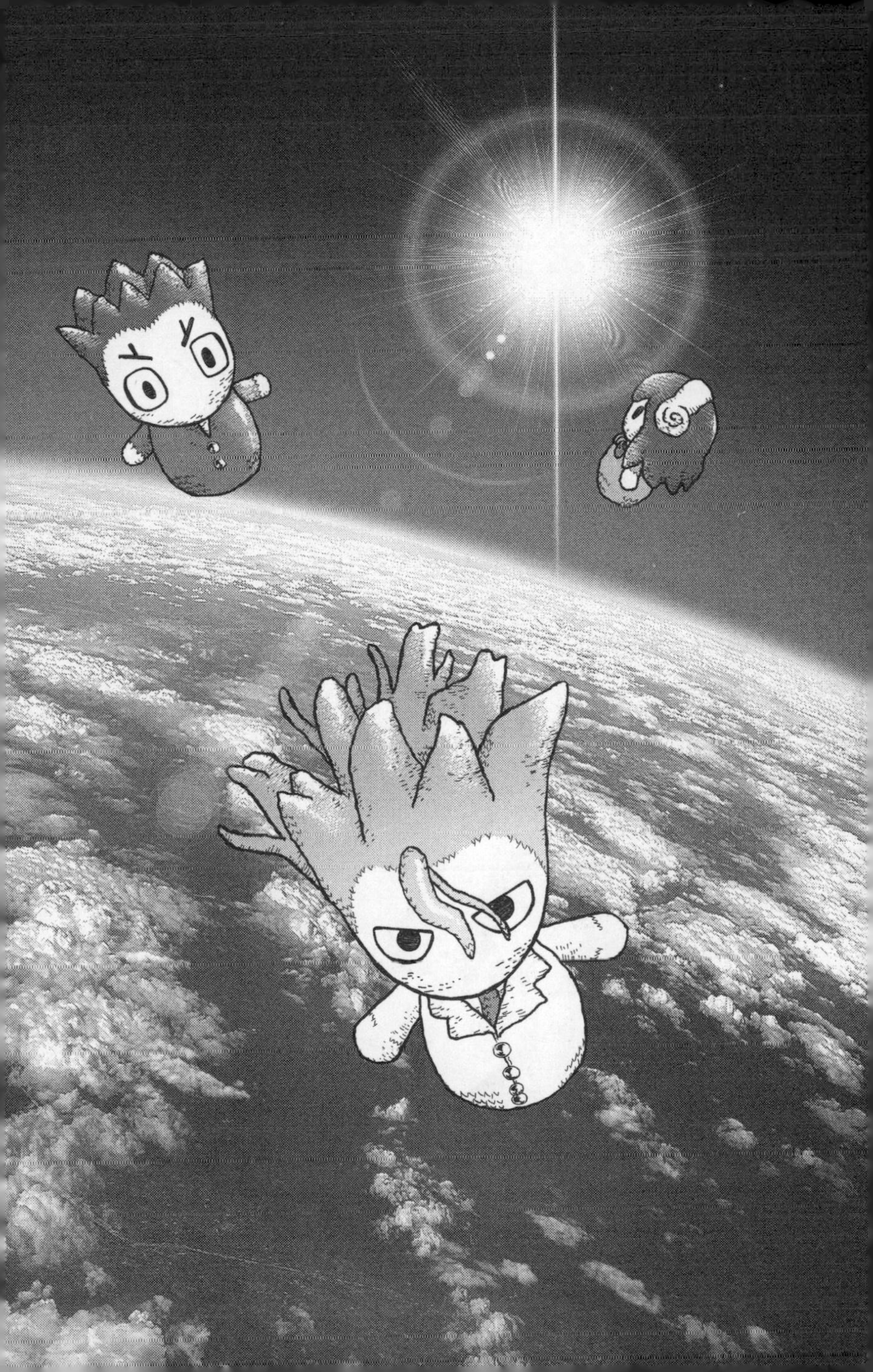

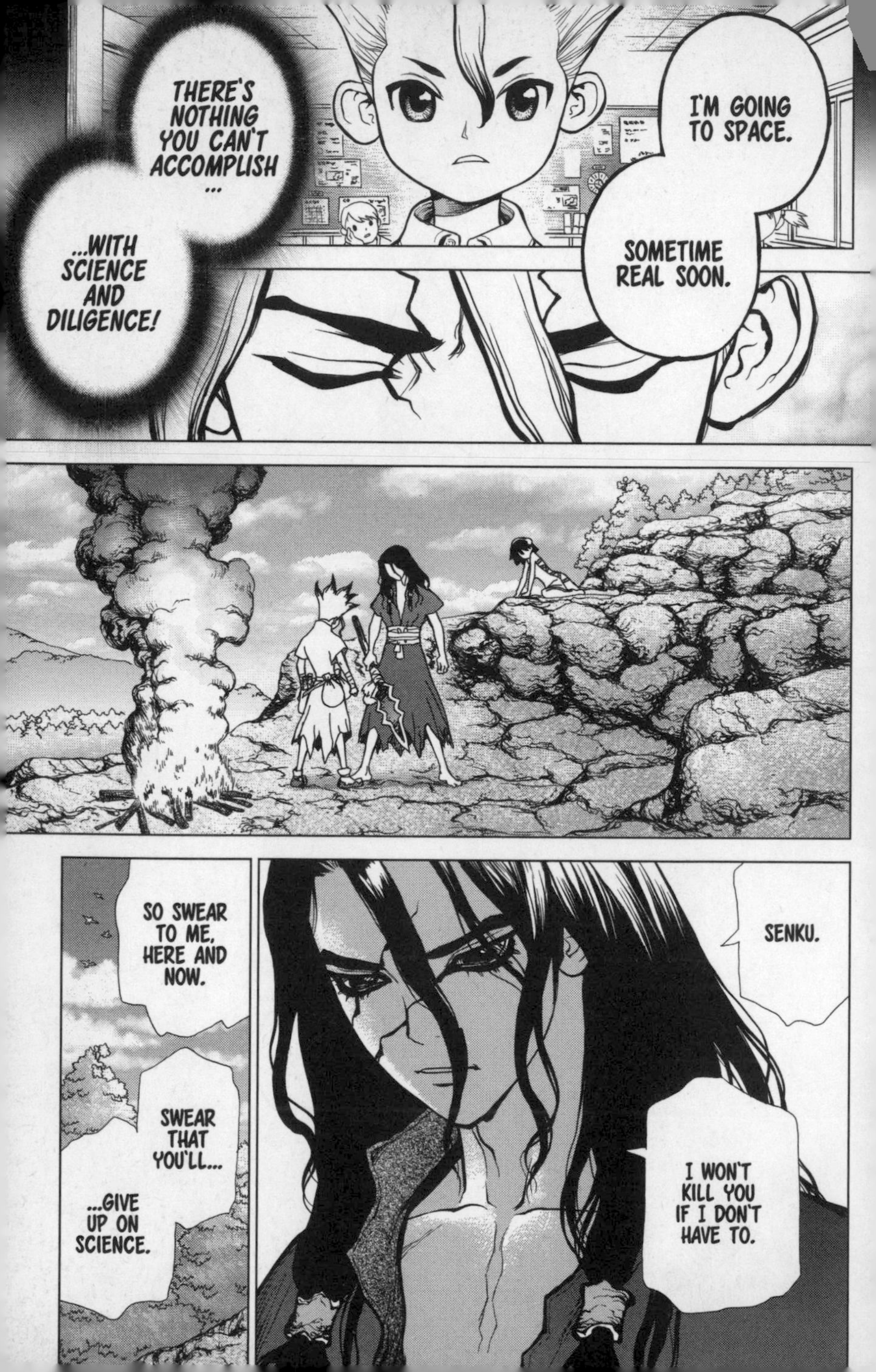
I'M GOING TO SPACE.
SOMETIME REAL SOON.
THERE'S NOTHING YOU CAN'T ACCOMPLISH ...
...WITH SCIENCE AND DILIGENCE!
SENKU.
I WON'T KILL YOU IF I DON'T HAVE TO.
SO SWEAR TO ME, HERE AND NOW.
SWEAR THAT YOU'LL...
...GIVE UP ON SCIENCE.

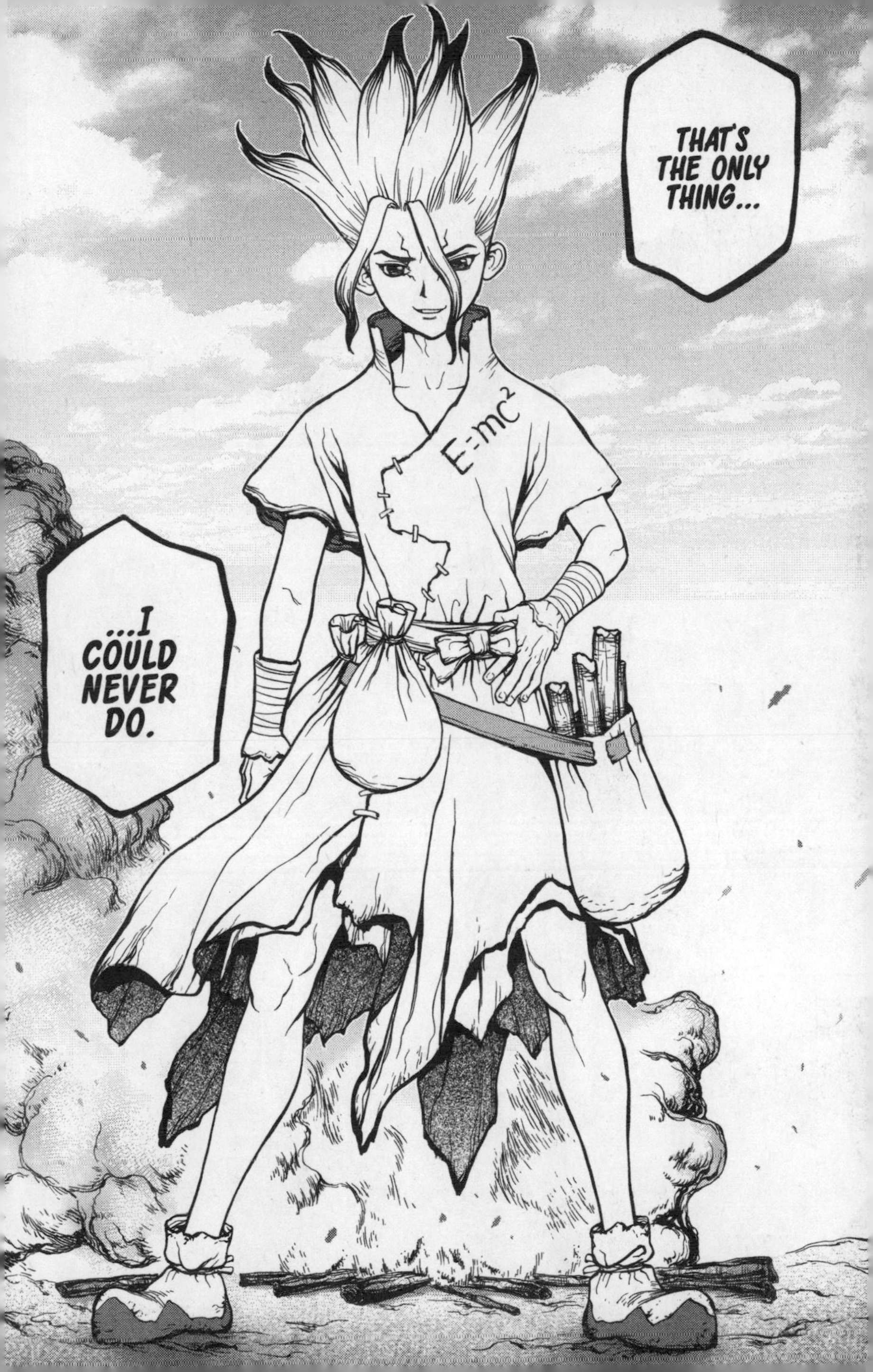
THAT'S THE ONLY THING...
...I COULD NEVER DO.
E=mc²

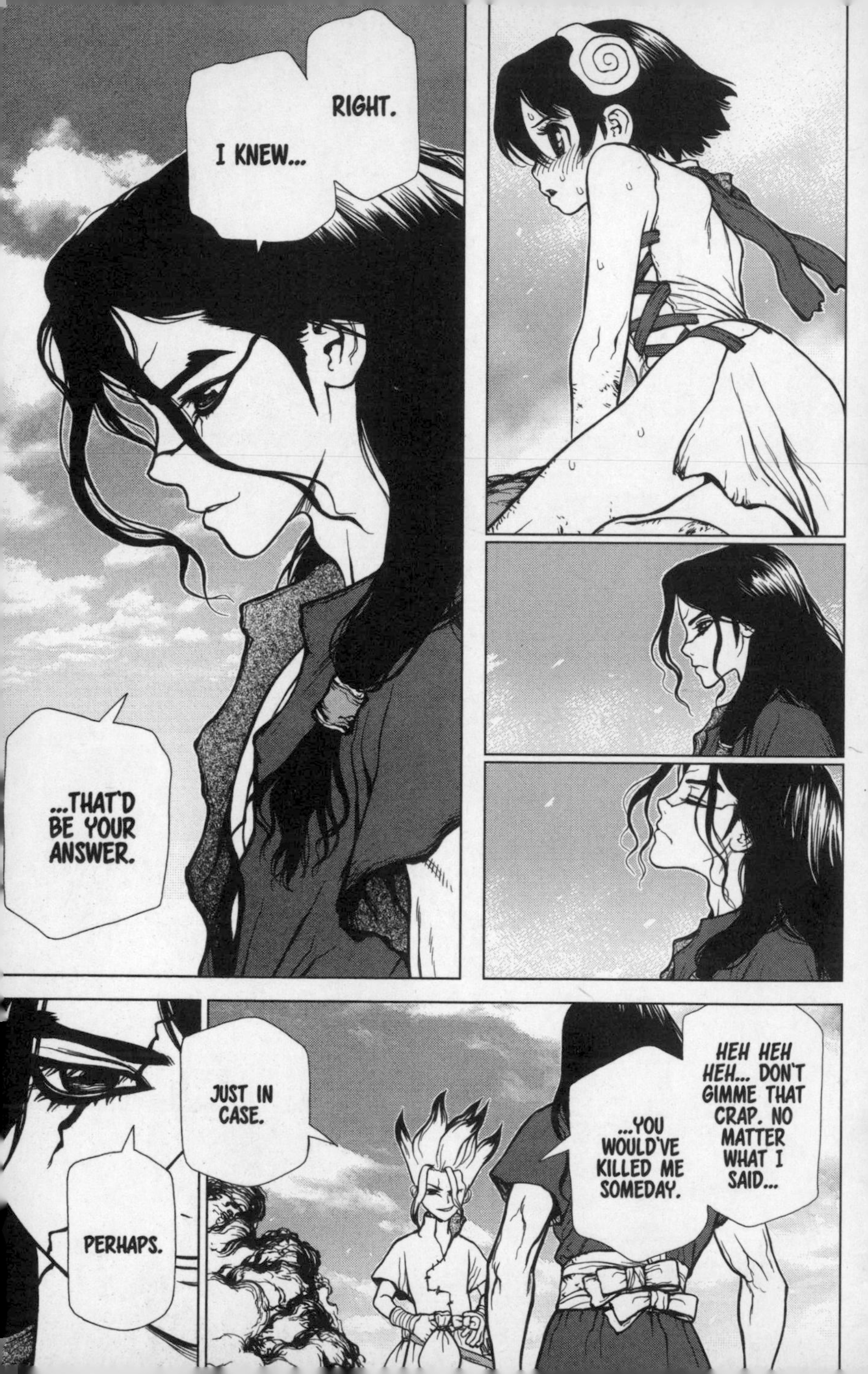
RIGHT. I KNEW...
...THAT'D BE YOUR ANSWER.
HEH HEH HEH... DON'T GIMME THAT CRAP. NO MATTER WHAT I SAID...
...YOU WOULD'VE KILLED ME SOMEDAY.
JUST IN CASE.
PERHAPS.

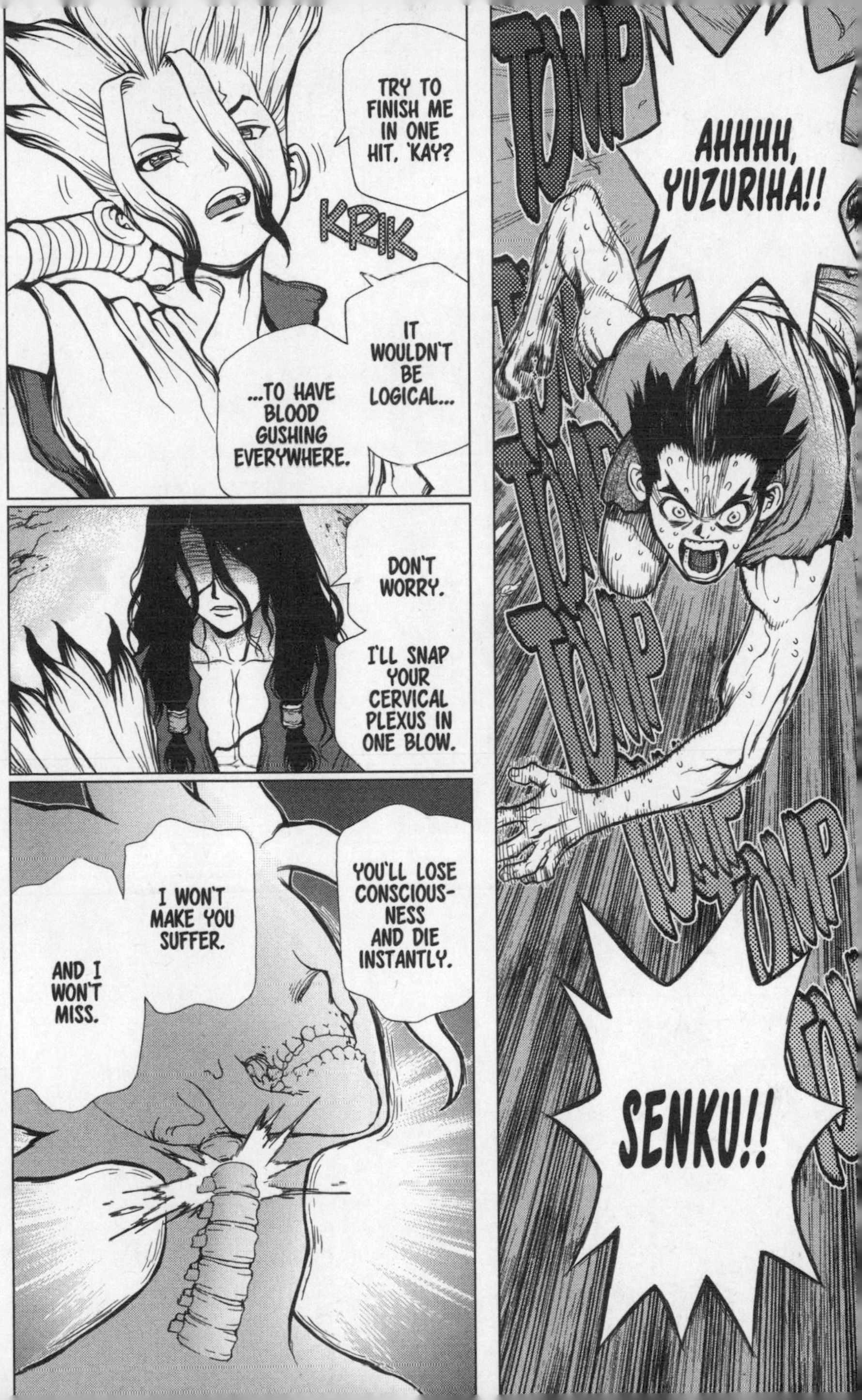
TOMP
AHHHH, YUZURIHA!!
TOMP
TOMP
SENKU!!
TRY TO FINISH ME IN ONE HIT, 'KAY?
KRIK
IT WOULDN'T BE LOGICAL...
...TO HAVE BLOOD GUSHING EVERYWHERE.
DON'T WORRY.
I'LL SNAP YOUR CERVICAL PLEXUS IN ONE BLOW.
YOU'LL LOSE CONSCIOUSNESS AND DIE INSTANTLY.
I WON'T MAKE YOU SUFFER.
AND I WON'T MISS.

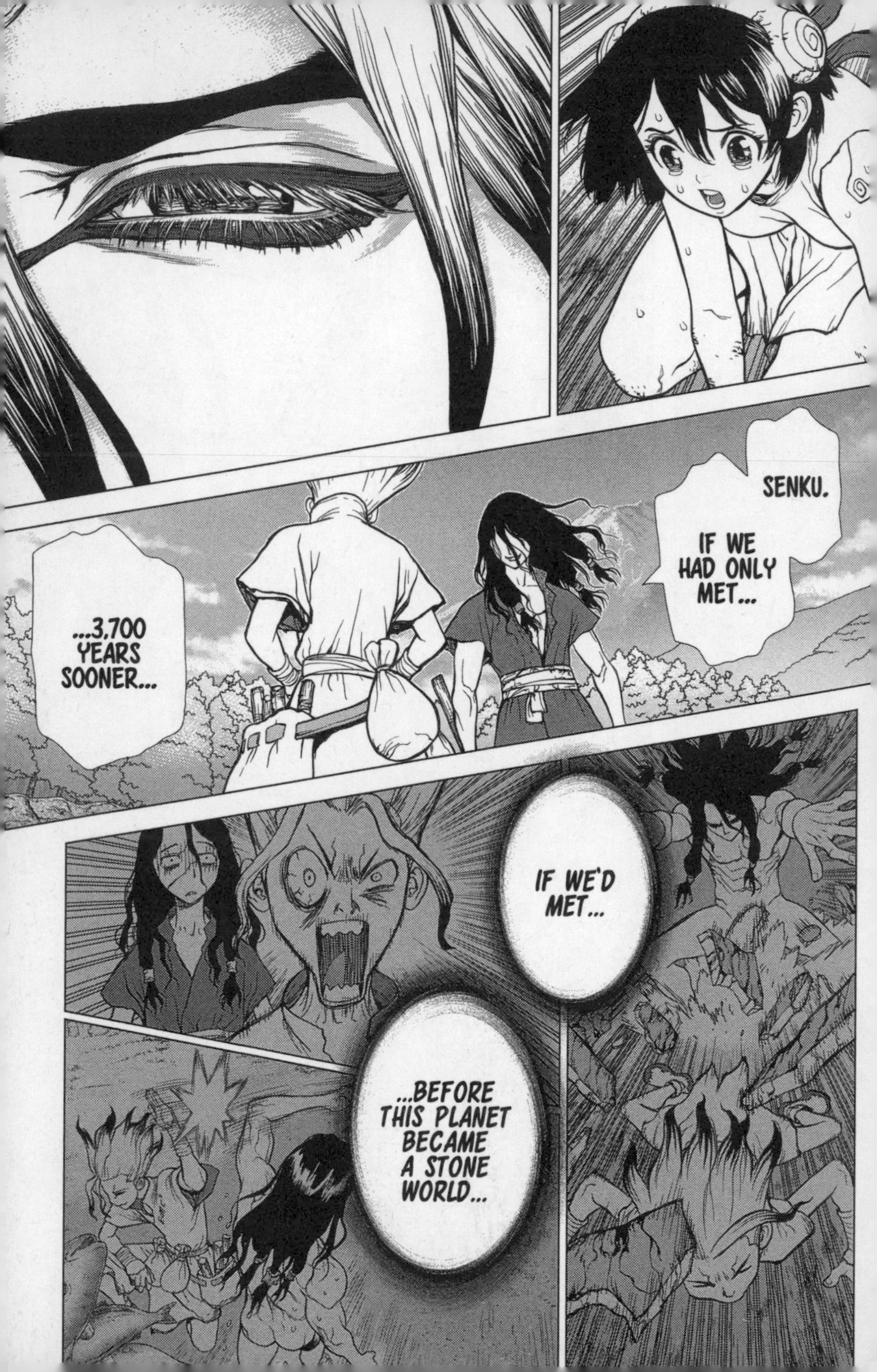
SENKU.
IF WE HAD ONLY MET...
...3,700 YEARS SOONER...
IF WE'D MET...
...BEFORE THIS PLANET BECAME A STONE WORLD...

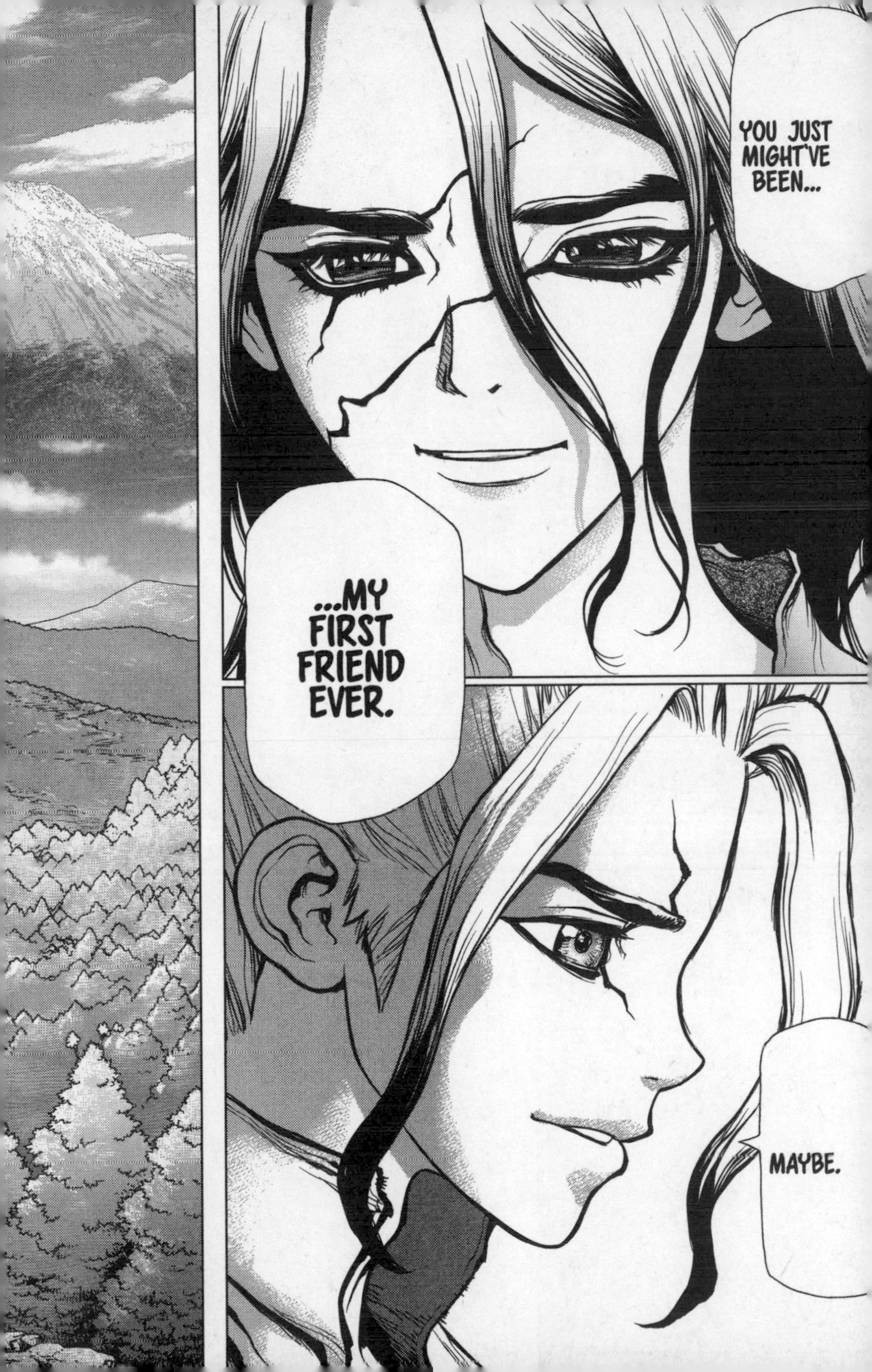
YOU JUST MIGHT'VE BEEN...
...MY FIRST FRIEND EVER.
MAYBE.

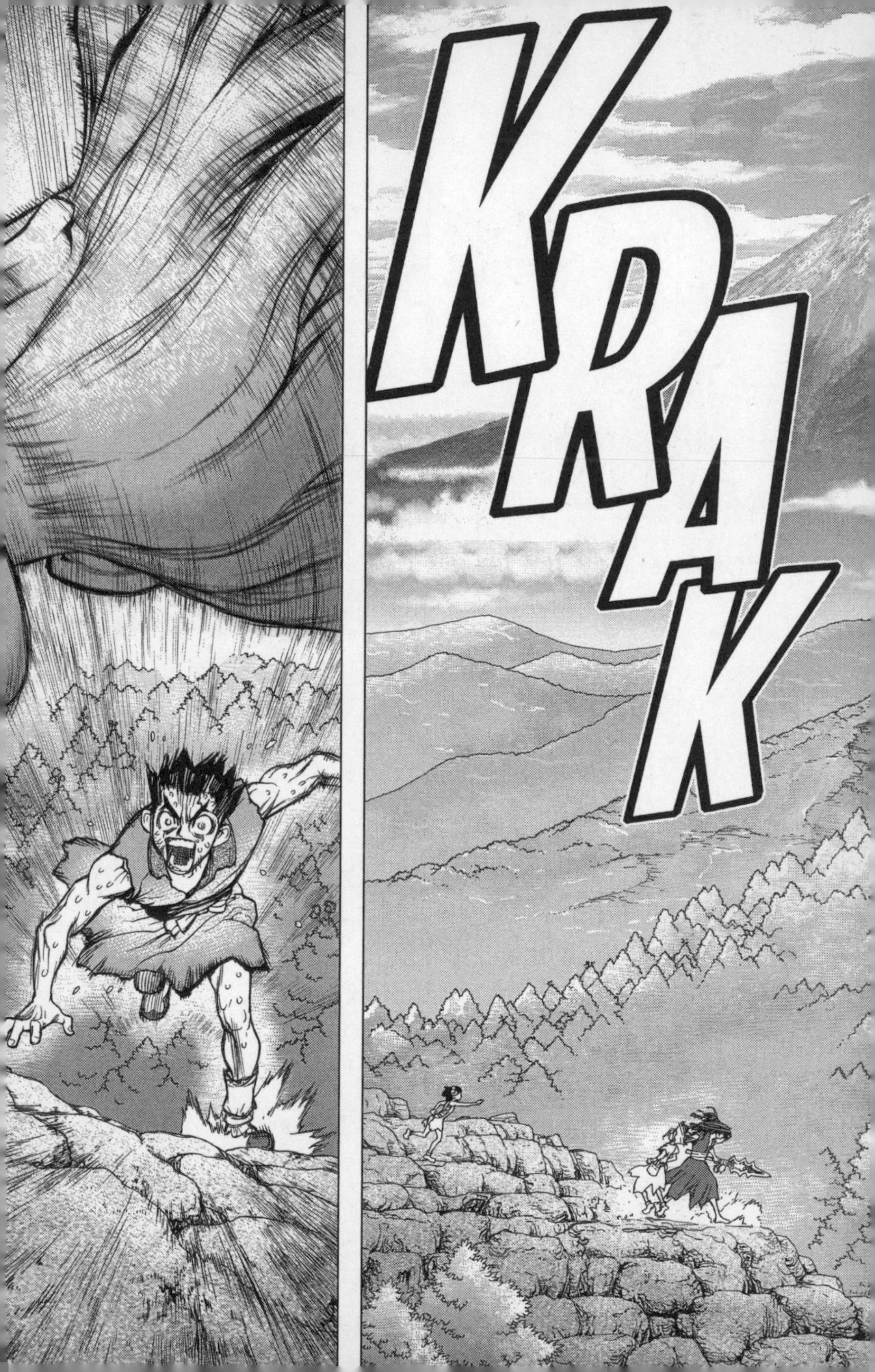
KRAK

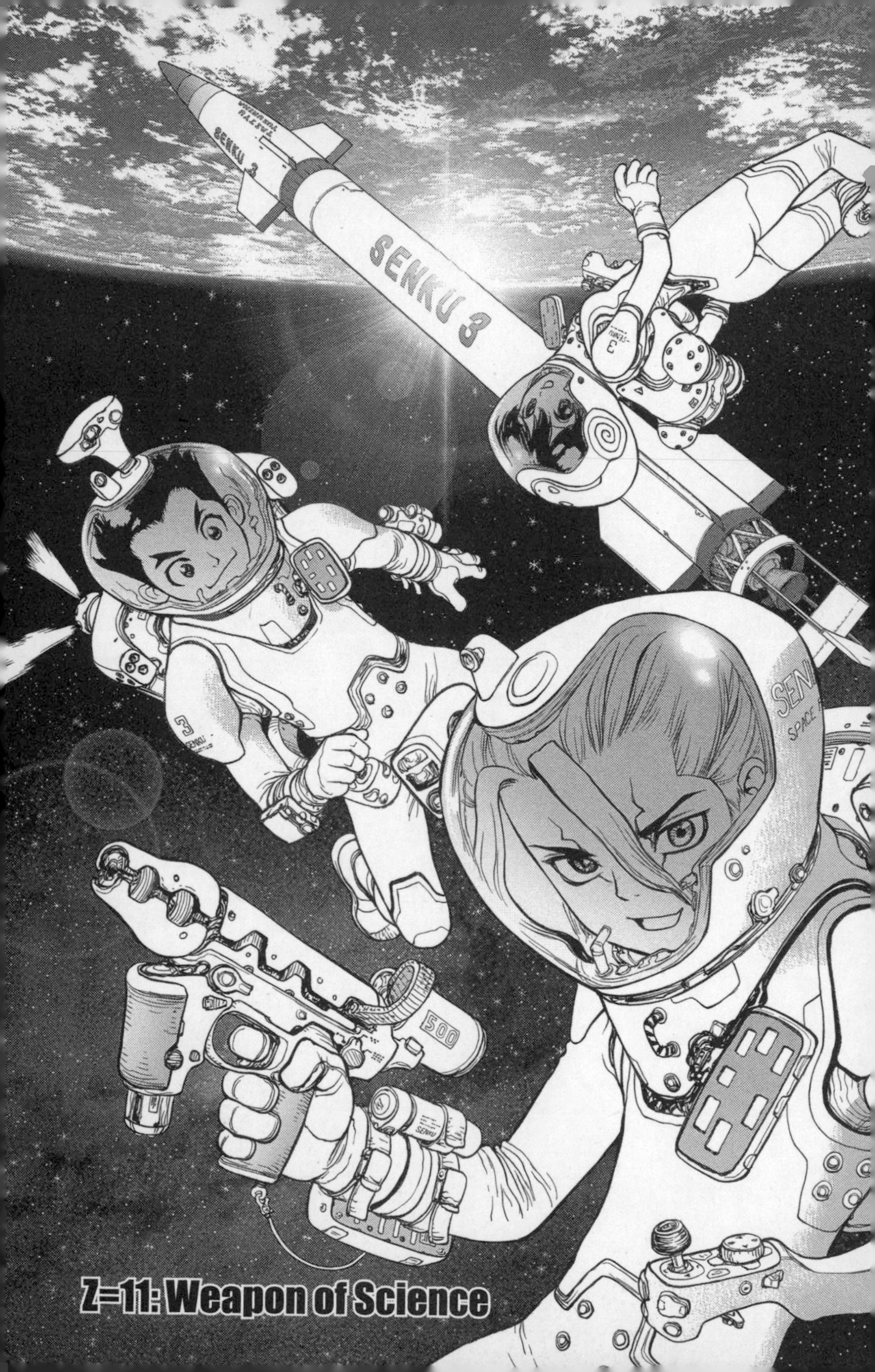
SENKU 3

Z=11: Weapon of Science

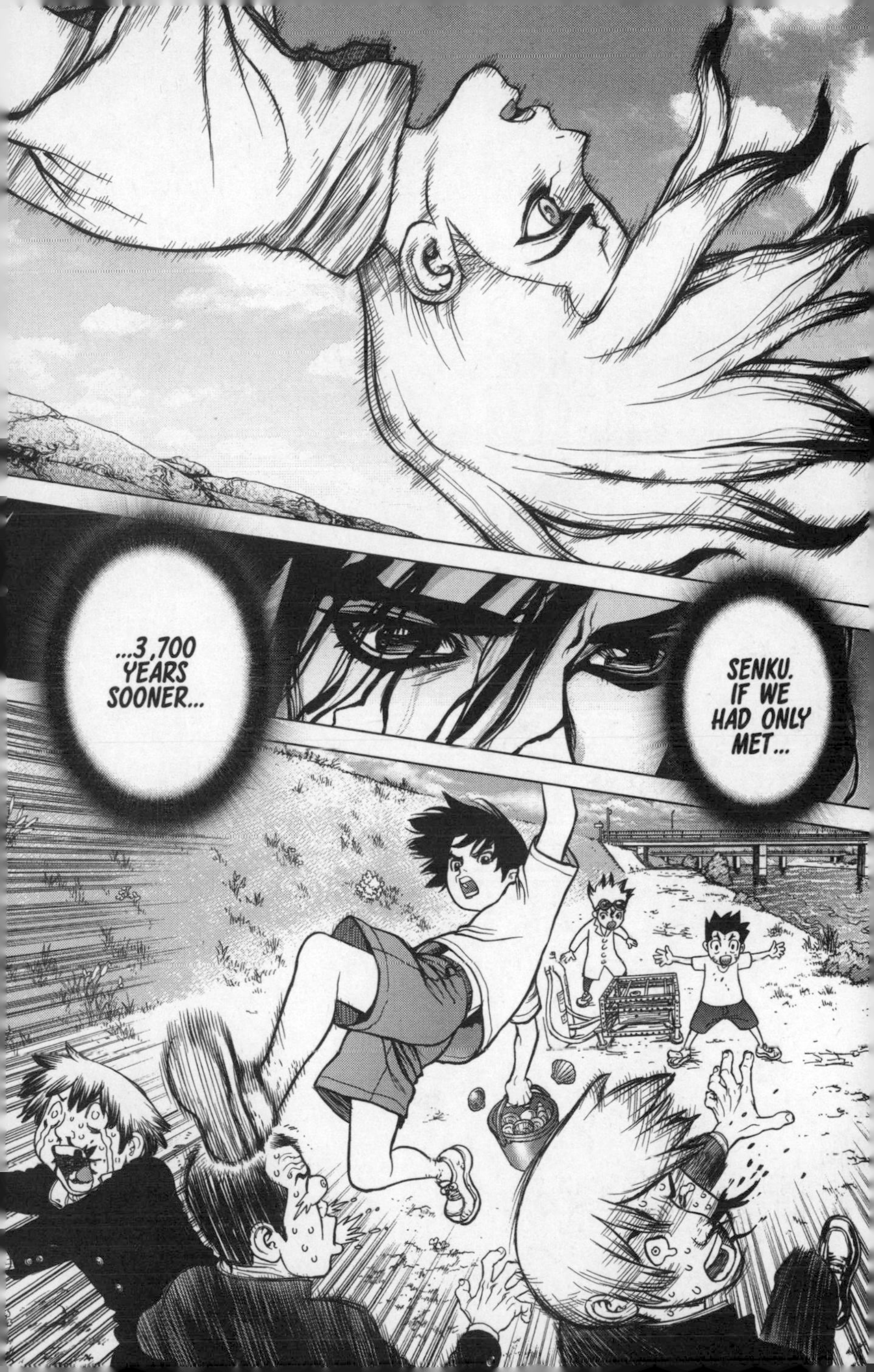
SENKU. IF WE HAD ONLY MET...
...3,700 YEARS SOONER...

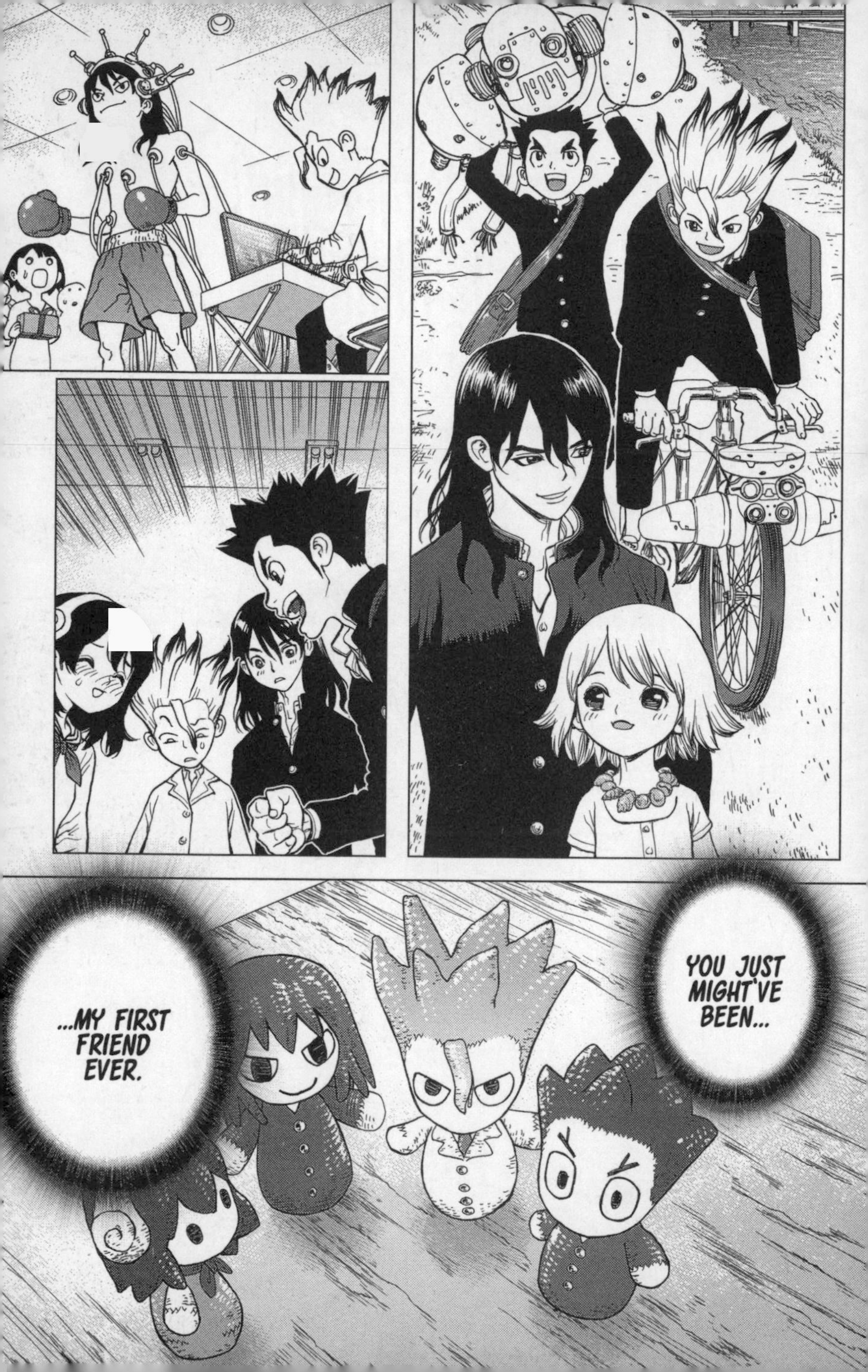
YOU JUST MIGHT'VE BEEN...
...MY FIRST FRIEND EVER.

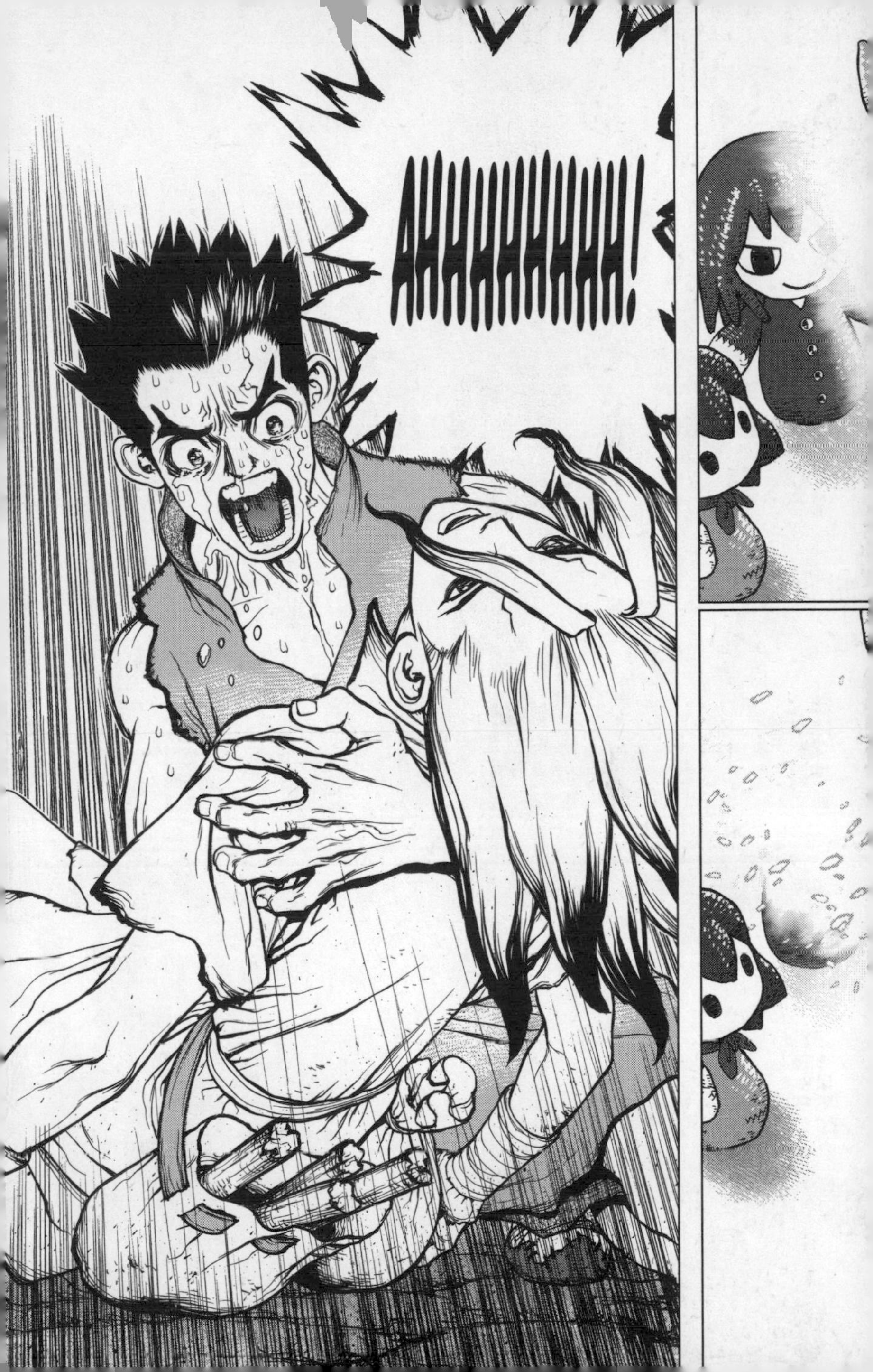
AHHHHHHHHHH!

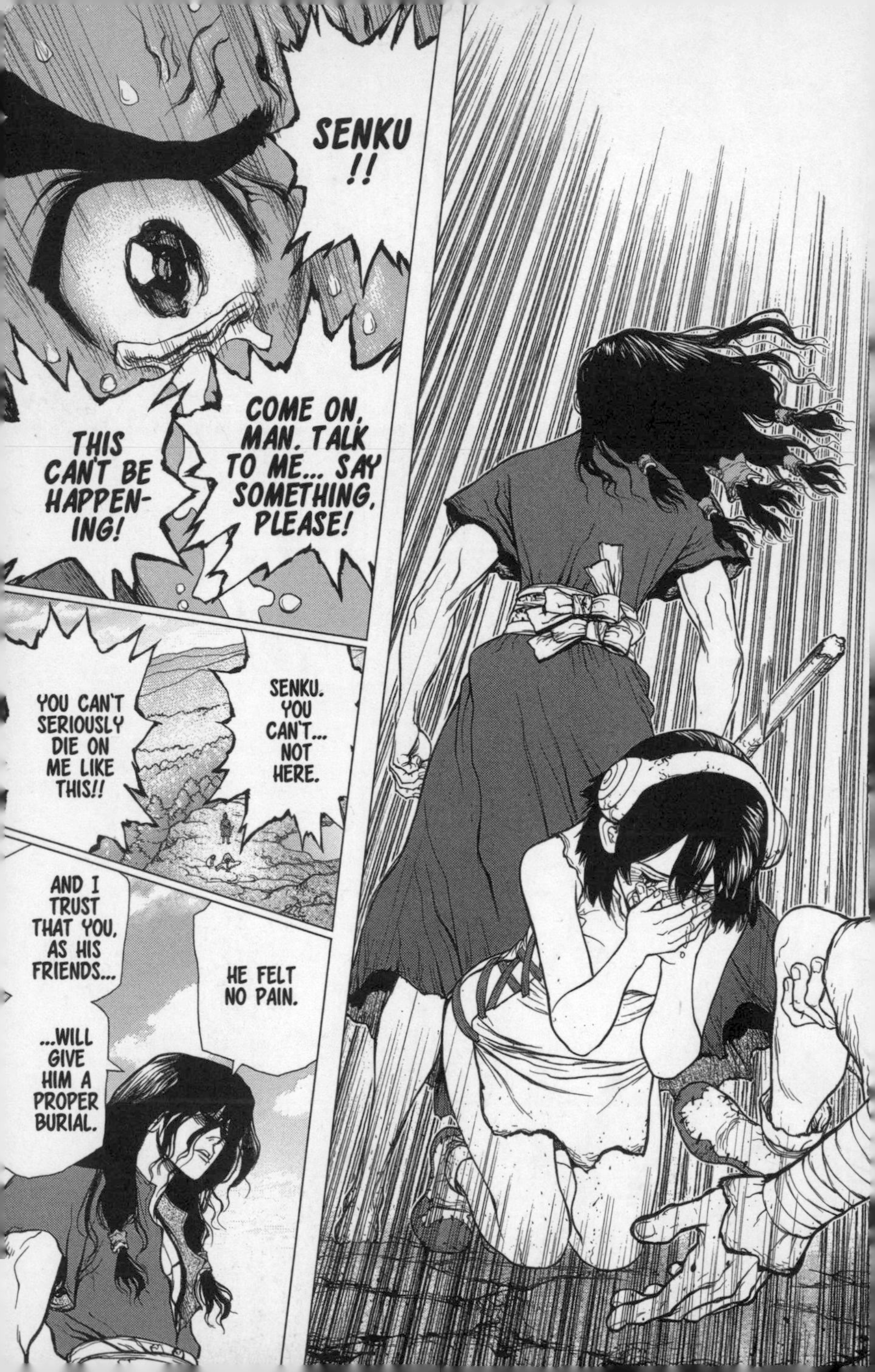

SENKU!!
COME ON, MAN. TALK TO ME... SAY SOMETHING, PLEASE!
THIS CAN'T BE HAPPEN-ING!
SENKU. YOU CAN'T... NOT HERE.
YOU CAN'T SERIOUSLY DIE ON ME LIKE THIS!!
HE FELT NO PAIN.
AND I TRUST THAT YOU, AS HIS FRIENDS...
...WILL GIVE HIM A PROPER BURIAL.

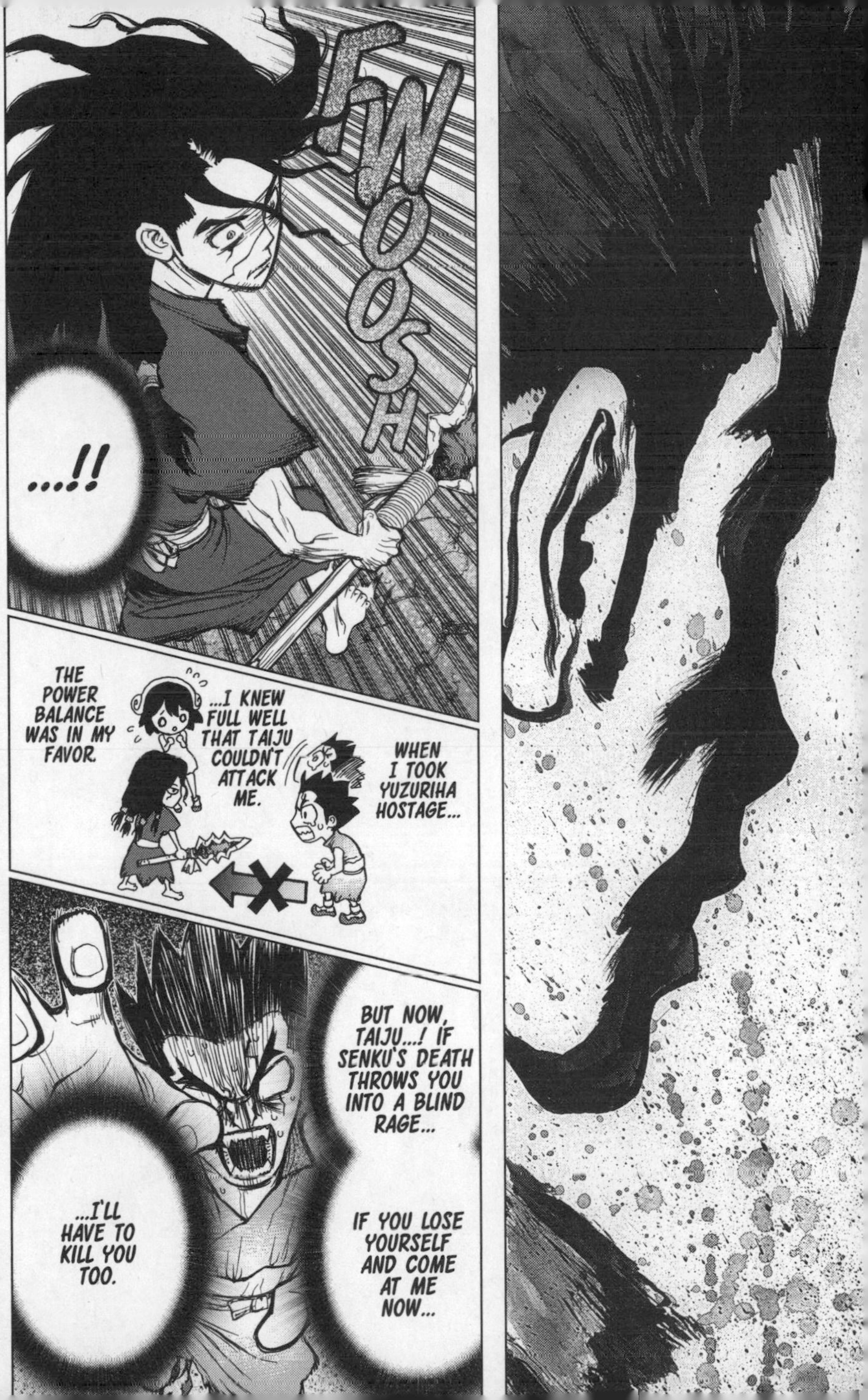
FWOOSH
...!!
WHEN I TOOK YUZURIHA HOSTAGE...
...I KNEW FULL WELL THAT TAIJU COULDN'T ATTACK ME.
THE POWER BALANCE WAS IN MY FAVOR.
BUT NOW, TAIJU...! IF SENKU'S DEATH THROWS YOU INTO A BLIND RAGE...
IF YOU LOSE YOURSELF AND COME AT ME NOW...
...I'LL HAVE TO KILL YOU TOO.

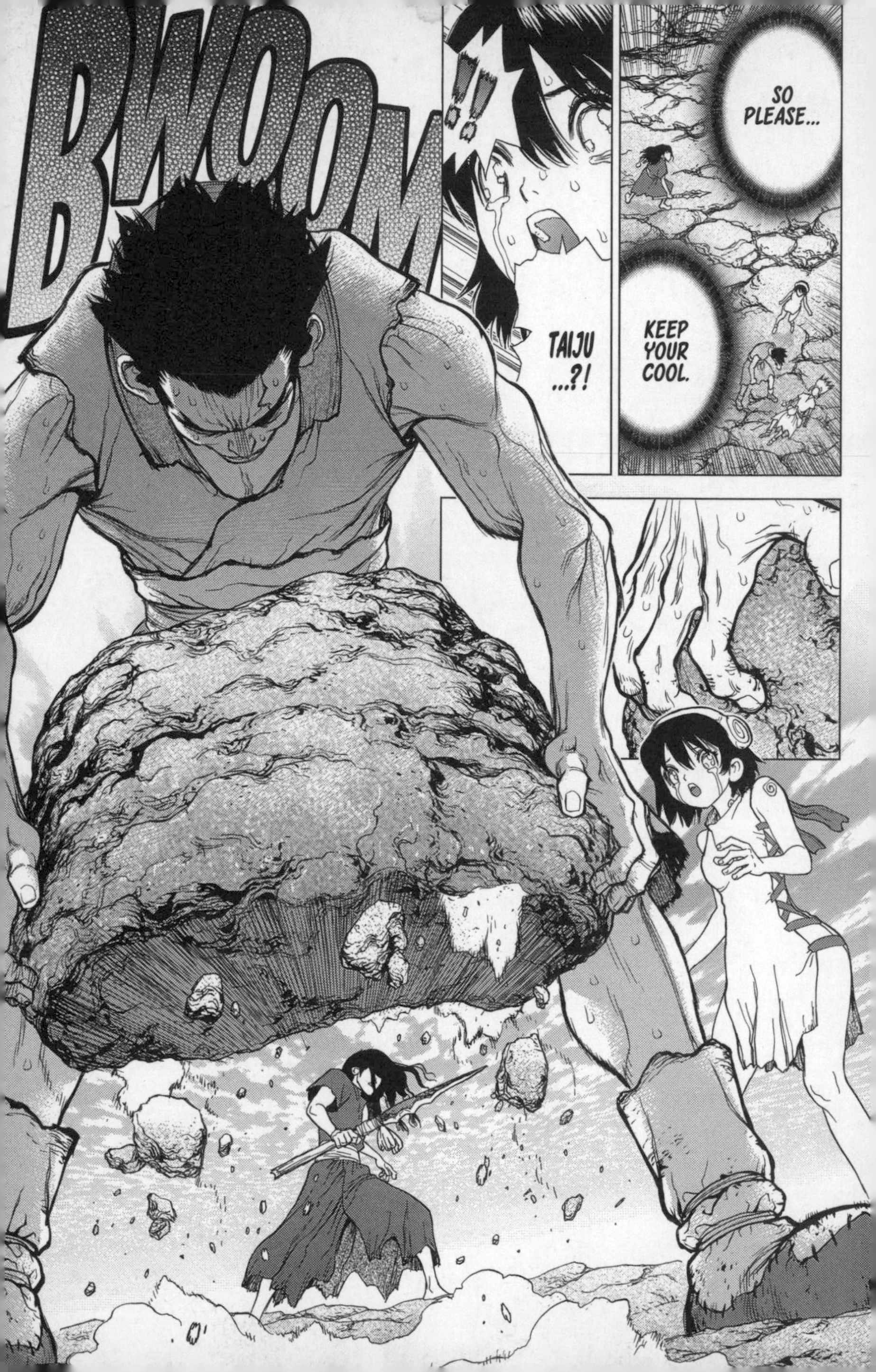
SO PLEASE...
KEEP YOUR COOL.
!!
TAIJU ...?!
BWOOM

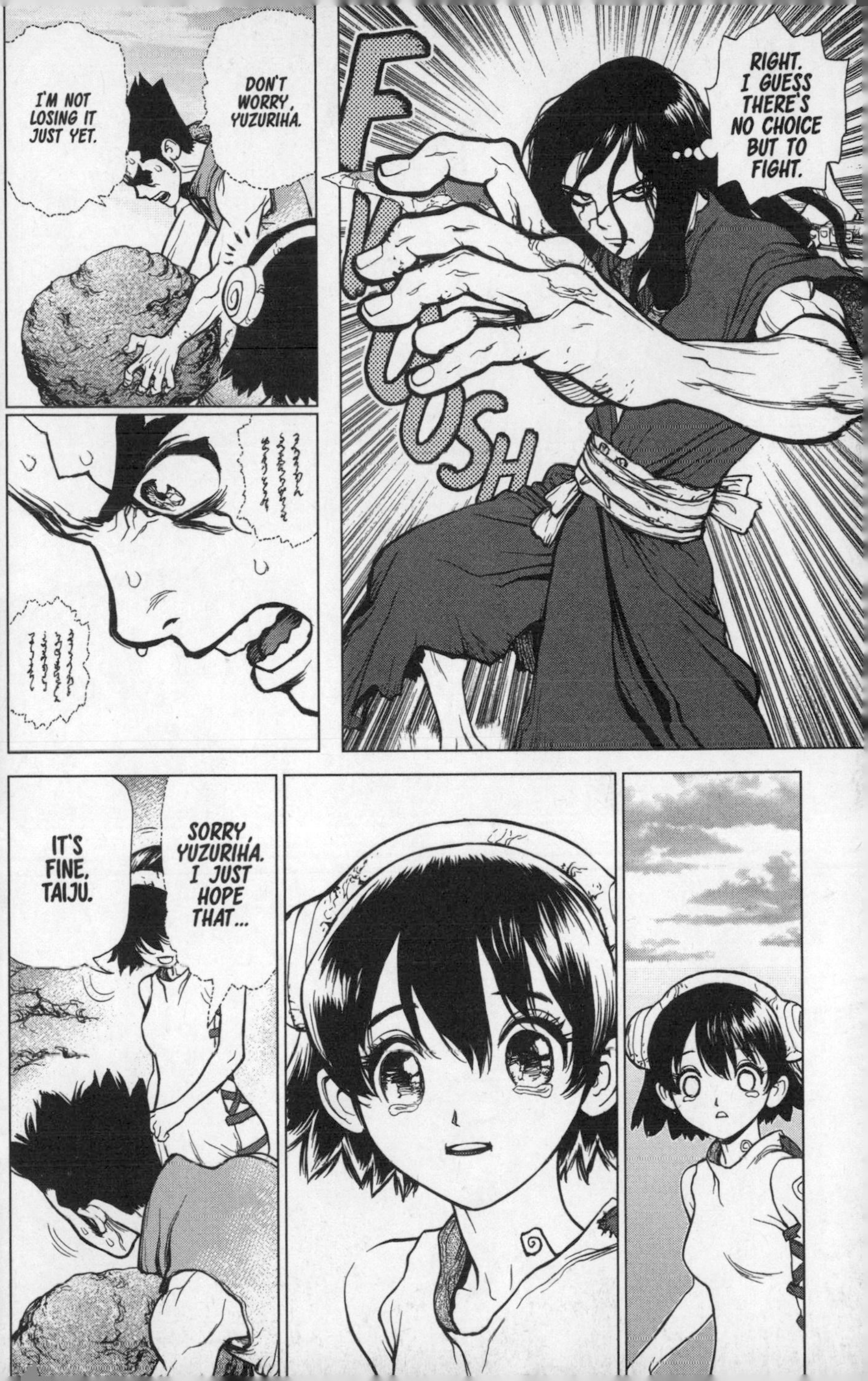
RIGHT. I GUESS THERE'S NO CHOICE BUT TO FIGHT.
FWOOSH
DON'T WORRY, YUZURIHA.
I'M NOT LOSING IT JUST YET.
SORRY, YUZURIHA. I JUST HOPE THAT...
IT'S FINE, TAIJU.

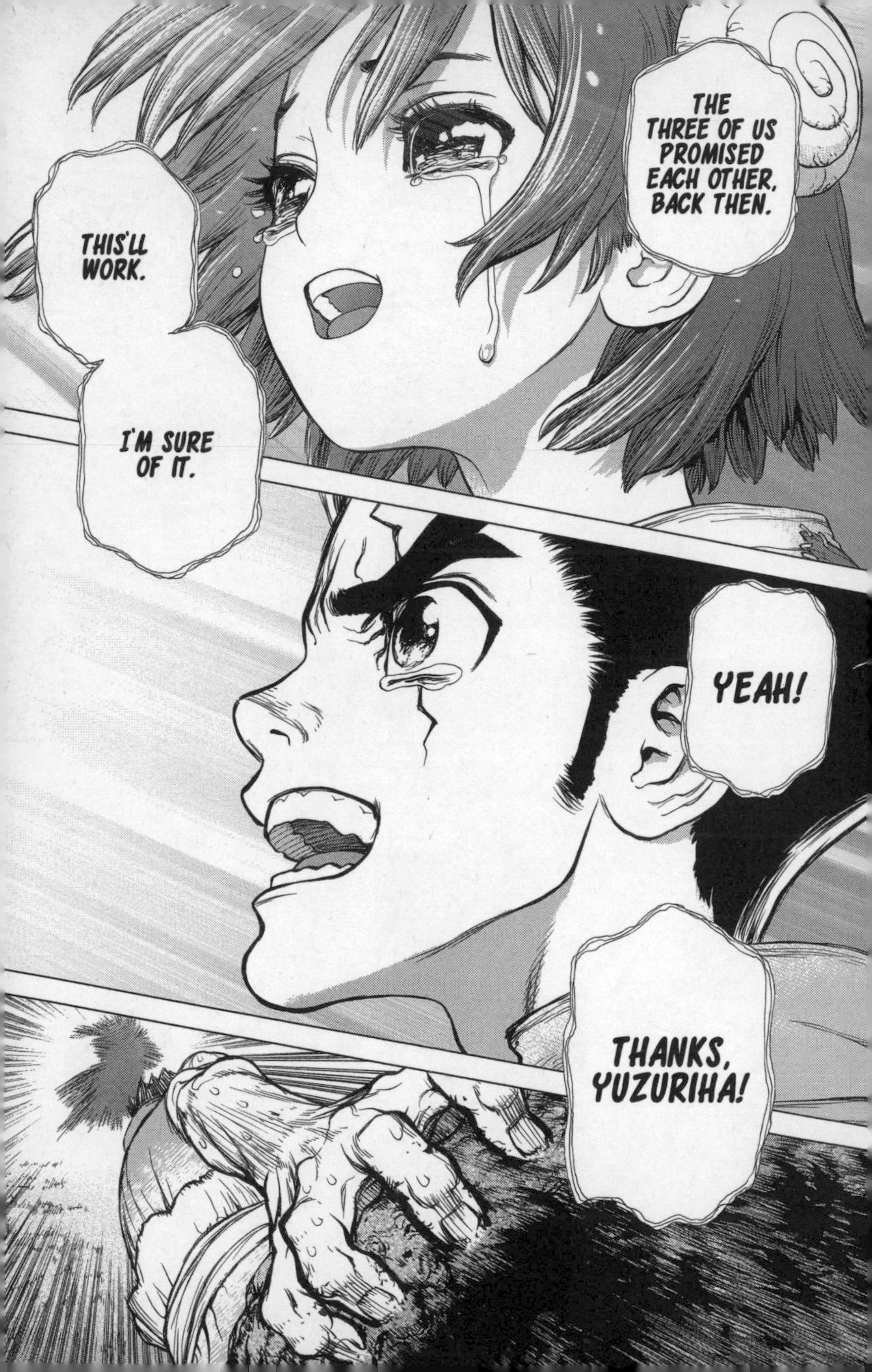
THE THREE OF US PROMISED EACH OTHER, BACK THEN.
THIS'LL WORK.
I'M SURE OF IT.
YEAH!
THANKS, YUZURIHA!

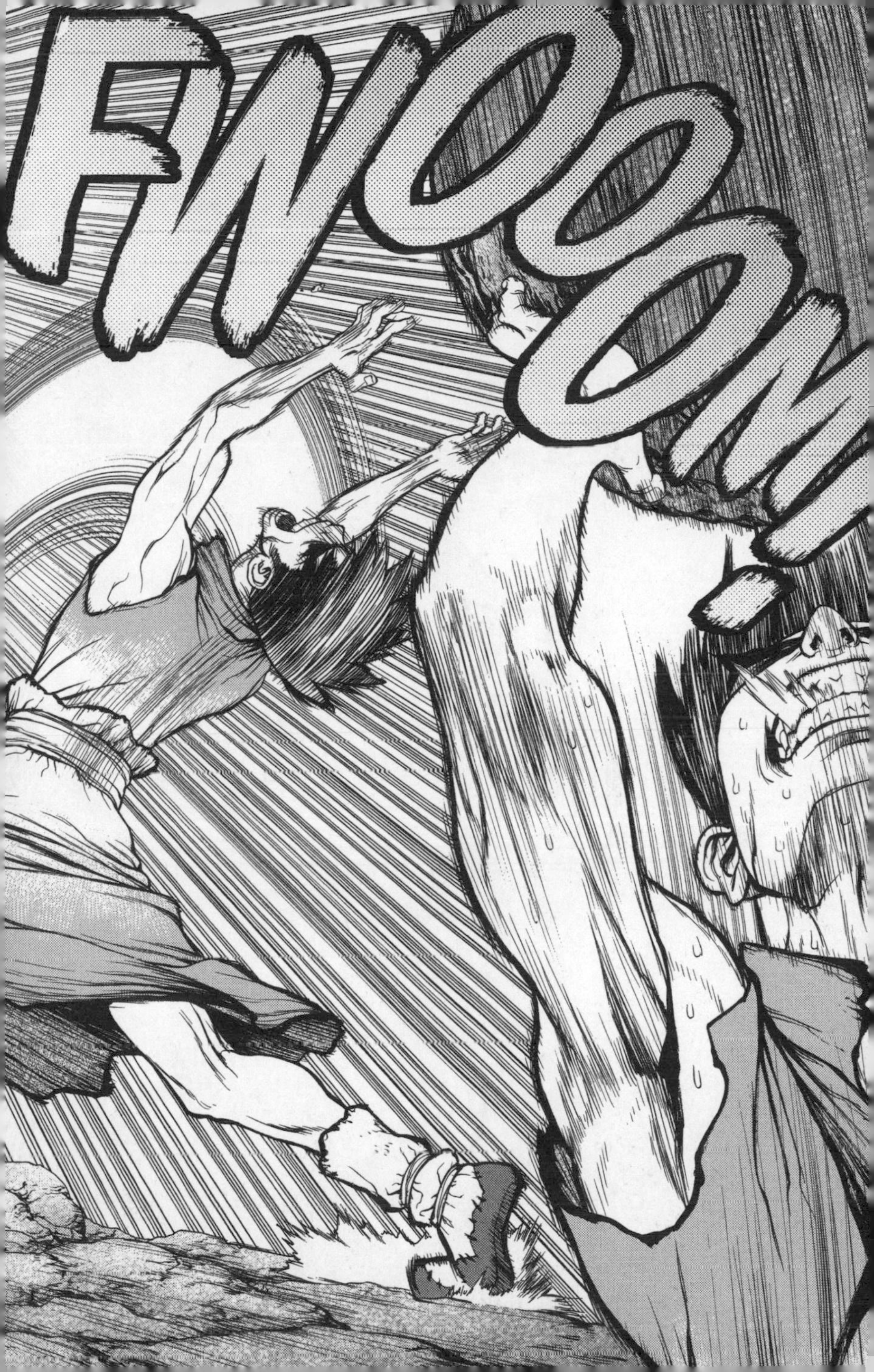
FWOOOM

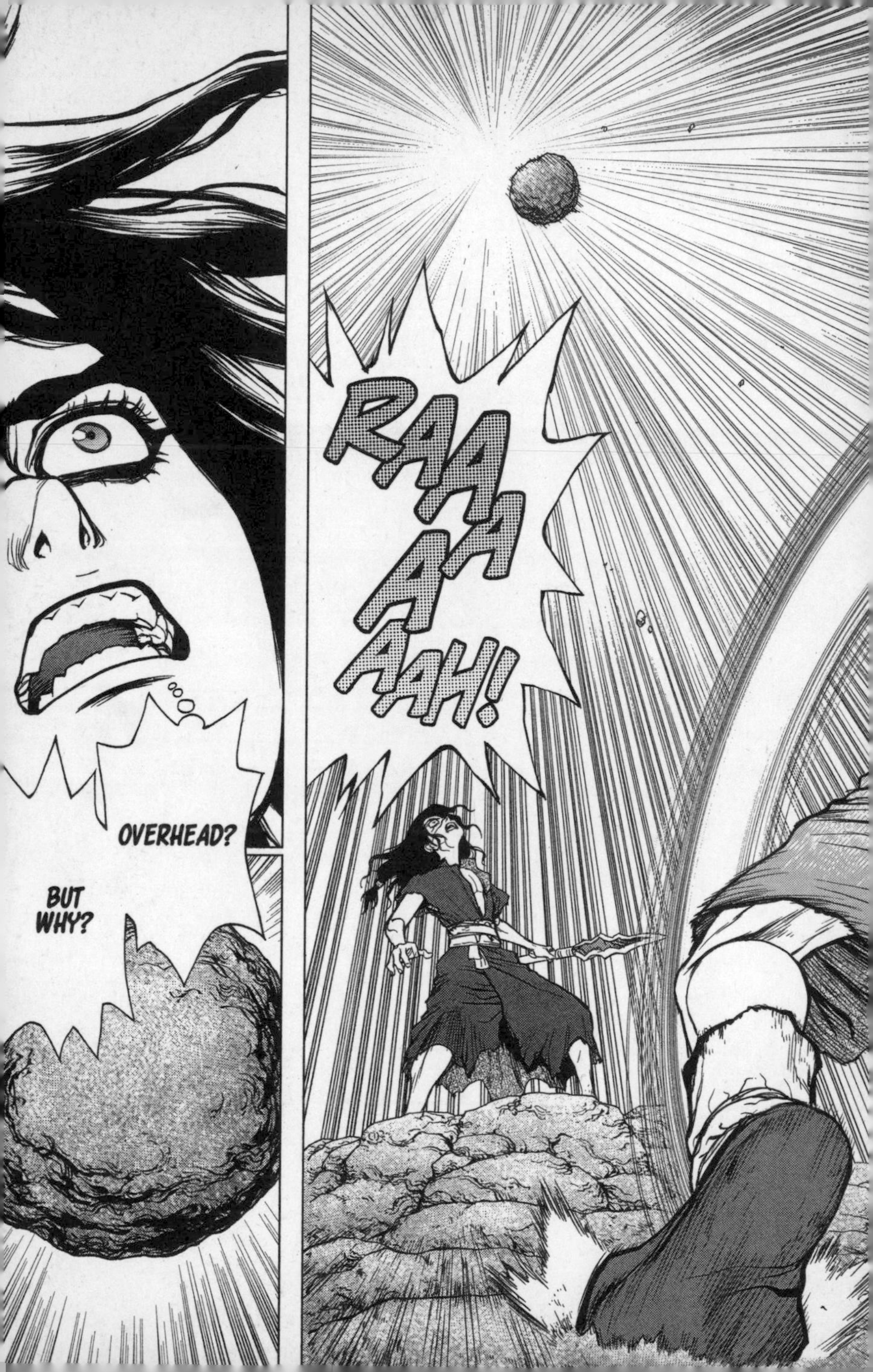
RAAAAAAH!
OVERHEAD?
BUT WHY?

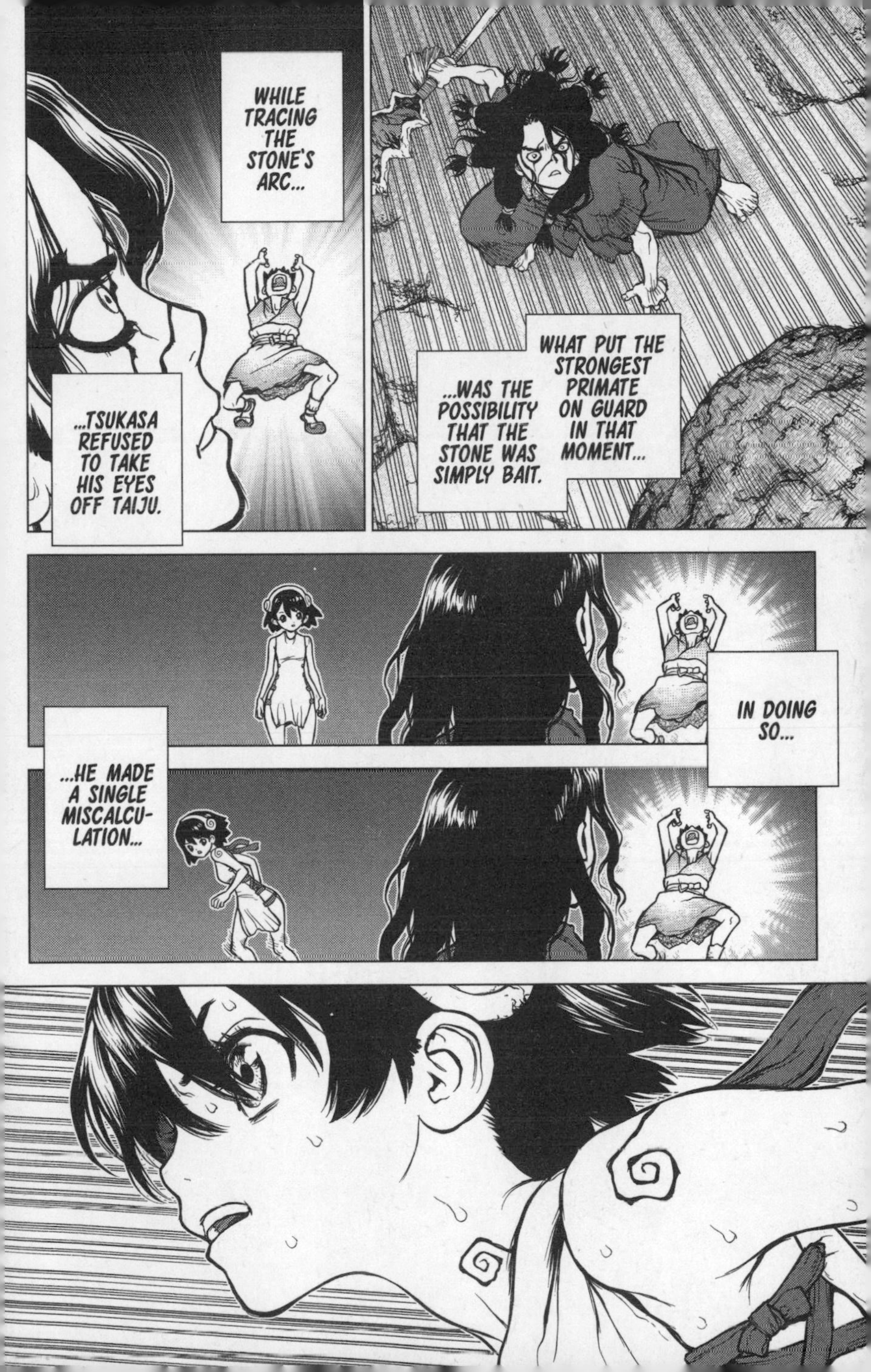
WHAT PUT THE STRONGEST PRIMATE ON GUARD IN THAT MOMENT...
...WAS THE POSSIBILITY THAT THE STONE WAS SIMPLY BAIT.
WHILE TRACING THE STONE'S ARC...
...TSUKASA REFUSED TO TAKE HIS EYES OFF TAIJU.
IN DOING SO...
...HE MADE A SINGLE MISCALCULATION...

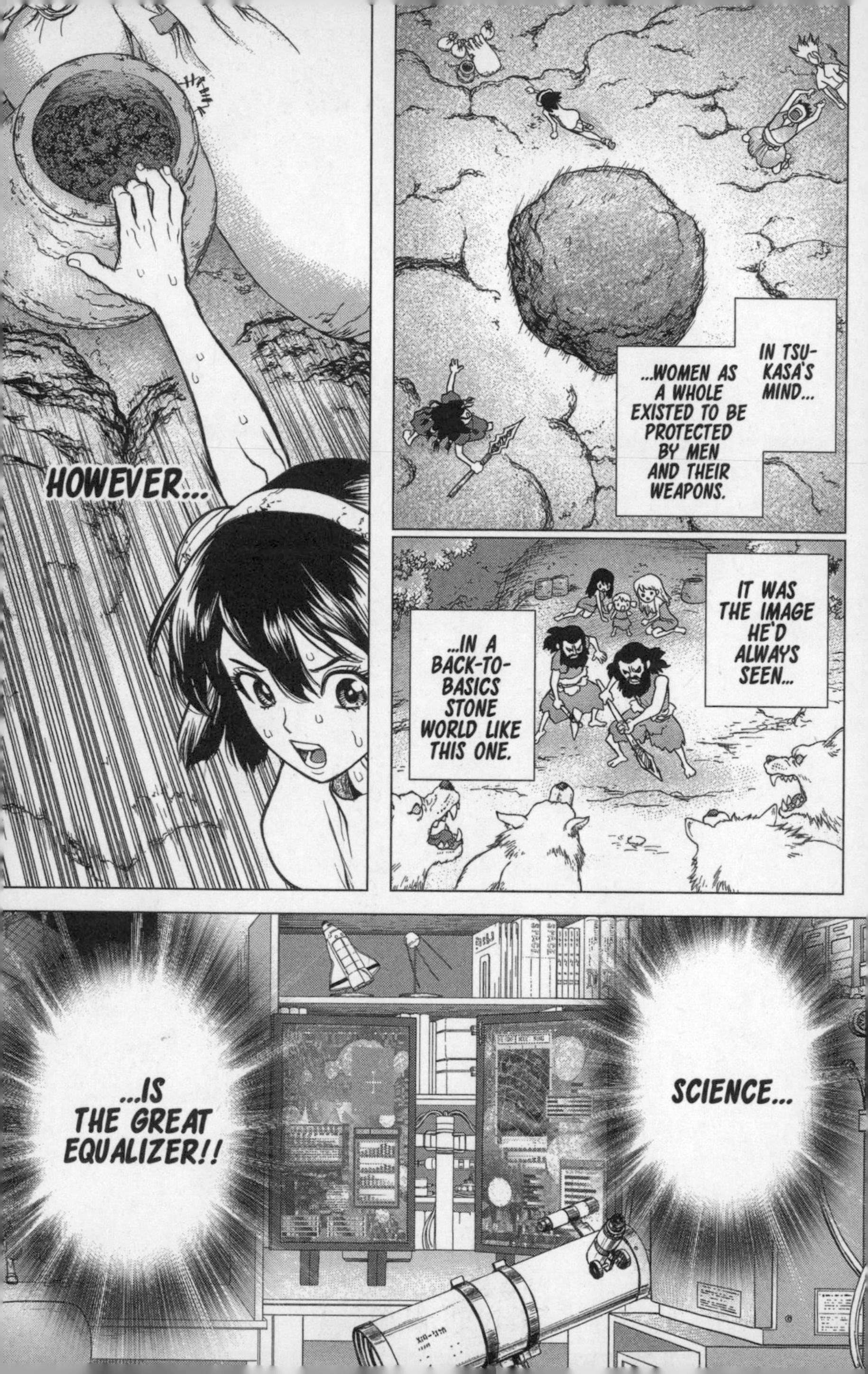
IN TSU-KASA'S MIND...
...WOMEN AS A WHOLE EXISTED TO BE PROTECTED BY MEN AND THEIR WEAPONS.
IT WAS THE IMAGE HE'D ALWAYS SEEN...
...IN A BACK-TO-BASICS STONE WORLD LIKE THIS ONE.
HOWEVER...
SCIENCE...
...IS THE GREAT EQUALIZER!!

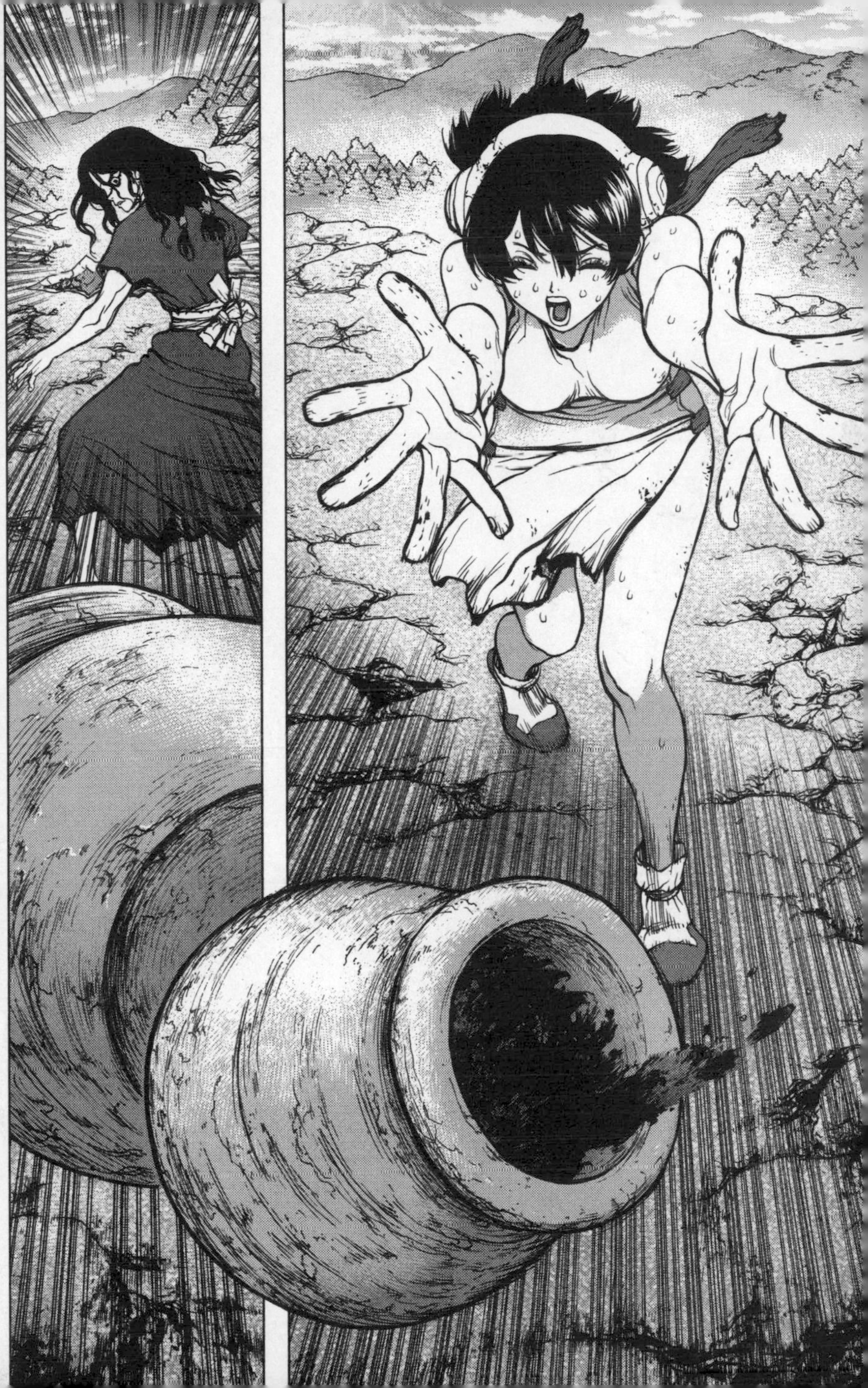

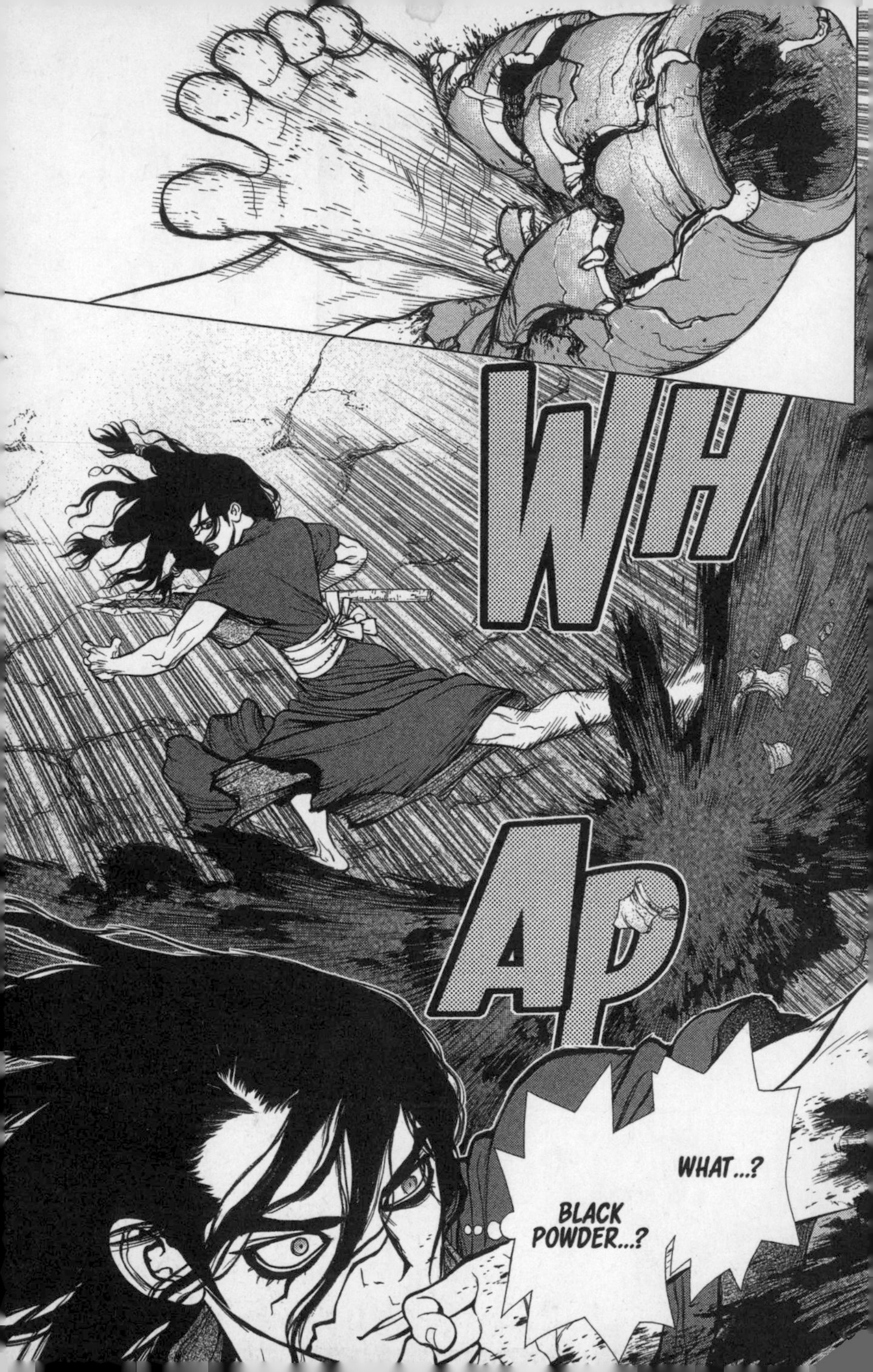
WHAP
WHAT...?
BLACK POWDER...?

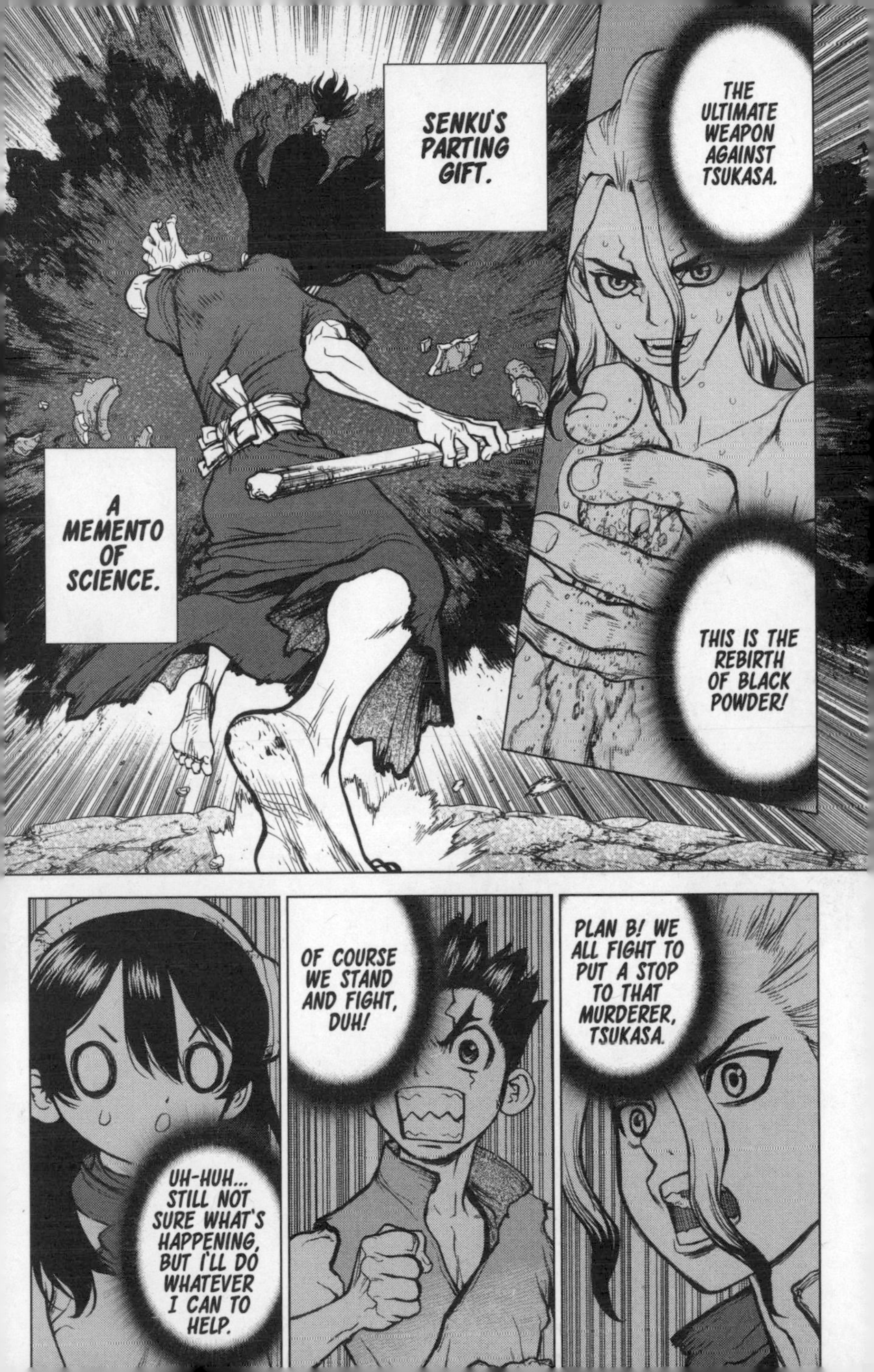
THE ULTIMATE WEAPON AGAINST TSUKASA.
THIS IS THE REBIRTH OF BLACK POWDER!
SENKU'S PARTING GIFT.
A MEMENTO OF SCIENCE.
PLAN B! WE ALL FIGHT TO PUT A STOP TO THAT MURDERER, TSUKASA.
OF COURSE WE STAND AND FIGHT, DUH!
UH-HUH... STILL NOT SURE WHAT'S HAPPENING, BUT I'LL DO WHATEVER I CAN TO HELP.

AT THAT MOMENT, THE THREE OF US MADE A PROMISE.

WE'D FIGHT TOGETHER!

ME, YUZURIHA AND SENKU TOO!!

WE'D COMBINE OUR STRENGTH AND FIGHT.

PSSH

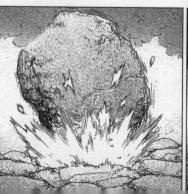

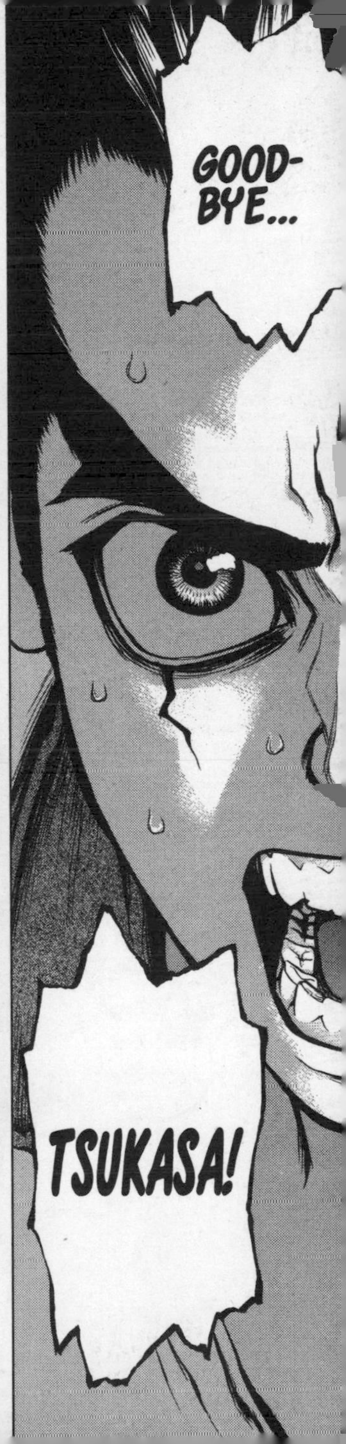
GOOD-BYE...
TSUKASA!
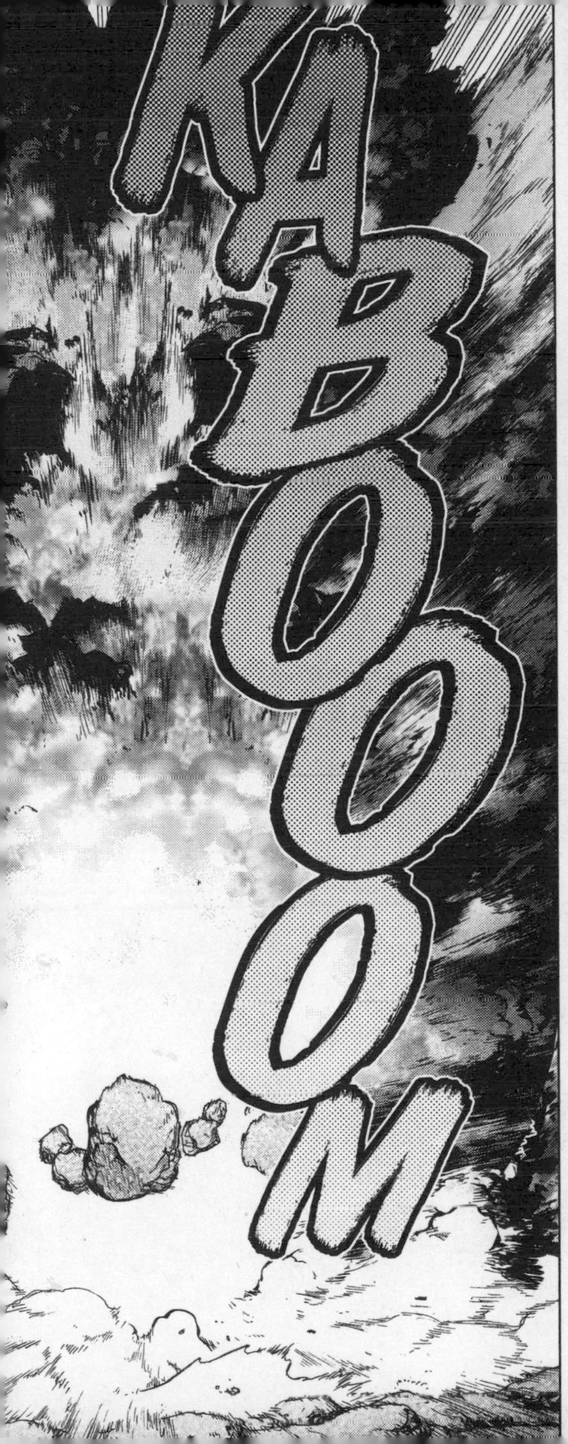
KABOOOM

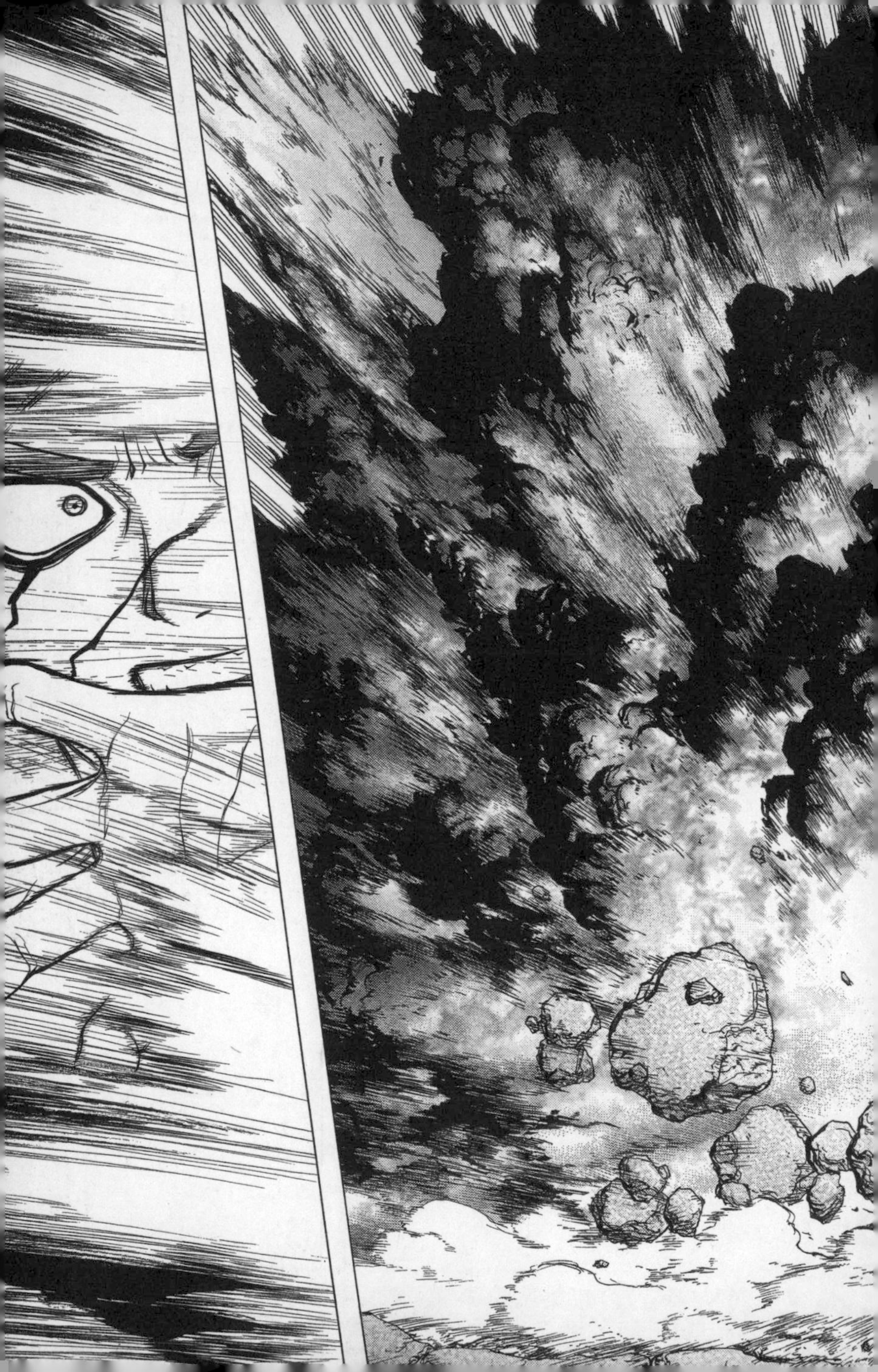

MECHA SENKU Q&A

SEARCH Question Corner

When Senku arrives at the Great Buddha of Kamakura, he spits out the coordinates just like that. Does he just know the coordinates of everything? That's nuts!!

Y.N. from Tokyo **SEARCH**

HEH HEH HEH... I KNOW EXACTLY WHERE WE ARE.

WE'RE 35.19 DEGREES NORTH...

...BY 139.32 DEGREES EAST!

You'd have to have superpowers to do that. I just memorized this one. That's all.

Senku may act all casual about it, but there is a valid explanation!

The Great Buddha lies at 35.1900 north latitude. That's precisely 19 seconds! Its longitude is 139.3208, which places it remarkably close to an even 32 seconds! "Did they build it there with that in mind?" "And in an era when taking measurements like that would've been difficult!" "What a crazy coincidence!!" A good scientist never leaves the little questions unasked!!

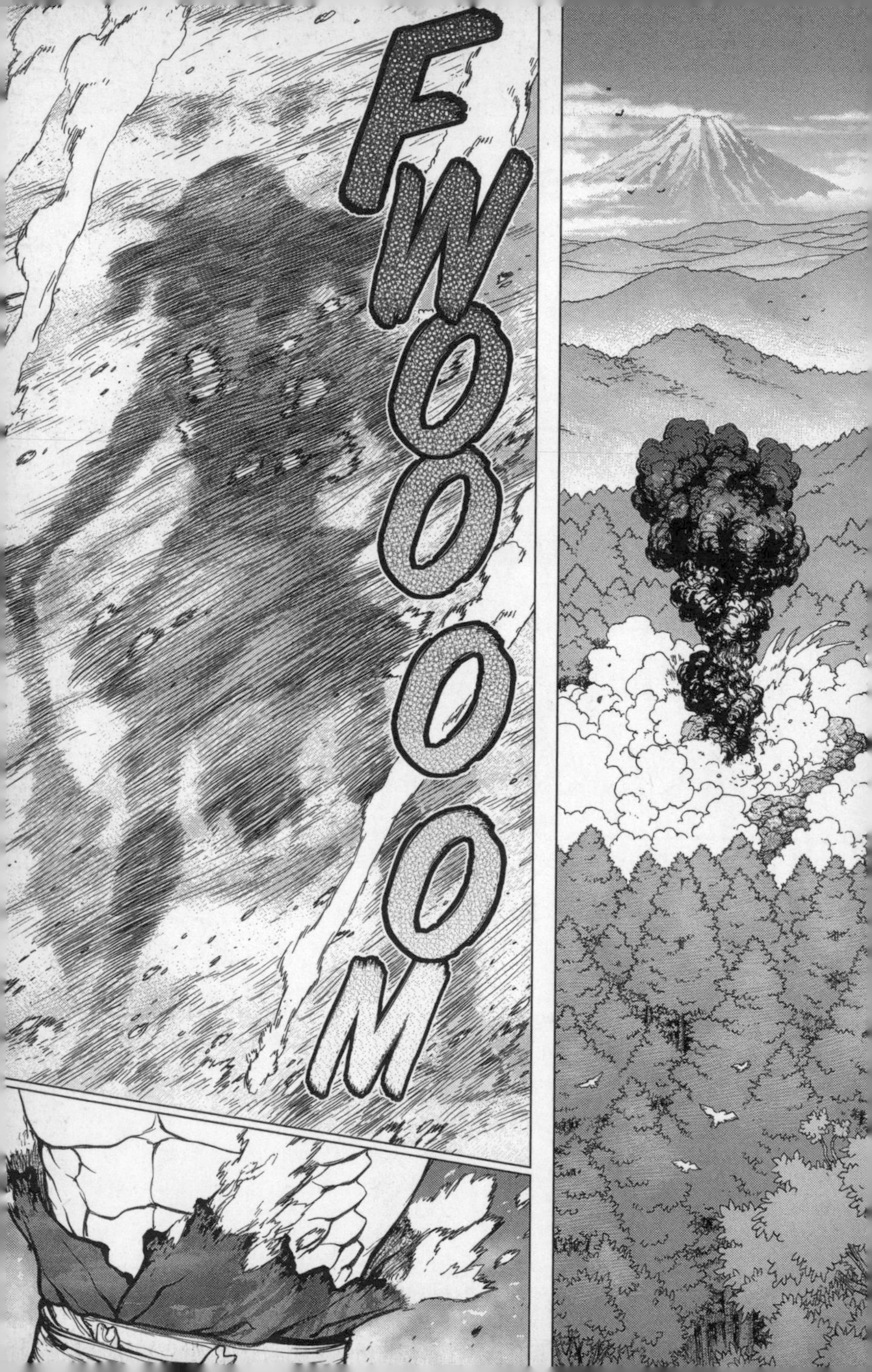
FWOOOOM

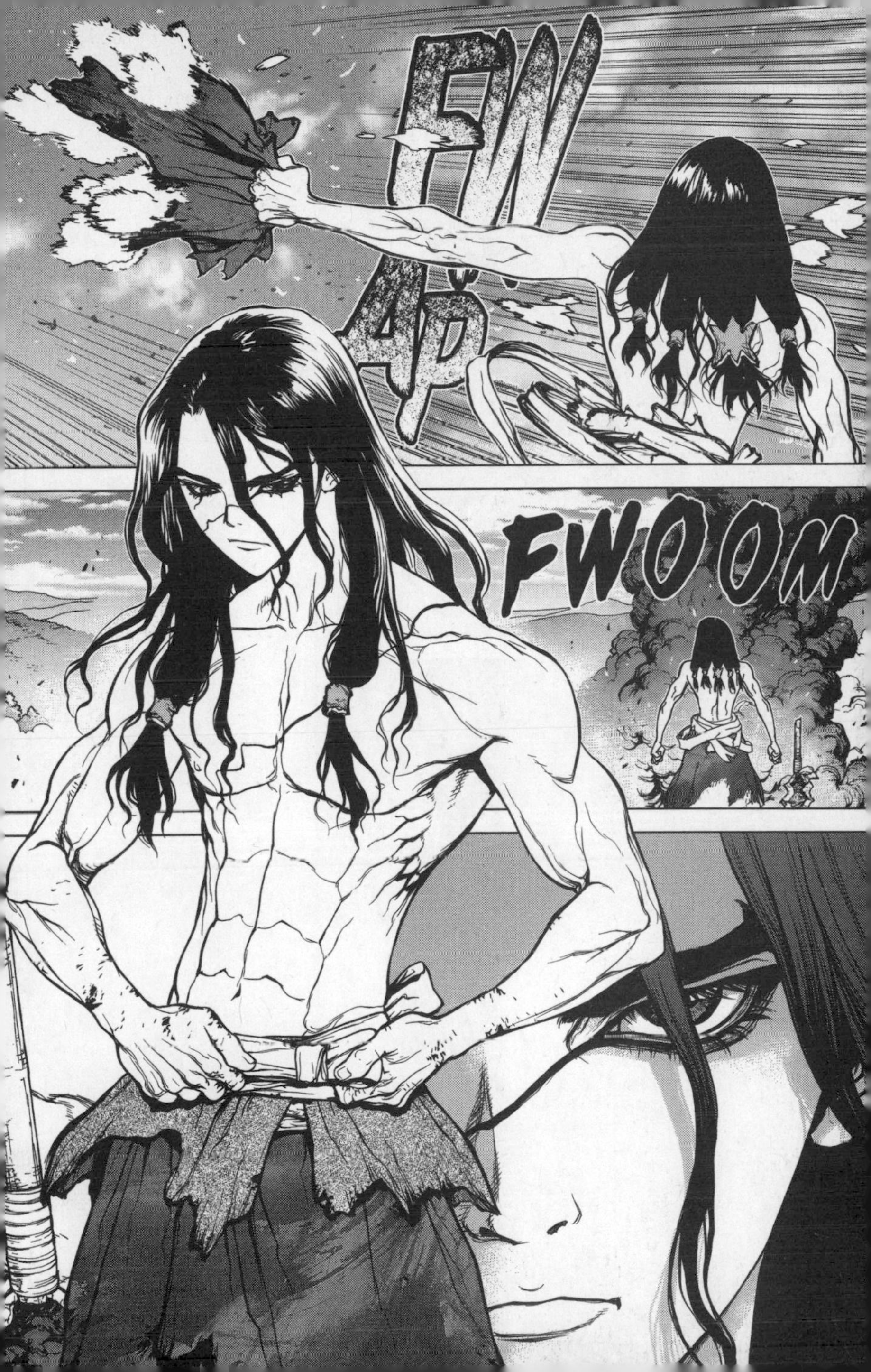
FWAP
FWOOM

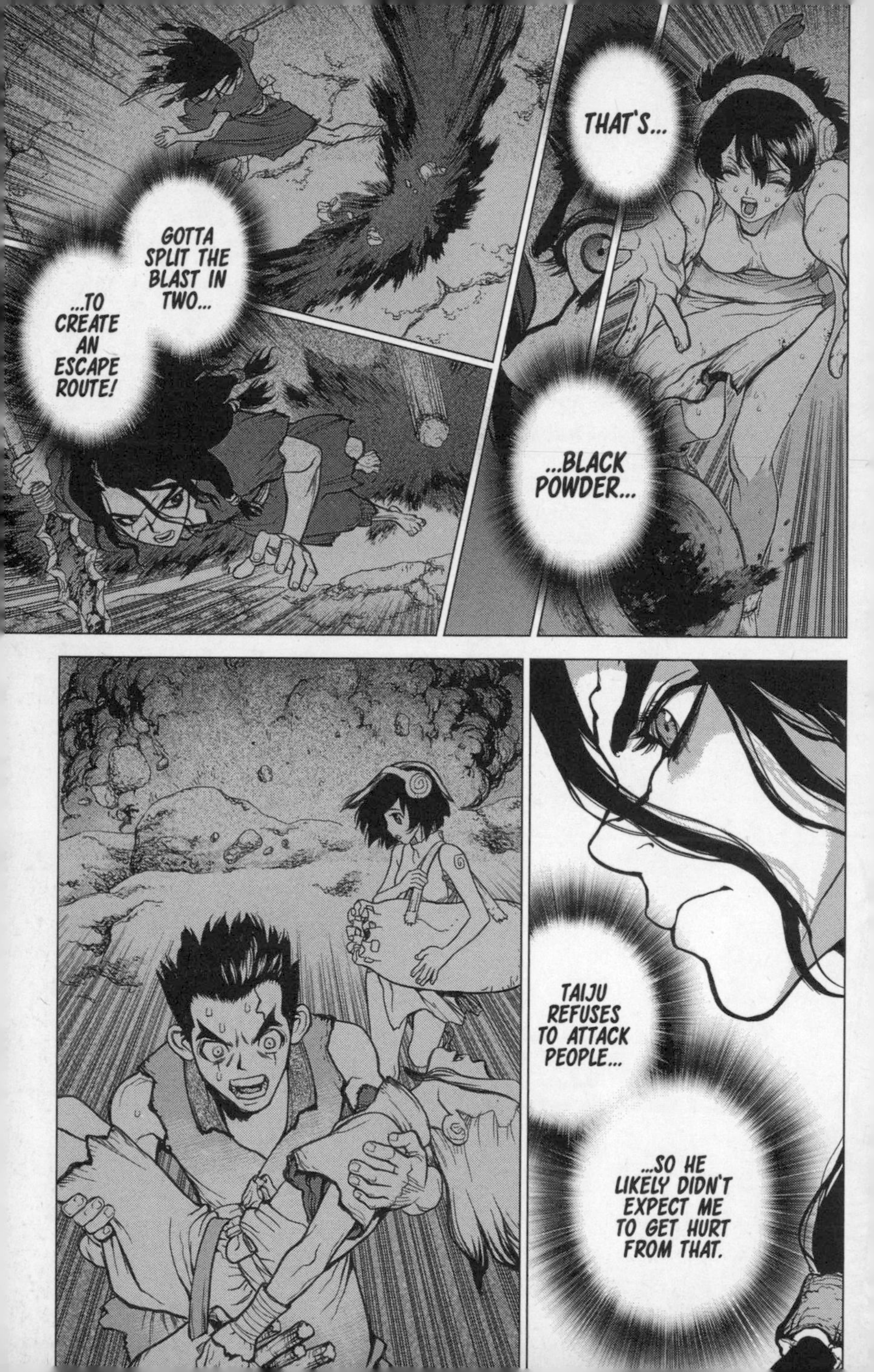
THAT'S...
...BLACK POWDER...
GOTTA SPLIT THE BLAST IN TWO...
...TO CREATE AN ESCAPE ROUTE!
TAIJU REFUSES TO ATTACK PEOPLE...
...SO HE LIKELY DIDN'T EXPECT ME TO GET HURT FROM THAT.

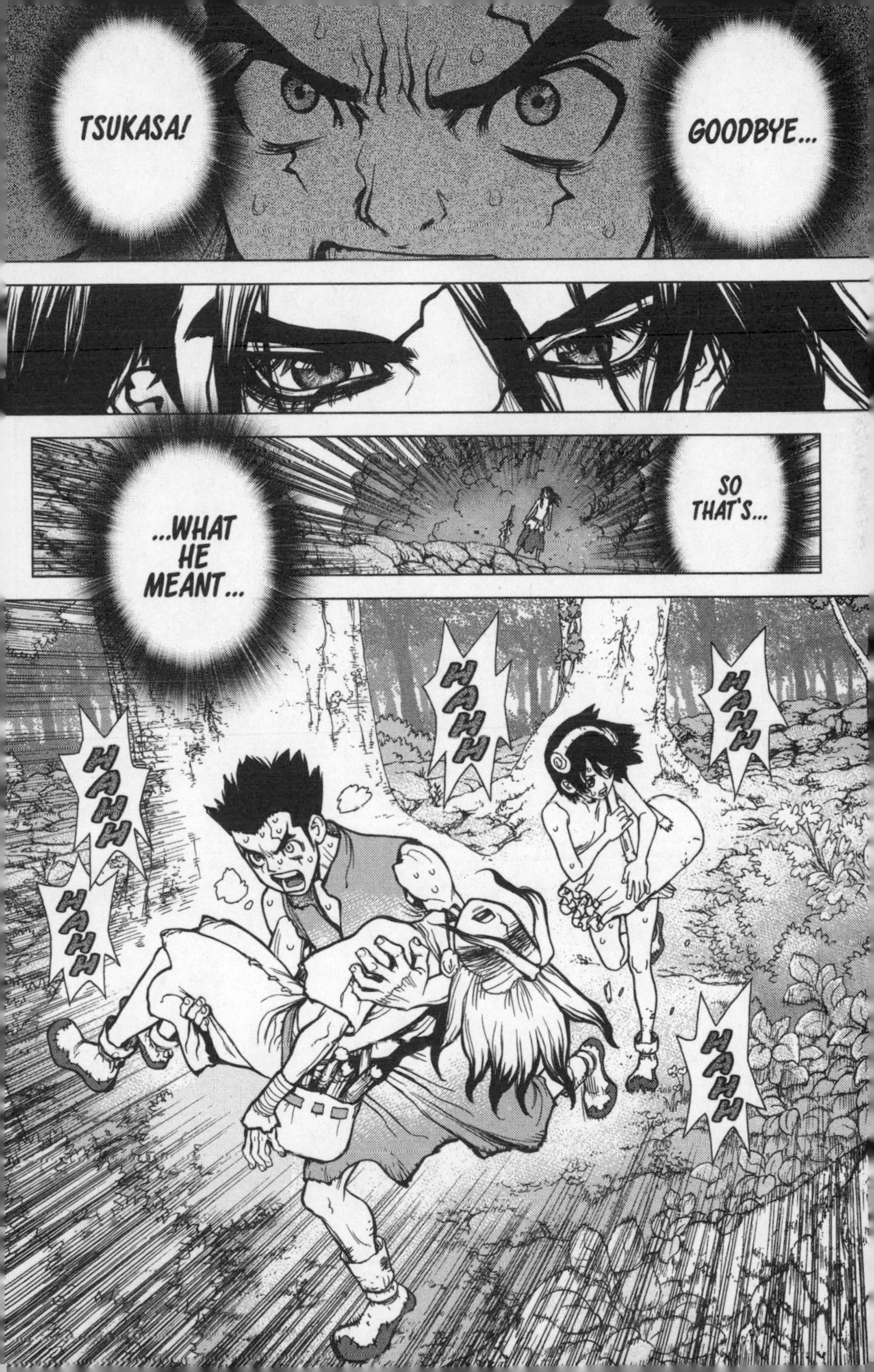
GOODBYE...
TSUKASA!
SO THAT'S...
...WHAT HE MEANT...
HAHH
HAHH
HAHH
HAHH
HAHH
HAHH

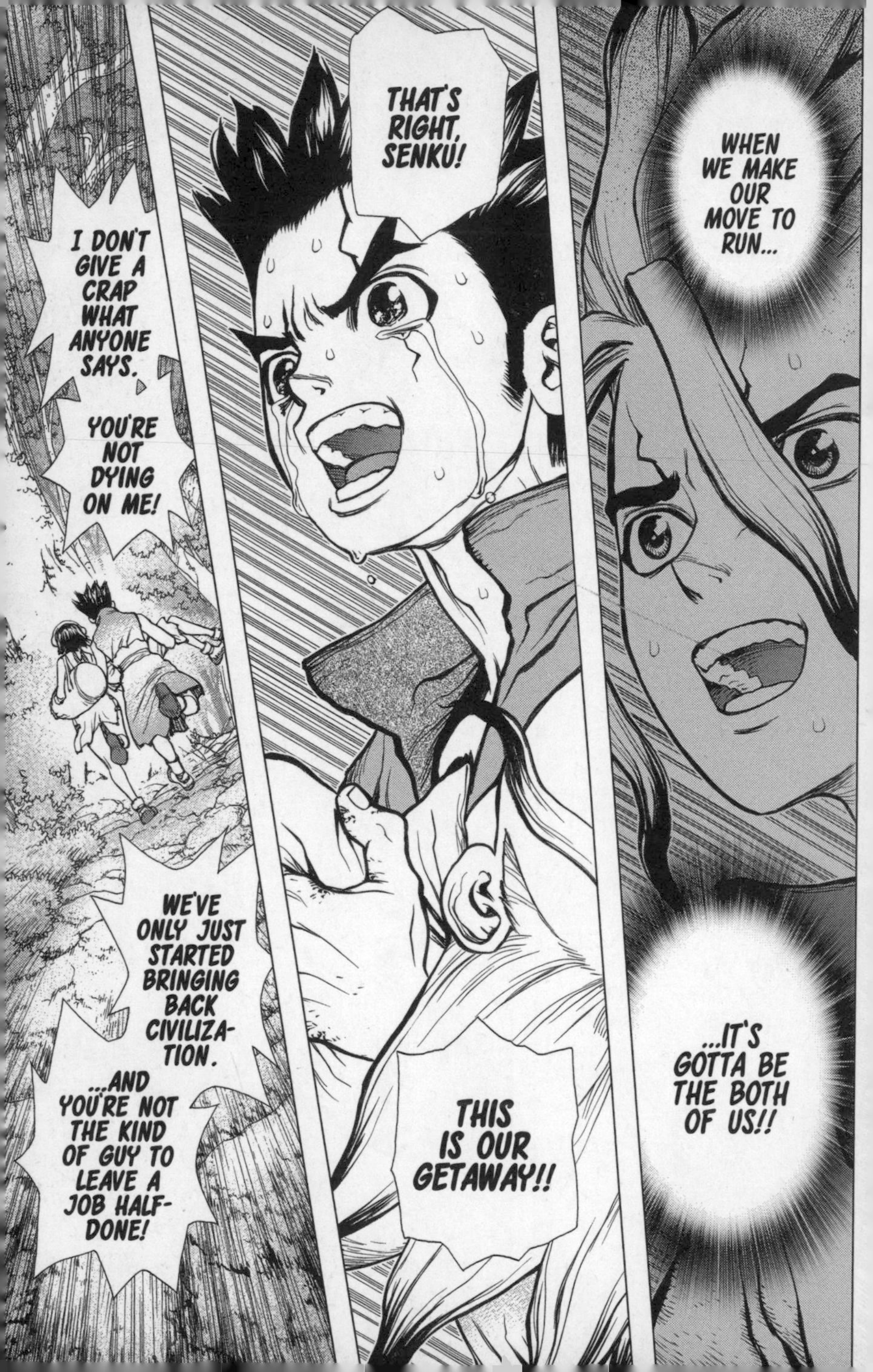
WHEN WE MAKE OUR MOVE TO RUN...
...IT'S GOTTA BE THE BOTH OF US!!
THAT'S RIGHT, SENKU!
THIS IS OUR GETAWAY!!
I DON'T GIVE A CRAP WHAT ANYONE SAYS.
YOU'RE NOT DYING ON ME!
WE'VE ONLY JUST STARTED BRINGING BACK CIVILIZA-TION.
...AND YOU'RE NOT THE KIND OF GUY TO LEAVE A JOB HALF-DONE!

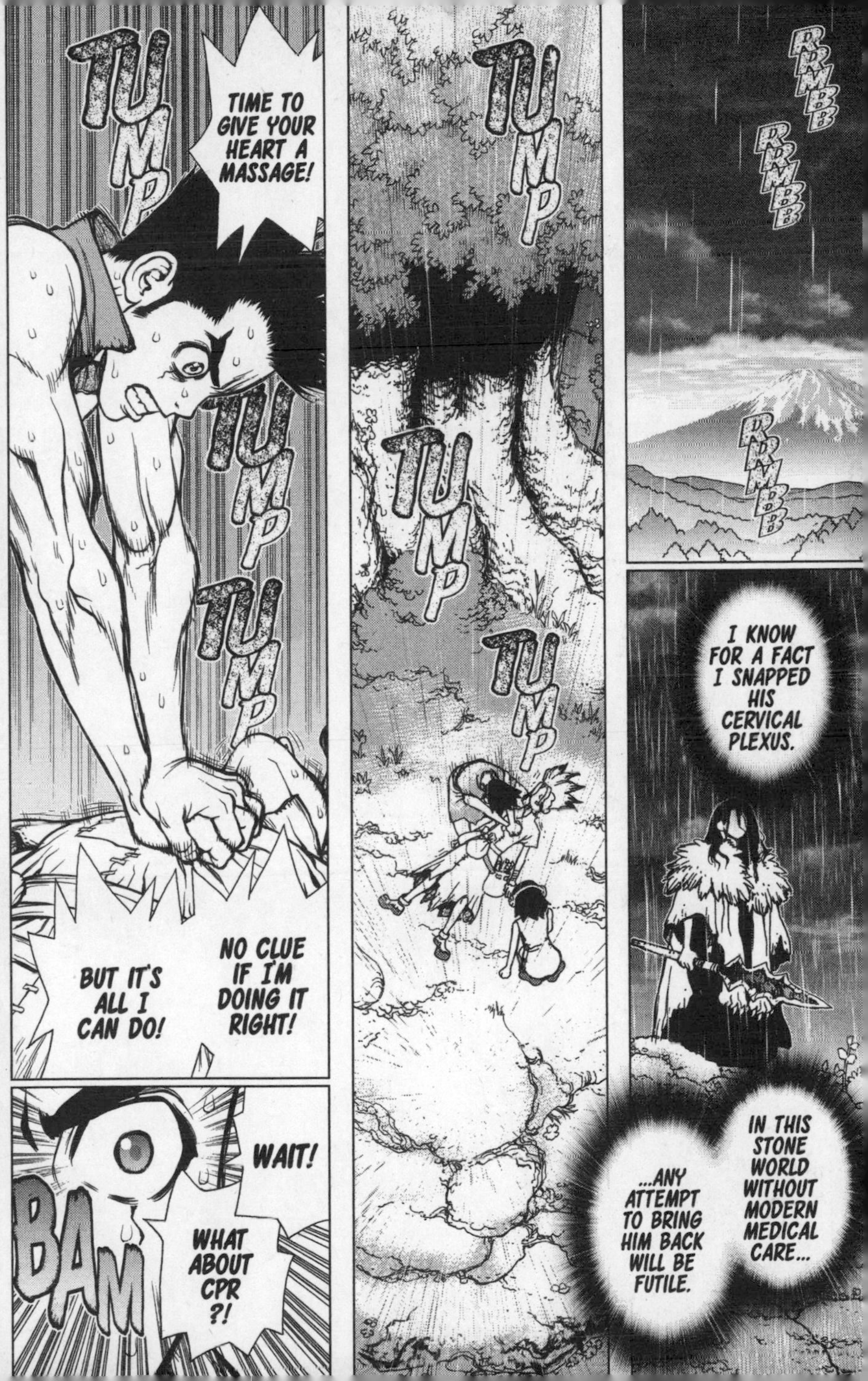
RRMBB
RRMBB
RRMBB
I KNOW FOR A FACT I SNAPPED HIS CERVICAL PLEXUS.
IN THIS STONE WORLD WITHOUT MODERN MEDICAL CARE...
...ANY ATTEMPT TO BRING HIM BACK WILL BE FUTILE.
TUMP
TUMP
TUMP
TIME TO GIVE YOUR HEART A MASSAGE!
TUMP
TUMP
TUMP
NO CLUE IF I'M DOING IT RIGHT!
BUT IT'S ALL I CAN DO!
WAIT!
WHAT ABOUT CPR ?!
BAM

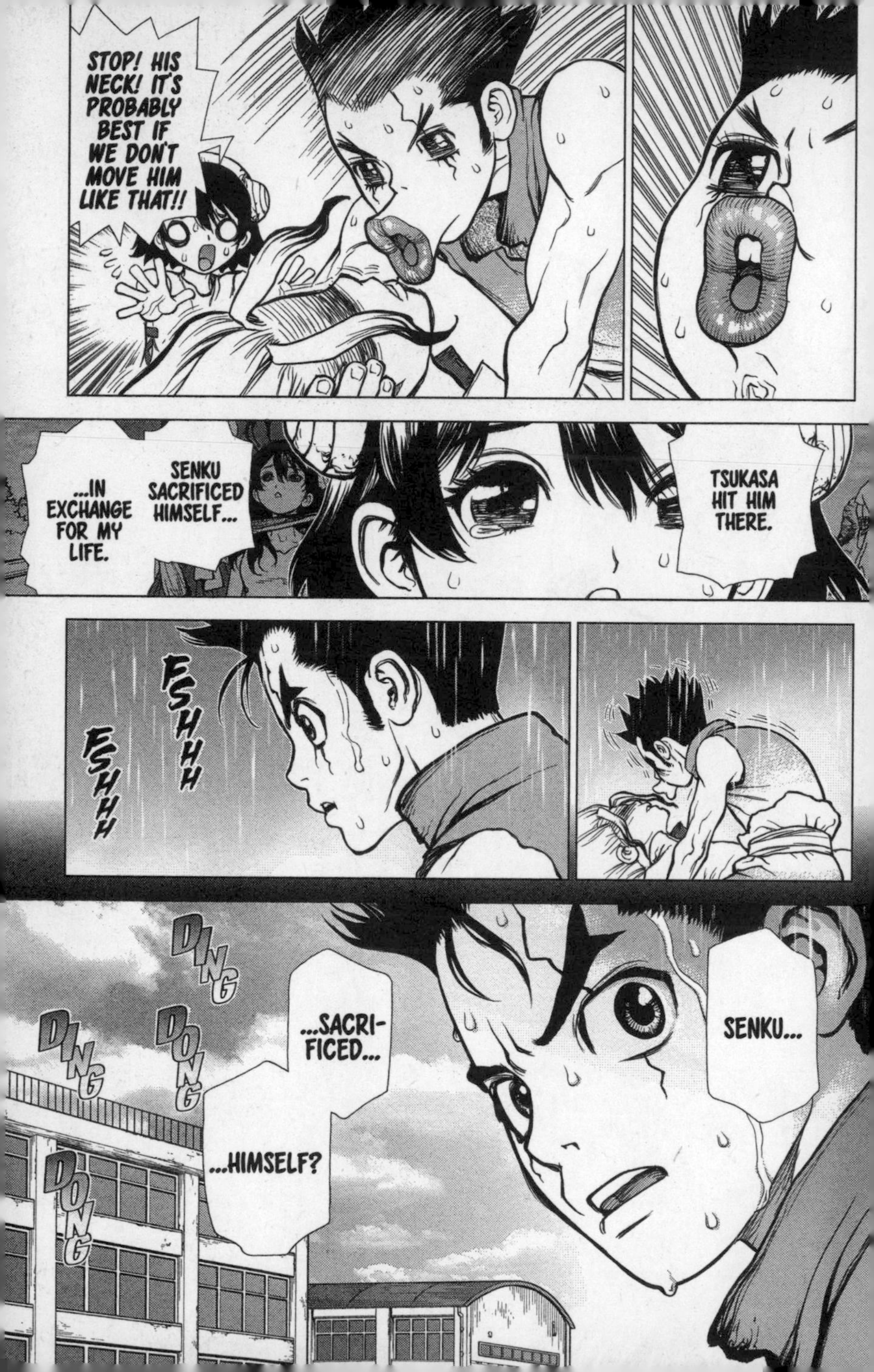
STOP! HIS NECK! IT'S PROBABLY BEST IF WE DON'T MOVE HIM LIKE THAT!!
TSUKASA HIT HIM THERE.
SENKU SACRIFICED HIMSELF...
...IN EXCHANGE FOR MY LIFE.
FSHHH
FSHHH
SENKU...
...SACRIFICED...
...HIMSELF?
DING
DONG
DING
DONG

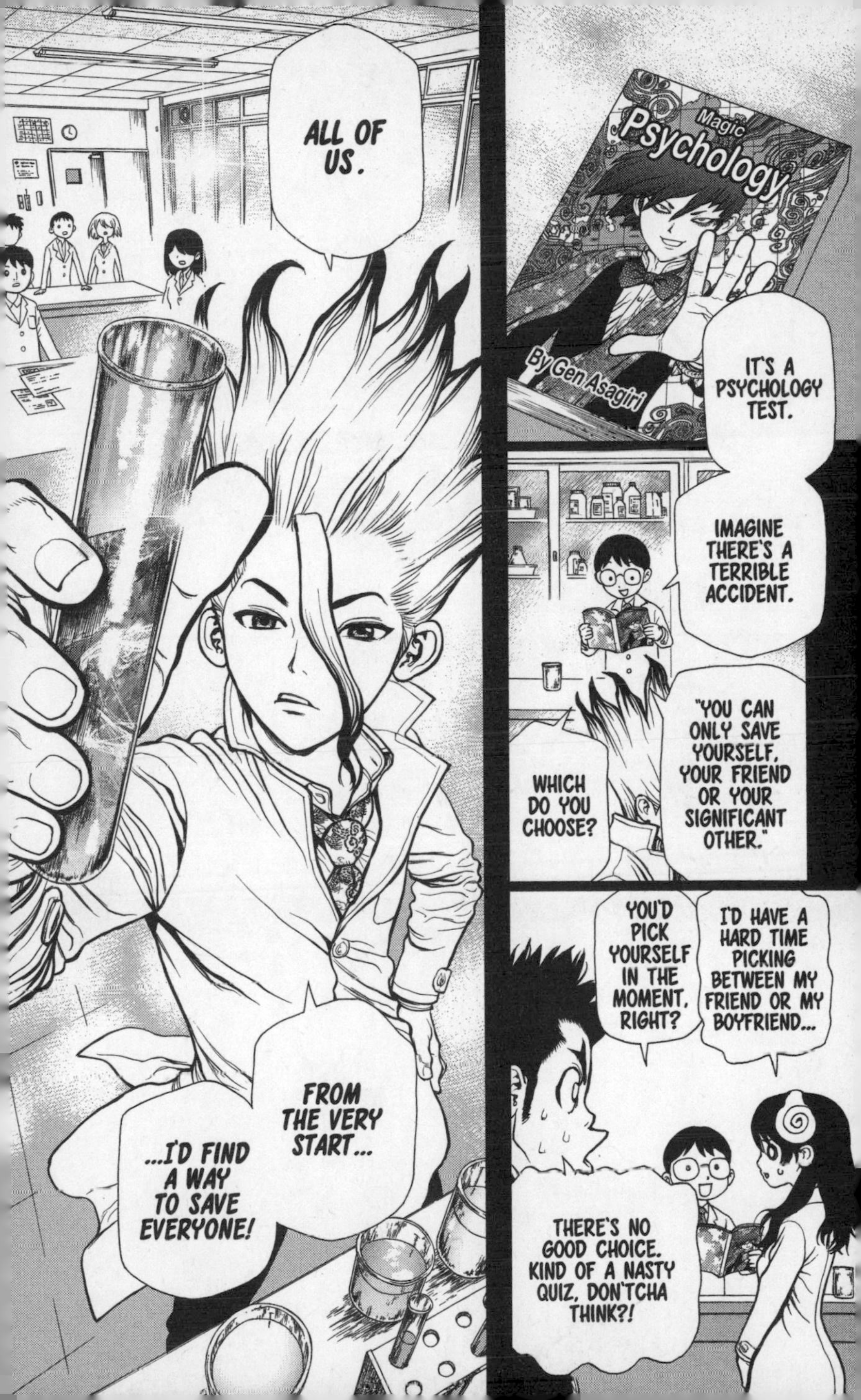
Magic Psychology
By Gen Asagiri
IT'S A PSYCHOLOGY TEST.
IMAGINE THERE'S A TERRIBLE ACCIDENT.
"YOU CAN ONLY SAVE YOURSELF, YOUR FRIEND OR YOUR SIGNIFICANT OTHER."
WHICH DO YOU CHOOSE?
I'D HAVE A HARD TIME PICKING BETWEEN MY FRIEND OR MY BOYFRIEND...
YOU'D PICK YOURSELF IN THE MOMENT, RIGHT?
THERE'S NO GOOD CHOICE. KIND OF A NASTY QUIZ, DON'TCHA THINK?!
ALL OF US.
FROM THE VERY START...
...I'D FIND A WAY TO SAVE EVERYONE!

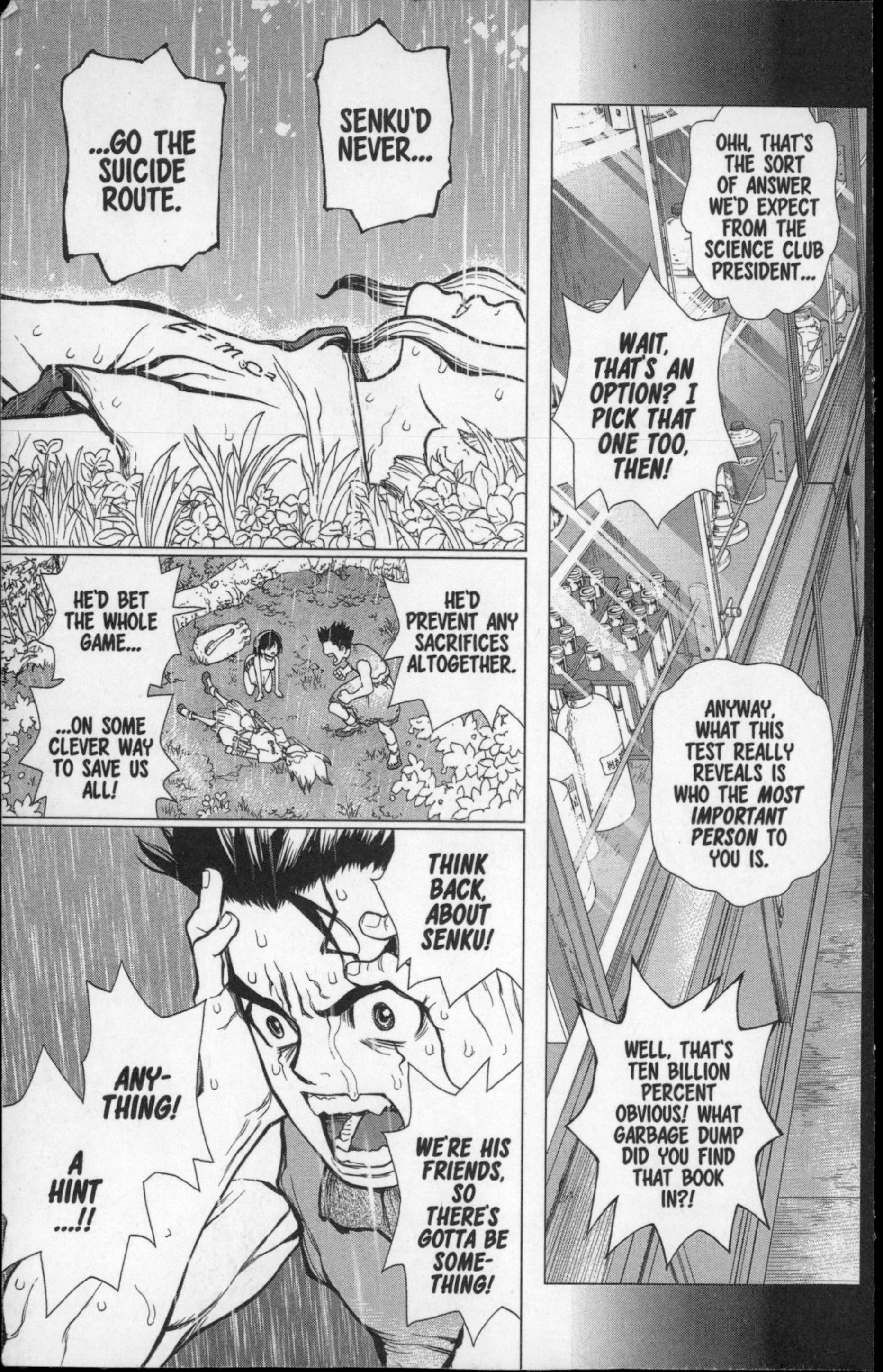
SENKU'D NEVER...
...GO THE SUICIDE ROUTE.
HE'D PREVENT ANY SACRIFICES ALTOGETHER.
HE'D BET THE WHOLE GAME...
...ON SOME CLEVER WAY TO SAVE US ALL!
THINK BACK, ABOUT SENKU!
ANY-THING!
A HINT ...!!
WE'RE HIS FRIENDS, SO THERE'S GOTTA BE SOME-THING!
OHH, THAT'S THE SORT OF ANSWER WE'D EXPECT FROM THE SCIENCE CLUB PRESIDENT...
WAIT, THAT'S AN OPTION? I PICK THAT ONE TOO, THEN!
ANYWAY, WHAT THIS TEST REALLY REVEALS IS WHO THE MOST IMPORTANT PERSON TO YOU IS.
WELL, THAT'S TEN BILLION PERCENT OBVIOUS! WHAT GARBAGE DUMP DID YOU FIND THAT BOOK IN?!

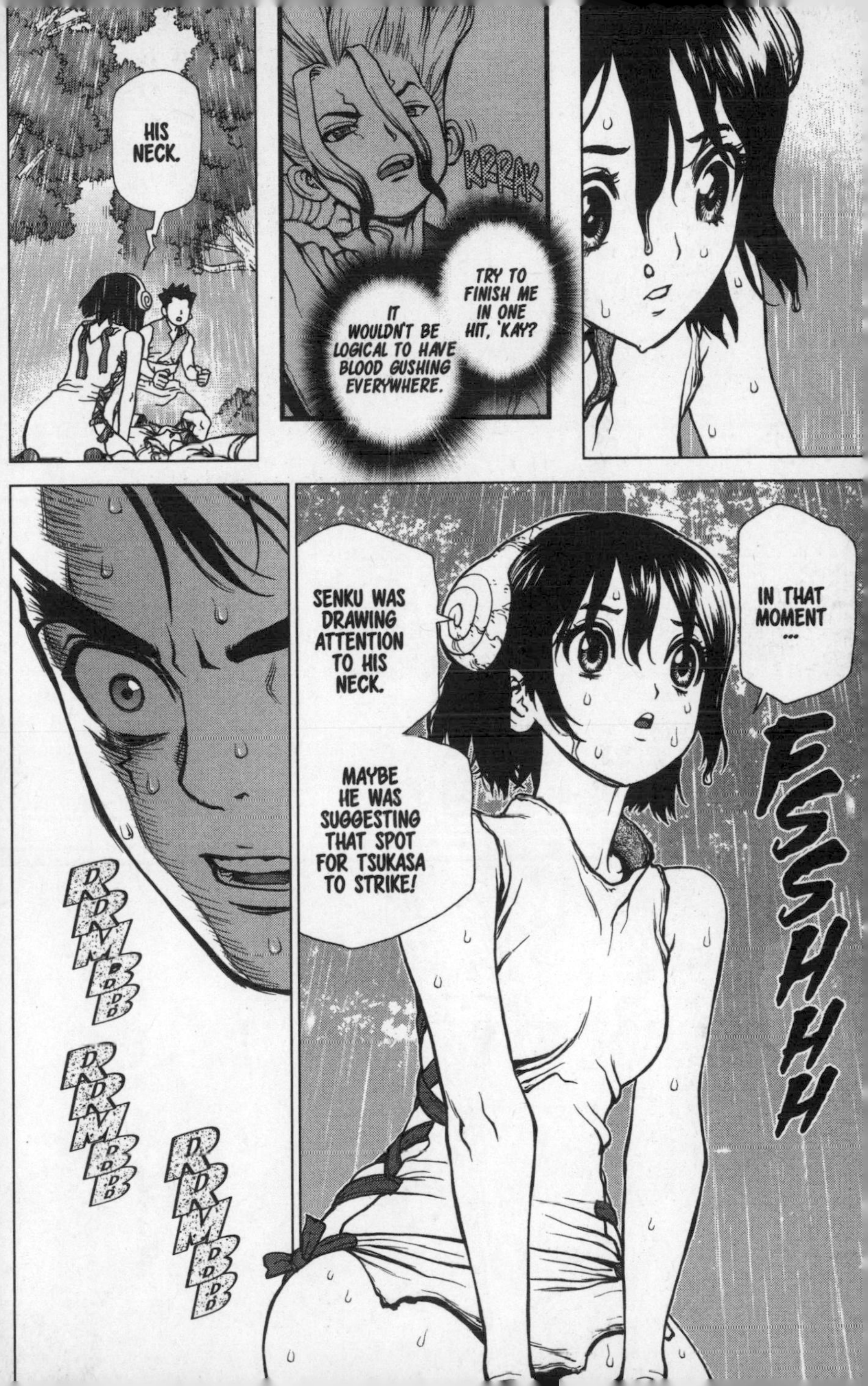
KRRAK
TRY TO FINISH ME IN ONE HIT, 'KAY?
IT WOULDN'T BE LOGICAL TO HAVE BLOOD GUSHING EVERYWHERE.
HIS NECK.
IN THAT MOMENT...
FSSHHH
SENKU WAS DRAWING ATTENTION TO HIS NECK.
MAYBE HE WAS SUGGESTING THAT SPOT FOR TSUKASA TO STRIKE!
RRMBB
RRMBB
RRMBB

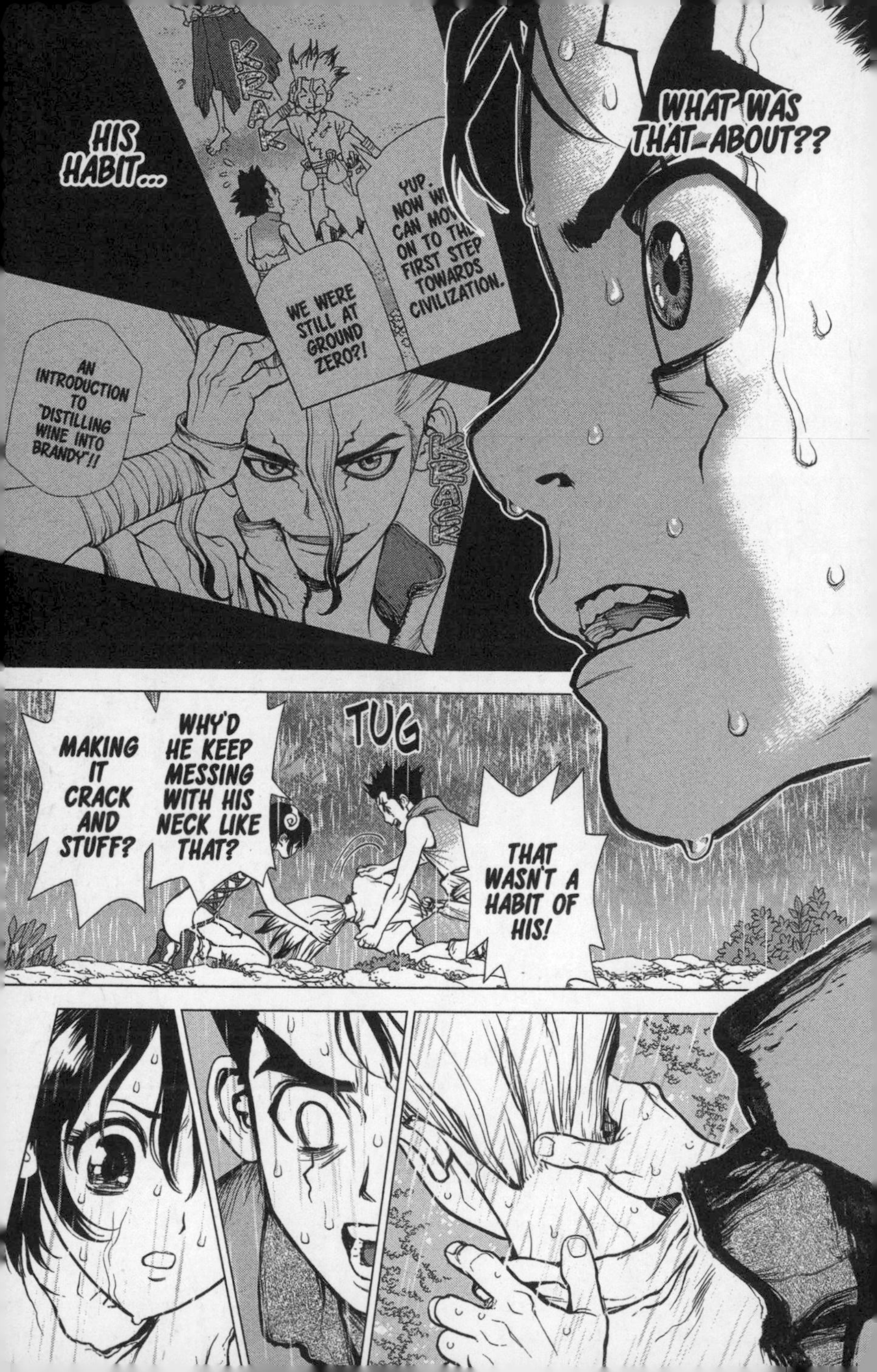
WHAT WAS THAT-ABOUT??
HIS HABIT...
KRAK
YUP. NOW WE CAN MOVE ON TO THE FIRST STEP TOWARDS CIVILIZATION.
WE WERE STILL AT GROUND ZERO?!
AN INTRODUCTION TO "DISTILLING WINE INTO BRANDY"!!
TUG
THAT WASN'T A HABIT OF HIS!
WHY'D HE KEEP MESSING WITH HIS NECK LIKE THAT?
MAKING IT CRACK AND STUFF?

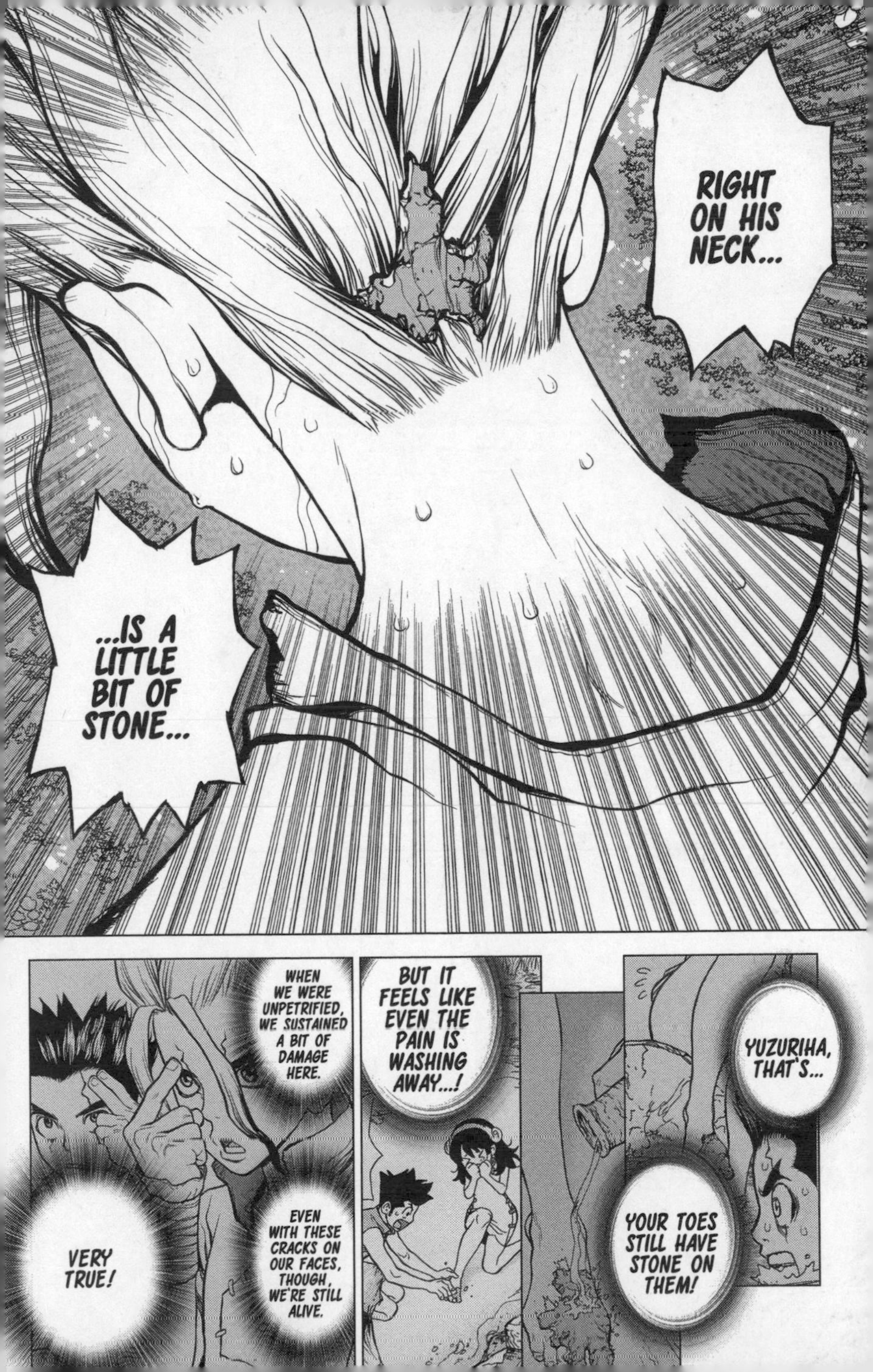
RIGHT ON HIS NECK...
...IS A LITTLE BIT OF STONE...
YUZURIHA, THAT'S...
YOUR TOES STILL HAVE STONE ON THEM!
BUT IT FEELS LIKE EVEN THE PAIN IS WASHING AWAY...!
WHEN WE WERE UNPETRIFIED, WE SUSTAINED A BIT OF DAMAGE HERE.
EVEN WITH THESE CRACKS ON OUR FACES, THOUGH, WE'RE STILL ALIVE.
VERY TRUE!

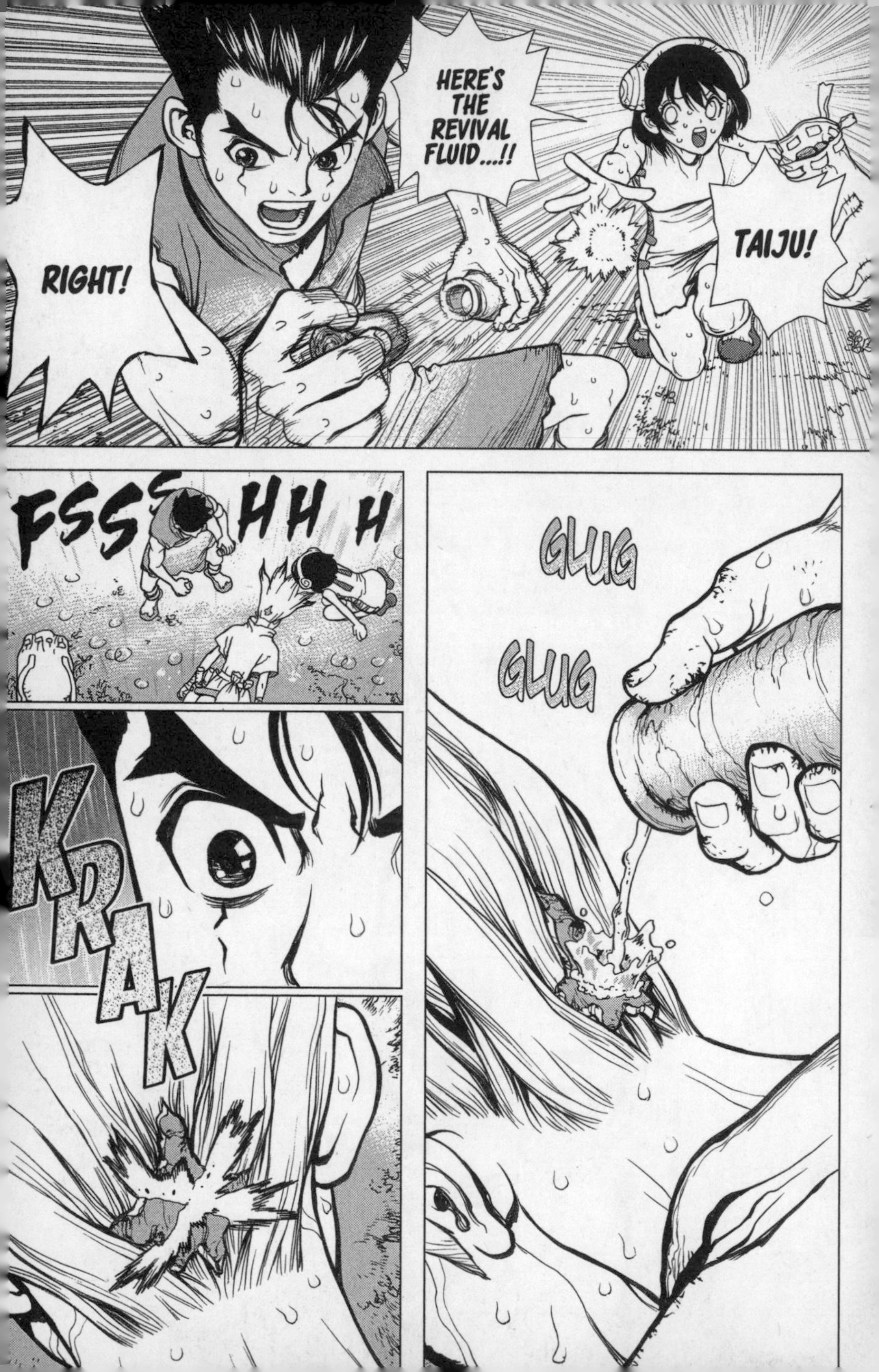
TAIJU!
HERE'S THE REVIVAL FLUID...!!
RIGHT!
GLUG
GLUG
FSSSHHH H
KRAK

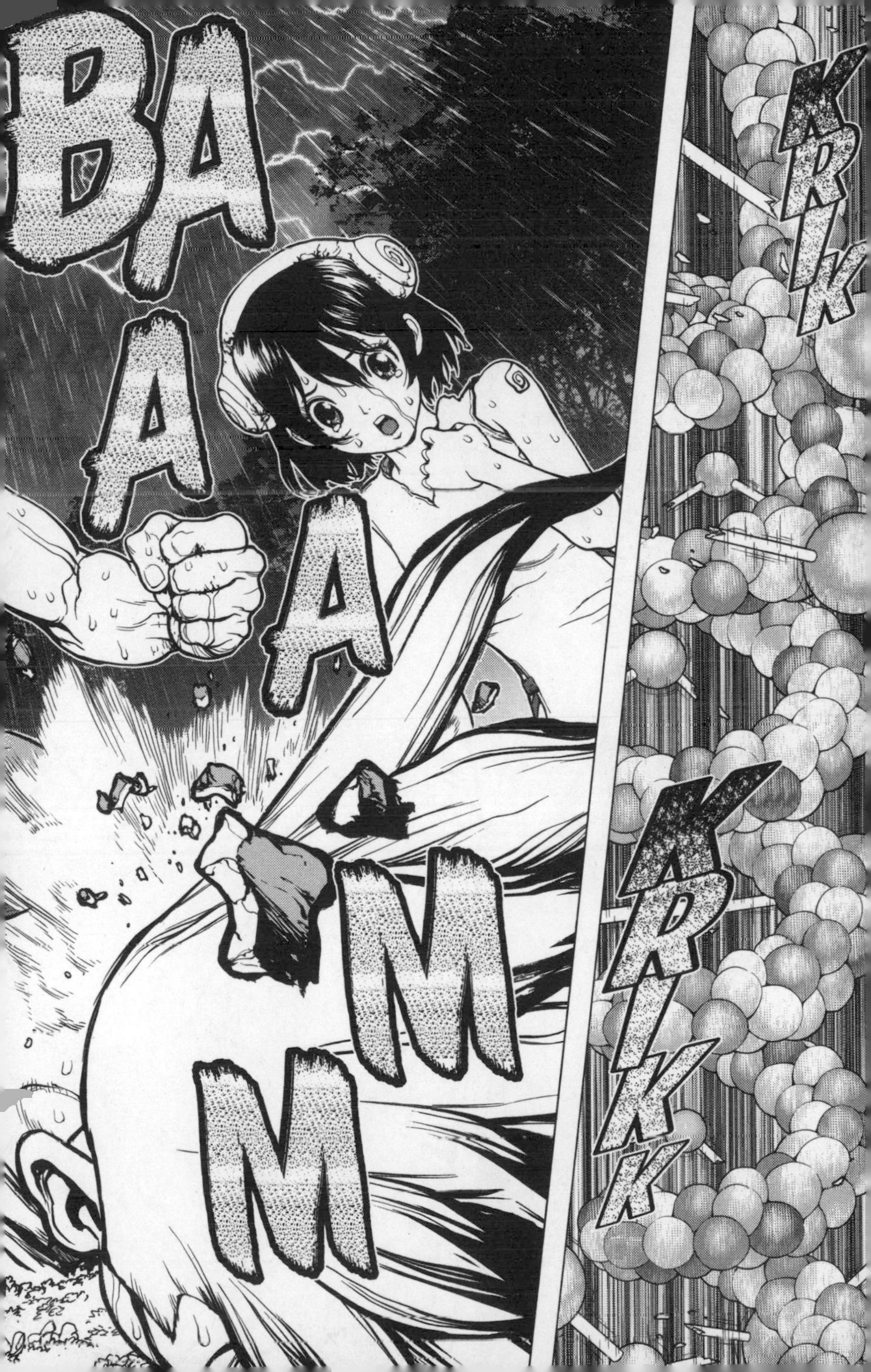
KRIK
KRIK
KRIKK
BAAAMMM

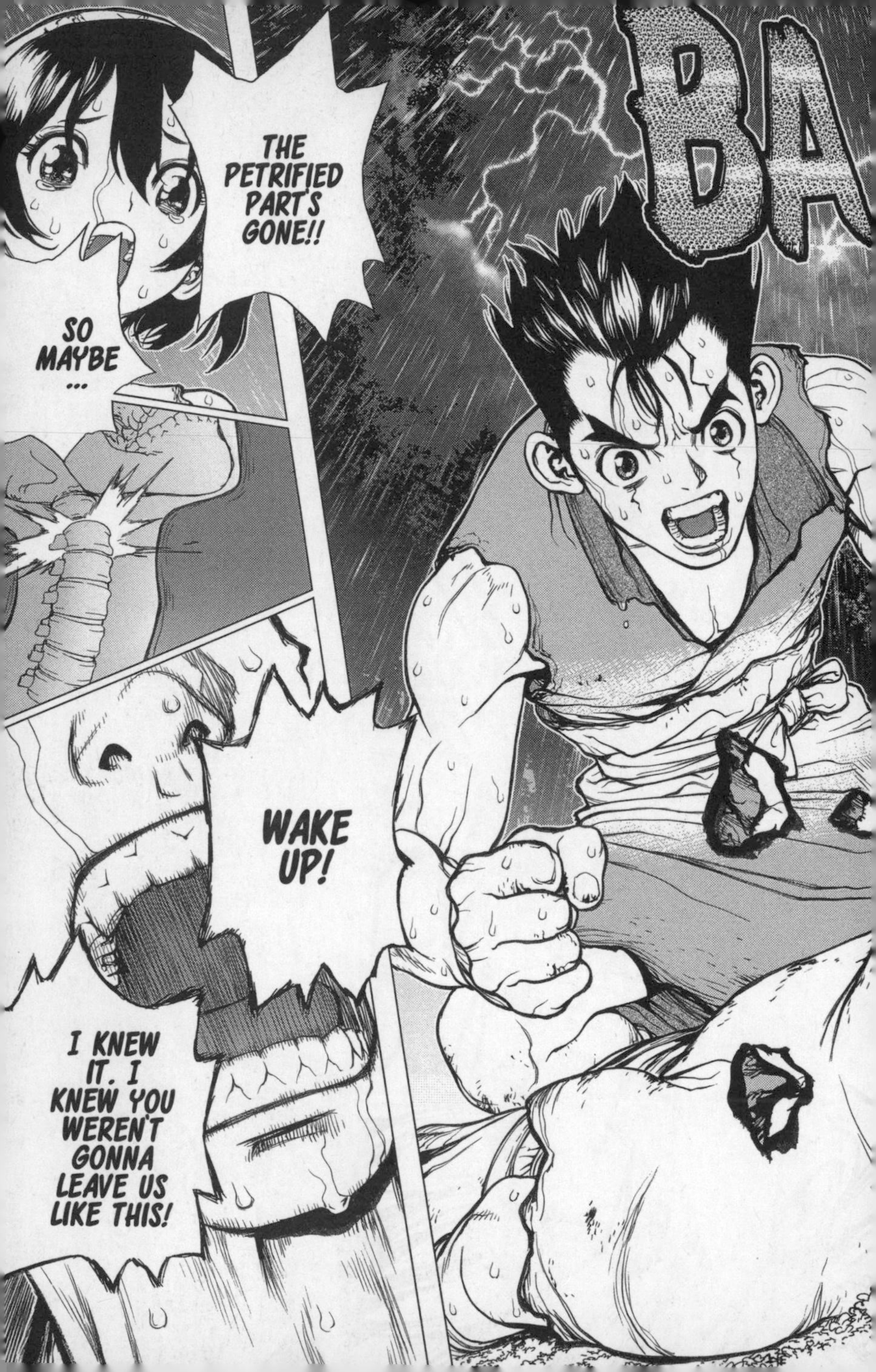
BA
WAKE UP!
I KNEW IT. I KNEW YOU WEREN'T GONNA LEAVE US LIKE THIS!
THE PETRIFIED PART'S GONE!!
SO MAYBE ...

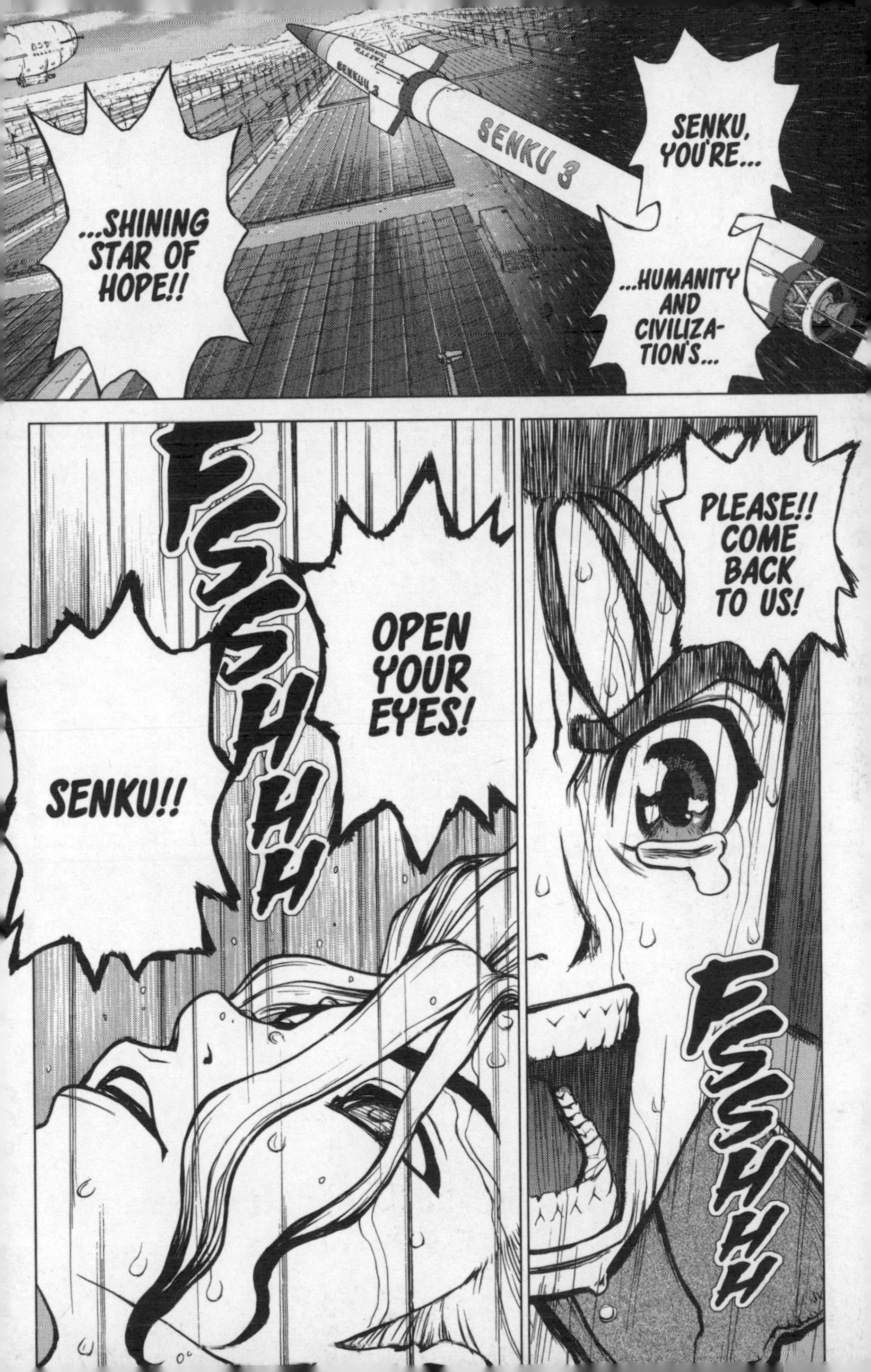
SENKU 3
SENKU, YOU'RE...
...HUMANITY AND CIVILIZA-TION'S...
...SHINING STAR OF HOPE!!
PLEASE!! COME BACK TO US!
FSSHHH
OPEN YOUR EYES!
SENKU!!
FSSHHH

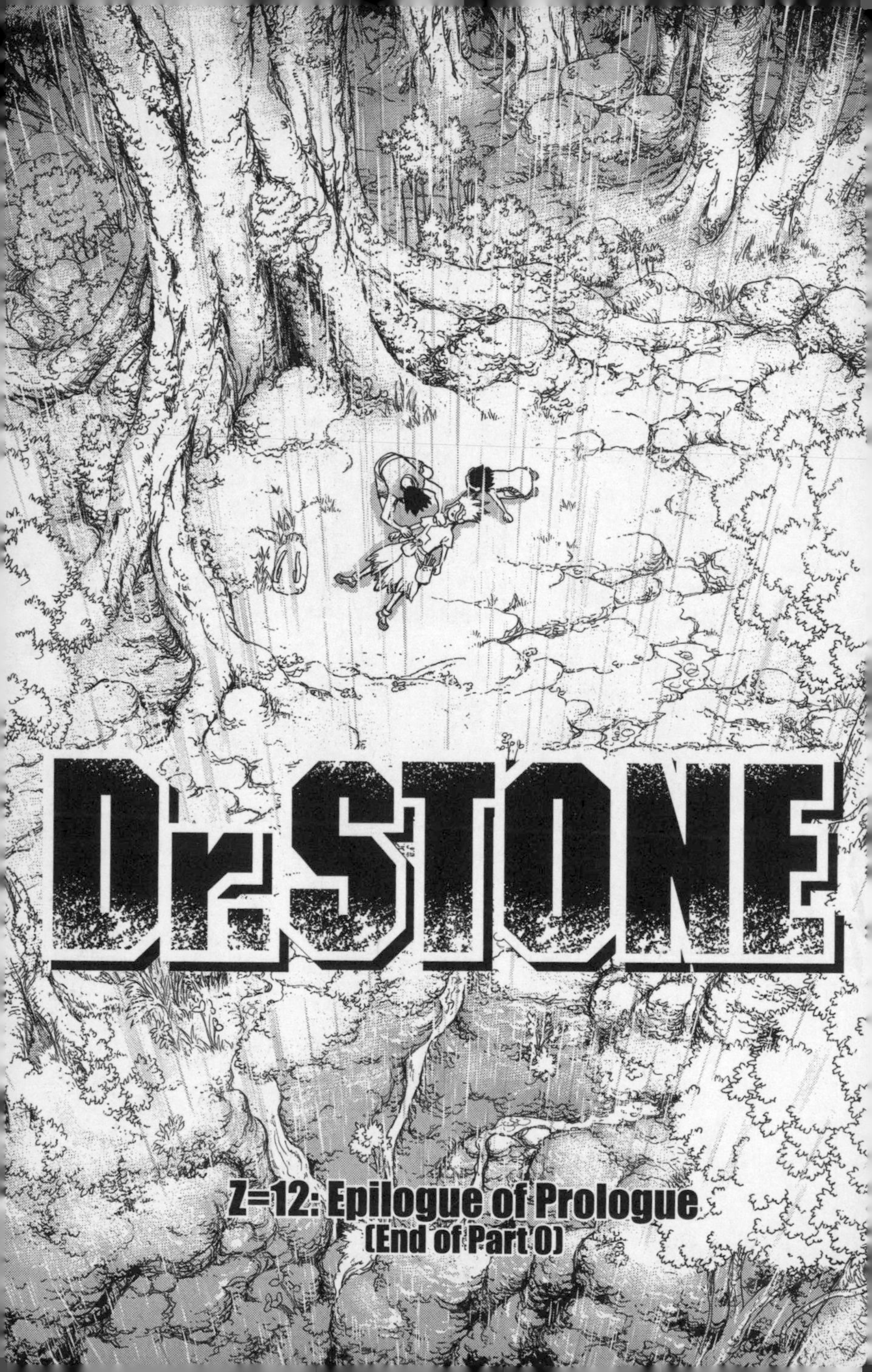
Dr.STONE
Z=12: Epilogue of Prologue
(End of Part 0)

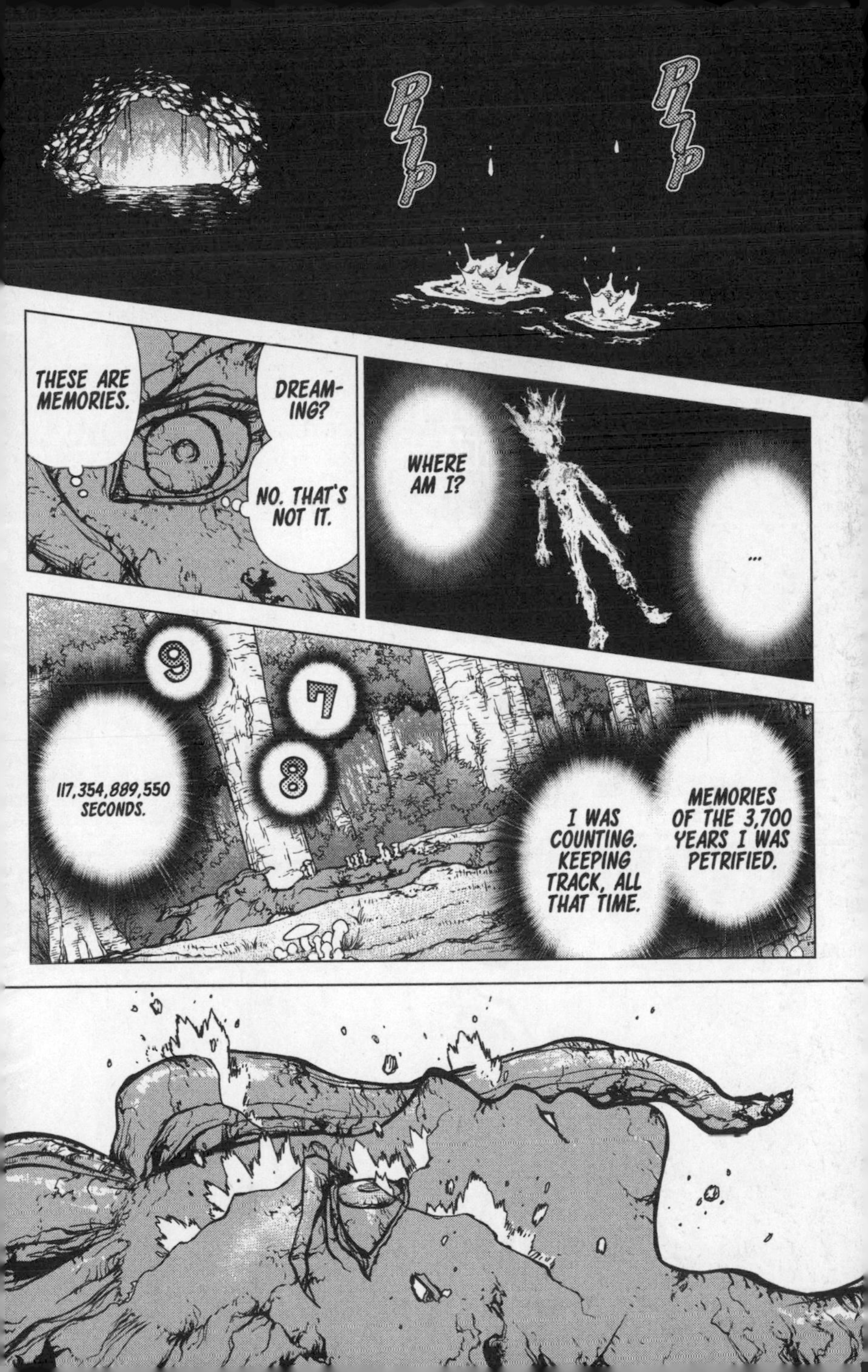
RIP
RIP
...
WHERE AM I?
DREAM-ING?
NO. THAT'S NOT IT.
THESE ARE MEMORIES.
MEMORIES OF THE 3,700 YEARS I WAS PETRIFIED.
I WAS COUNTING. KEEPING TRACK, ALL THAT TIME.
7
8
9
117,354,889,550 SECONDS.

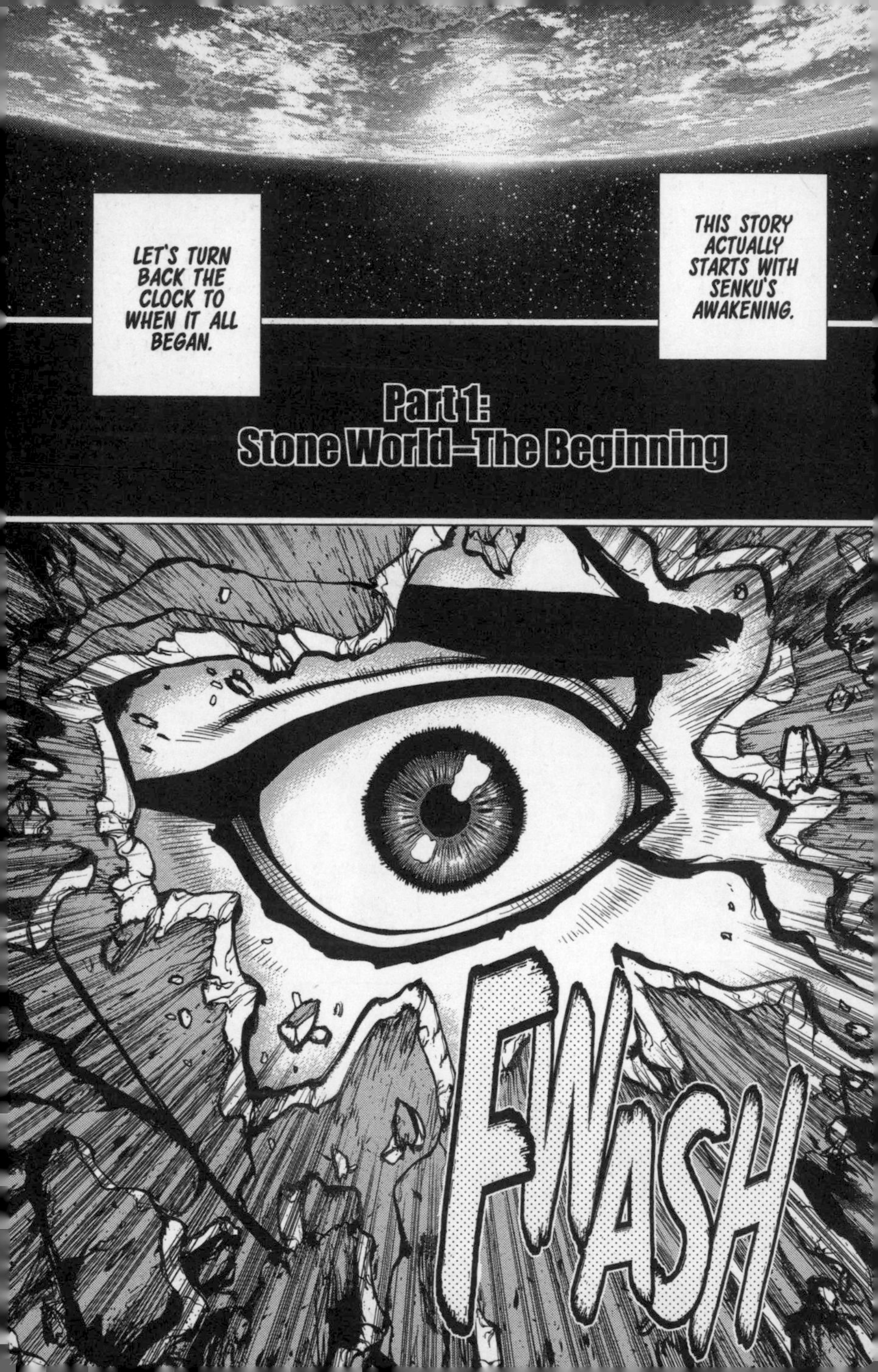
THIS STORY ACTUALLY STARTS WITH SENKU'S AWAKENING.
LET'S TURN BACK THE CLOCK TO WHEN IT ALL BEGAN.
Part 1:
Stone World—The Beginning
FWASH

MECHA SENKU Q&A

SEARCH Question Corner

They call Tsukasa "History's Strongest Primate High Schooler," but how strong is he, really?

The Naked Professor from Osaka **SEARCH**

FROM NOW ON...

...I'LL DO THE FIGHTING!!

He won MMA tournaments while still in high school. Tsukasa is heretofore undefeated!

He is so famous that even Taiju, who does not watch television, has heard of him!

Science Questions — How does one make gasoline out of plastic bottle caps?

Character Questions — If Taiju and Tsukasa really fought, who would win?

Questions That Aren't Really Questions — I wanna get petrified and challenge myself to count the seconds...

Now answering any and all queries!

My name is

MECHA SENKU!!

WHRRR KLANG

Dr. STONE

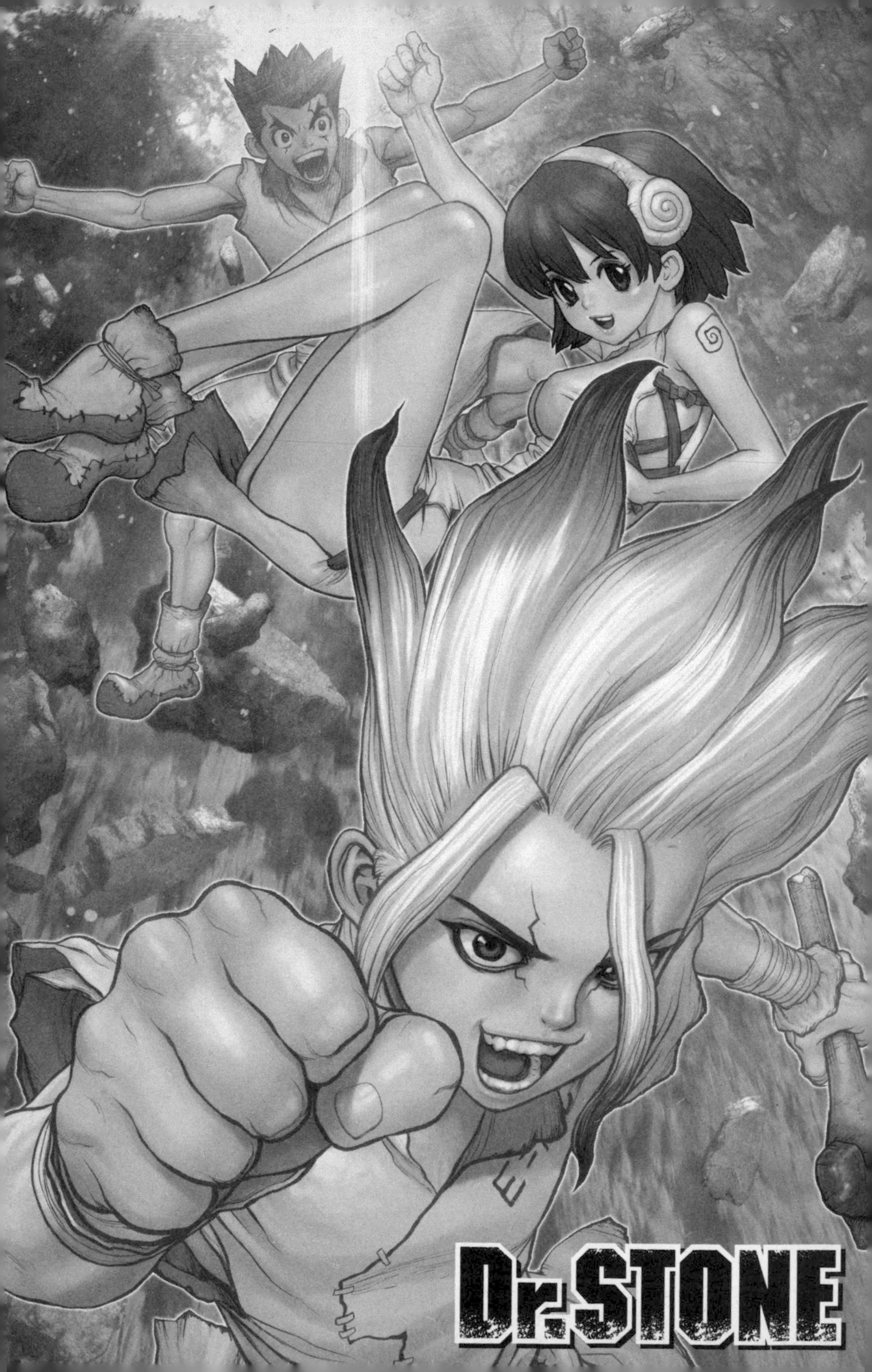
Dr.STONE

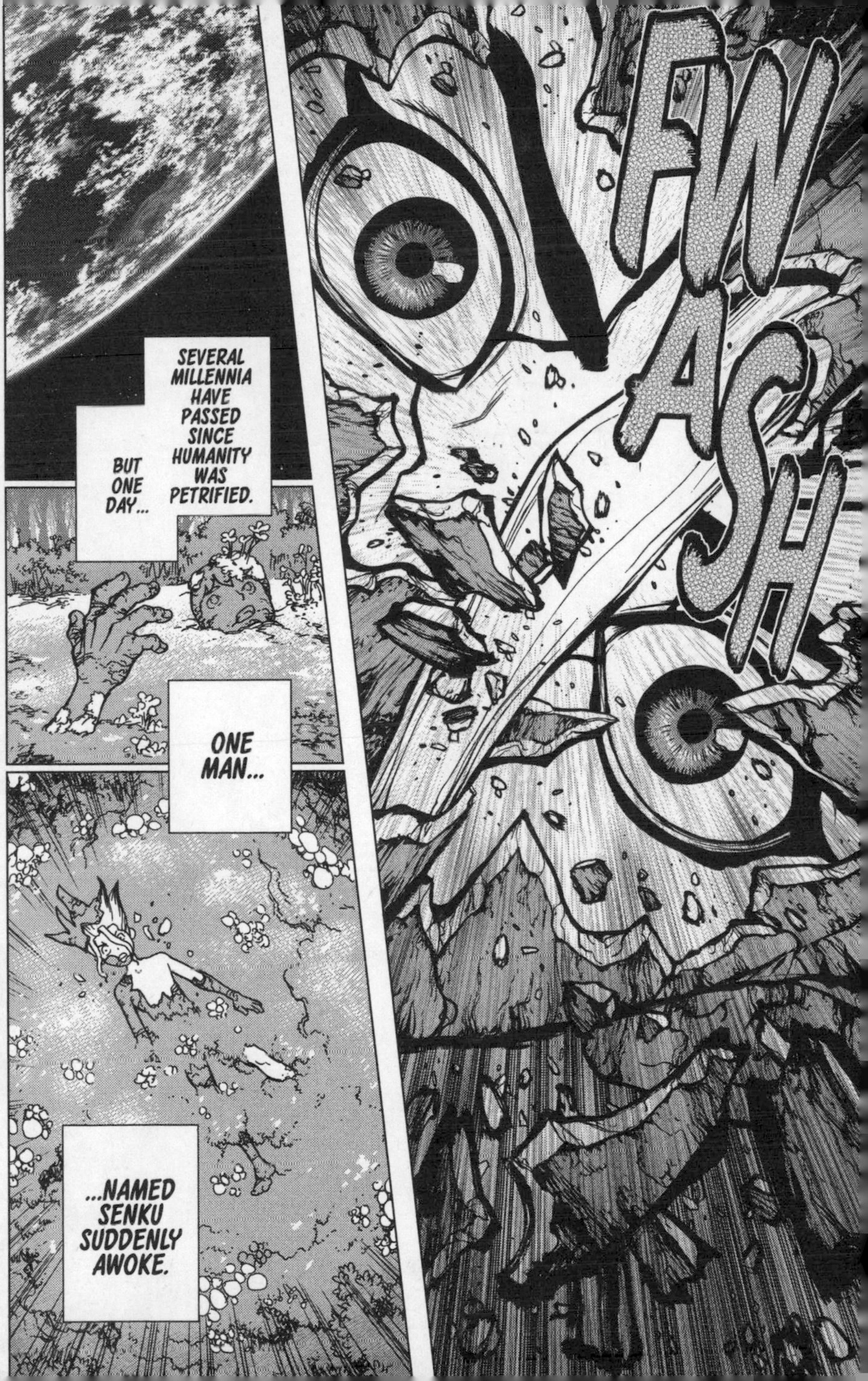
FWAASH
SEVERAL MILLENNIA HAVE PASSED SINCE HUMANITY WAS PETRIFIED.
BUT ONE DAY...
ONE MAN...
...NAMED SENKU SUDDENLY AWOKE.

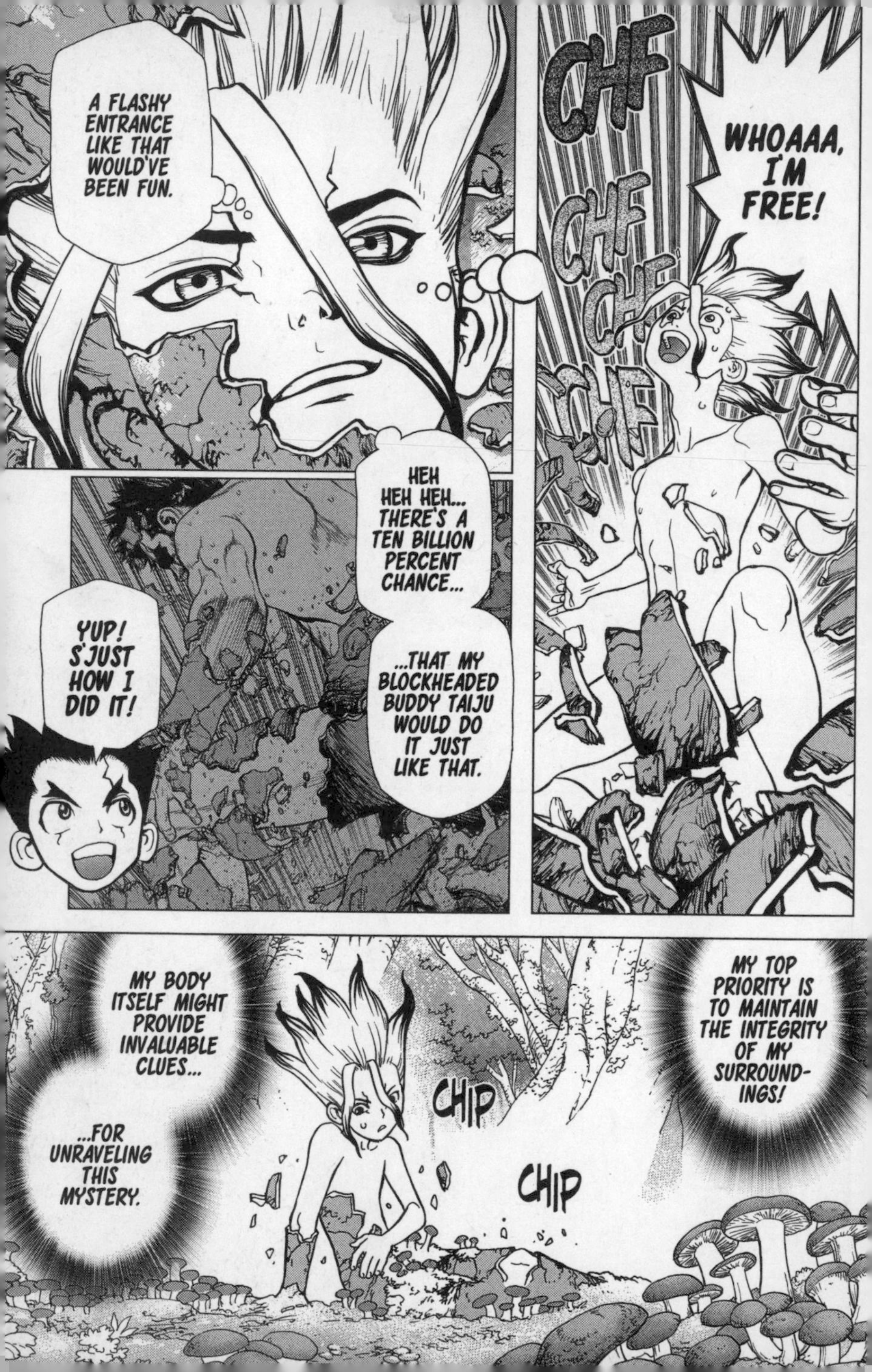
WHOAAA, I'M FREE!
CHF
CHF
CHF
CHF
CHF
A FLASHY ENTRANCE LIKE THAT WOULD'VE BEEN FUN.
HEH HEH HEH... THERE'S A TEN BILLION PERCENT CHANCE...
...THAT MY BLOCKHEADED BUDDY TAIJU WOULD DO IT JUST LIKE THAT.
YUP! S'JUST HOW I DID IT!
MY TOP PRIORITY IS TO MAINTAIN THE INTEGRITY OF MY SURROUND-INGS!
CHIP
CHIP
MY BODY ITSELF MIGHT PROVIDE INVALUABLE CLUES...
...FOR UNRAVELING THIS MYSTERY.

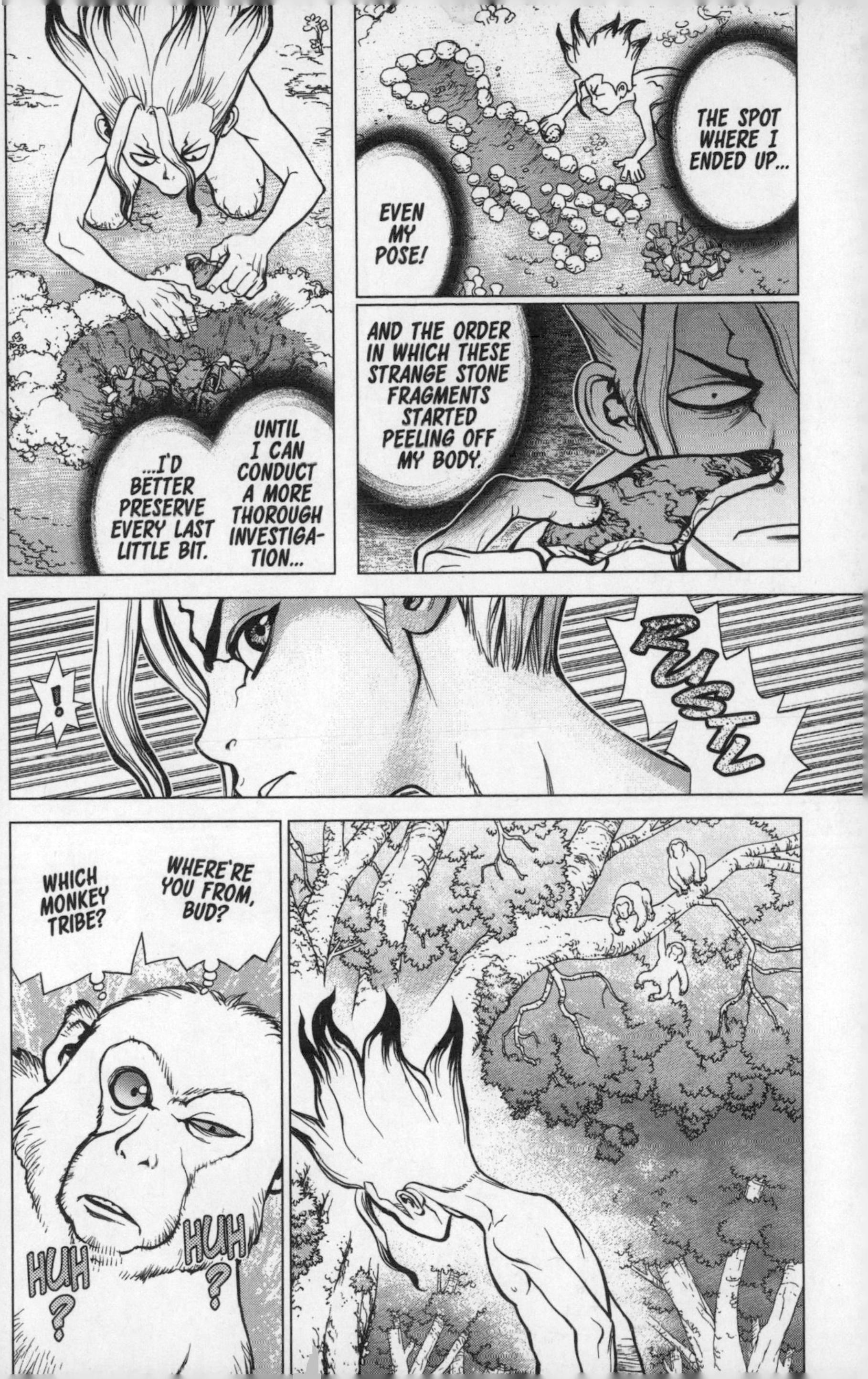
THE SPOT WHERE I ENDED UP...
EVEN MY POSE!
AND THE ORDER IN WHICH THESE STRANGE STONE FRAGMENTS STARTED PEELING OFF MY BODY.
UNTIL I CAN CONDUCT A MORE THOROUGH INVESTIGA-TION...
...I'D BETTER PRESERVE EVERY LAST LITTLE BIT.
RUSTL
!
WHERE'RE YOU FROM, BUD?
WHICH MONKEY TRIBE?
HUH?
HUH?

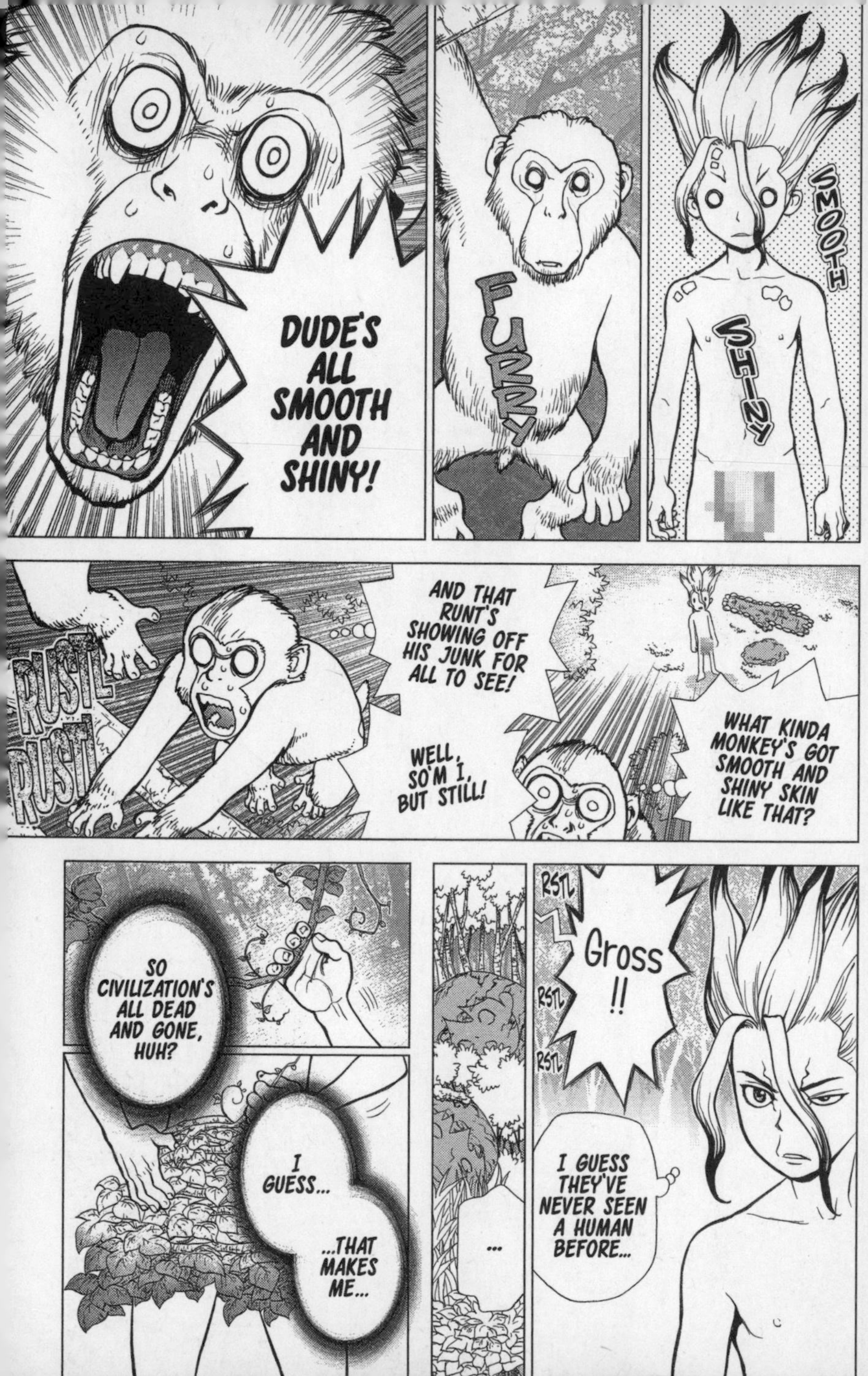
SMOOTH
SHINY
FURRY
DUDE'S ALL SMOOTH AND SHINY!
WHAT KINDA MONKEY'S GOT SMOOTH AND SHINY SKIN LIKE THAT?
WELL, SO'M I, BUT STILL!
AND THAT RUNT'S SHOWING OFF HIS JUNK FOR ALL TO SEE!
RUSTL RUSTL
RSTL
RSTL
RSTL
Gross !!
I GUESS THEY'VE NEVER SEEN A HUMAN BEFORE...
...
SO CIVILIZATION'S ALL DEAD AND GONE, HUH?
I GUESS...
...THAT MAKES ME...

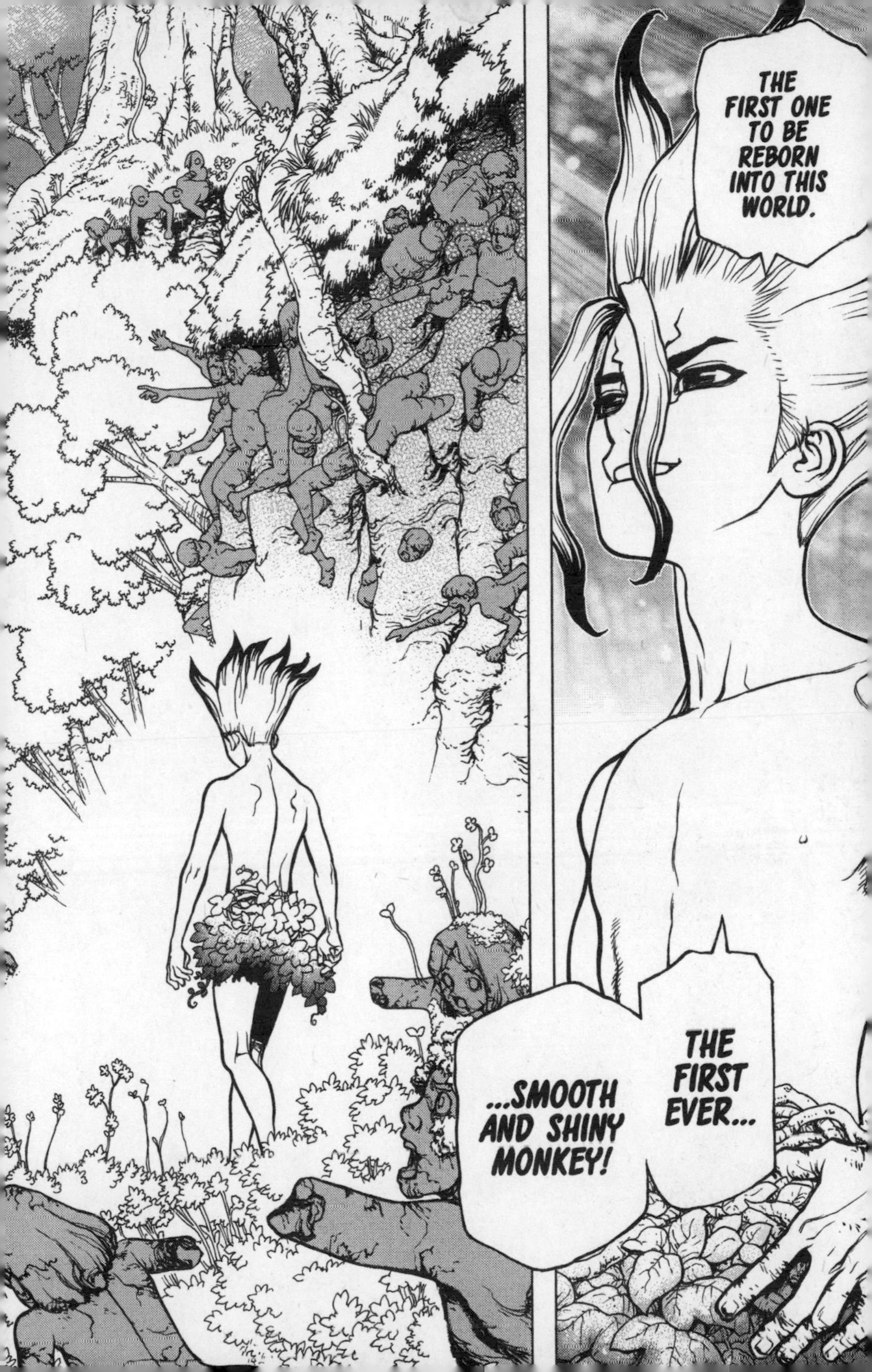
THE FIRST ONE TO BE REBORN INTO THIS WORLD.
THE FIRST EVER...
...SMOOTH AND SHINY MONKEY!

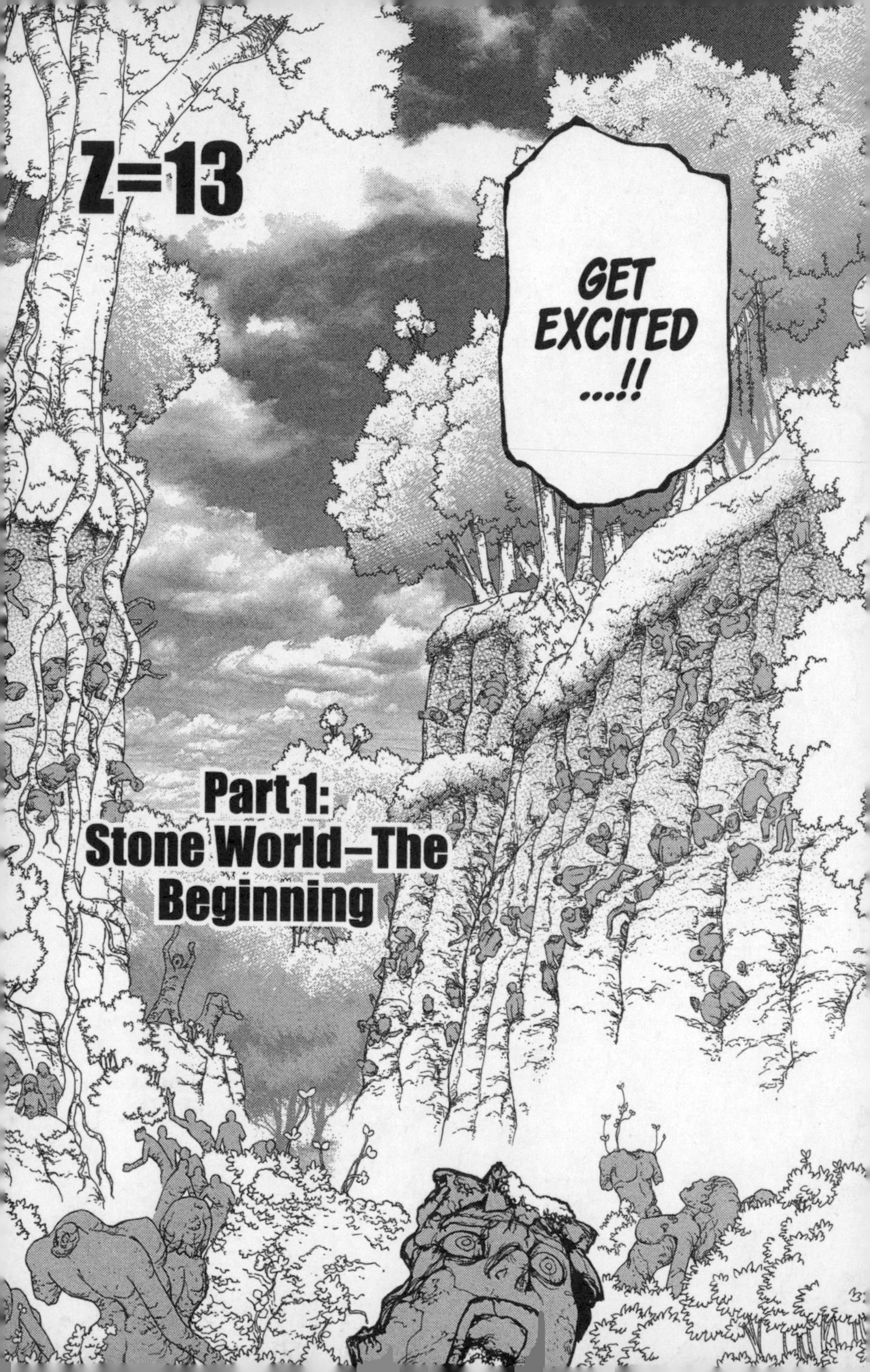
GET EXCITED ....!!
Z=13
Part 1: Stone World–The Beginning

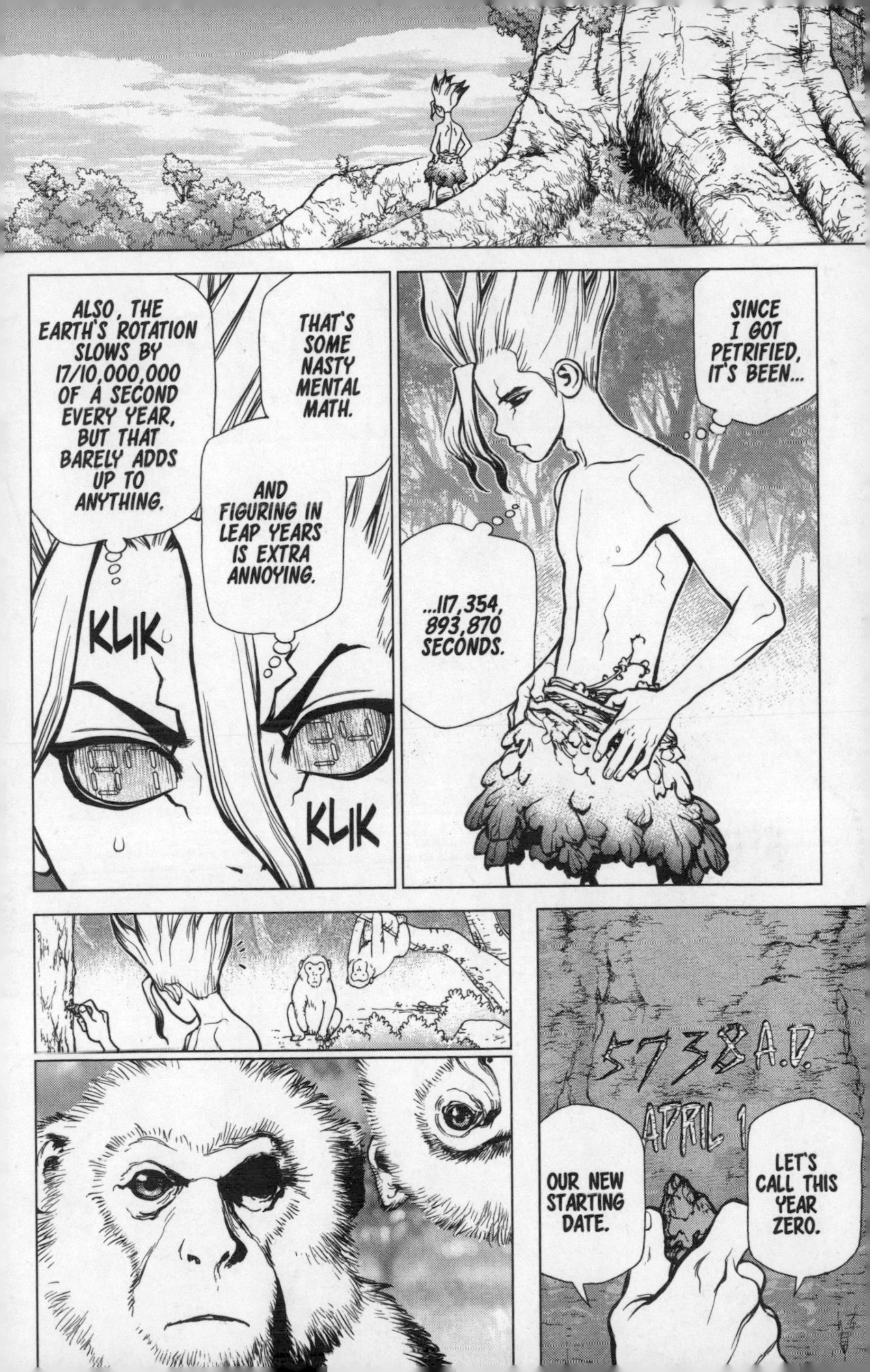
SINCE I GOT PETRIFIED, IT'S BEEN...
...117,354, 893,870 SECONDS.
THAT'S SOME NASTY MENTAL MATH.
ALSO, THE EARTH'S ROTATION SLOWS BY 17/10,000,000 OF A SECOND EVERY YEAR, BUT THAT BARELY ADDS UP TO ANYTHING.
AND FIGURING IN LEAP YEARS IS EXTRA ANNOYING.
KLIK
KLIK
5738 A.D.
APRIL 1
LET'S CALL THIS YEAR ZERO.
OUR NEW STARTING DATE.

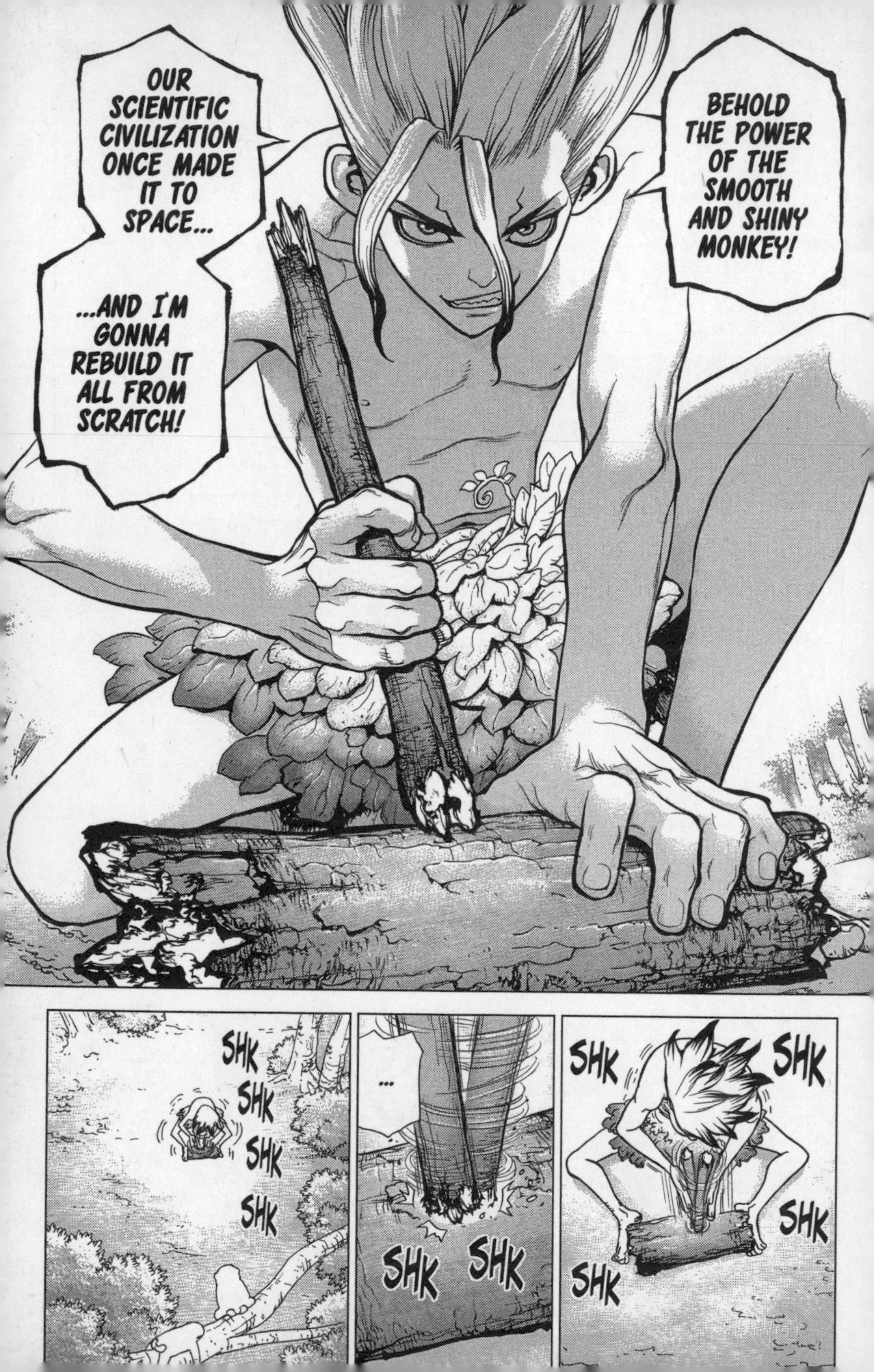
BEHOLD THE POWER OF THE SMOOTH AND SHINY MONKEY!
OUR SCIENTIFIC CIVILIZATION ONCE MADE IT TO SPACE...
...AND I'M GONNA REBUILD IT ALL FROM SCRATCH!
SHK
SHK
SHK
SHK
SHK
SHK
SHK
SHK
...
SHK
SHK
SHK
SHK
SHK
SHK

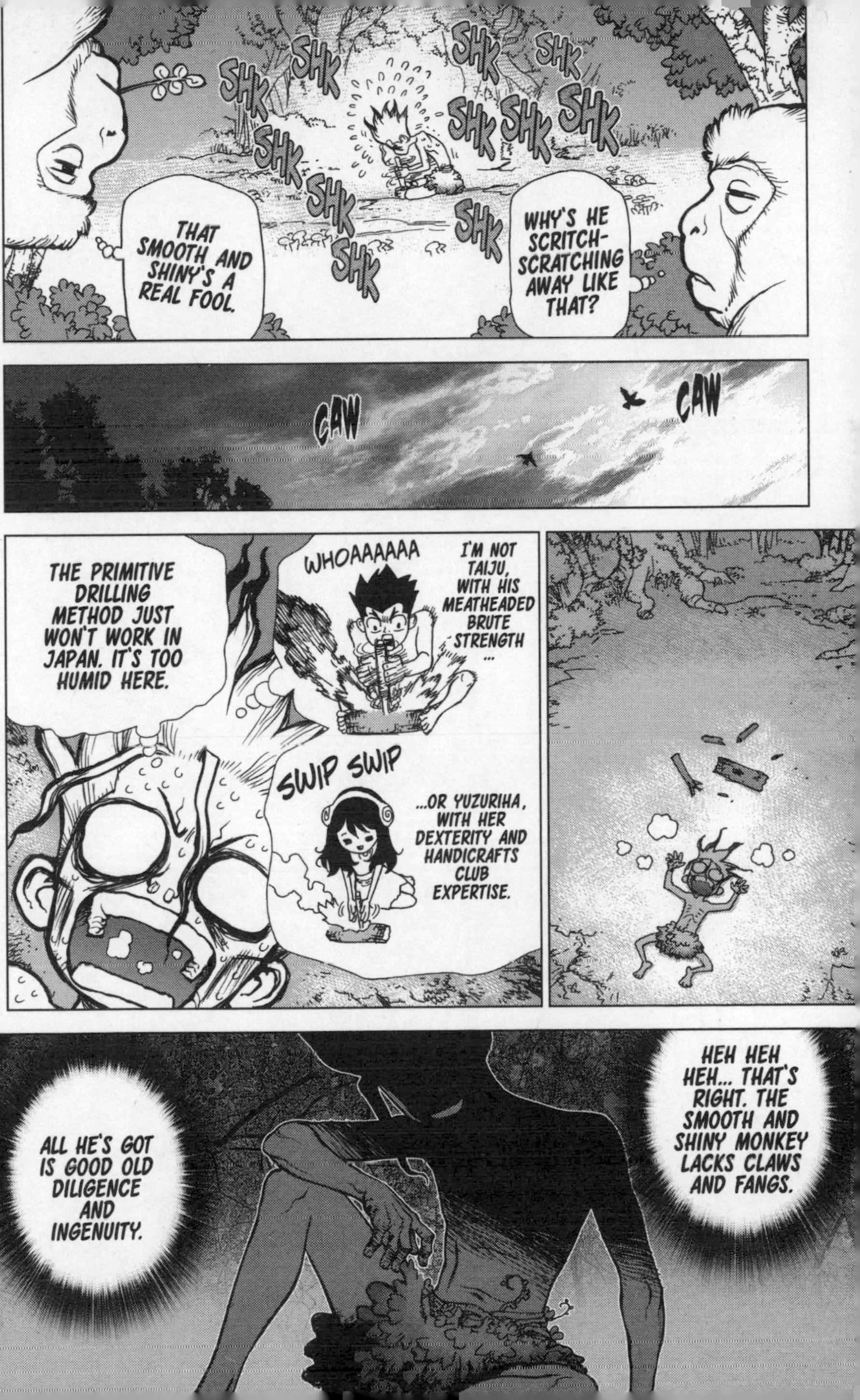
SHK SHK SHK SHK SHK SHK SHK SHK SHK SHK SHK SHK
WHY'S HE SCRITCH-SCRATCHING AWAY LIKE THAT?
THAT SMOOTH AND SHINY'S A REAL FOOL.
CAW
CAW
I'M NOT TAIJU, WITH HIS MEATHEADED BRUTE STRENGTH...
WHOAAAAAA
THE PRIMITIVE DRILLING METHOD JUST WON'T WORK IN JAPAN. IT'S TOO HUMID HERE.
...OR YUZURIHA, WITH HER DEXTERITY AND HANDICRAFTS CLUB EXPERTISE.
SWIP SWIP
HEH HEH HEH... THAT'S RIGHT. THE SMOOTH AND SHINY MONKEY LACKS CLAWS AND FANGS.
ALL HE'S GOT IS GOOD OLD DILIGENCE AND INGENUITY.

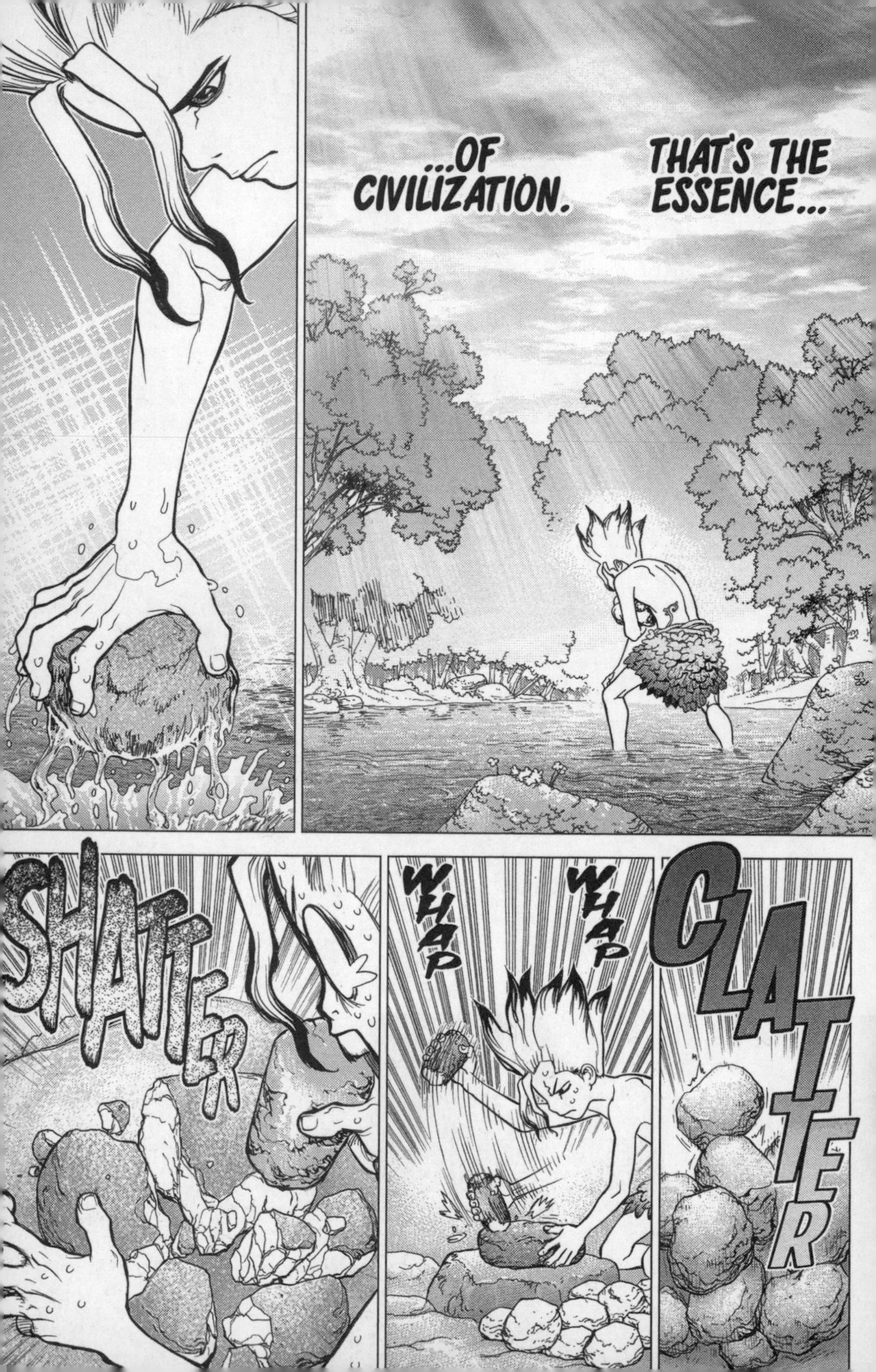
THAT'S THE ESSENCE...
...OF CIVILIZATION.
CLATTER
WHAP
WHAP
SHATTER

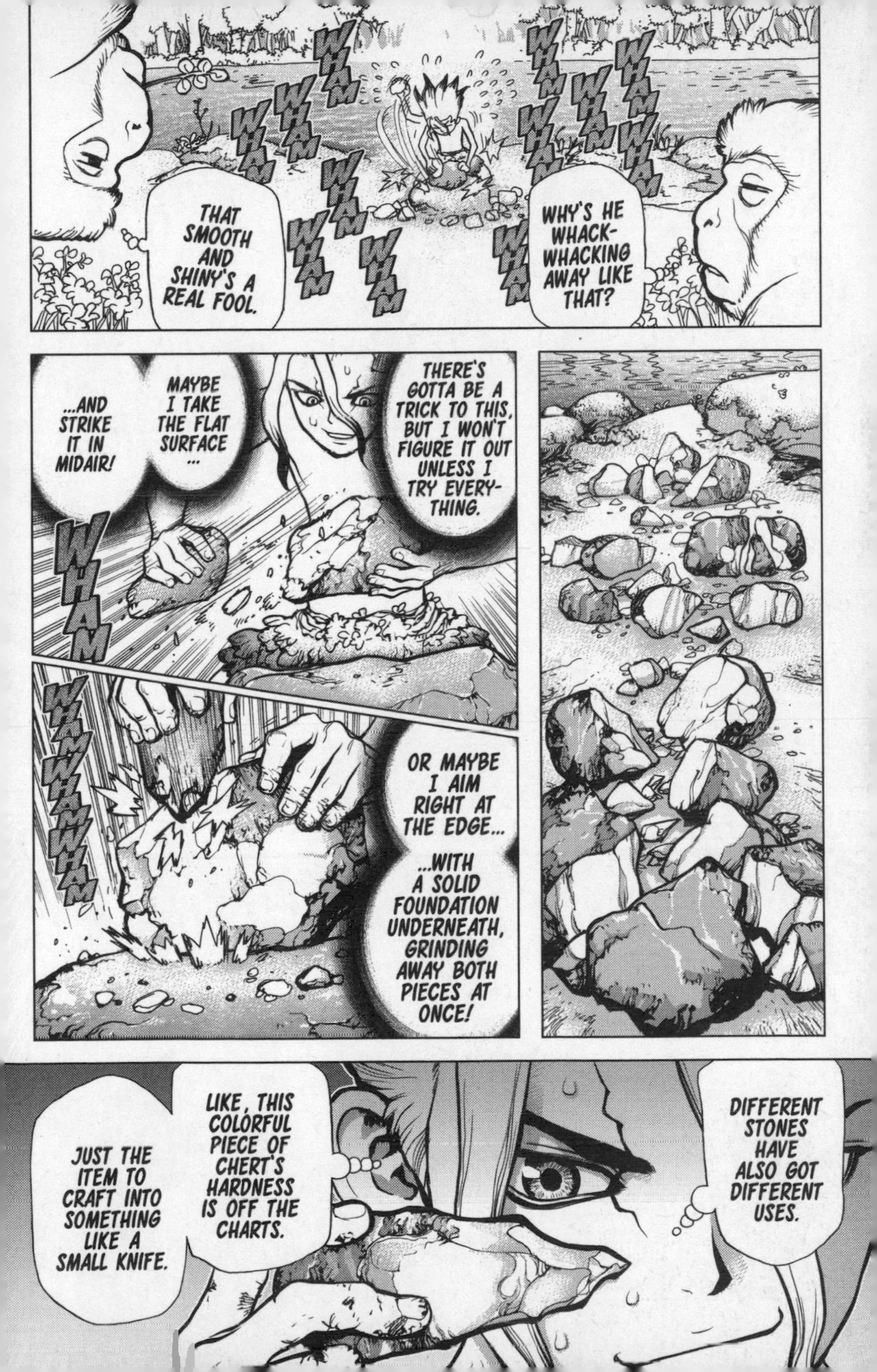
WHAM WHAM WHAM
WHY'S HE WHACK-WHACKING AWAY LIKE THAT?
WHAM WHAM WHAM WHAM WHAM
THAT SMOOTH AND SHINY'S A REAL FOOL.
THERE'S GOTTA BE A TRICK TO THIS, BUT I WON'T FIGURE IT OUT UNLESS I TRY EVERY-THING.
MAYBE I TAKE THE FLAT SURFACE...
...AND STRIKE IT IN MIDAIR!
WHAM
OR MAYBE I AIM RIGHT AT THE EDGE...
...WITH A SOLID FOUNDATION UNDERNEATH, GRINDING AWAY BOTH PIECES AT ONCE!
WHAMWHAMWHAM
DIFFERENT STONES HAVE ALSO GOT DIFFERENT USES.
LIKE, THIS COLORFUL PIECE OF CHERT'S HARDNESS IS OFF THE CHARTS.
JUST THE ITEM TO CRAFT INTO SOMETHING LIKE A SMALL KNIFE.

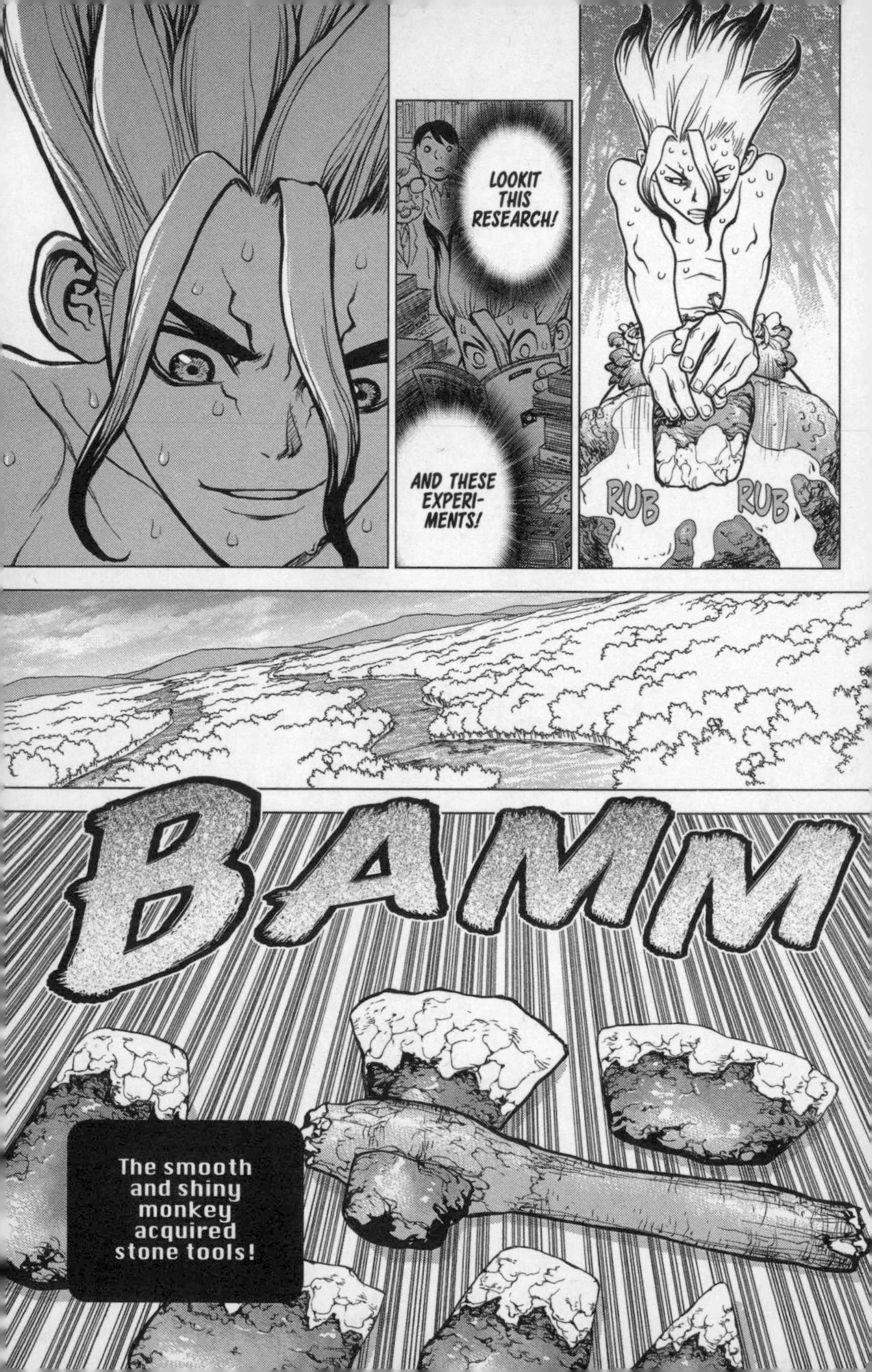
RUB RUB
LOOKIT THIS RESEARCH!
AND THESE EXPERI-MENTS!
BAMM
The smooth and shiny monkey acquired stone tools!

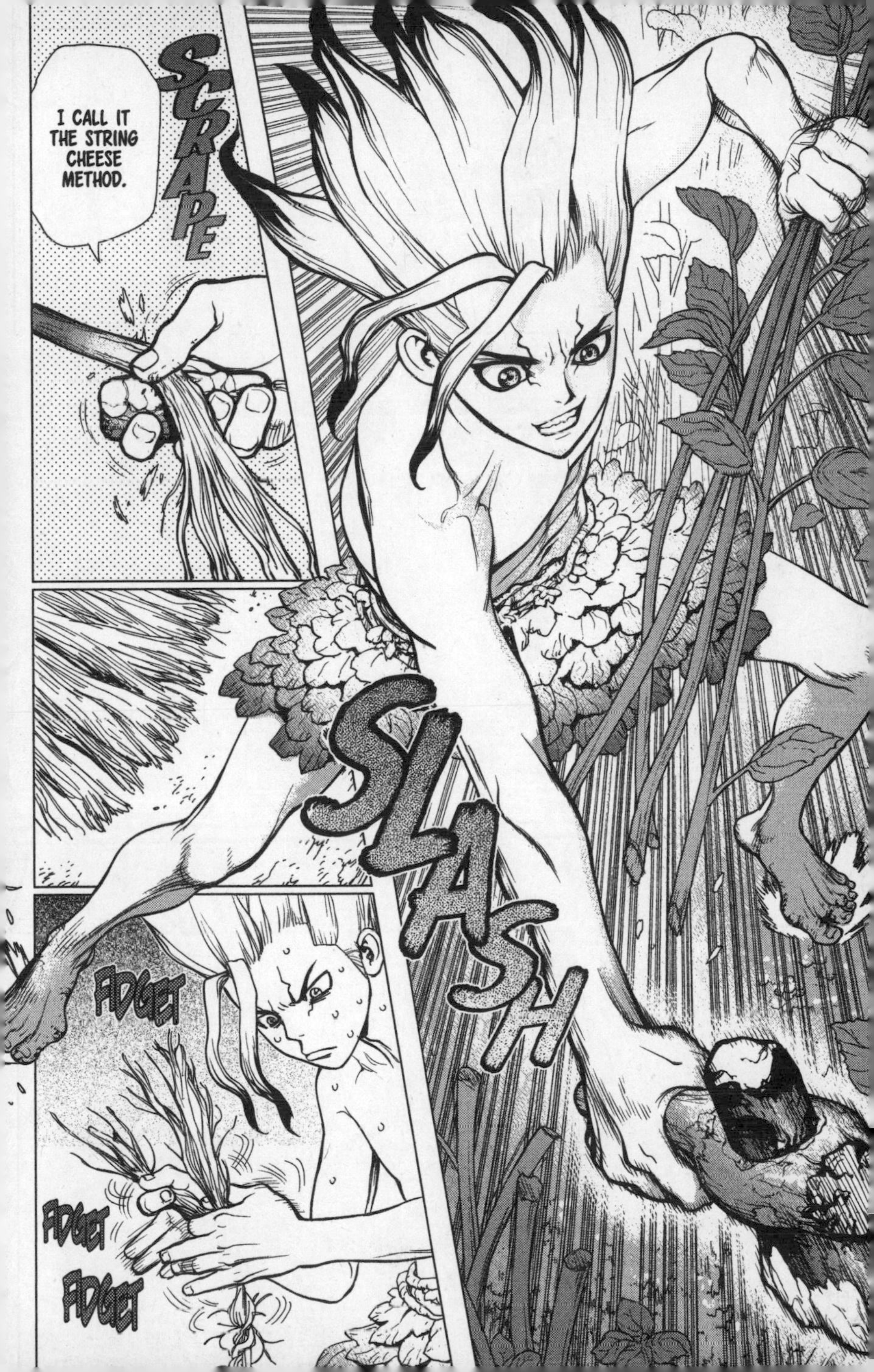

SLASH
I CALL IT THE STRING CHEESE METHOD.
SCRAPE
FIDGET
FIDGET
FIDGET

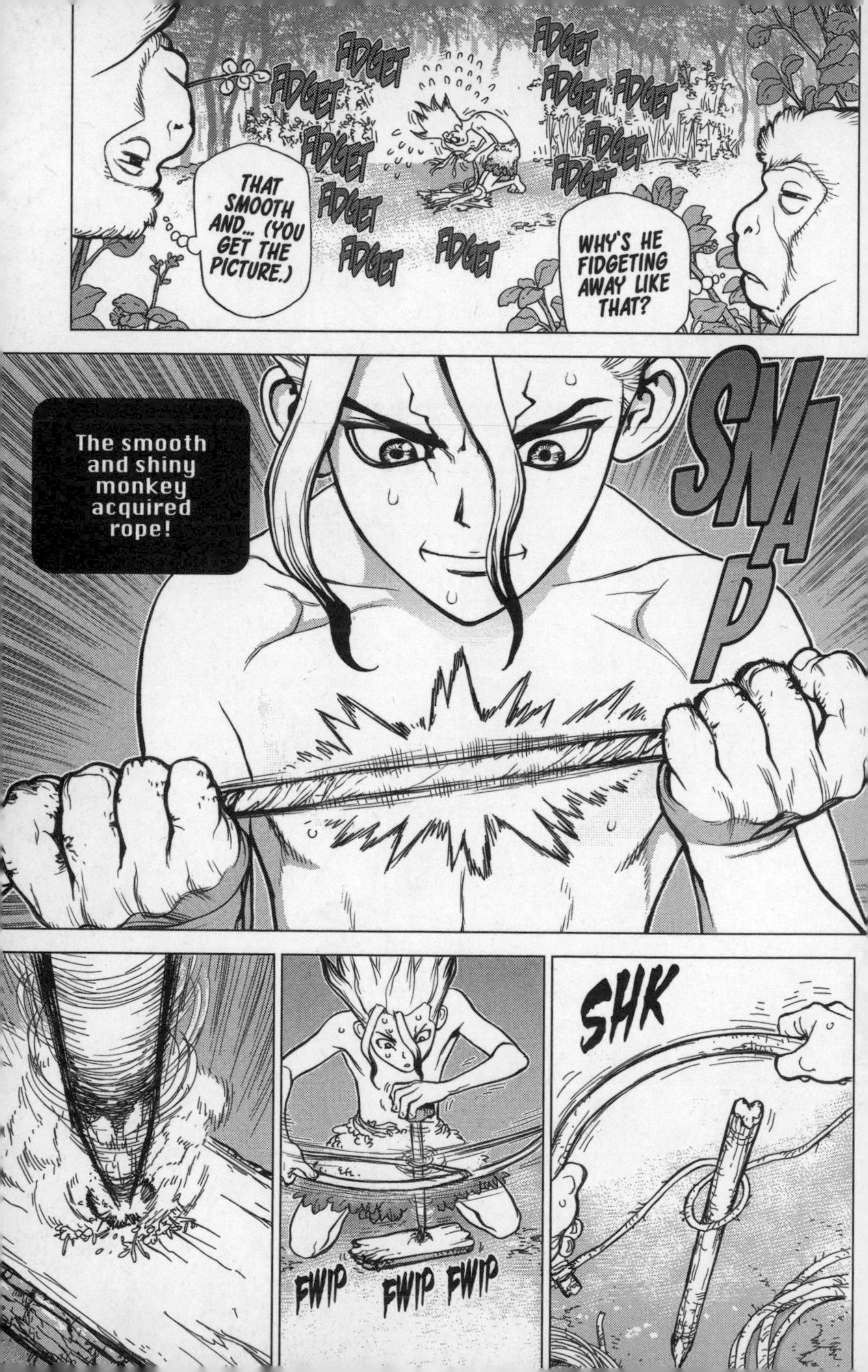
FIDGET
FIDGET FIDGET
FIDGET
FIDGET
WHY'S HE FIDGETING AWAY LIKE THAT?
FIDGET
FIDGET
FIDGET
FIDGET
FIDGET
FIDGET
THAT SMOOTH AND... (YOU GET THE PICTURE.)
SNAP
The smooth and shiny monkey acquired rope!
SHK
FWIP FWIP FWIP

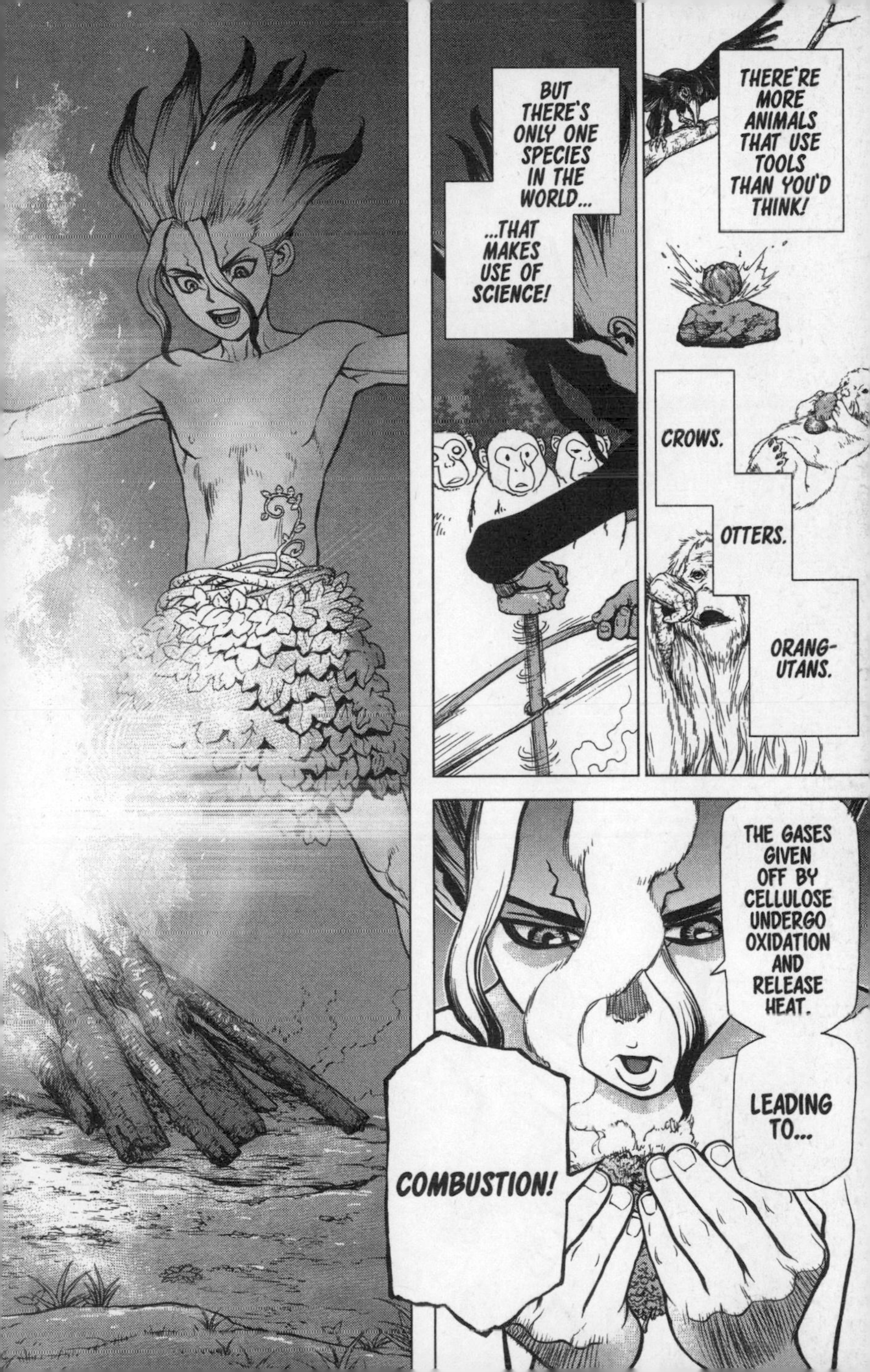
THERE'RE MORE ANIMALS THAT USE TOOLS THAN YOU'D THINK!
CROWS.
OTTERS.
ORANG-UTANS.
BUT THERE'S ONLY ONE SPECIES IN THE WORLD...
...THAT MAKES USE OF SCIENCE!
THE GASES GIVEN OFF BY CELLULOSE UNDERGO OXIDATION AND RELEASE HEAT.
LEADING TO...
COMBUSTION!

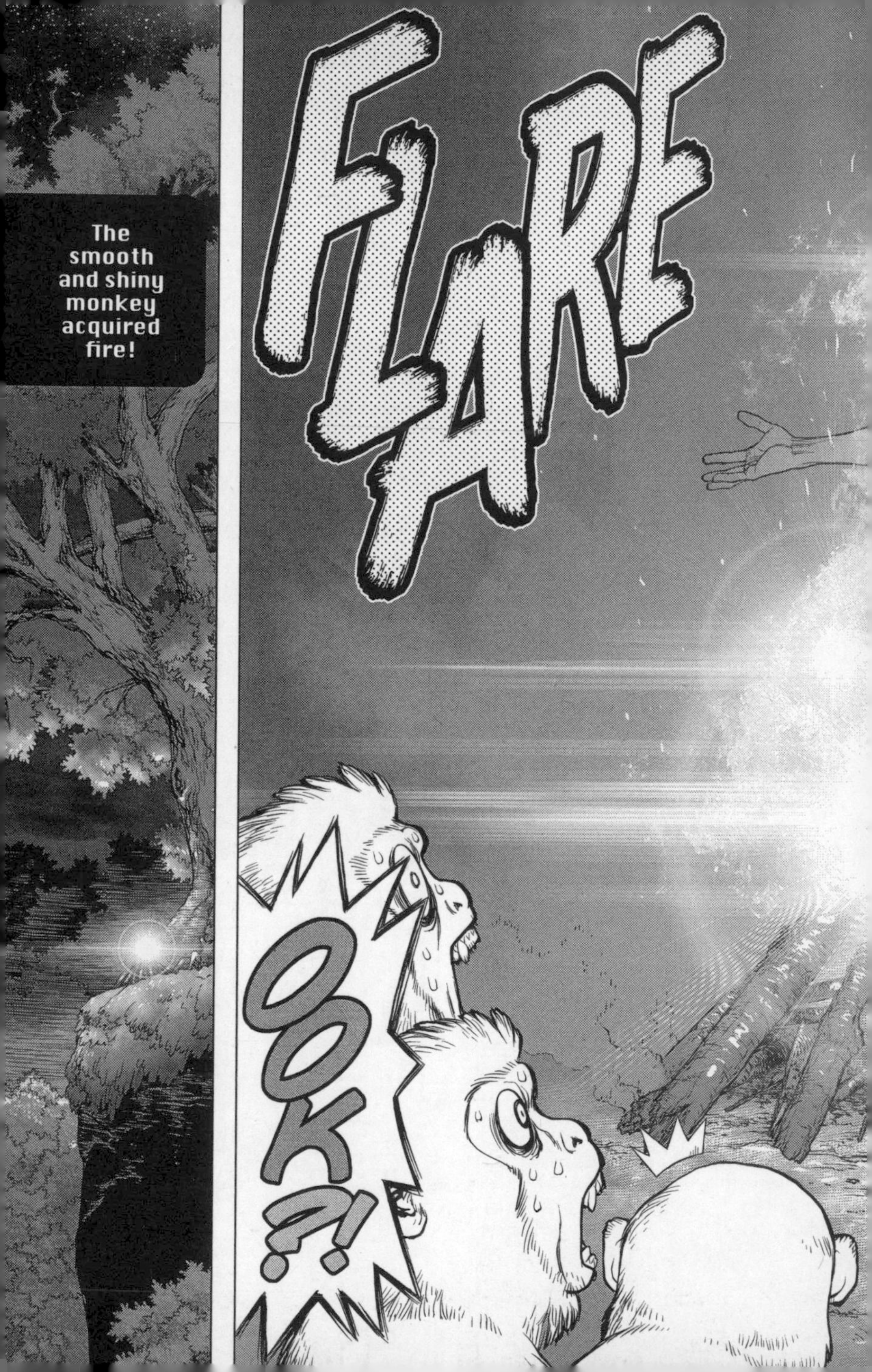
FLARE
OOOK?!
The smooth and shiny monkey acquired fire!

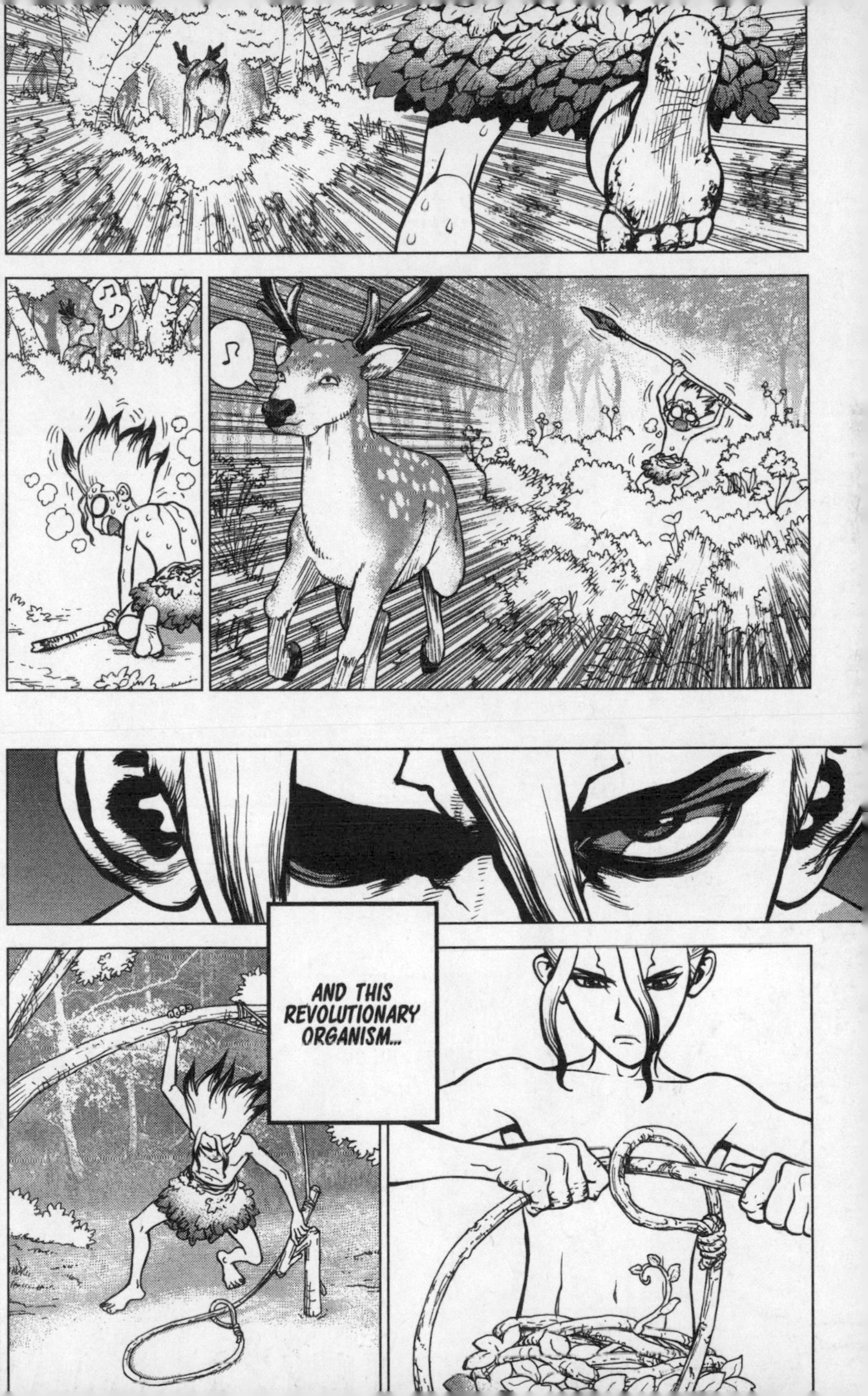
AND THIS REVOLUTIONARY ORGANISM...

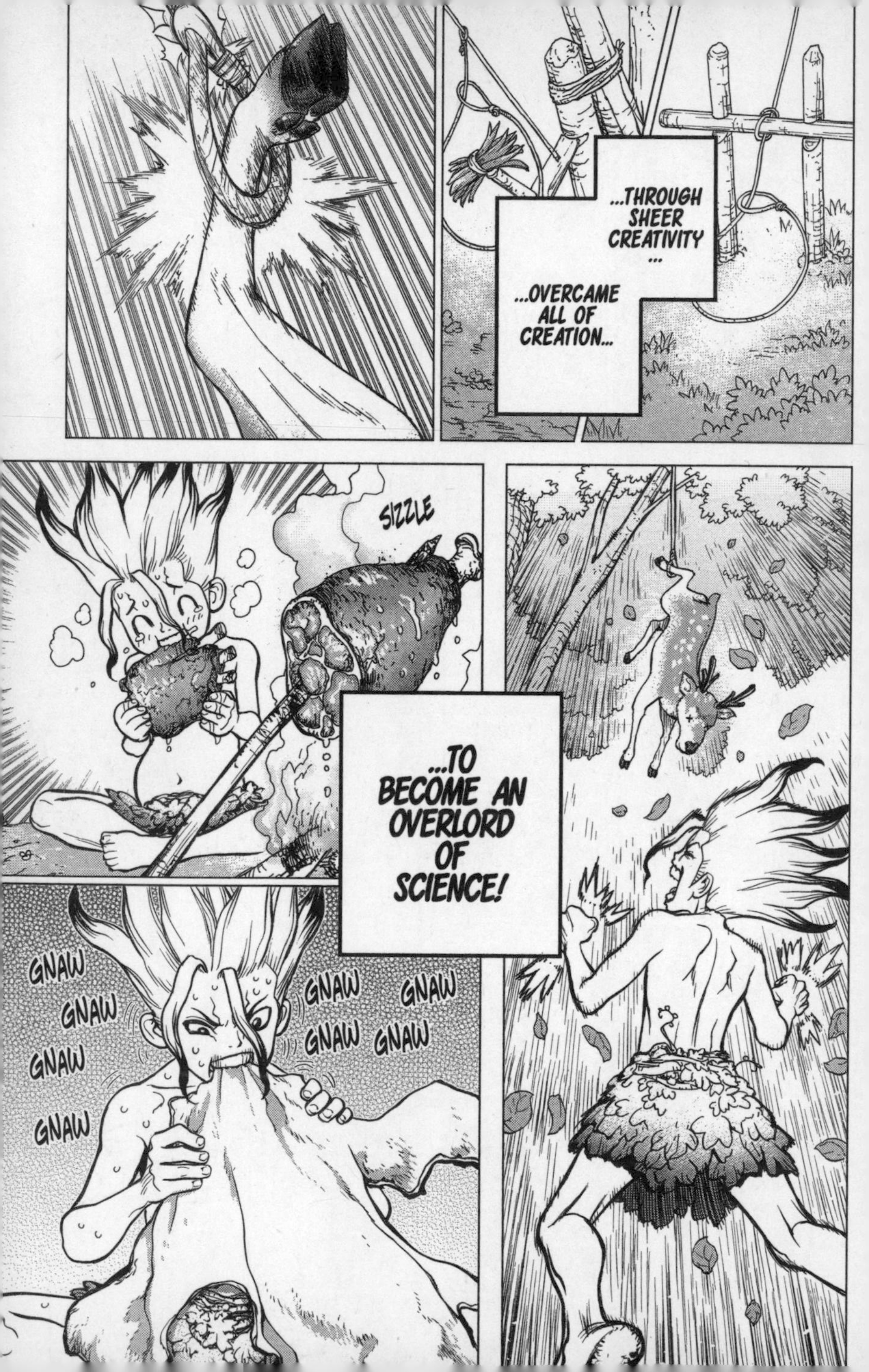
...THROUGH SHEER CREATIVITY ...
...OVERCAME ALL OF CREATION...
...TO BECOME AN OVERLORD OF SCIENCE!
SIZZLE
GNAW GNAW GNAW GNAW GNAW GNAW GNAW GNAW

TMP

TMP TMP

TMP

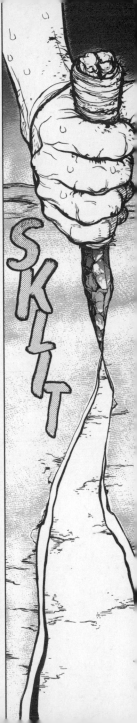

SKLLT

THE SMOOTH AND SHINY MONKEY...

...AIN'T SO SMOOTH 'N' SHINY NO MORE?!

HEH HEH HEH... DID I FORGET TO INTRODUCE MYSELF?

IT'S A PLEASURE TO MEET YOU ALL.

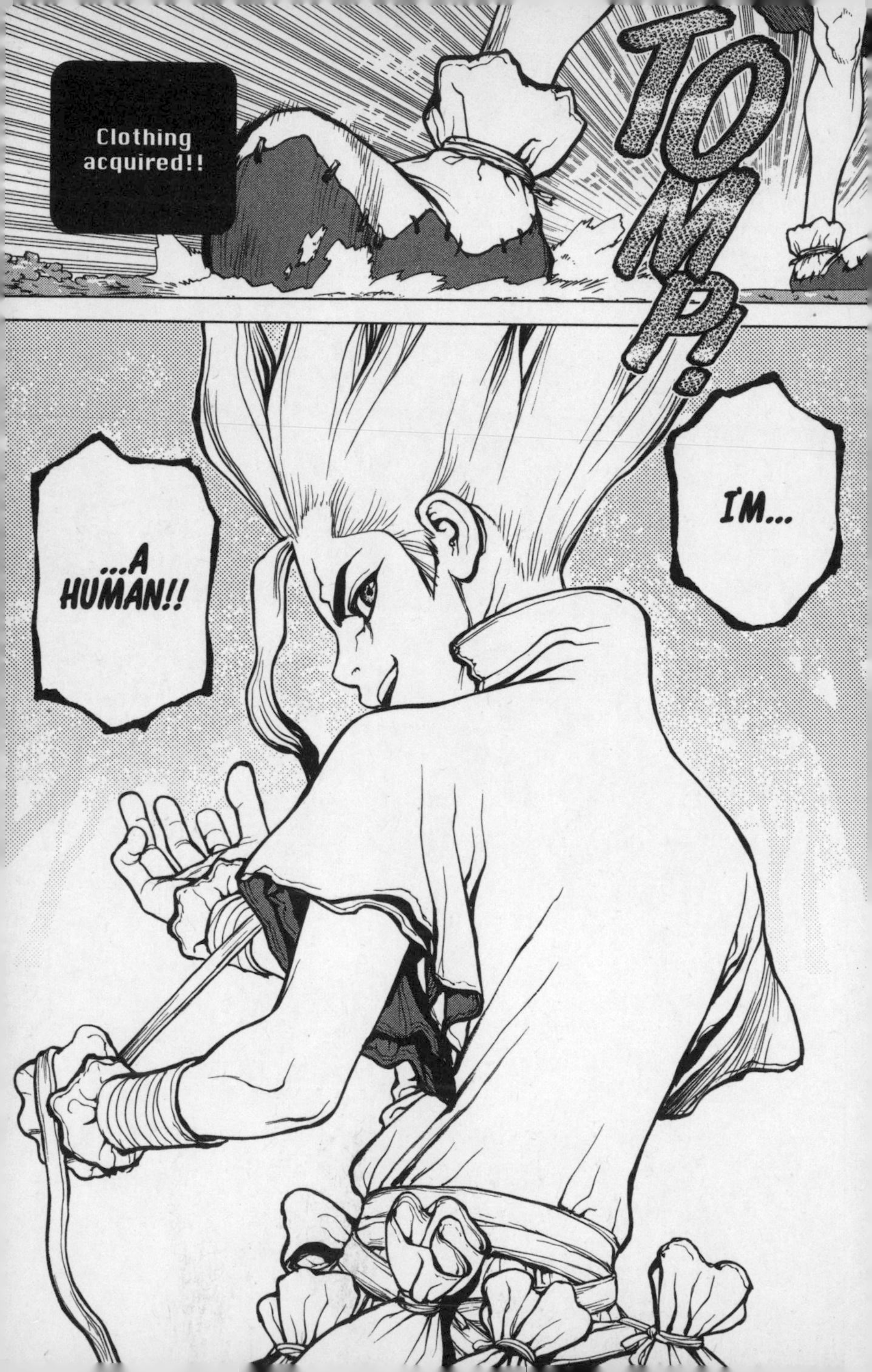
Clothing acquired!!
TOMP!
I'M...
...A HUMAN!!

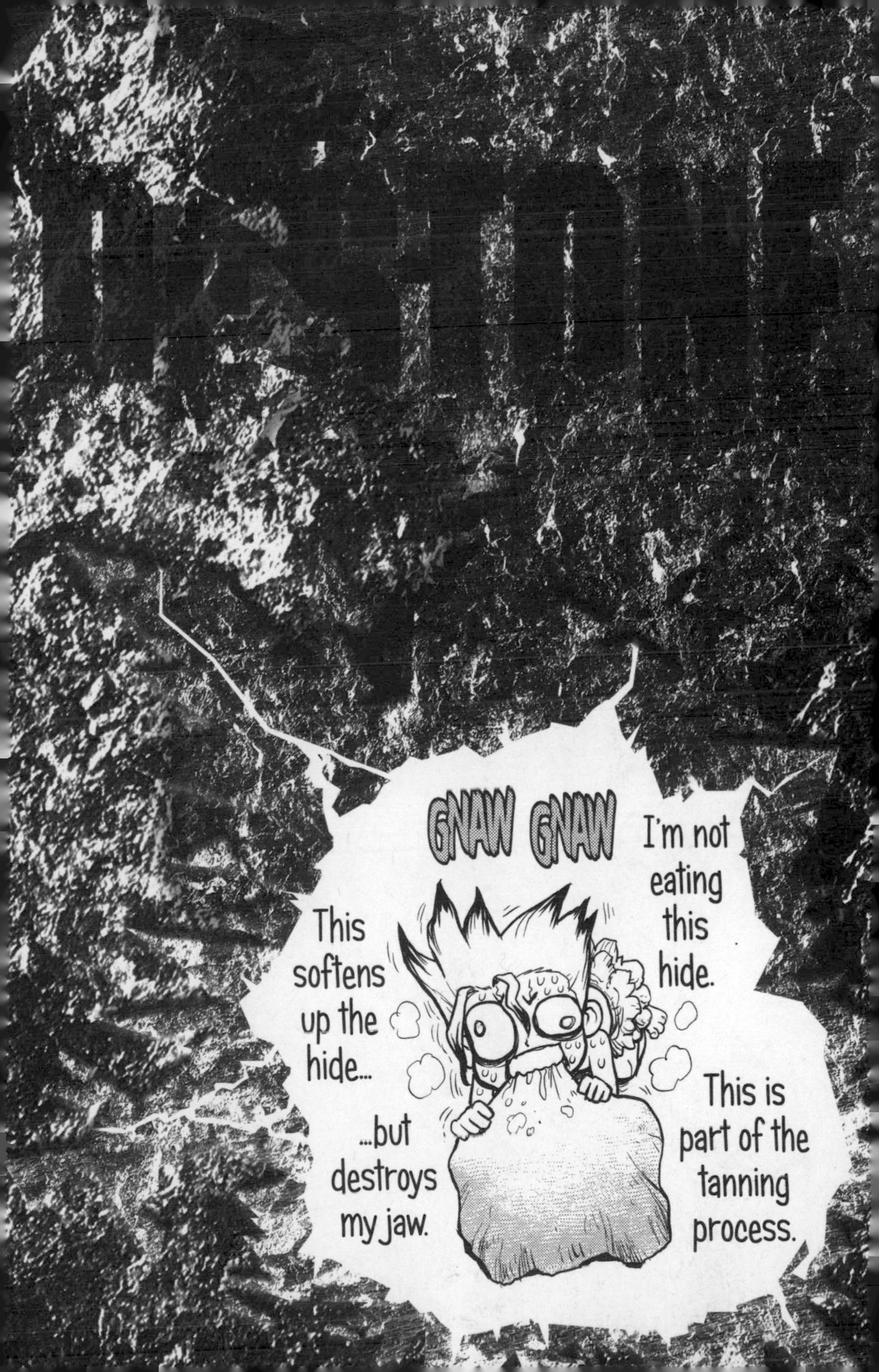
GNAW GNAW
I'm not eating this hide.
This is part of the tanning process.
This softens up the hide...
...but destroys my jaw.

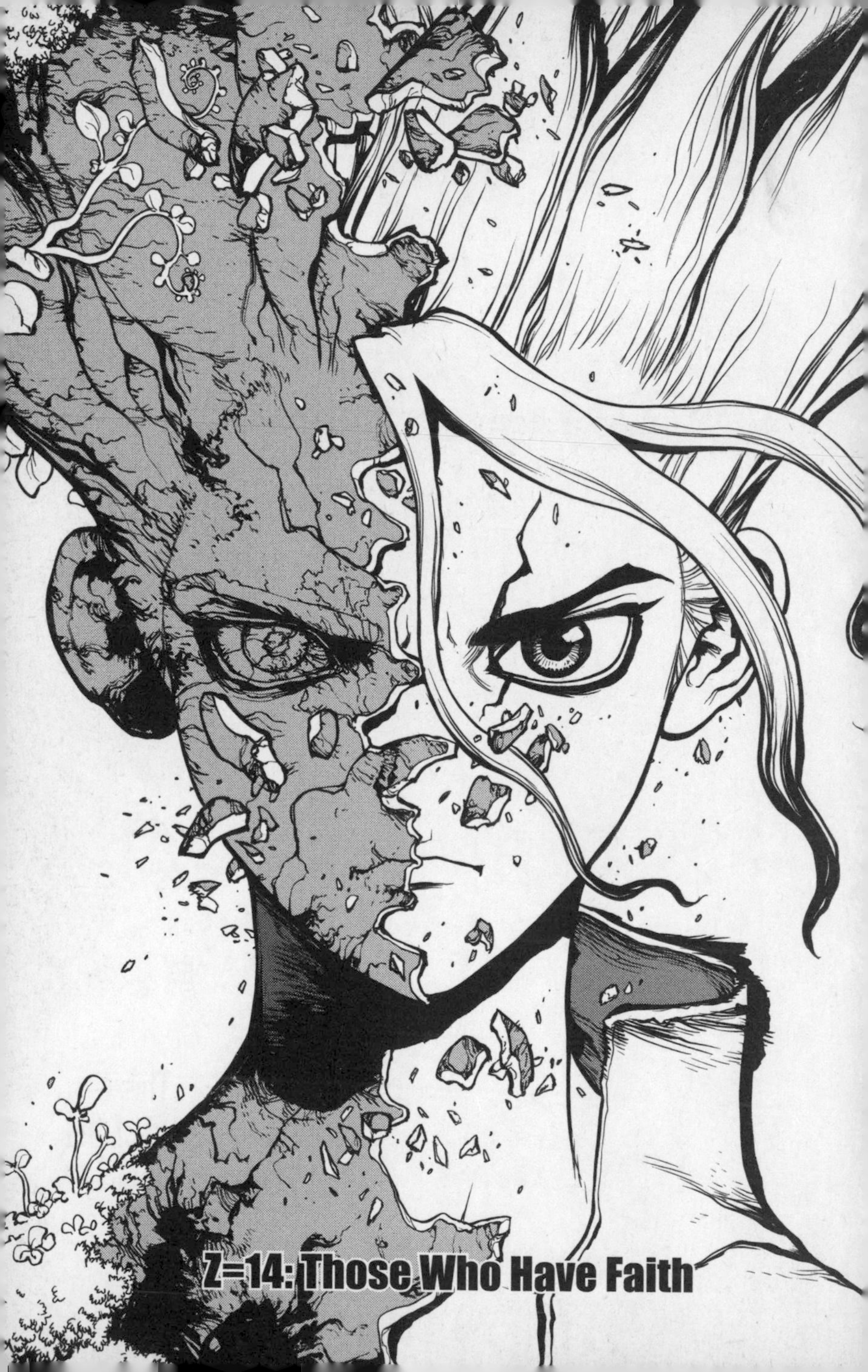
Z=14: Those Who Have Faith

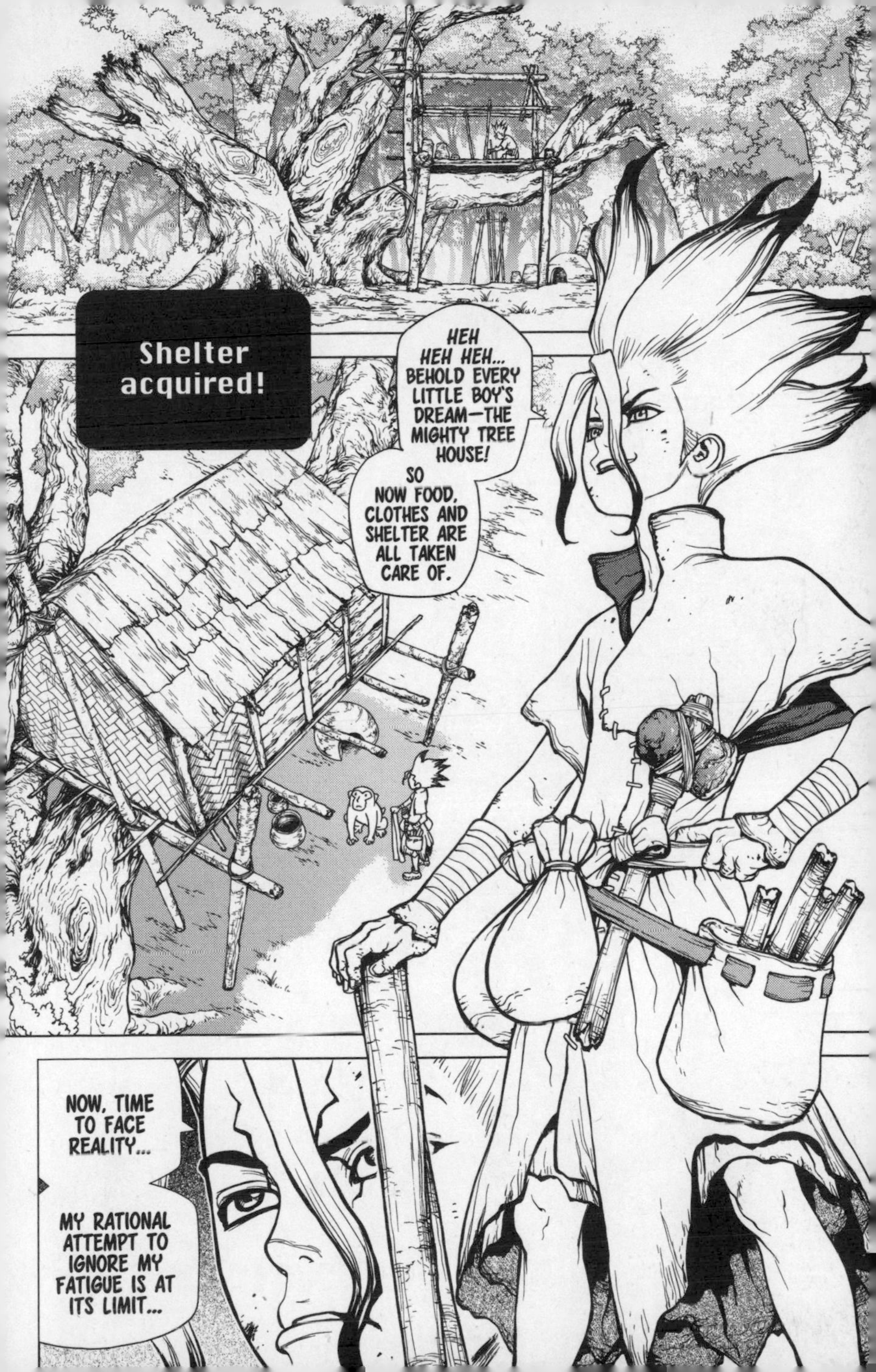
Shelter acquired!
HEH HEH HEH... BEHOLD EVERY LITTLE BOY'S DREAM—THE MIGHTY TREE HOUSE!
SO NOW FOOD, CLOTHES AND SHELTER ARE ALL TAKEN CARE OF.
NOW, TIME TO FACE REALITY...
MY RATIONAL ATTEMPT TO IGNORE MY FATIGUE IS AT ITS LIMIT...

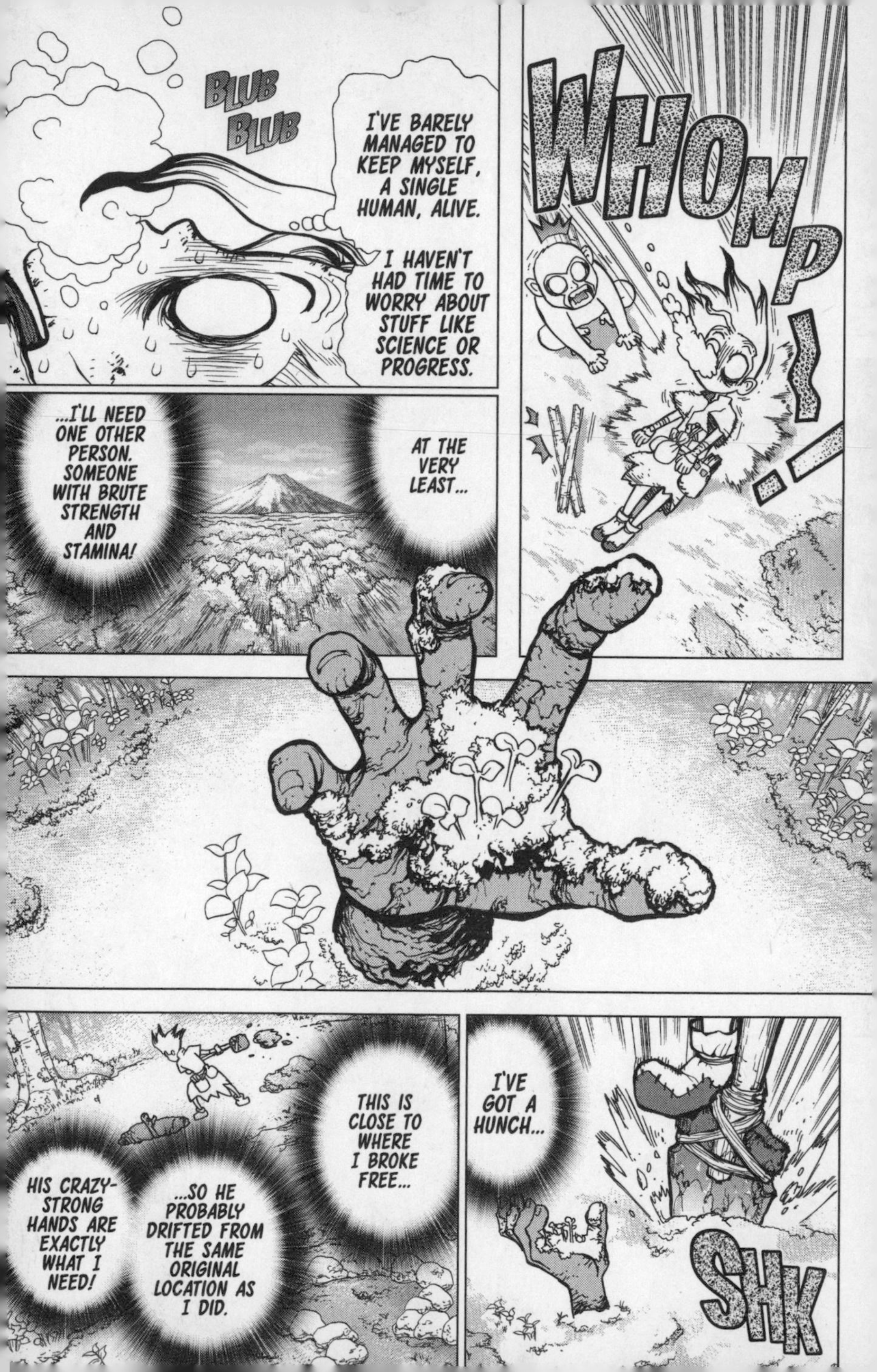
WHOMP!!
BLUB BLUB
I'VE BARELY MANAGED TO KEEP MYSELF, A SINGLE HUMAN, ALIVE.
I HAVEN'T HAD TIME TO WORRY ABOUT STUFF LIKE SCIENCE OR PROGRESS.
AT THE VERY LEAST...
...I'LL NEED ONE OTHER PERSON. SOMEONE WITH BRUTE STRENGTH AND STAMINA!
I'VE GOT A HUNCH...
SHK
THIS IS CLOSE TO WHERE I BROKE FREE...
...SO HE PROBABLY DRIFTED FROM THE SAME ORIGINAL LOCATION AS I DID.
HIS CRAZY-STRONG HANDS ARE EXACTLY WHAT I NEED!

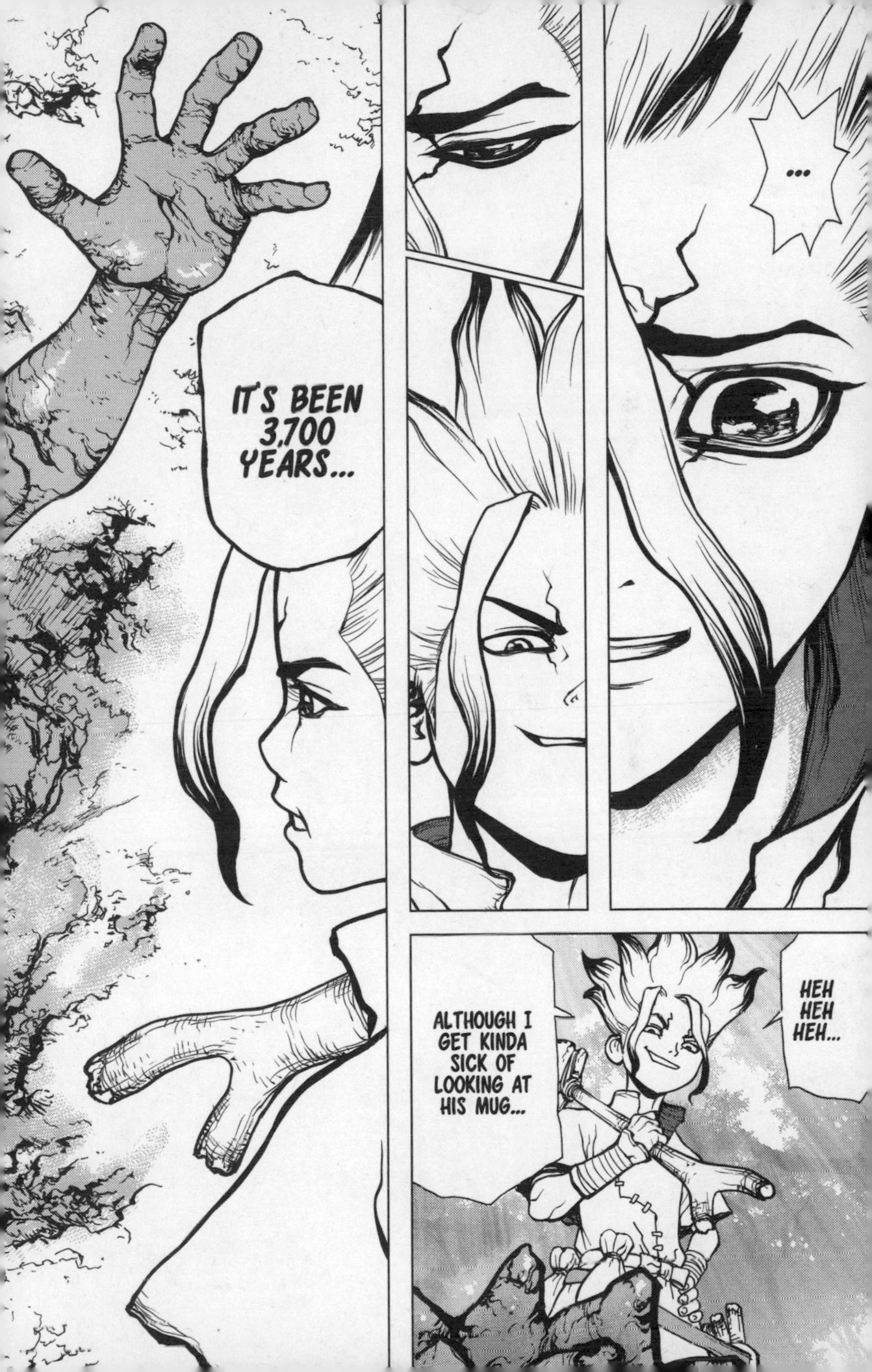
...
HEH HEH HEH...
ALTHOUGH I GET KINDA SICK OF LOOKING AT HIS MUG...
IT'S BEEN 3,700 YEARS...

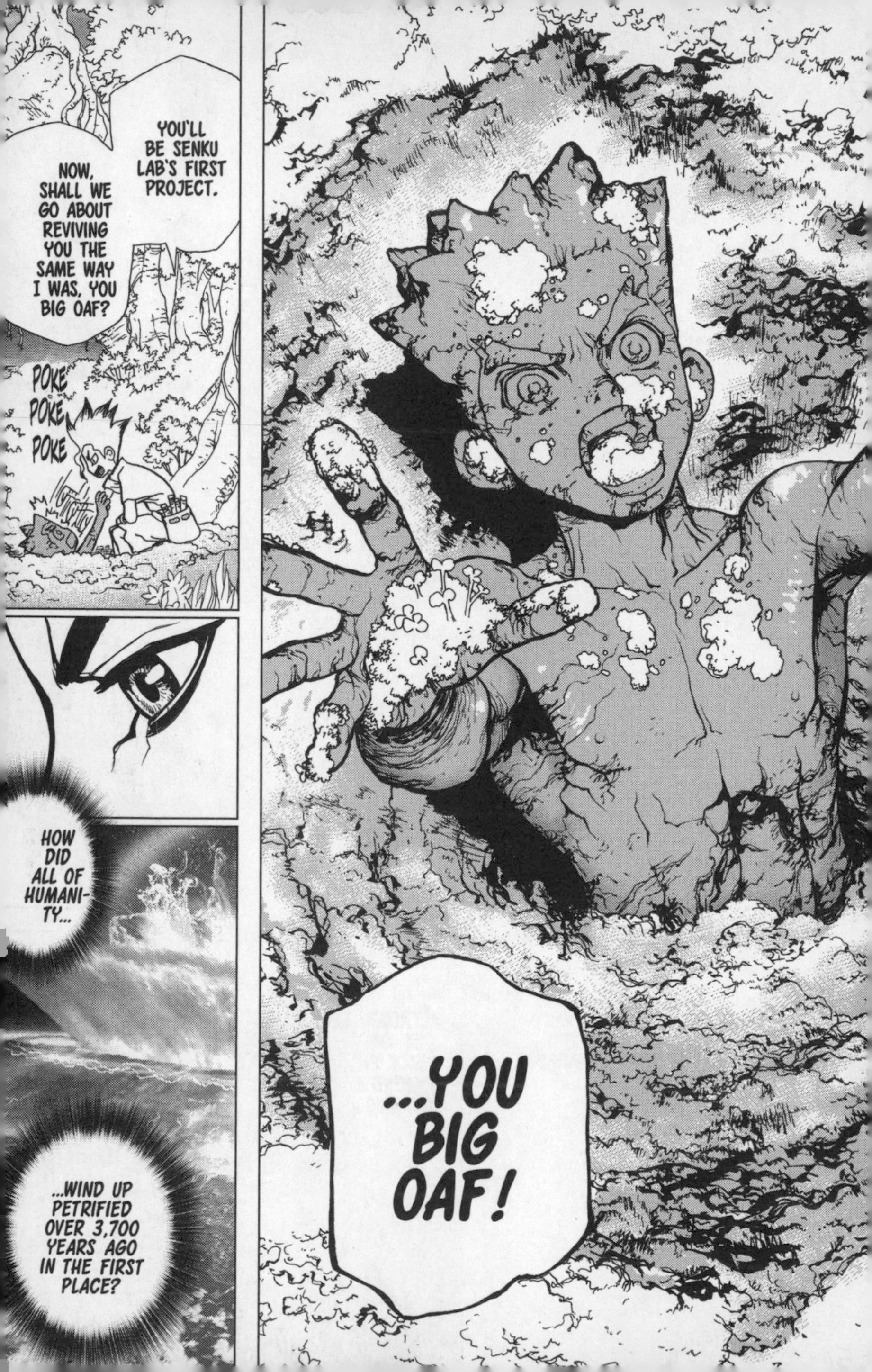
...YOU BIG OAF!
NOW, SHALL WE GO ABOUT REVIVING YOU THE SAME WAY I WAS, YOU BIG OAF?
YOU'LL BE SENKU LAB'S FIRST PROJECT.
POKE POKE POKE
HOW DID ALL OF HUMANI-TY...
...WIND UP PETRIFIED OVER 3,700 YEARS AGO IN THE FIRST PLACE?

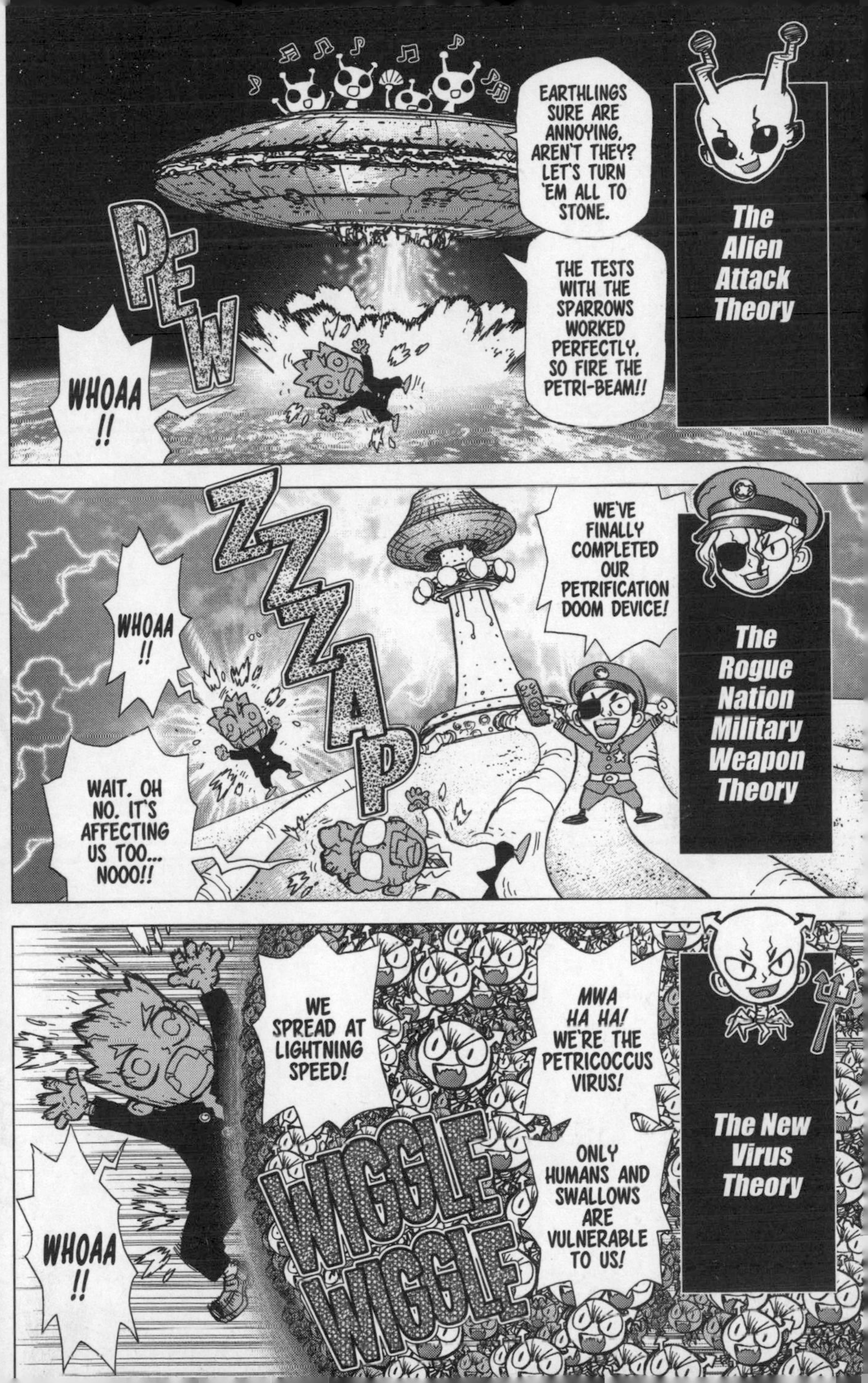
The Alien Attack Theory
EARTHLINGS SURE ARE ANNOYING, AREN'T THEY? LET'S TURN 'EM ALL TO STONE.
THE TESTS WITH THE SPARROWS WORKED PERFECTLY, SO FIRE THE PETRI-BEAM!!
PEW
WHOAA!!
The Rogue Nation Military Weapon Theory
WE'VE FINALLY COMPLETED OUR PETRIFICATION DOOM DEVICE!
ZZZAP
WHOAA!!
WAIT. OH NO. IT'S AFFECTING US TOO... NOOO!!
The New Virus Theory
MWA HA HA! WE'RE THE PETRICOCCUS VIRUS!
WE SPREAD AT LIGHTNING SPEED!
ONLY HUMANS AND SWALLOWS ARE VULNERABLE TO US!
WIGGLE WIGGLE
WHOAA!!

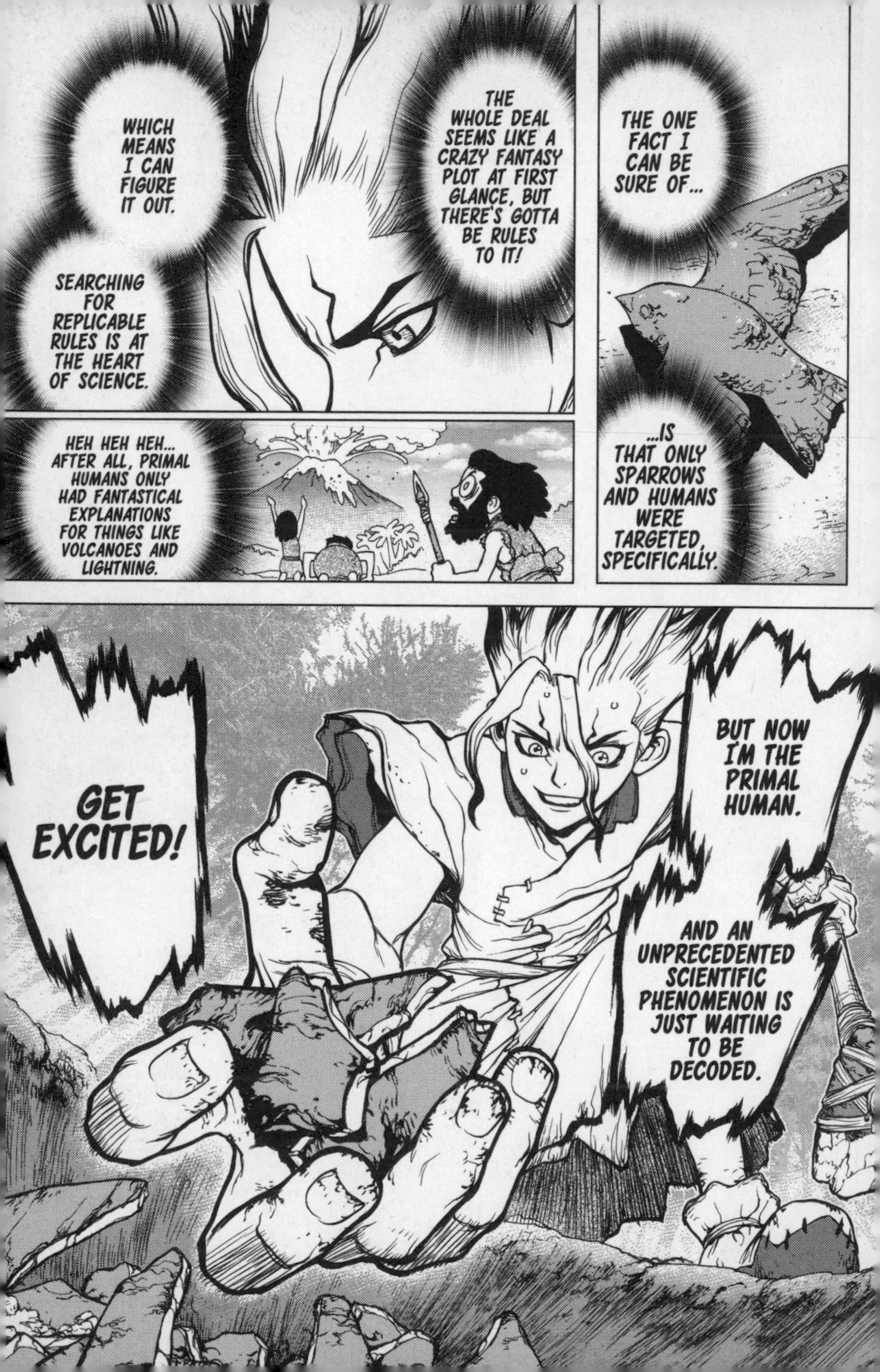
THE ONE FACT I CAN BE SURE OF...
...IS THAT ONLY SPARROWS AND HUMANS WERE TARGETED, SPECIFICALLY.
THE WHOLE DEAL SEEMS LIKE A CRAZY FANTASY PLOT AT FIRST GLANCE, BUT THERE'S GOTTA BE RULES TO IT!
WHICH MEANS I CAN FIGURE IT OUT.
SEARCHING FOR REPLICABLE RULES IS AT THE HEART OF SCIENCE.
HEH HEH HEH... AFTER ALL, PRIMAL HUMANS ONLY HAD FANTASTICAL EXPLANATIONS FOR THINGS LIKE VOLCANOES AND LIGHTNING.
BUT NOW I'M THE PRIMAL HUMAN.
AND AN UNPRECEDENTED SCIENTIFIC PHENOMENON IS JUST WAITING TO BE DECODED.
GET EXCITED!

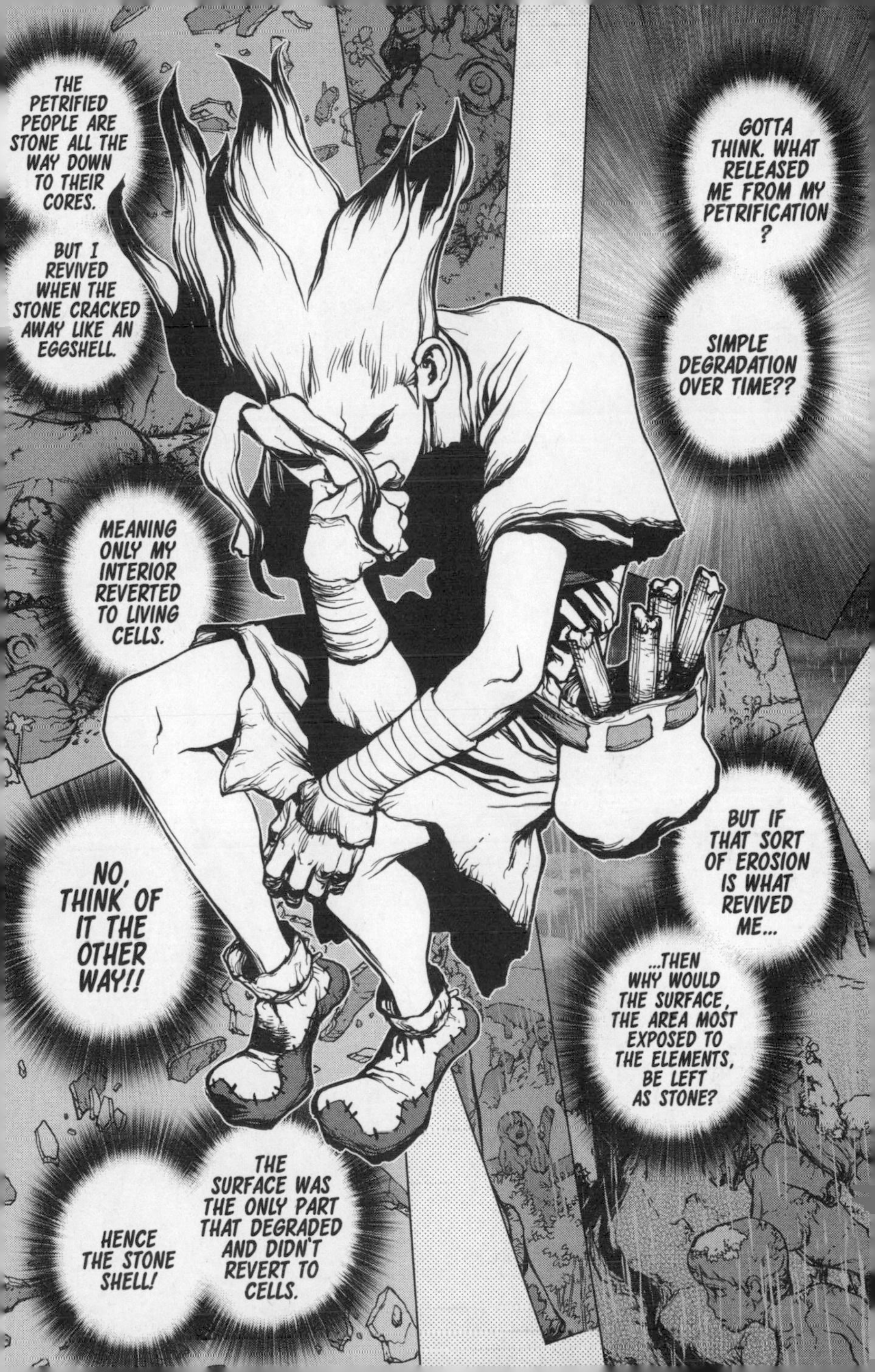
GOTTA THINK. WHAT RELEASED ME FROM MY PETRIFICATION?
SIMPLE DEGRADATION OVER TIME??
THE PETRIFIED PEOPLE ARE STONE ALL THE WAY DOWN TO THEIR CORES.
BUT I REVIVED WHEN THE STONE CRACKED AWAY LIKE AN EGGSHELL.
MEANING ONLY MY INTERIOR REVERTED TO LIVING CELLS.
BUT IF THAT SORT OF EROSION IS WHAT REVIVED ME...
...THEN WHY WOULD THE SURFACE, THE AREA MOST EXPOSED TO THE ELEMENTS, BE LEFT AS STONE?
NO, THINK OF IT THE OTHER WAY!!
THE SURFACE WAS THE ONLY PART THAT DEGRADED AND DIDN'T REVERT TO CELLS.
HENCE THE STONE SHELL!

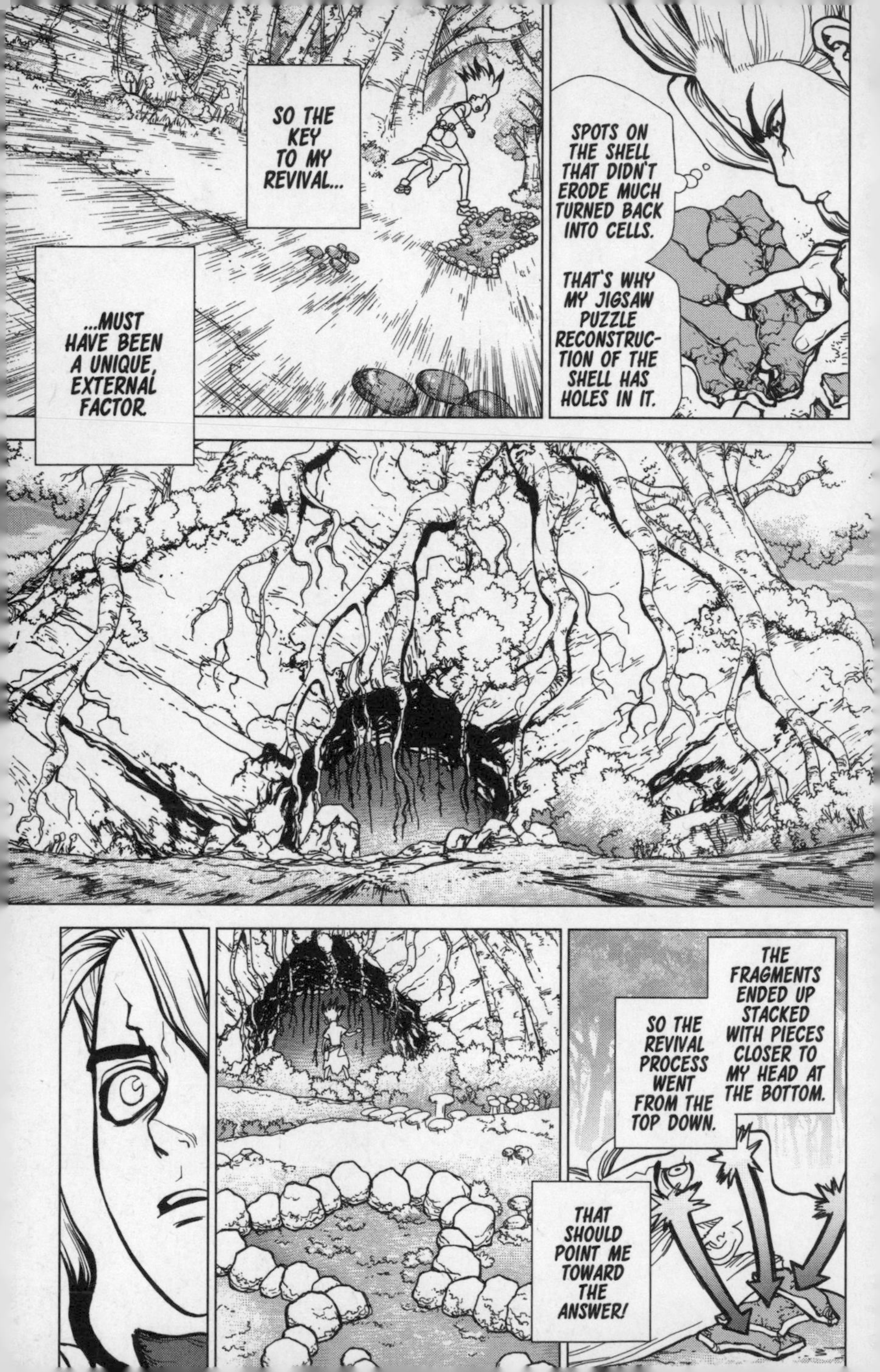
SPOTS ON THE SHELL THAT DIDN'T ERODE MUCH TURNED BACK INTO CELLS.
THAT'S WHY MY JIGSAW PUZZLE RECONSTRUCTION OF THE SHELL HAS HOLES IN IT.
SO THE KEY TO MY REVIVAL...
...MUST HAVE BEEN A UNIQUE, EXTERNAL FACTOR.
THE FRAGMENTS ENDED UP STACKED WITH PIECES CLOSER TO MY HEAD AT THE BOTTOM.
SO THE REVIVAL PROCESS WENT FROM THE TOP DOWN.
THAT SHOULD POINT ME TOWARD THE ANSWER!

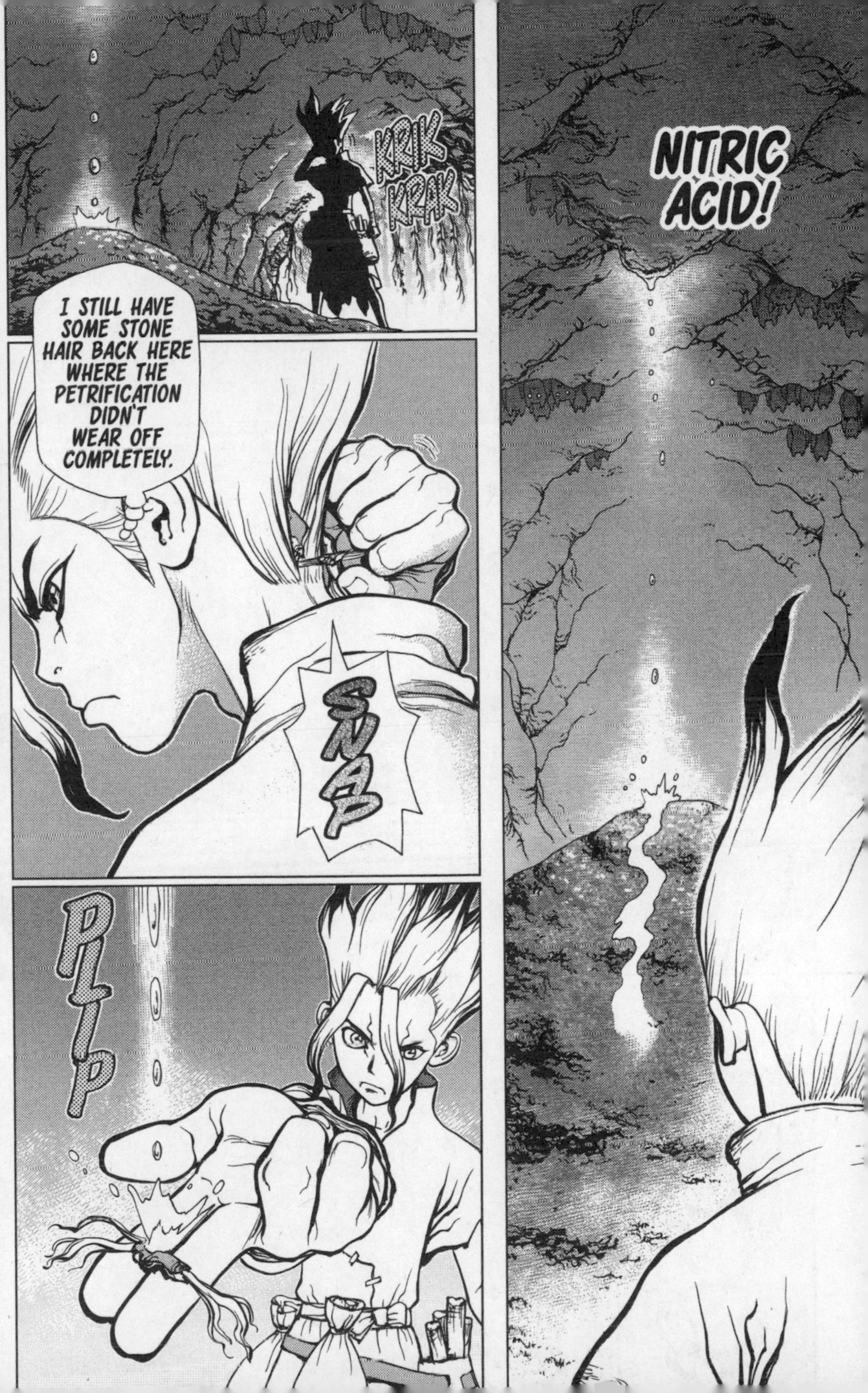
NITRIC ACID!
KRIK KRAK
I STILL HAVE SOME STONE HAIR BACK HERE WHERE THE PETRIFICATION DIDN'T WEAR OFF COMPLETELY.
SNAP
PLIP

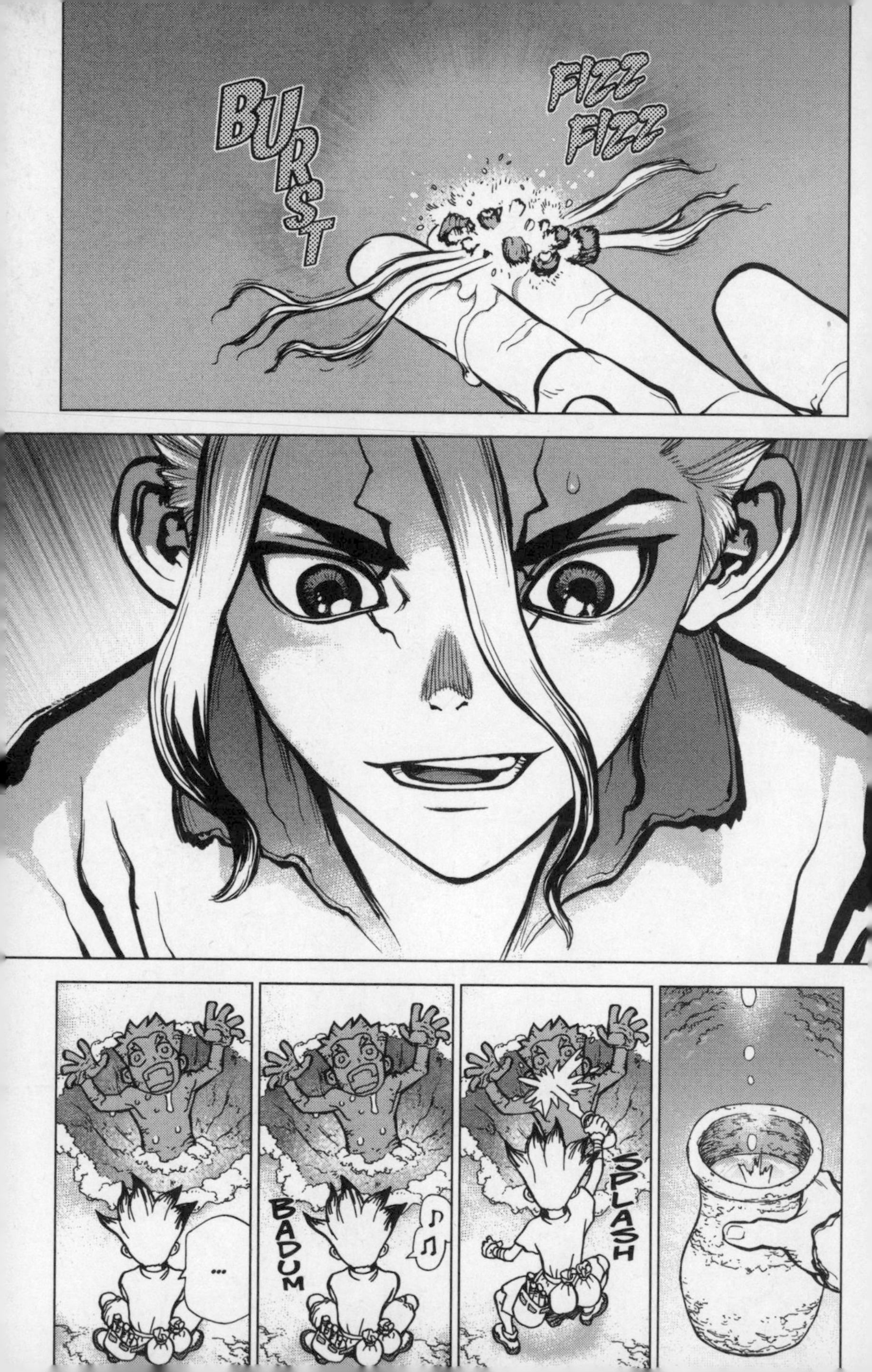
FIZZ FIZZ
BURST
SPLASH
♪♫
BADUM
...

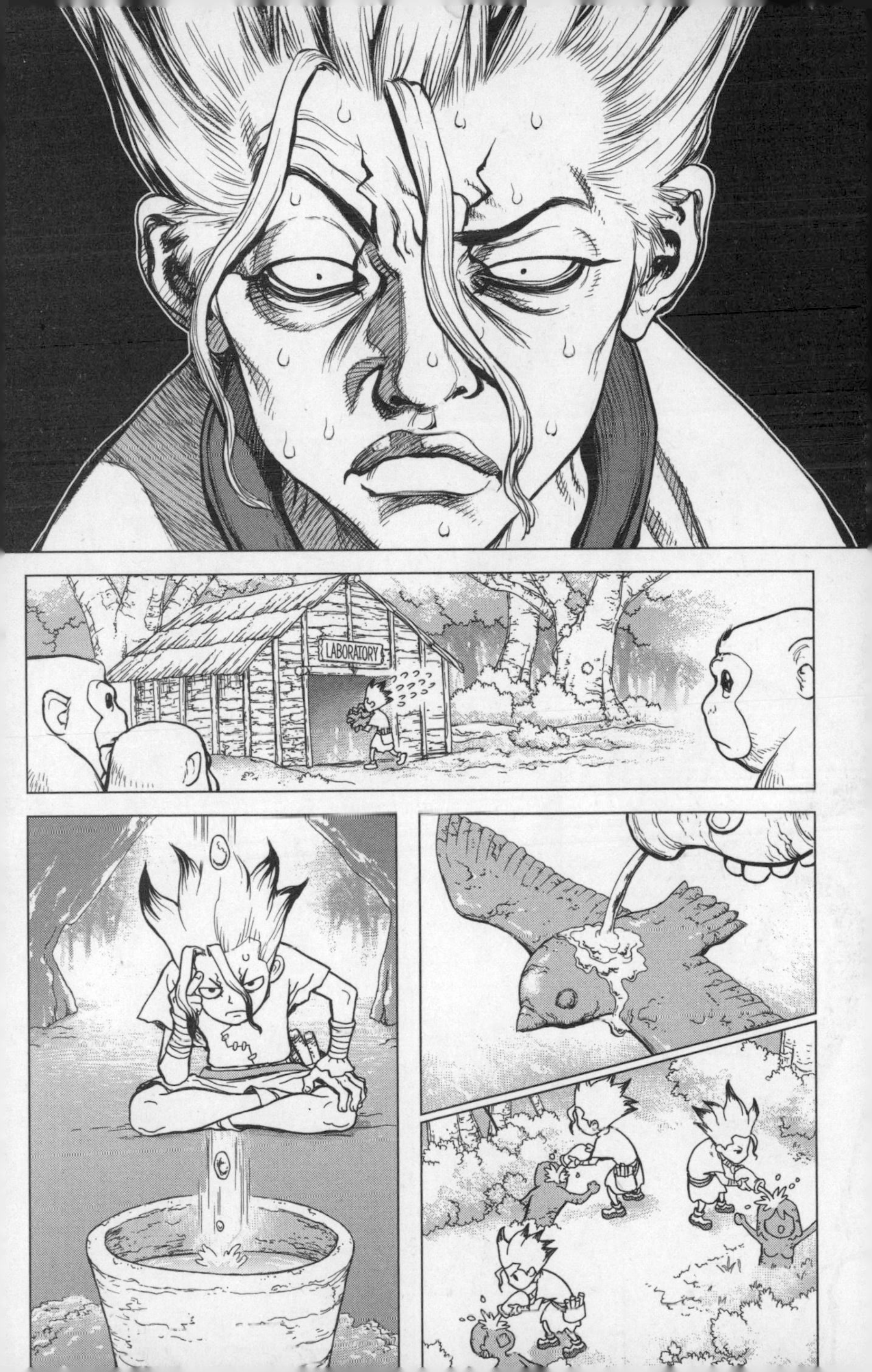
LABORATORY

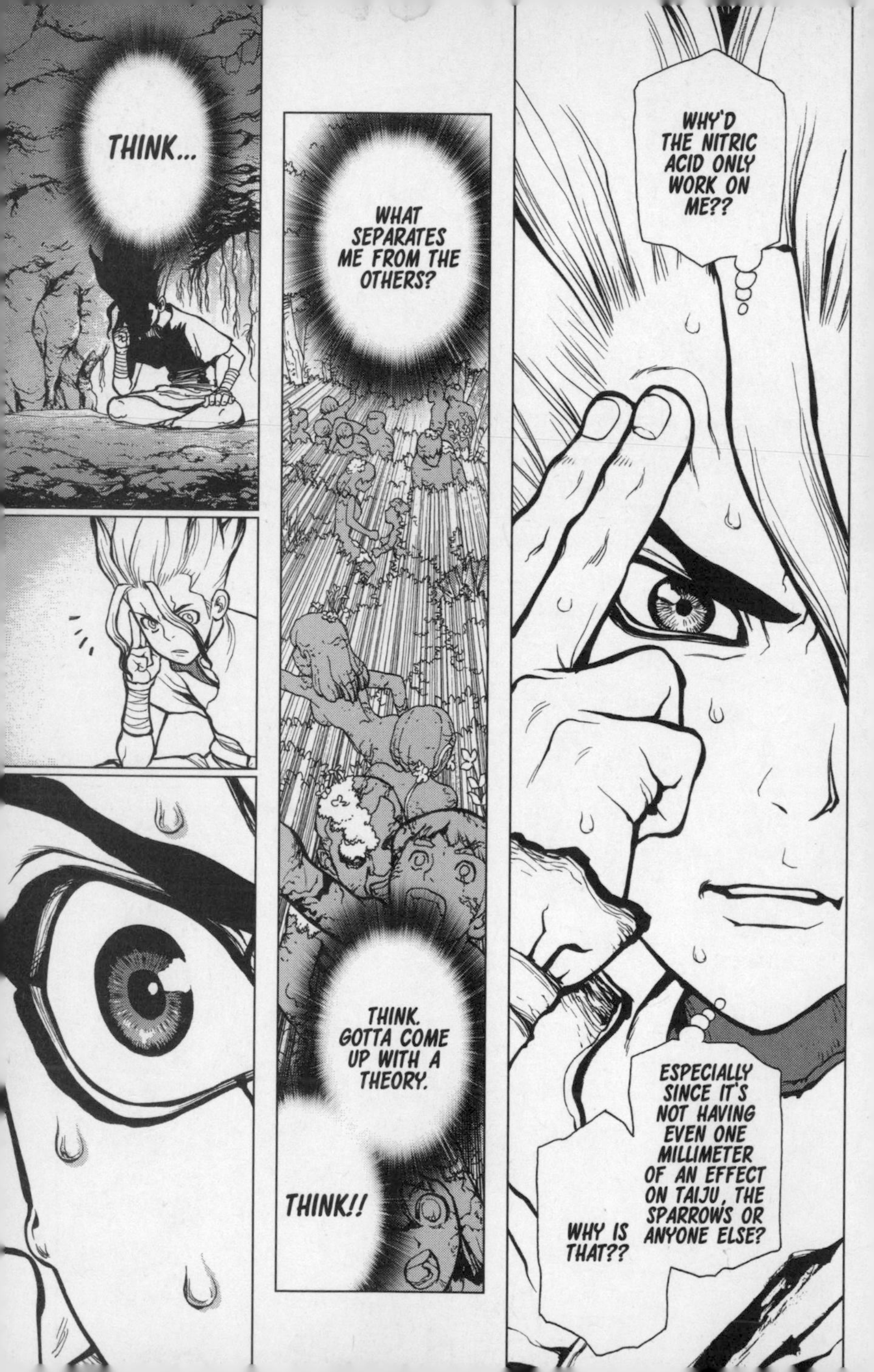
WHY'D THE NITRIC ACID ONLY WORK ON ME??
ESPECIALLY SINCE IT'S NOT HAVING EVEN ONE MILLIMETER OF AN EFFECT ON TAIJU, THE SPARROWS OR ANYONE ELSE?
WHY IS THAT??
WHAT SEPARATES ME FROM THE OTHERS?
THINK. GOTTA COME UP WITH A THEORY.
THINK!!
THINK...

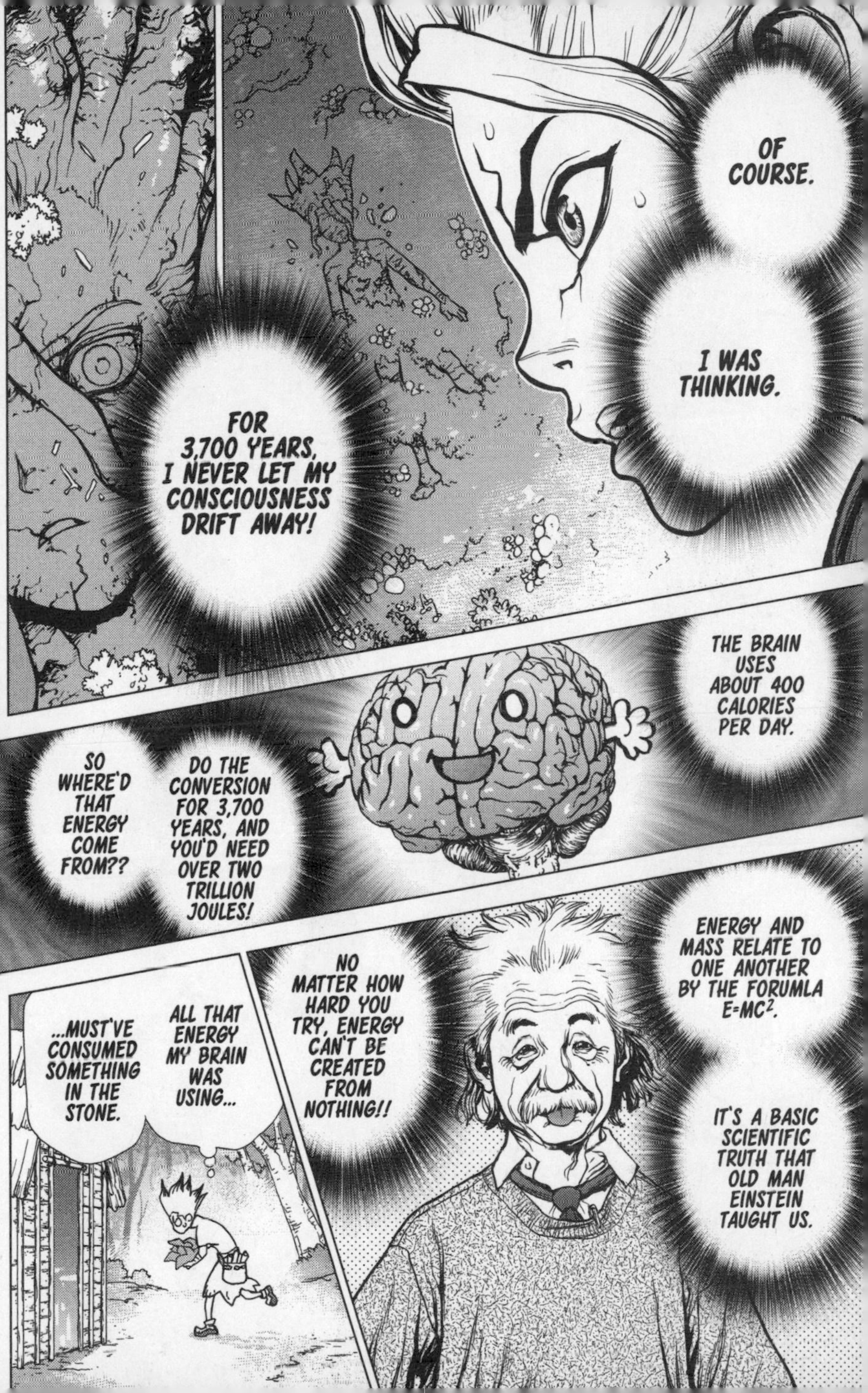
OF COURSE.
I WAS THINKING.
FOR 3,700 YEARS, I NEVER LET MY CONSCIOUSNESS DRIFT AWAY!
THE BRAIN USES ABOUT 400 CALORIES PER DAY.
DO THE CONVERSION FOR 3,700 YEARS, AND YOU'D NEED OVER TWO TRILLION JOULES!
SO WHERE'D THAT ENERGY COME FROM??
ENERGY AND MASS RELATE TO ONE ANOTHER BY THE FORUMLA $E=MC^2$.
IT'S A BASIC SCIENTIFIC TRUTH THAT OLD MAN EINSTEIN TAUGHT US.
NO MATTER HOW HARD YOU TRY, ENERGY CAN'T BE CREATED FROM NOTHING!!
ALL THAT ENERGY MY BRAIN WAS USING...
...MUST'VE CONSUMED SOMETHING IN THE STONE.

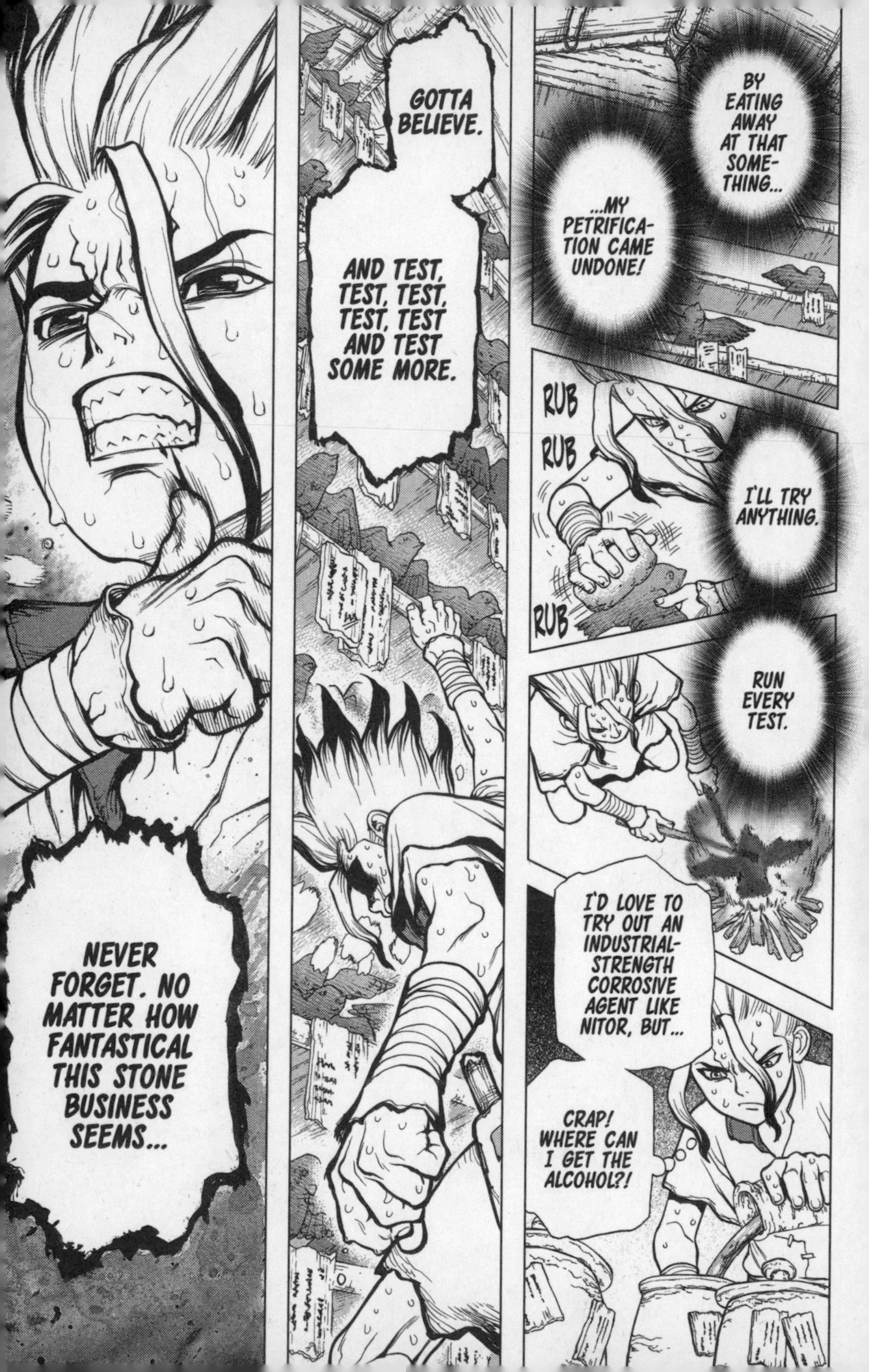
BY EATING AWAY AT THAT SOME-THING...
...MY PETRIFICA-TION CAME UNDONE!
I'LL TRY ANYTHING.
RUB
RUB
RUB
RUN EVERY TEST.
I'D LOVE TO TRY OUT AN INDUSTRIAL-STRENGTH CORROSIVE AGENT LIKE NITOR, BUT...
CRAP! WHERE CAN I GET THE ALCOHOL?!
GOTTA BELIEVE.
AND TEST, TEST, TEST, TEST, TEST AND TEST SOME MORE.
NEVER FORGET. NO MATTER HOW FANTASTICAL THIS STONE BUSINESS SEEMS...

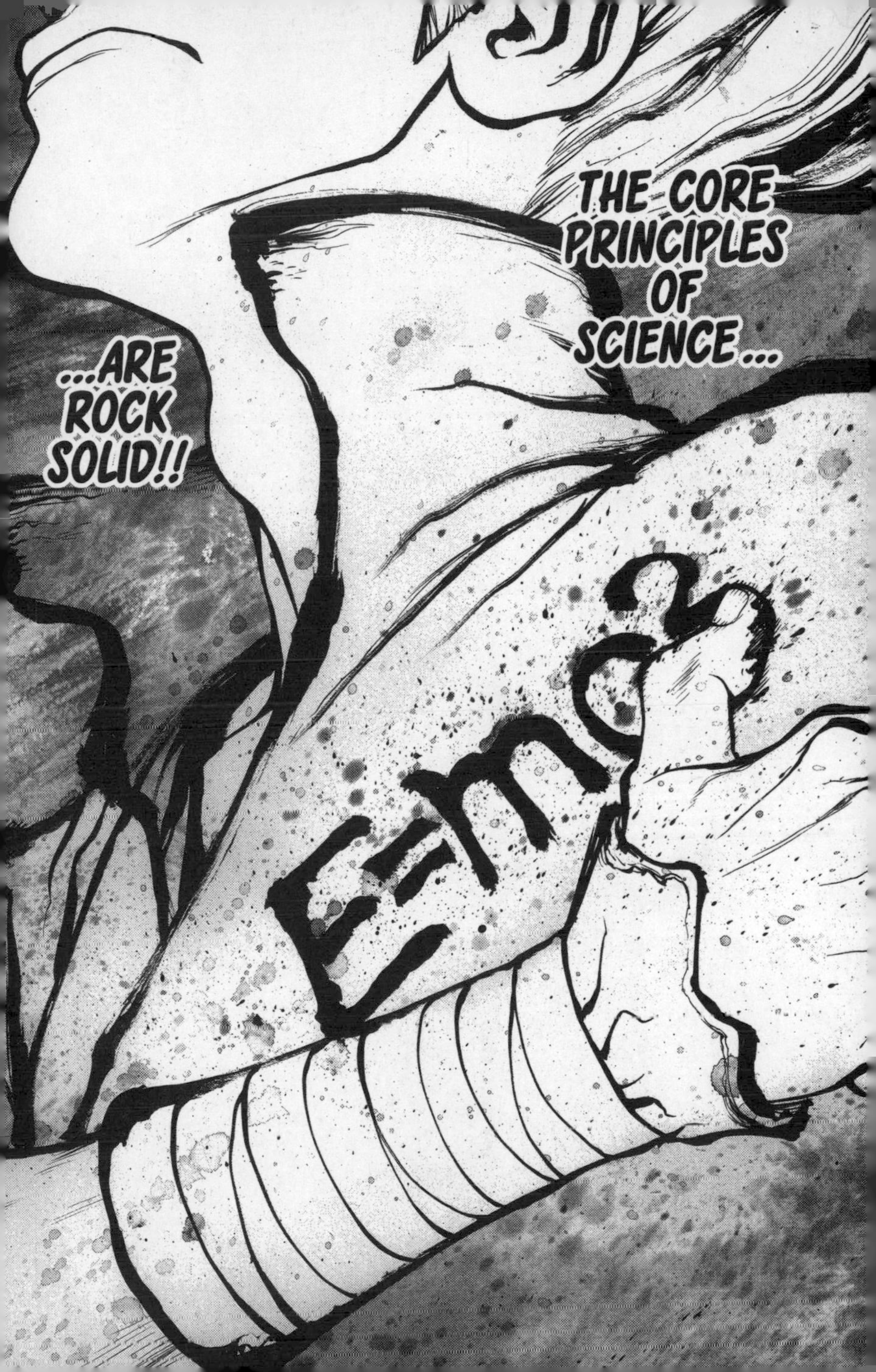
THE CORE PRINCIPLES OF SCIENCE...
...ARE ROCK SOLID!!
E=mc²

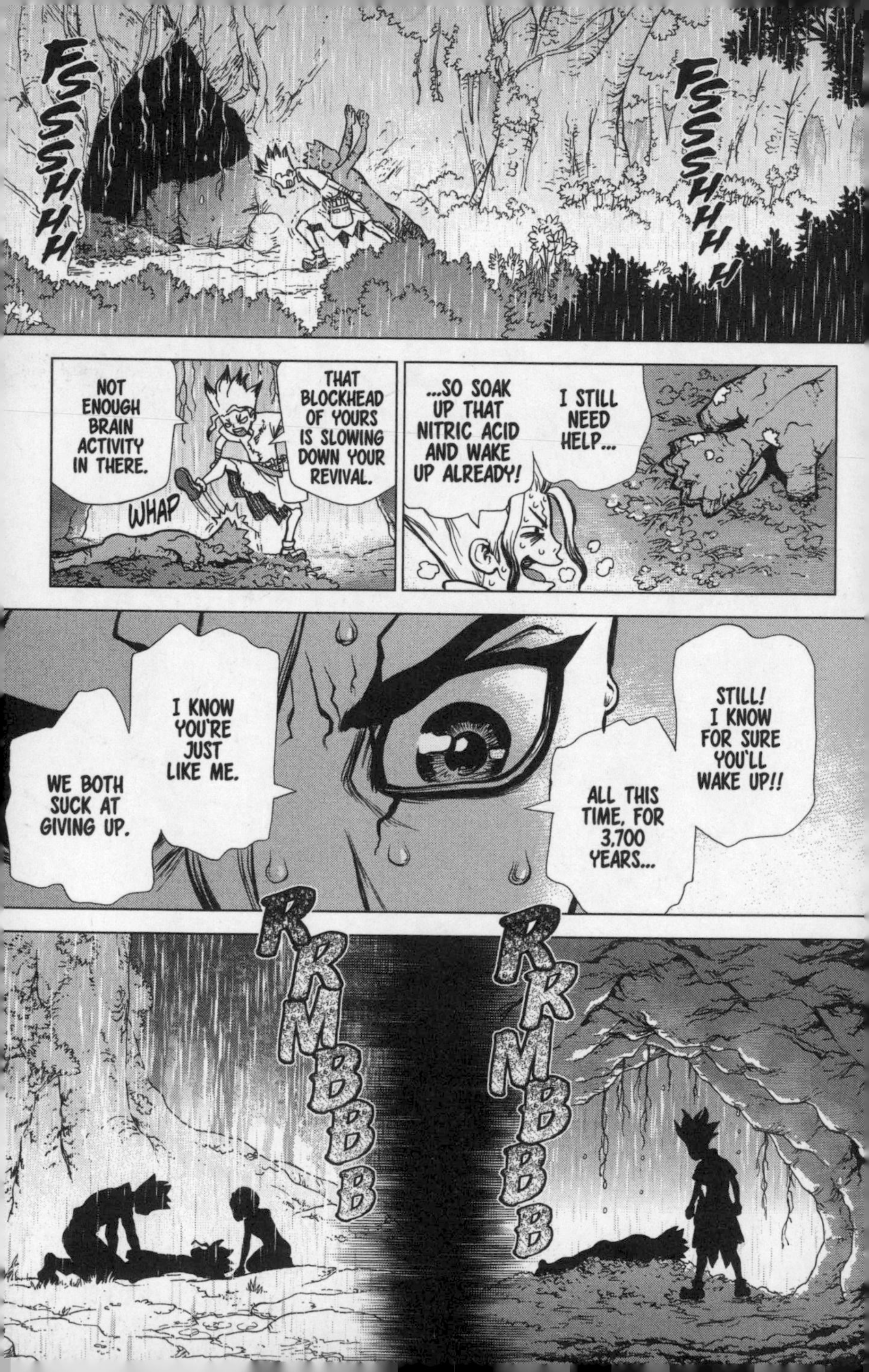
FSSSHHH
FSSSHHH
I STILL NEED HELP...
...SO SOAK UP THAT NITRIC ACID AND WAKE UP ALREADY!
THAT BLOCKHEAD OF YOURS IS SLOWING DOWN YOUR REVIVAL.
NOT ENOUGH BRAIN ACTIVITY IN THERE.
WHAP
STILL! I KNOW FOR SURE YOU'LL WAKE UP!!
ALL THIS TIME, FOR 3,700 YEARS...
I KNOW YOU'RE JUST LIKE ME.
WE BOTH SUCK AT GIVING UP.
RRMBBB
RRMBBB

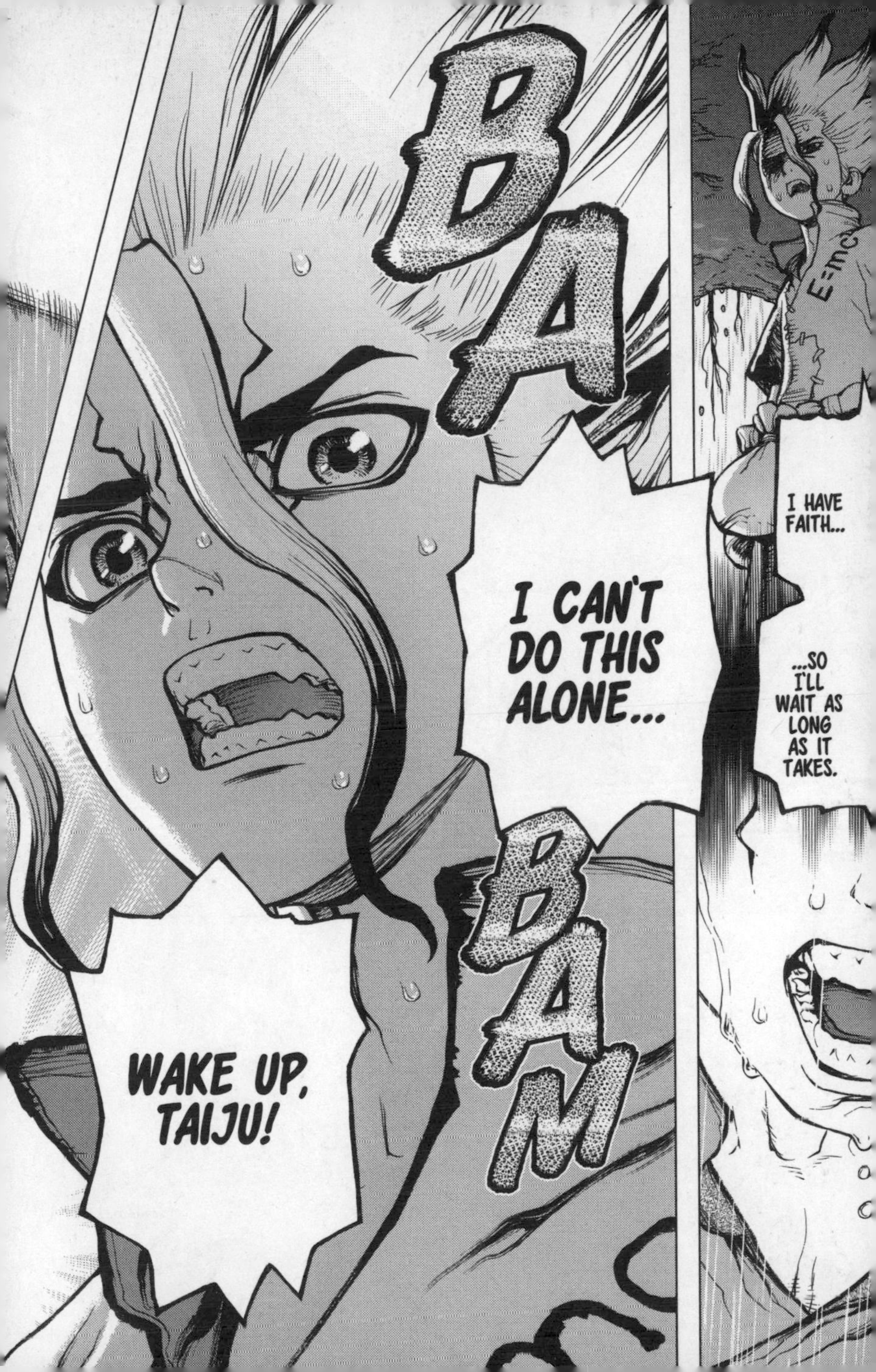
I HAVE FAITH...
...SO I'LL WAIT AS LONG AS IT TAKES.
BA
I CAN'T DO THIS ALONE...
BAM
WAKE UP, TAIJU!

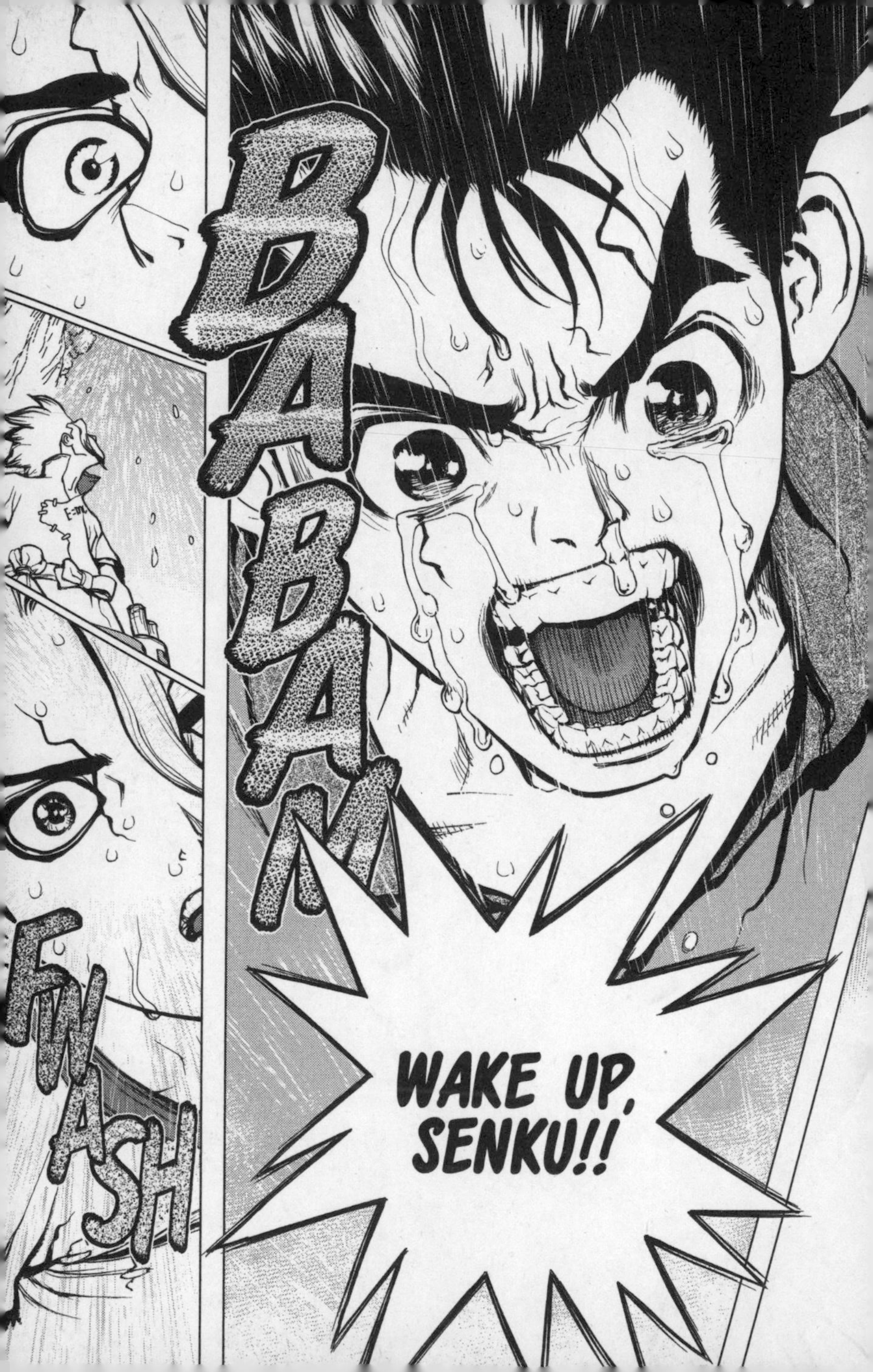
BABAM
WAKE UP, SENKU!!
FWASH

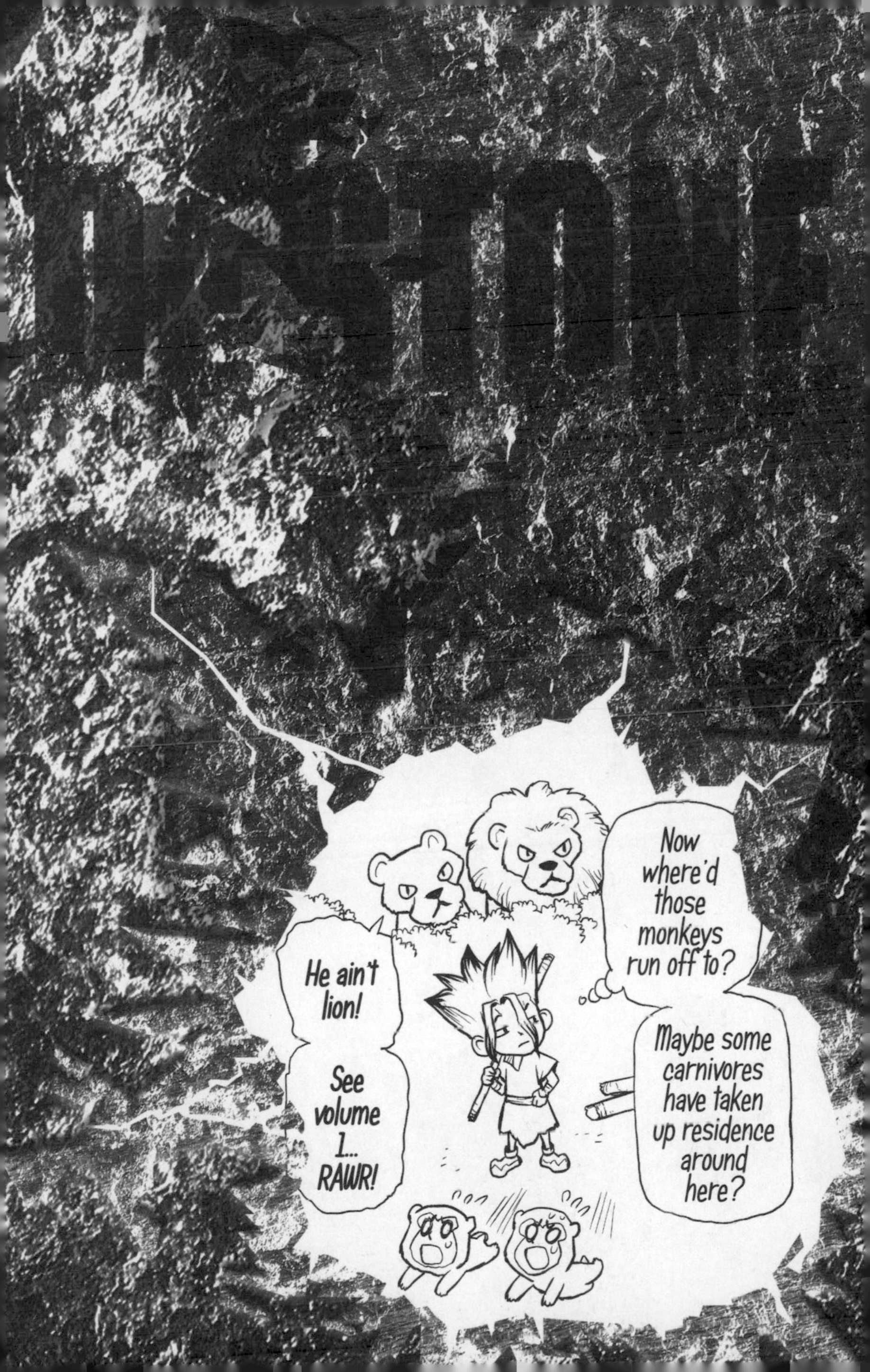
Now where'd those monkeys run off to?
Maybe some carnivores have taken up residence around here?
He ain't lion!
See volume 1... RAWR!

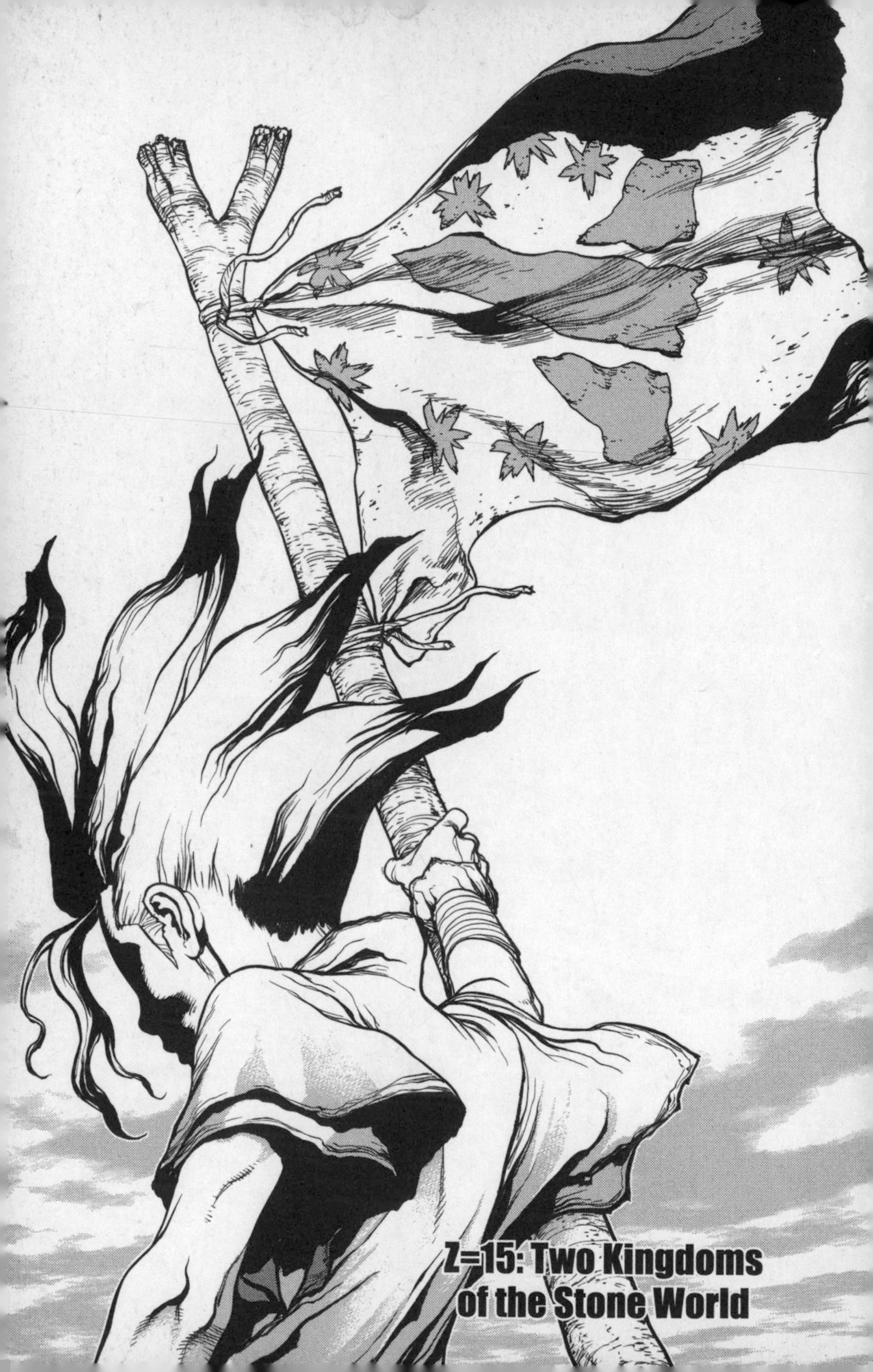
Z=15: Two Kingdoms
of the Stone World

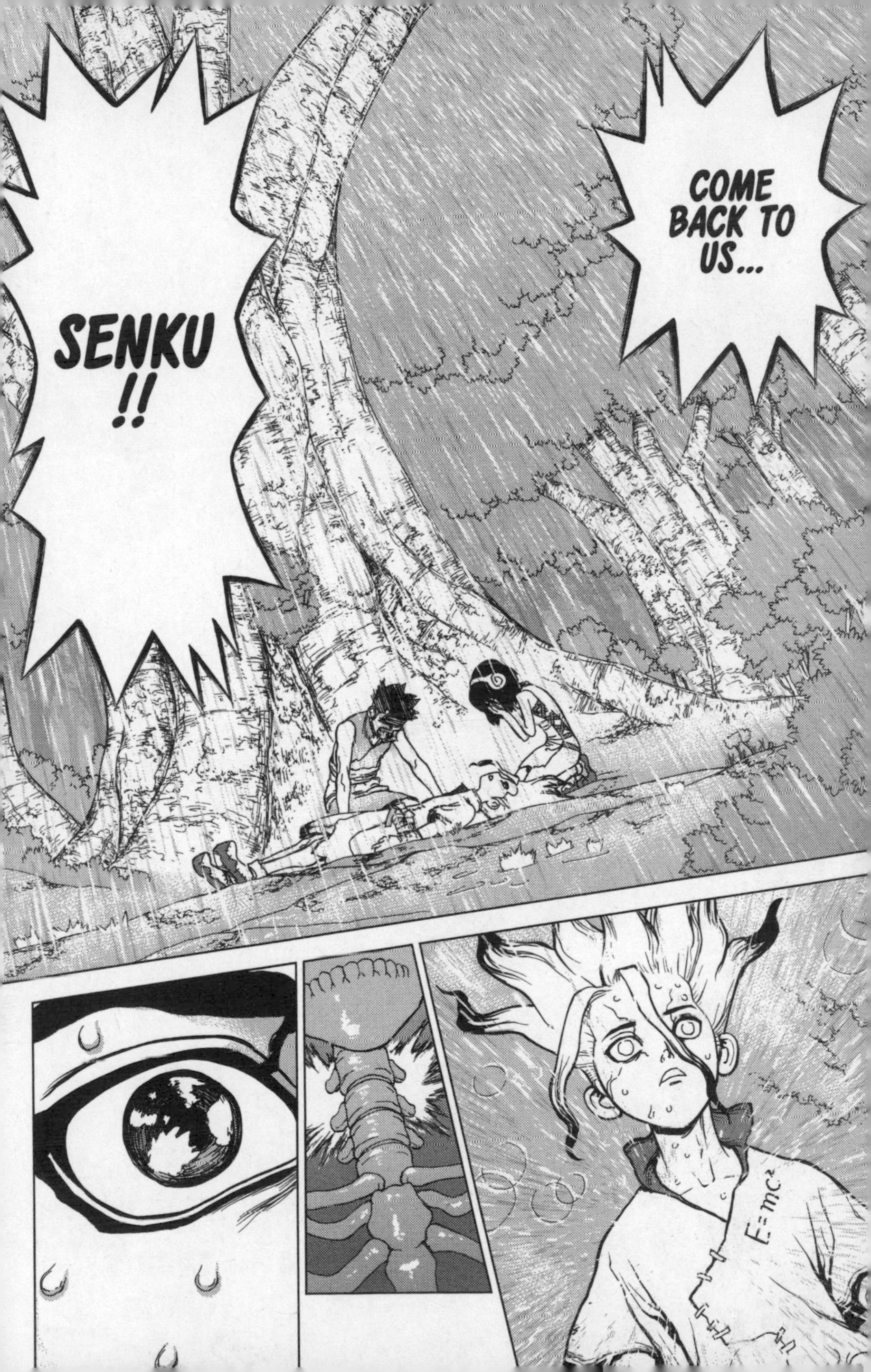
COME BACK TO US...
SENKU!!
E=mc²

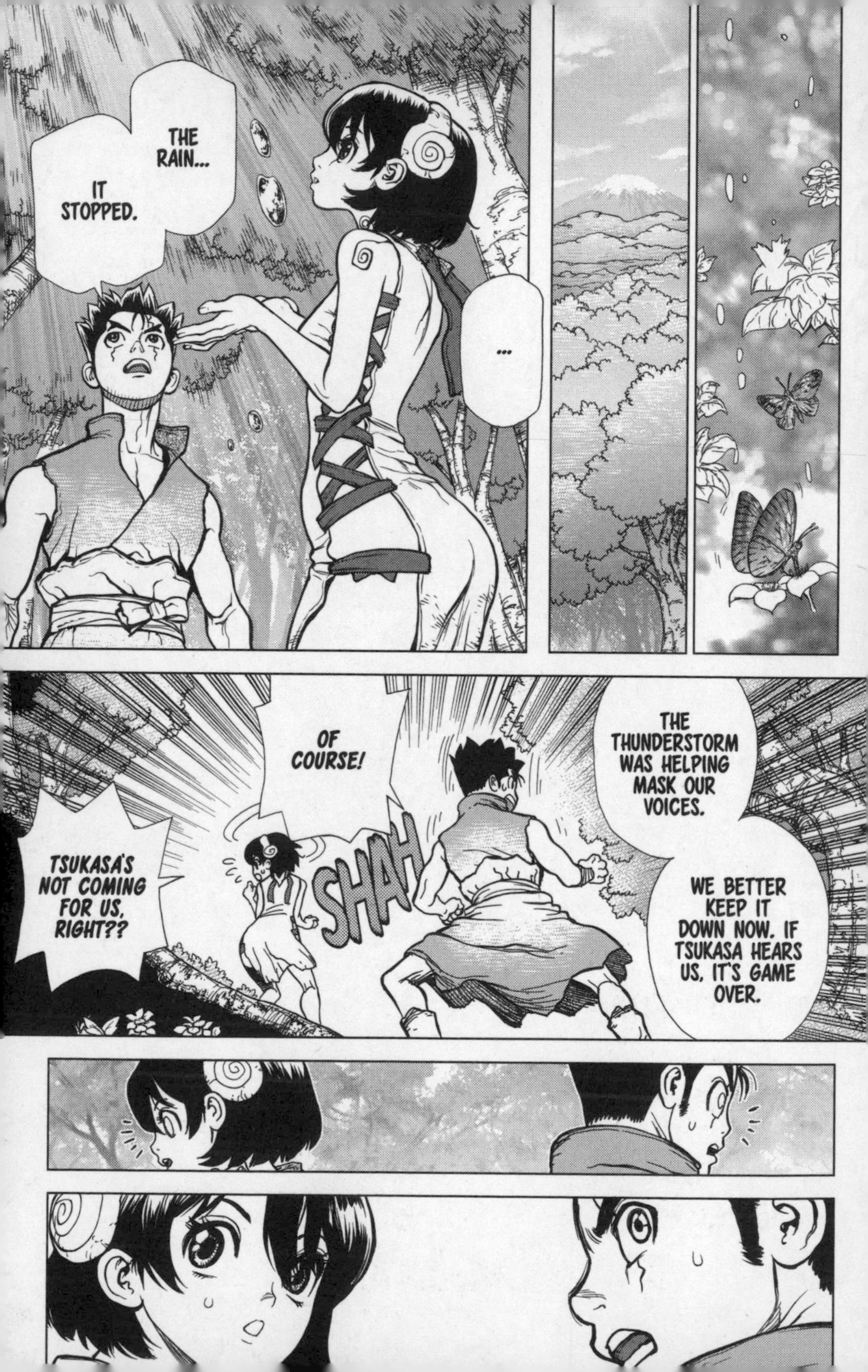
THE RAIN... IT STOPPED.
...
THE THUNDERSTORM WAS HELPING MASK OUR VOICES.
WE BETTER KEEP IT DOWN NOW. IF TSUKASA HEARS US, IT'S GAME OVER.
OF COURSE!
SHAH
TSUKASA'S NOT COMING FOR US, RIGHT??

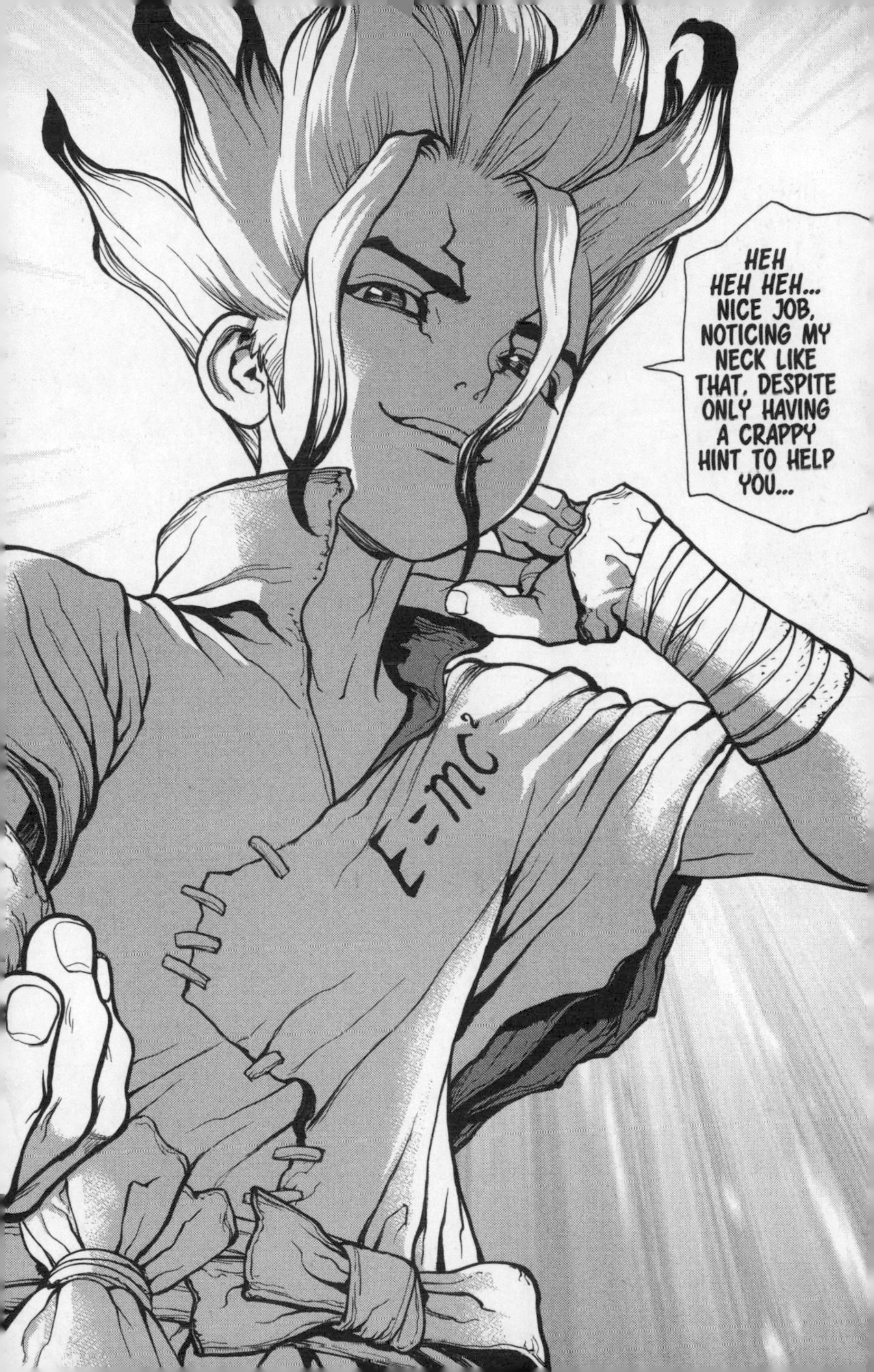
HEH HEH HEH... NICE JOB, NOTICING MY NECK LIKE THAT, DESPITE ONLY HAVING A CRAPPY HINT TO HELP YOU...

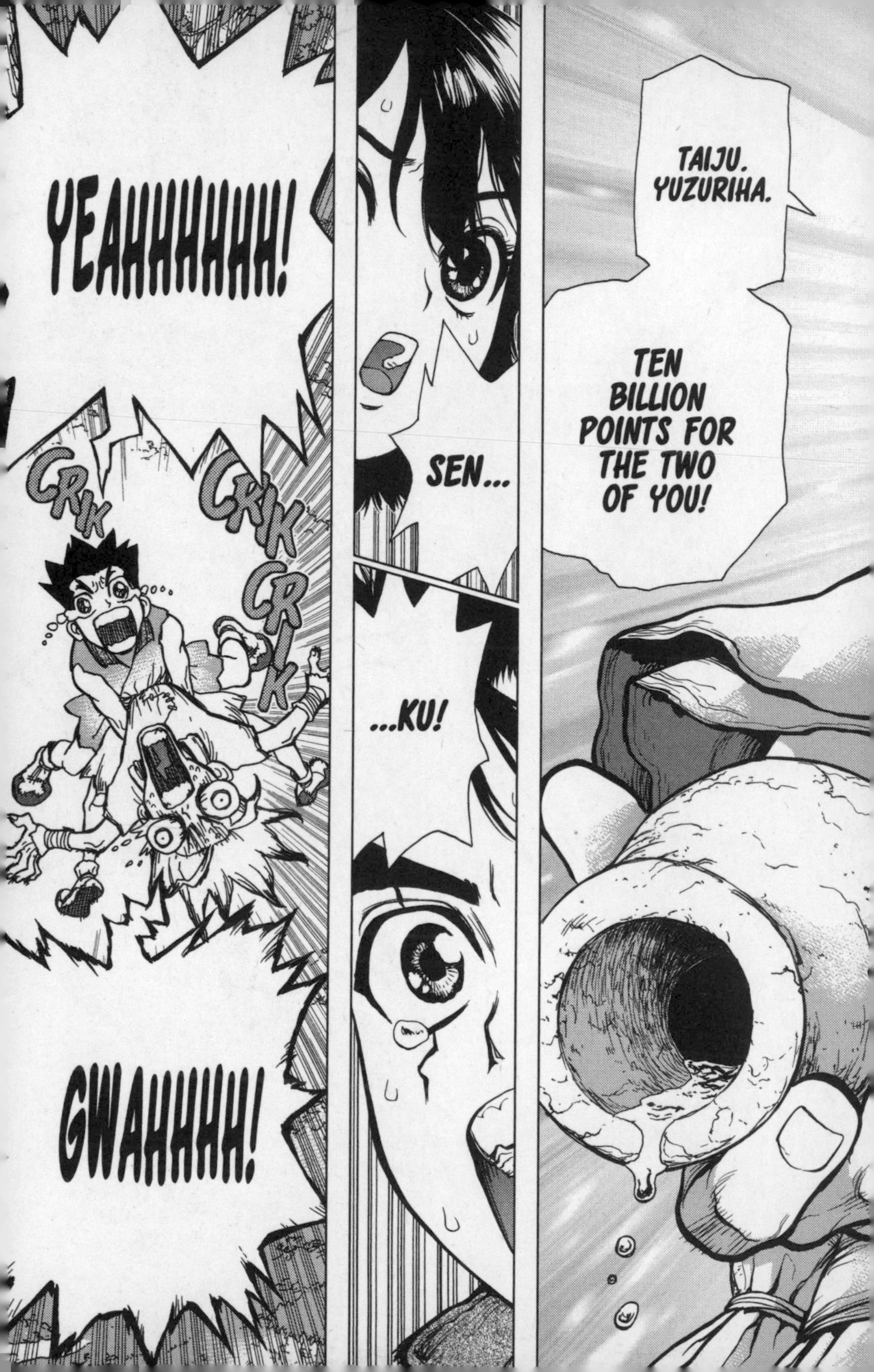
TAIJU. YUZURIHA.
TEN BILLION POINTS FOR THE TWO OF YOU!
SEN...
...KU!
YEAHHHHHH!
CRIK
CRIK
CRIK
GWAHHHH!

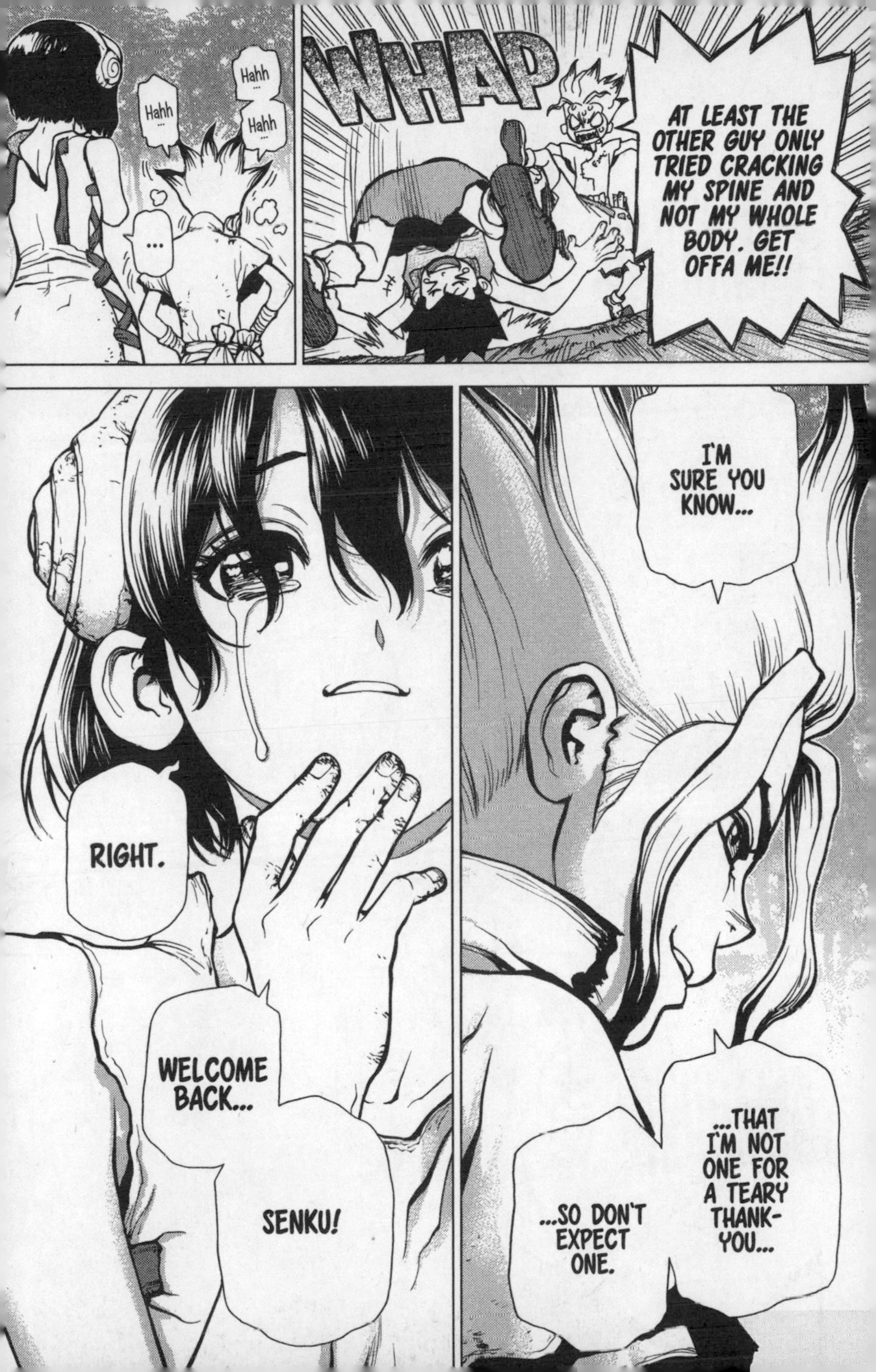
WHAP
AT LEAST THE OTHER GUY ONLY TRIED CRACKING MY SPINE AND NOT MY WHOLE BODY. GET OFFA ME!!
Hahh...
Hahh...
Hahh...
...
I'M SURE YOU KNOW...
...THAT I'M NOT ONE FOR A TEARY THANK-YOU...
...SO DON'T EXPECT ONE.
RIGHT.
WELCOME BACK...
SENKU!

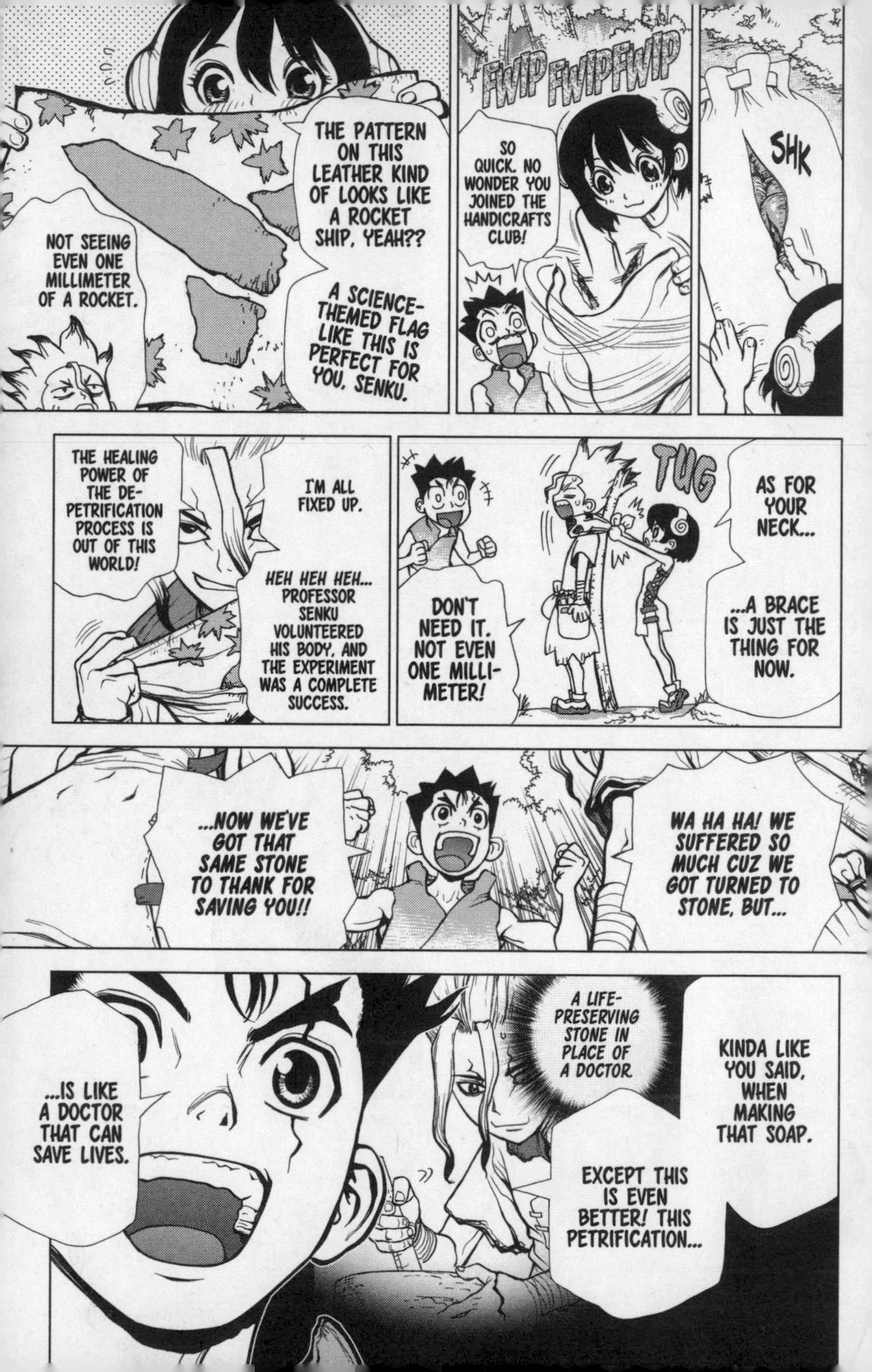
SHK
FWIP FWIP FWIP
SO QUICK. NO WONDER YOU JOINED THE HANDICRAFTS CLUB!
THE PATTERN ON THIS LEATHER KIND OF LOOKS LIKE A ROCKET SHIP, YEAH??
NOT SEEING EVEN ONE MILLIMETER OF A ROCKET.
A SCIENCE-THEMED FLAG LIKE THIS IS PERFECT FOR YOU, SENKU.
TUG
AS FOR YOUR NECK...
...A BRACE IS JUST THE THING FOR NOW.
DON'T NEED IT. NOT EVEN ONE MILLI-METER!
I'M ALL FIXED UP.
THE HEALING POWER OF THE DE-PETRIFICATION PROCESS IS OUT OF THIS WORLD!
HEH HEH HEH... PROFESSOR SENKU VOLUNTEERED HIS BODY, AND THE EXPERIMENT WAS A COMPLETE SUCCESS.
WA HA HA! WE SUFFERED SO MUCH CUZ WE GOT TURNED TO STONE, BUT...
...NOW WE'VE GOT THAT SAME STONE TO THANK FOR SAVING YOU!!
KINDA LIKE YOU SAID, WHEN MAKING THAT SOAP.
EXCEPT THIS IS EVEN BETTER! THIS PETRIFICATION...
...IS LIKE A DOCTOR THAT CAN SAVE LIVES.
A LIFE-PRESERVING STONE IN PLACE OF A DOCTOR.

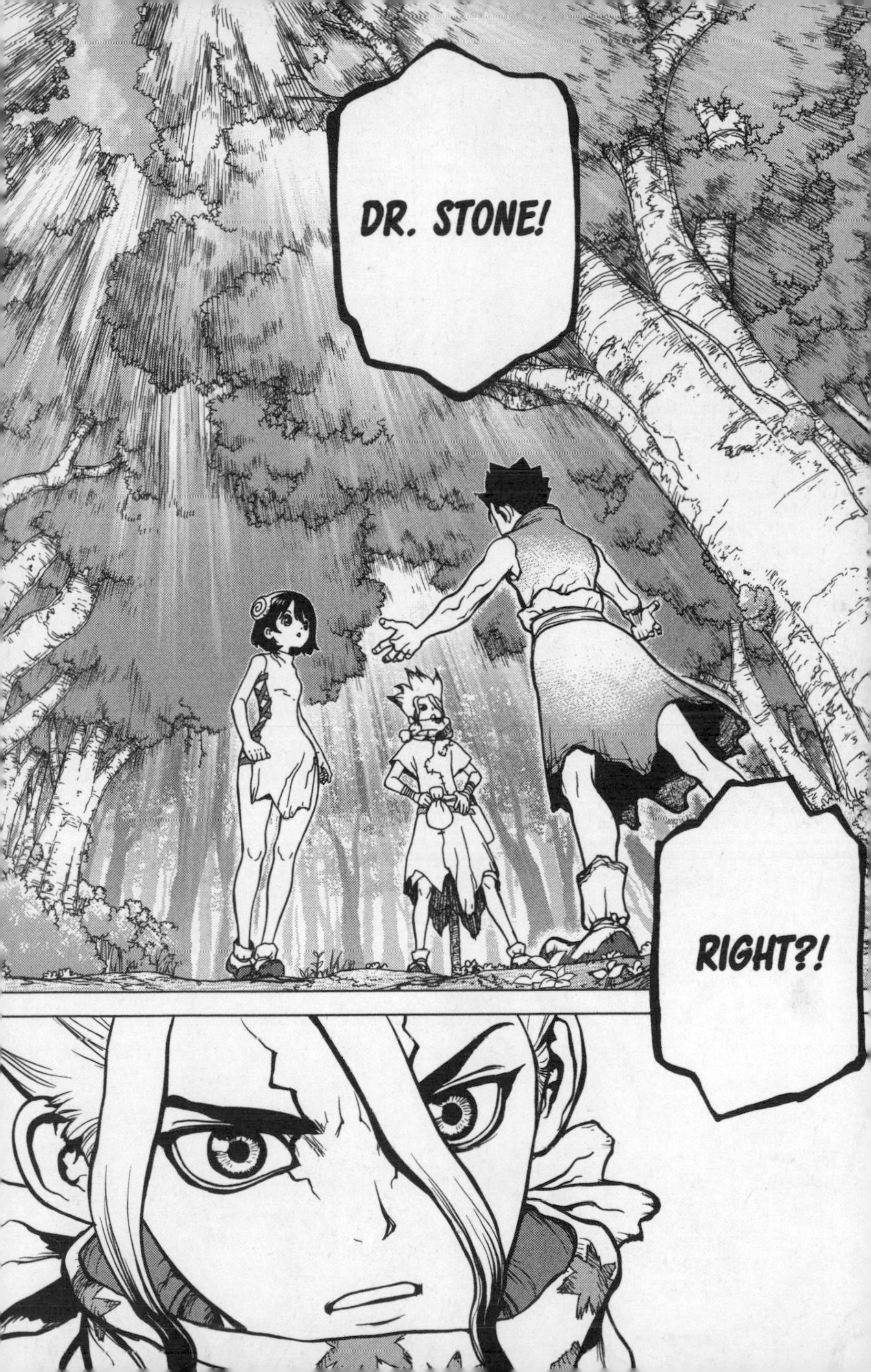
DR. STONE!
RIGHT?!

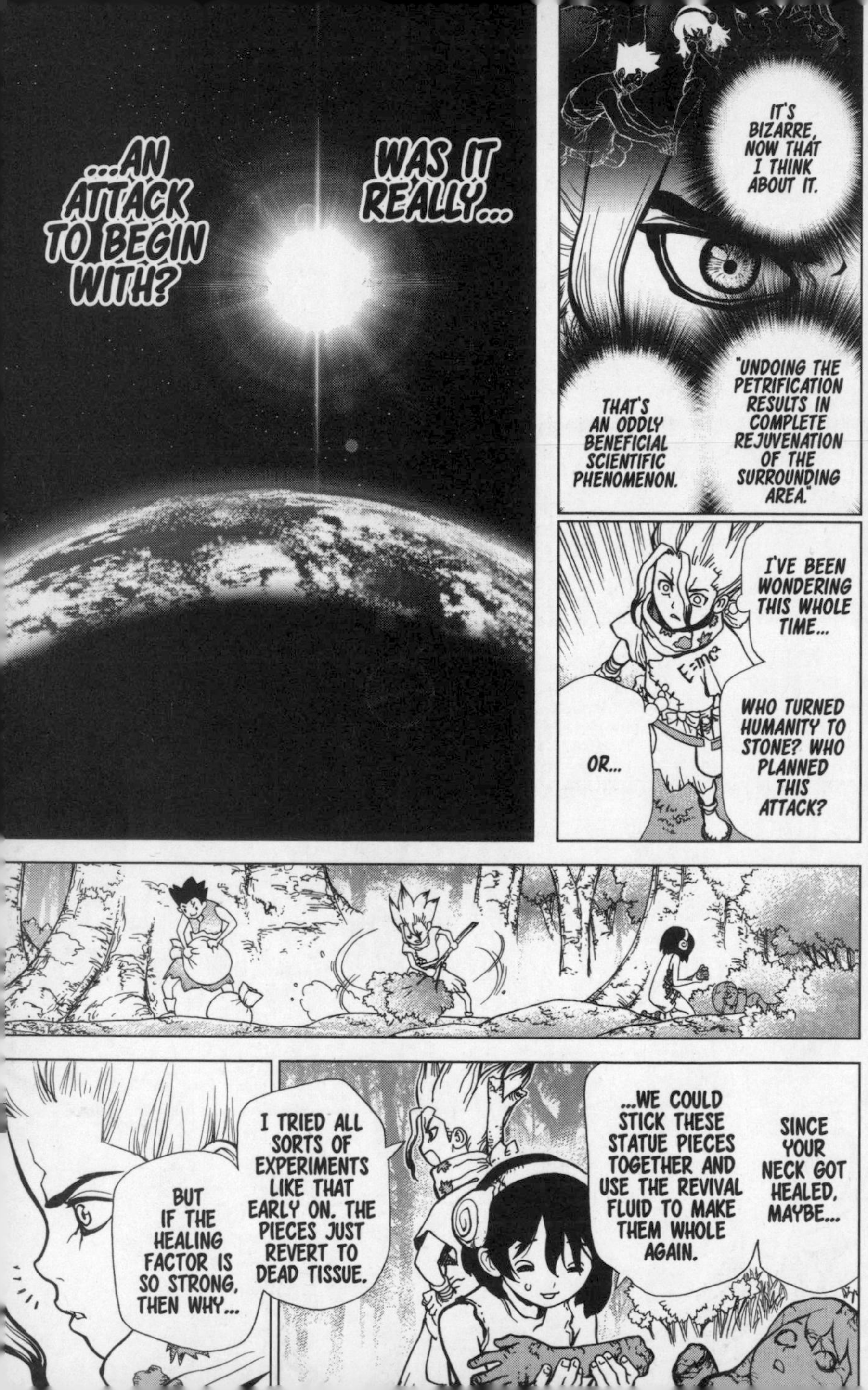
IT'S BIZARRE, NOW THAT I THINK ABOUT IT.
"UNDOING THE PETRIFICATION RESULTS IN COMPLETE REJUVENATION OF THE SURROUNDING AREA."
THAT'S AN ODDLY BENEFICIAL SCIENTIFIC PHENOMENON.
I'VE BEEN WONDERING THIS WHOLE TIME...
WHO TURNED HUMANITY TO STONE? WHO PLANNED THIS ATTACK?
OR...
WAS IT REALLY...
...AN ATTACK TO BEGIN WITH?
SINCE YOUR NECK GOT HEALED, MAYBE...
...WE COULD STICK THESE STATUE PIECES TOGETHER AND USE THE REVIVAL FLUID TO MAKE THEM WHOLE AGAIN.
I TRIED ALL SORTS OF EXPERIMENTS LIKE THAT EARLY ON. THE PIECES JUST REVERT TO DEAD TISSUE.
BUT IF THE HEALING FACTOR IS SO STRONG, THEN WHY...

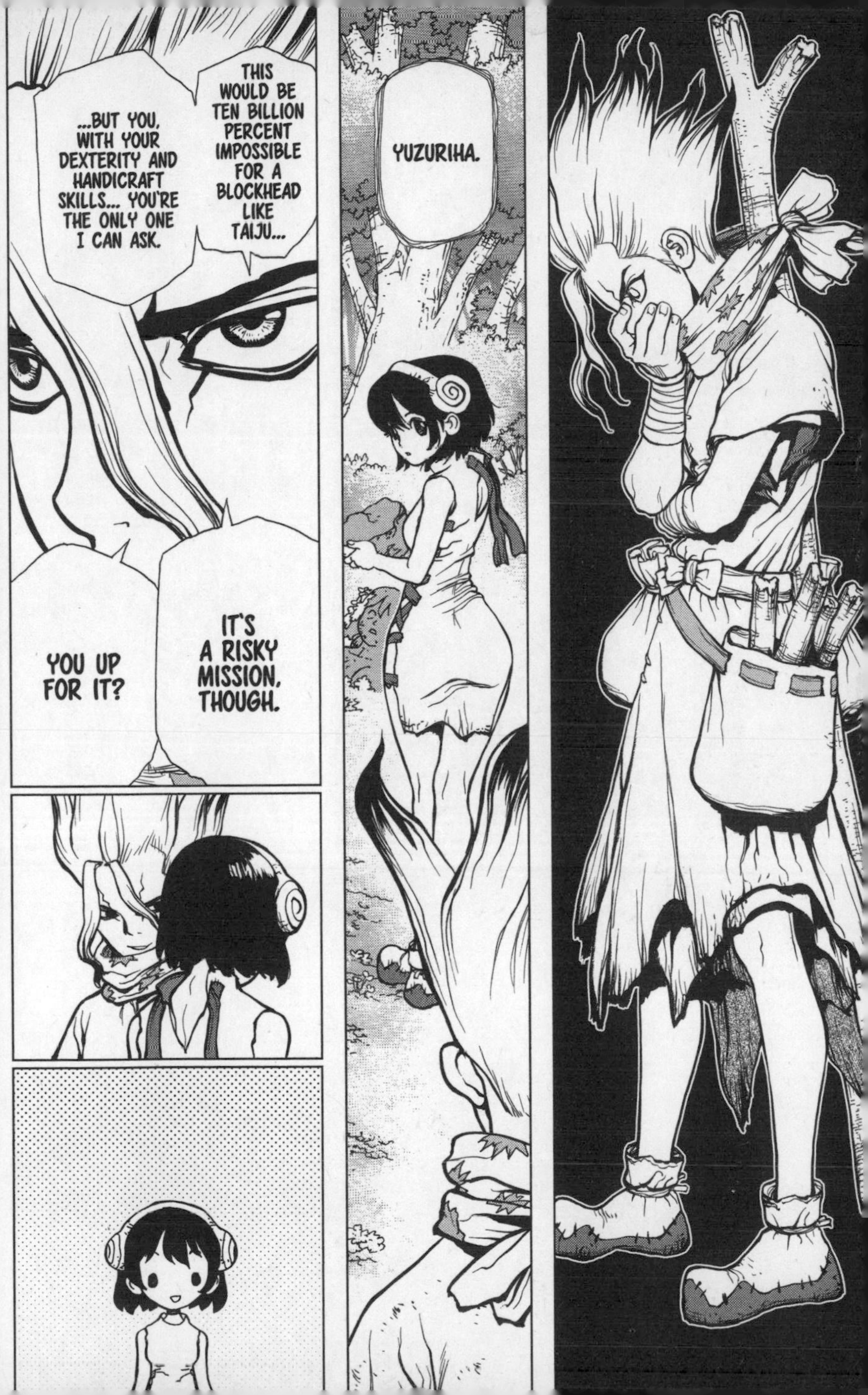
YUZURIHA.
THIS WOULD BE TEN BILLION PERCENT IMPOSSIBLE FOR A BLOCKHEAD LIKE TAIJU...
...BUT YOU, WITH YOUR DEXTERITY AND HANDICRAFT SKILLS... YOU'RE THE ONLY ONE I CAN ASK.
IT'S A RISKY MISSION, THOUGH.
YOU UP FOR IT?

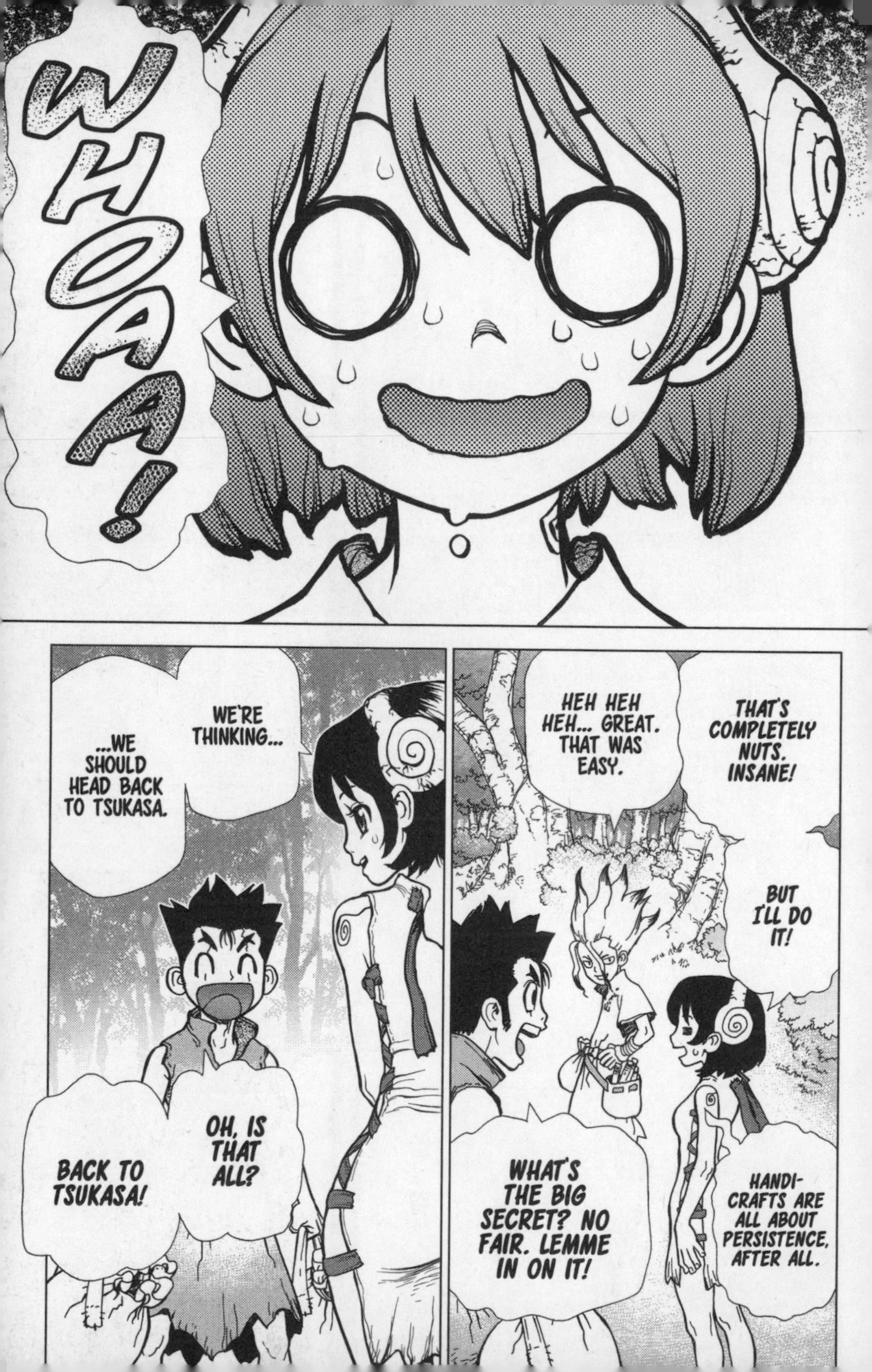
WHOAA!
THAT'S COMPLETELY NUTS. INSANE!
HEH HEH HEH... GREAT. THAT WAS EASY.
BUT I'LL DO IT!
HANDI-CRAFTS ARE ALL ABOUT PERSISTENCE, AFTER ALL.
WHAT'S THE BIG SECRET? NO FAIR. LEMME IN ON IT!
WE'RE THINKING...
...WE SHOULD HEAD BACK TO TSUKASA.
OH, IS THAT ALL?
BACK TO TSUKASA!

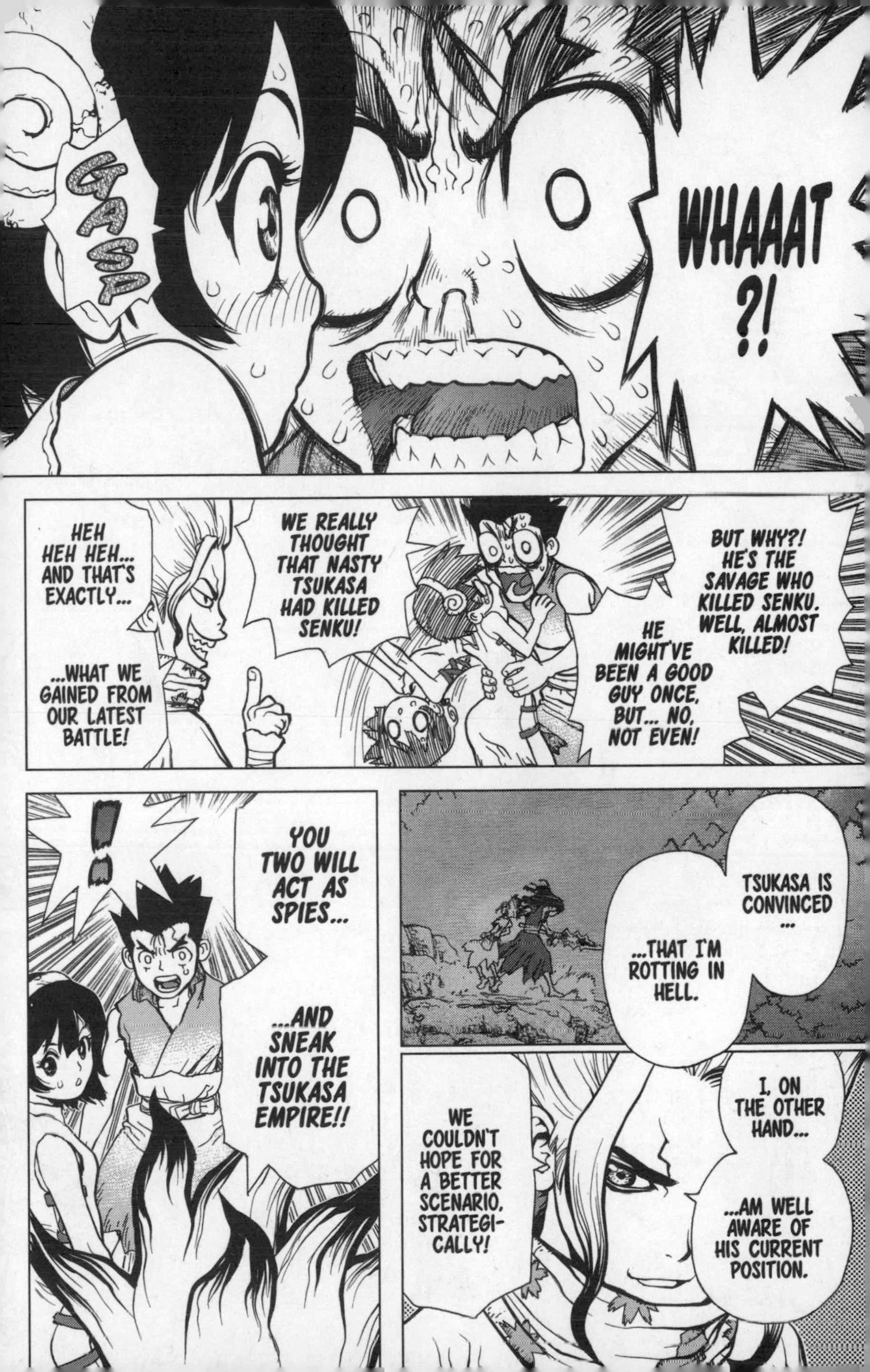
WHAAAT ?!
GASP
BUT WHY?! HE'S THE SAVAGE WHO KILLED SENKU. WELL, ALMOST KILLED!
HE MIGHT'VE BEEN A GOOD GUY ONCE, BUT... NO, NOT EVEN!
WE REALLY THOUGHT THAT NASTY TSUKASA HAD KILLED SENKU!
HEH HEH HEH... AND THAT'S EXACTLY...
...WHAT WE GAINED FROM OUR LATEST BATTLE!
TSUKASA IS CONVINCED ...
...THAT I'M ROTTING IN HELL.
I, ON THE OTHER HAND...
...AM WELL AWARE OF HIS CURRENT POSITION.
WE COULDN'T HOPE FOR A BETTER SCENARIO, STRATEGI-CALLY!
YOU TWO WILL ACT AS SPIES...
...AND SNEAK INTO THE TSUKASA EMPIRE!!
!

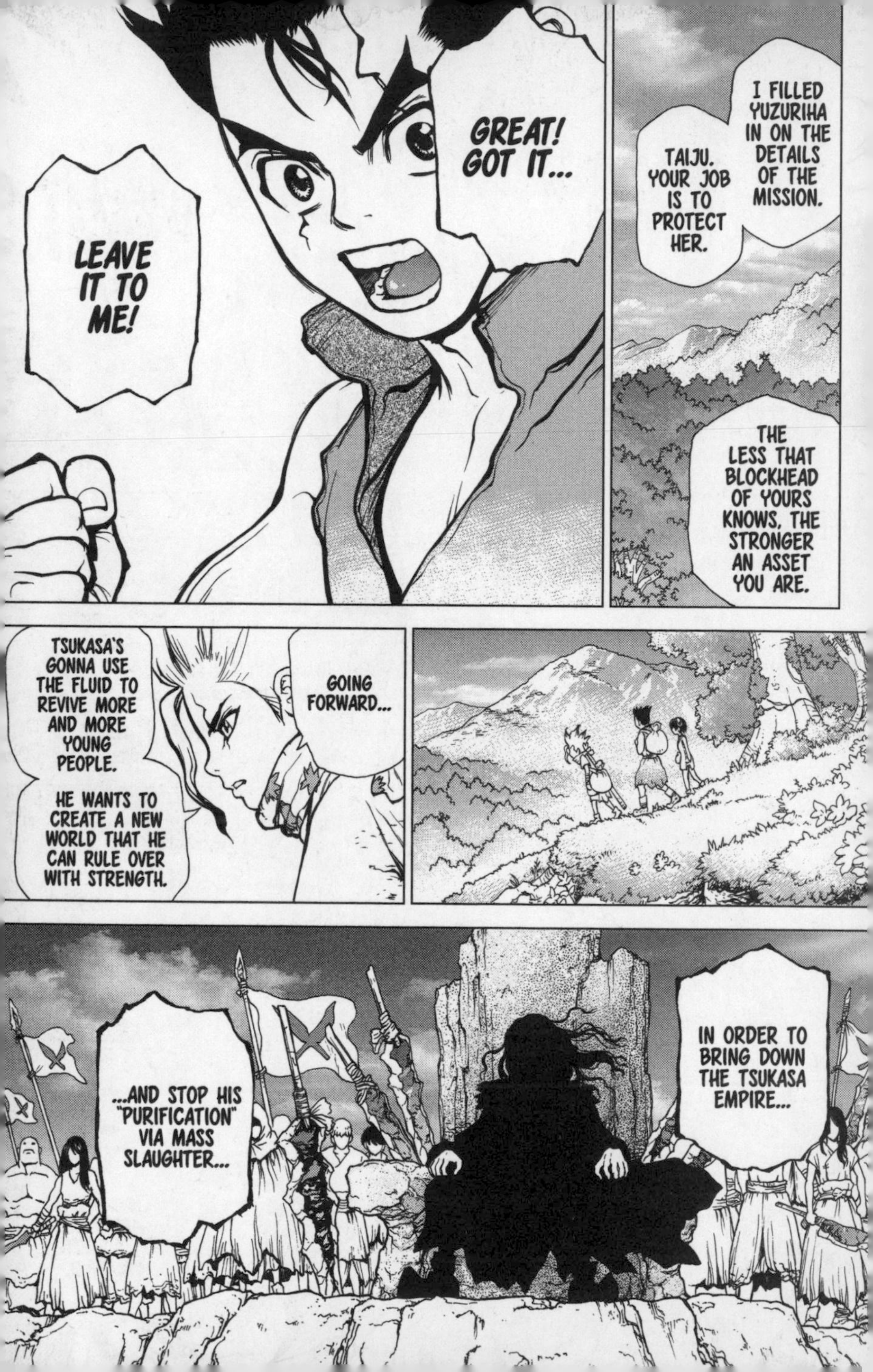
I FILLED YUZURIHA IN ON THE DETAILS OF THE MISSION.
TAIJU. YOUR JOB IS TO PROTECT HER.
THE LESS THAT BLOCKHEAD OF YOURS KNOWS, THE STRONGER AN ASSET YOU ARE.
GREAT! GOT IT...
LEAVE IT TO ME!
GOING FORWARD...
TSUKASA'S GONNA USE THE FLUID TO REVIVE MORE AND MORE YOUNG PEOPLE.
HE WANTS TO CREATE A NEW WORLD THAT HE CAN RULE OVER WITH STRENGTH.
IN ORDER TO BRING DOWN THE TSUKASA EMPIRE...
...AND STOP HIS "PURIFICATION" VIA MASS SLAUGHTER...

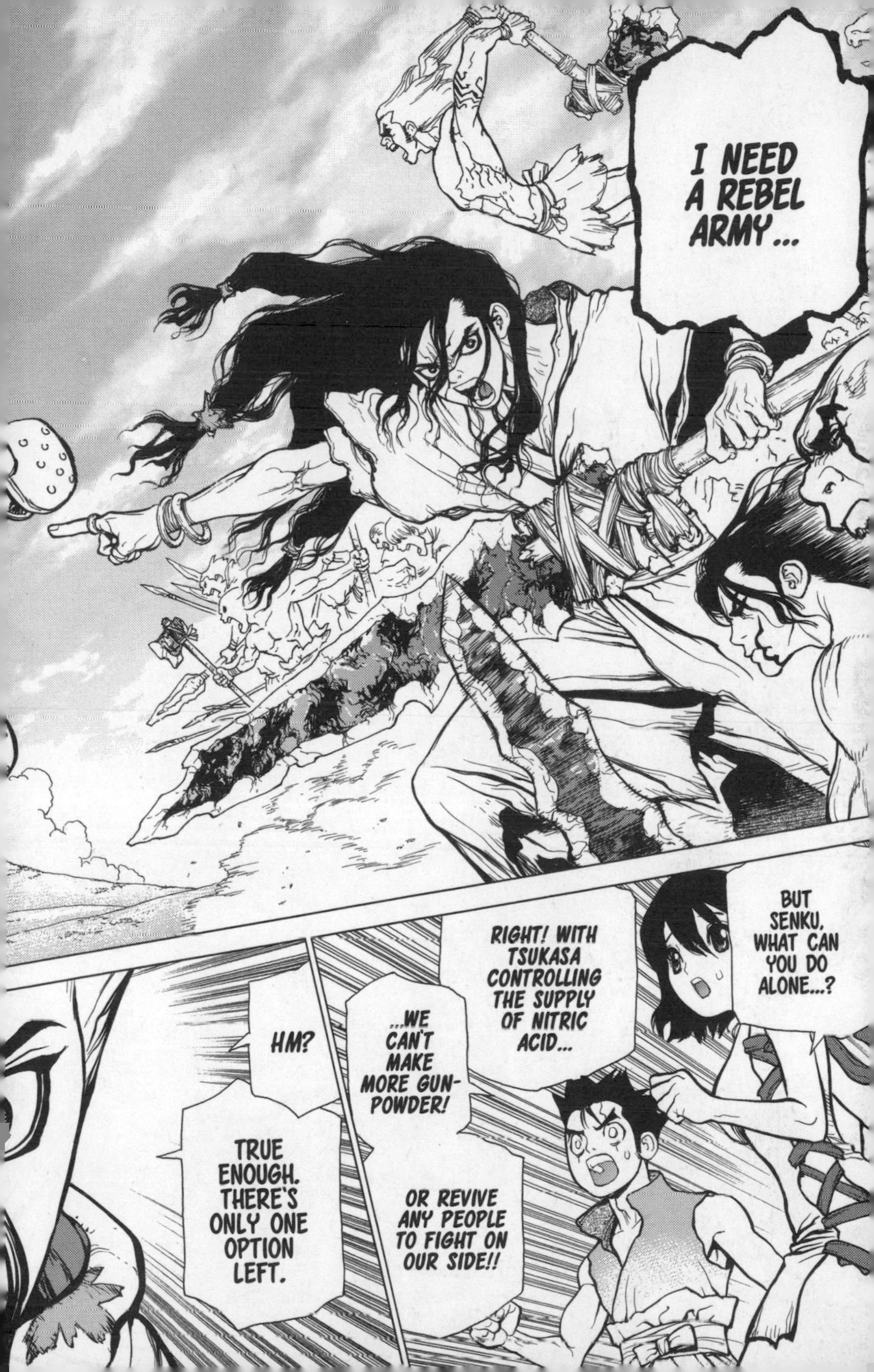
I NEED A REBEL ARMY...
BUT SENKU, WHAT CAN YOU DO ALONE...?
RIGHT! WITH TSUKASA CONTROLLING THE SUPPLY OF NITRIC ACID...
...WE CAN'T MAKE MORE GUN-POWDER!
OR REVIVE ANY PEOPLE TO FIGHT ON OUR SIDE!!
HM?
TRUE ENOUGH. THERE'S ONLY ONE OPTION LEFT.

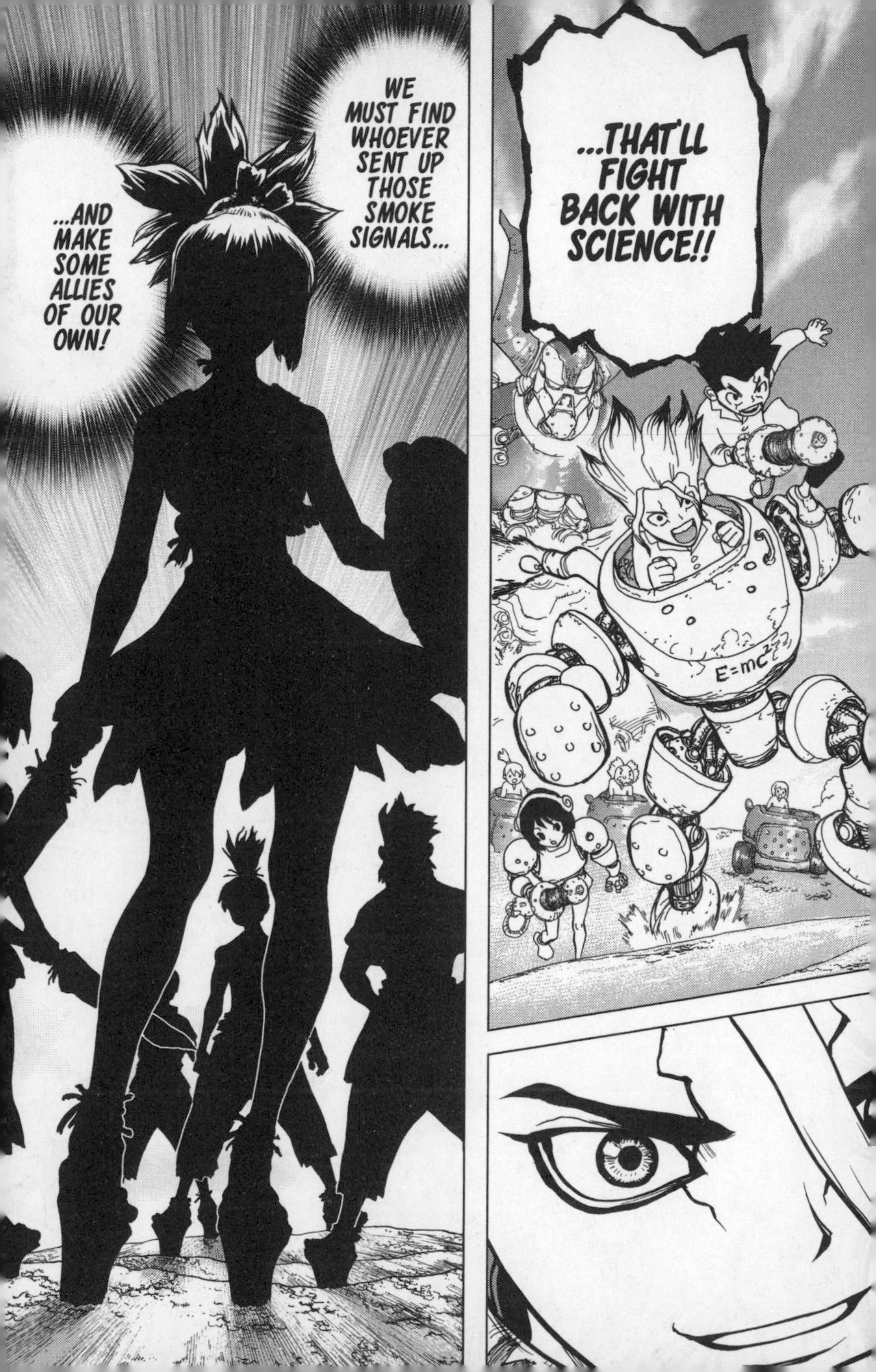
WE MUST FIND WHOEVER SENT UP THOSE SMOKE SIGNALS...
...AND MAKE SOME ALLIES OF OUR OWN!
...THAT'LL FIGHT BACK WITH SCIENCE!!
$E=mc^2$

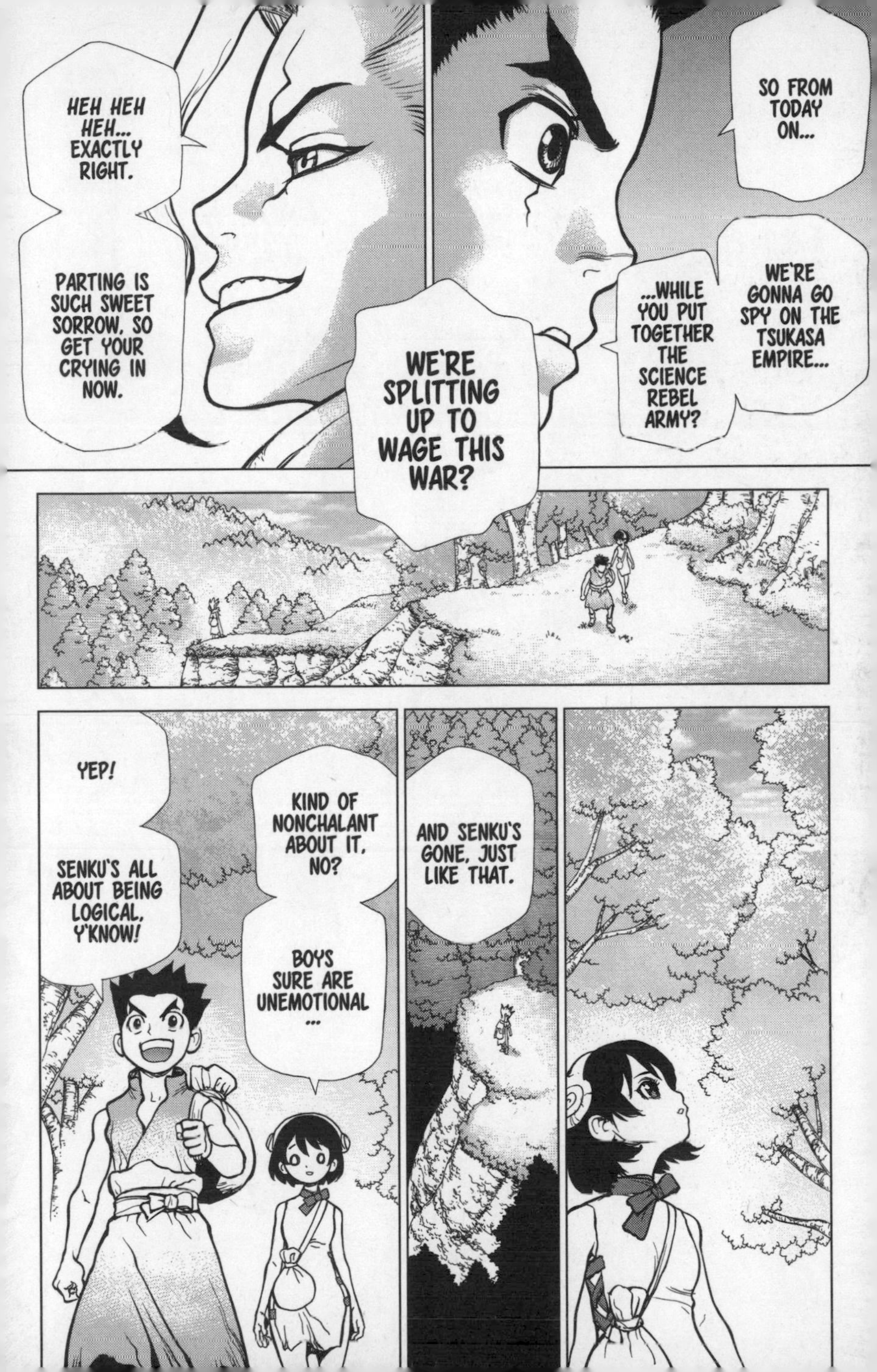
SO FROM TODAY ON...
WE'RE GONNA GO SPY ON THE TSUKASA EMPIRE...
...WHILE YOU PUT TOGETHER THE SCIENCE REBEL ARMY?
WE'RE SPLITTING UP TO WAGE THIS WAR?
HEH HEH HEH... EXACTLY RIGHT.
PARTING IS SUCH SWEET SORROW, SO GET YOUR CRYING IN NOW.
AND SENKU'S GONE, JUST LIKE THAT.
KIND OF NONCHALANT ABOUT IT, NO?
YEP!
SENKU'S ALL ABOUT BEING LOGICAL, Y'KNOW!
BOYS SURE ARE UNEMOTIONAL...

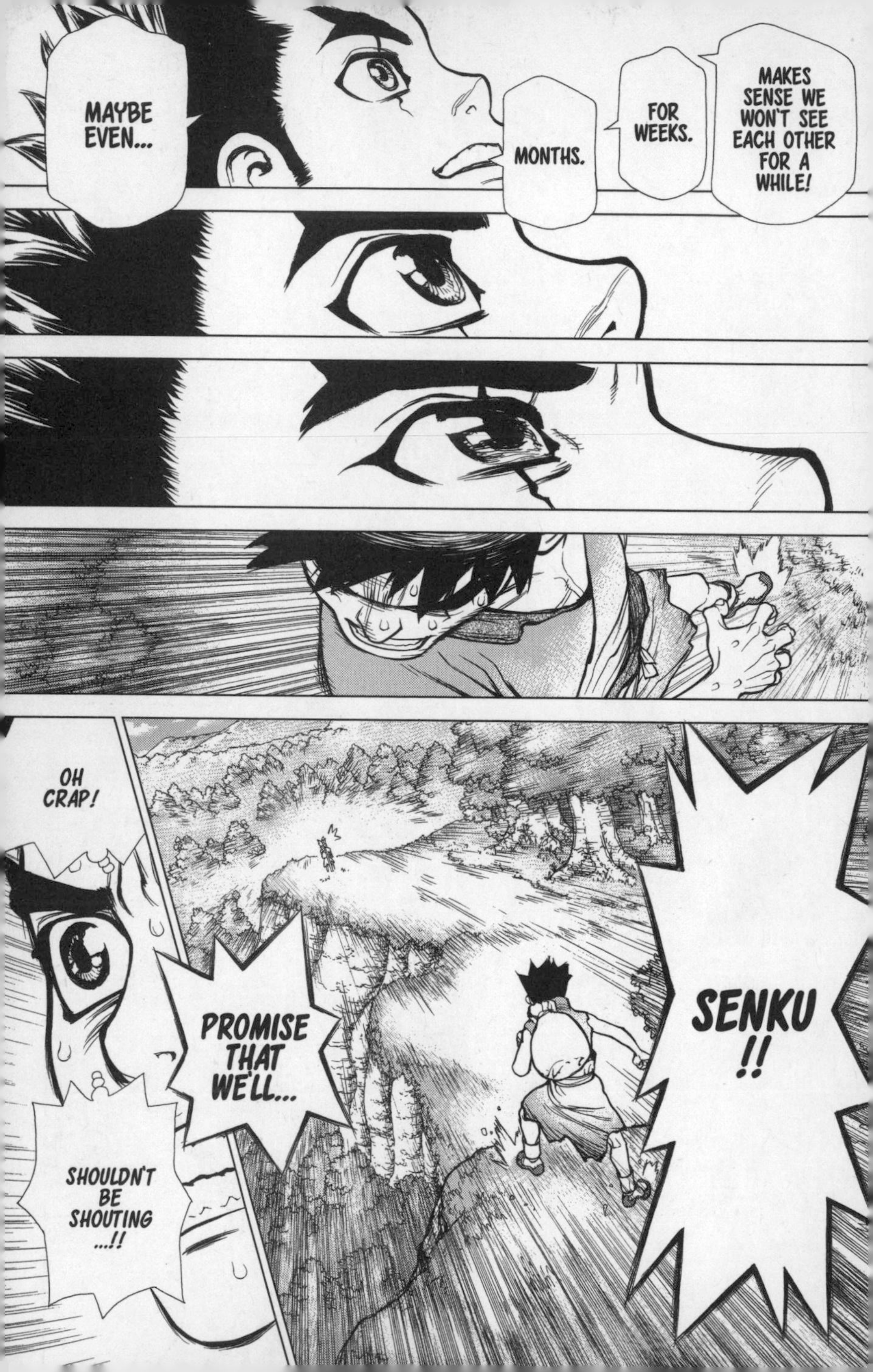
MAKES SENSE WE WON'T SEE EACH OTHER FOR A WHILE!
FOR WEEKS.
MONTHS.
MAYBE EVEN...
SENKU!!
PROMISE THAT WE'LL...
OH CRAP!
SHOULDN'T BE SHOUTING ...!!

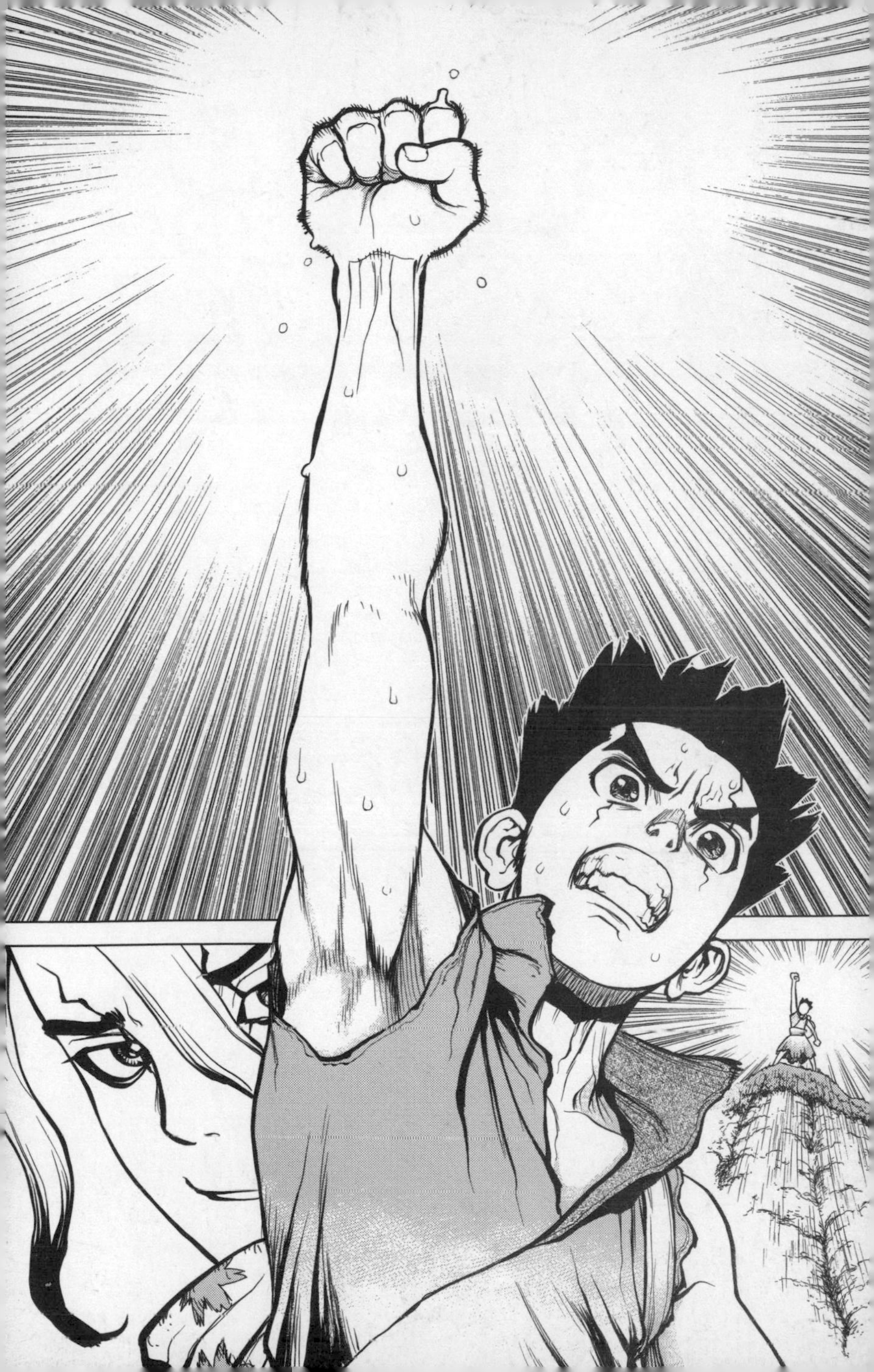

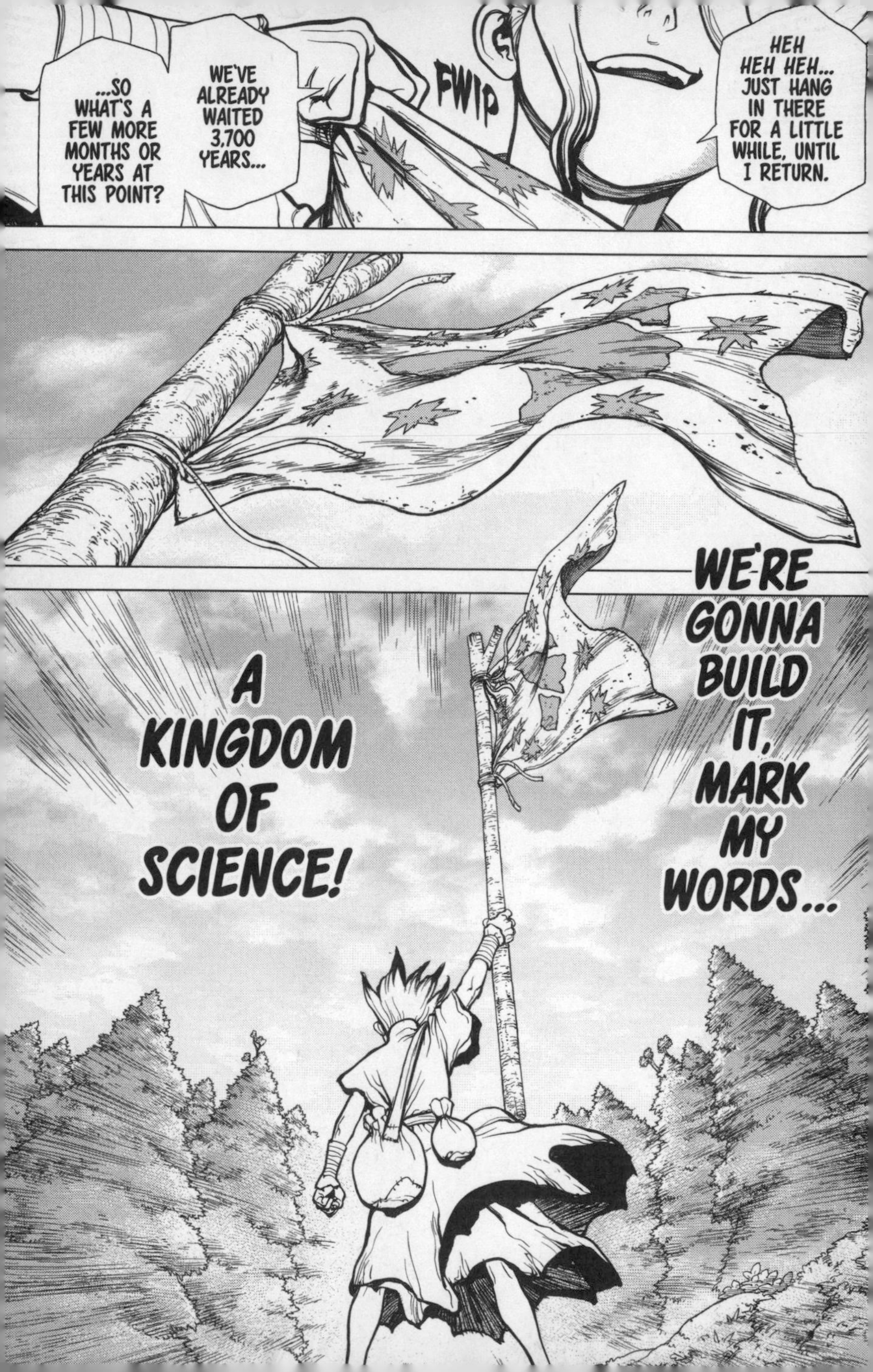
HEH HEH HEH... JUST HANG IN THERE FOR A LITTLE WHILE, UNTIL I RETURN.
FWIP
WE'VE ALREADY WAITED 3,700 YEARS...
...SO WHAT'S A FEW MORE MONTHS OR YEARS AT THIS POINT?
WE'RE GONNA BUILD IT, MARK MY WORDS...
A KINGDOM OF SCIENCE!

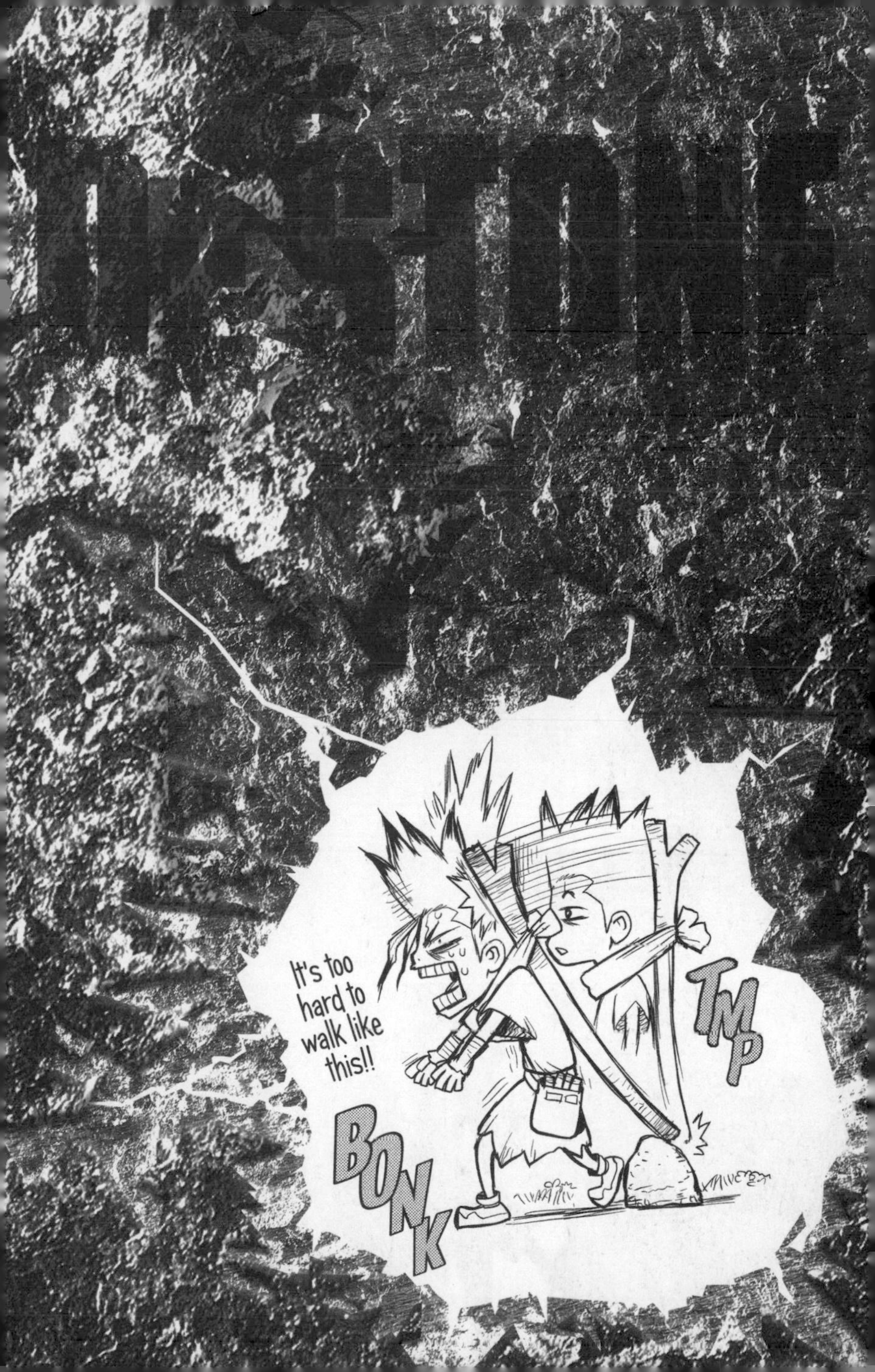
It's too hard to walk like this!!
TMP
BONK

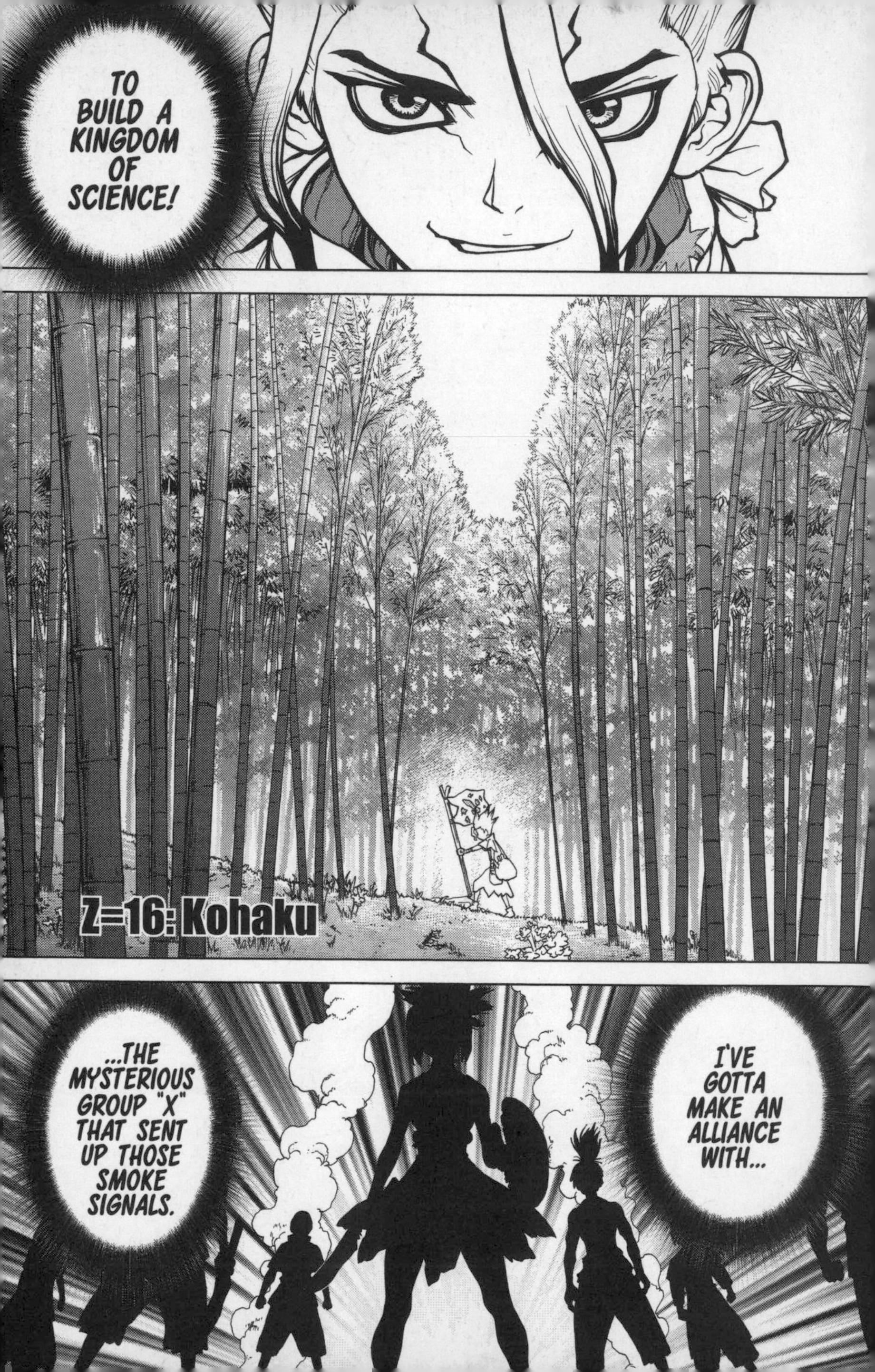
TO BUILD A KINGDOM OF SCIENCE!
Z=16: Kohaku
I'VE GOTTA MAKE AN ALLIANCE WITH...
...THE MYSTERIOUS GROUP "X" THAT SENT UP THOSE SMOKE SIGNALS.

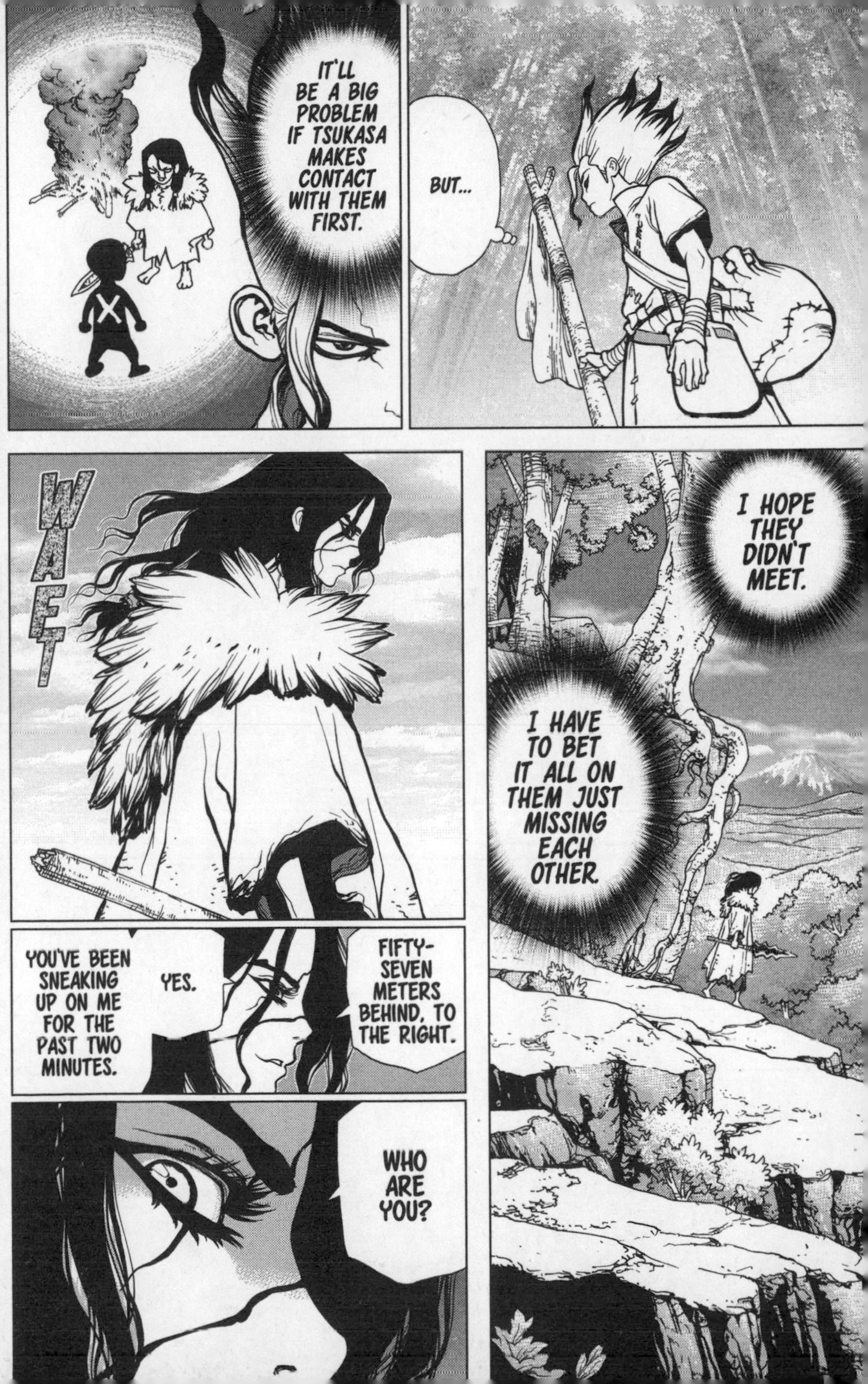
BUT...
IT'LL BE A BIG PROBLEM IF TSUKASA MAKES CONTACT WITH THEM FIRST.
I HOPE THEY DIDN'T MEET.
I HAVE TO BET IT ALL ON THEM JUST MISSING EACH OTHER.
WAFT
FIFTY-SEVEN METERS BEHIND, TO THE RIGHT.
YES.
YOU'VE BEEN SNEAKING UP ON ME FOR THE PAST TWO MINUTES.
WHO ARE YOU?

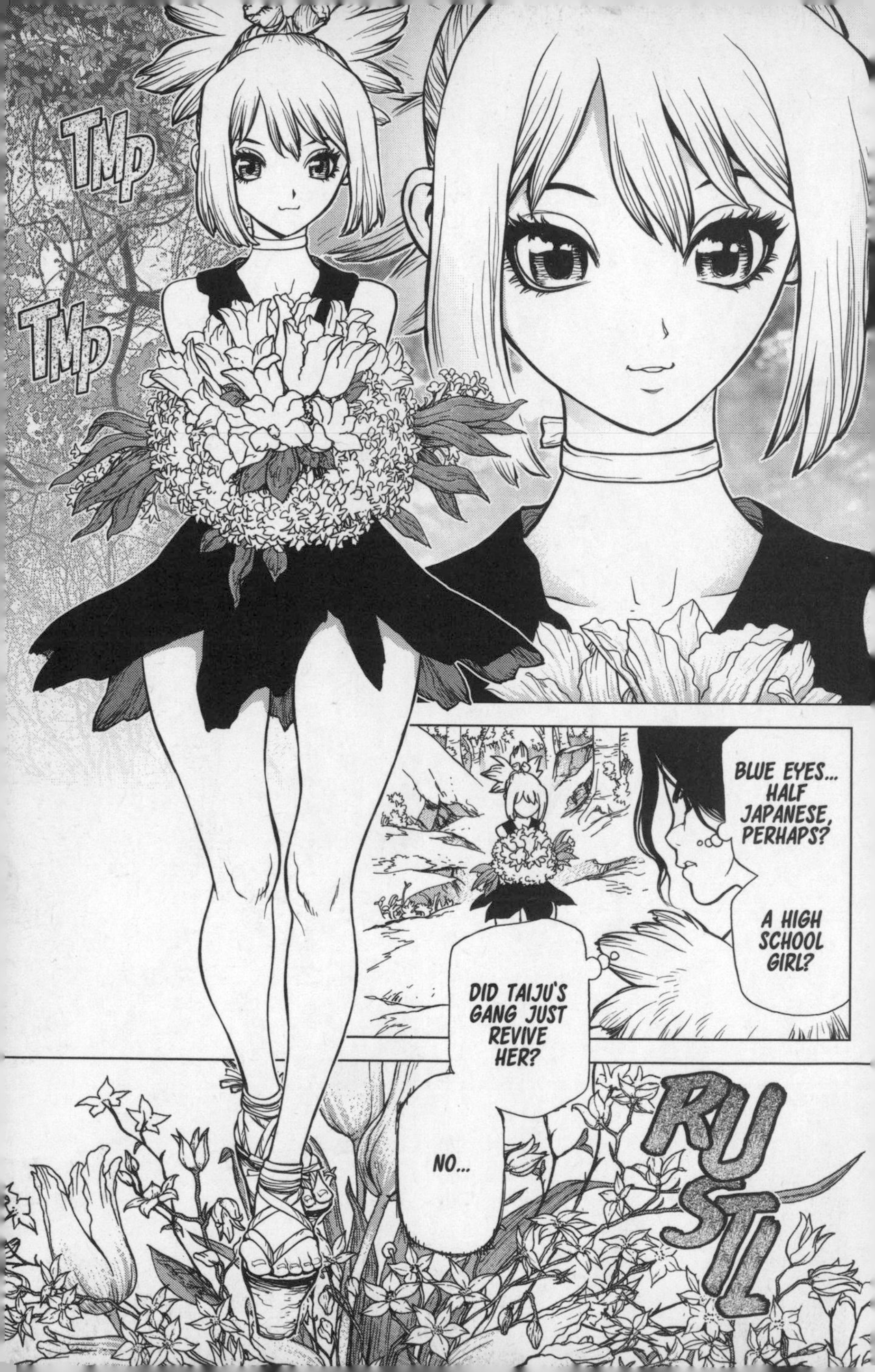
BLUE EYES... HALF JAPANESE, PERHAPS?
A HIGH SCHOOL GIRL?
DID TAIJU'S GANG JUST REVIVE HER?
NO...
RUSTL
TMP
TMP

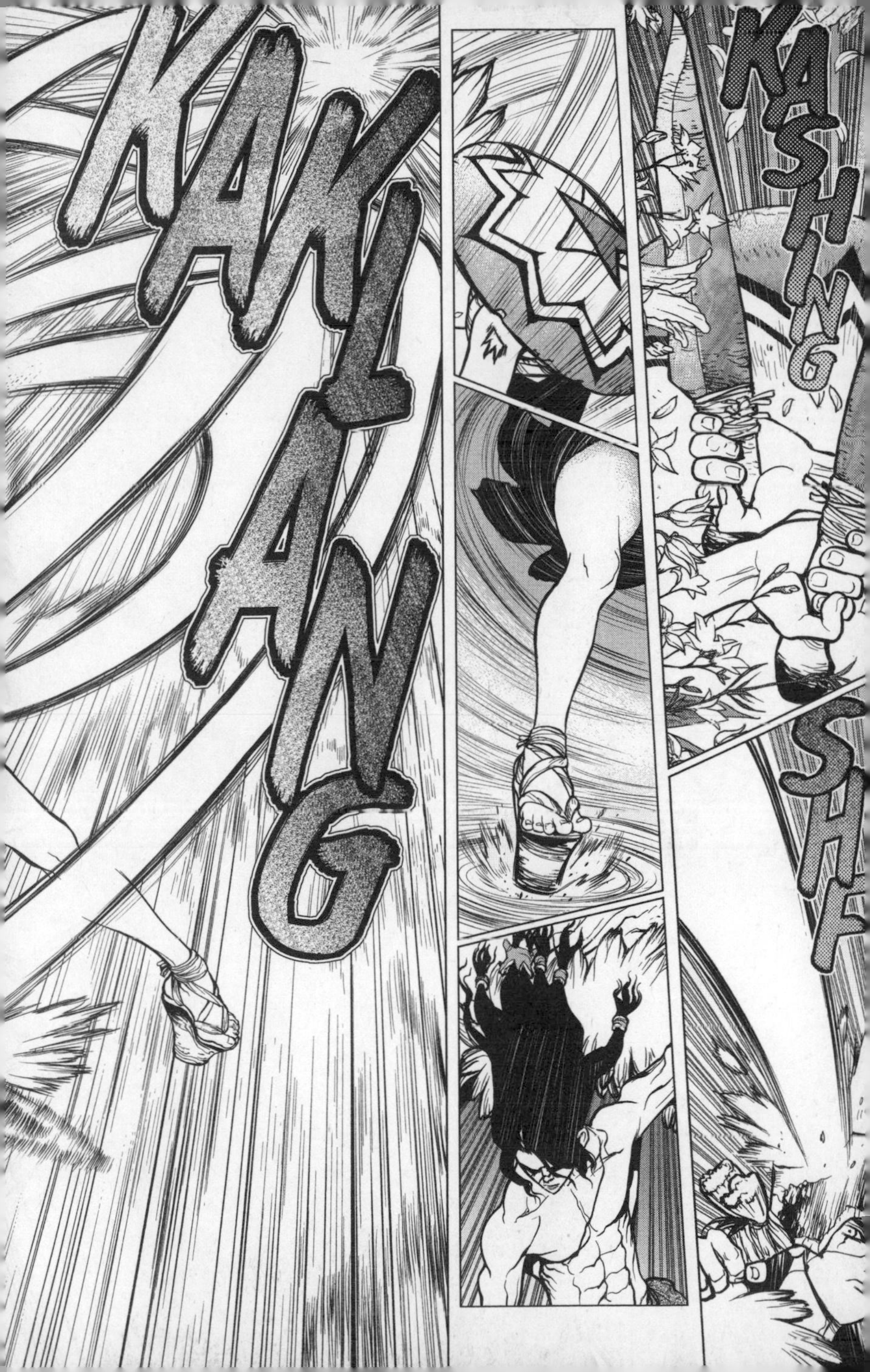
KASHING
SHF
KAKLANG

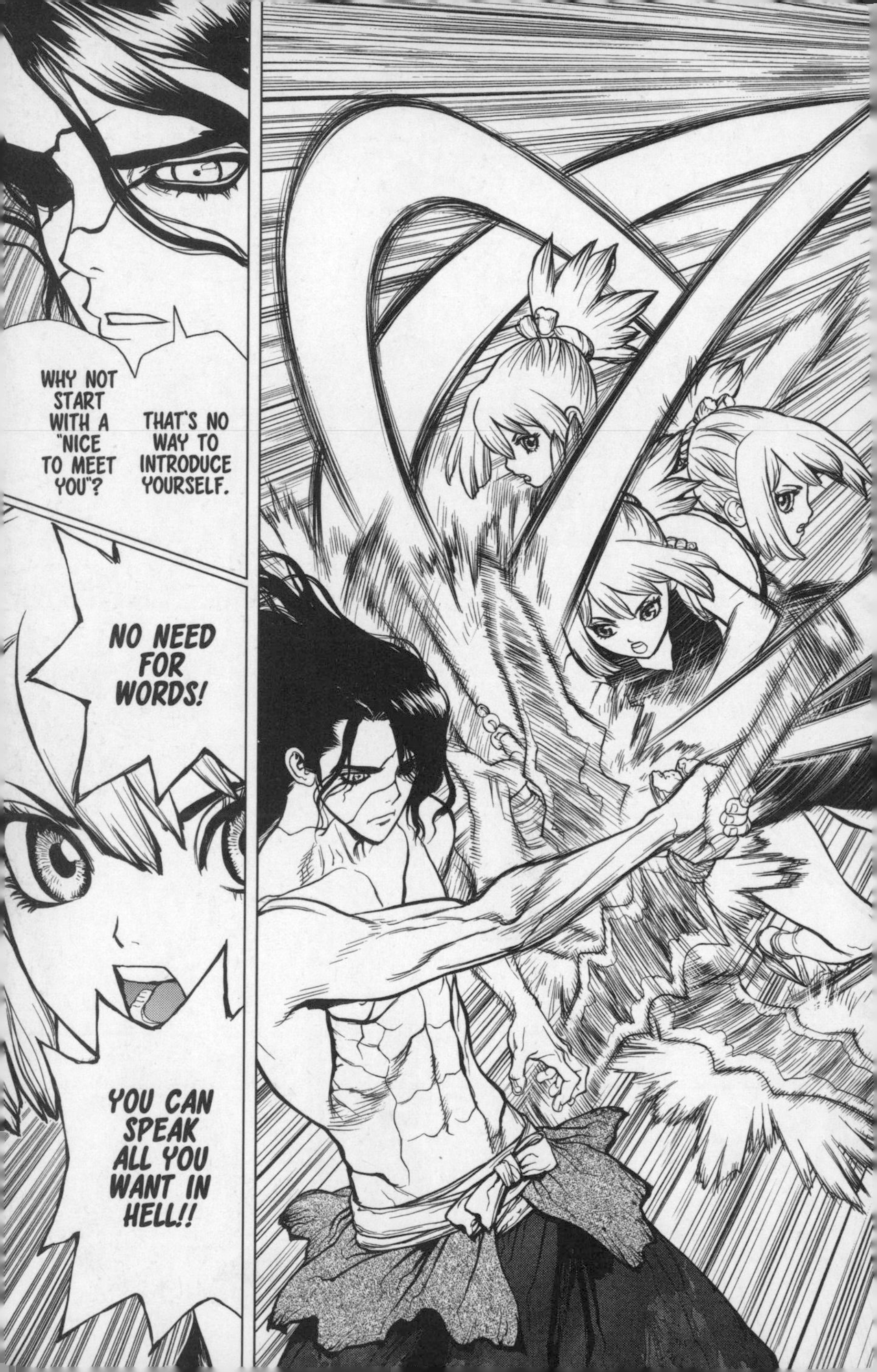
THAT'S NO WAY TO INTRODUCE YOURSELF.
WHY NOT START WITH A "NICE TO MEET YOU"?
NO NEED FOR WORDS!
YOU CAN SPEAK ALL YOU WANT IN HELL!!

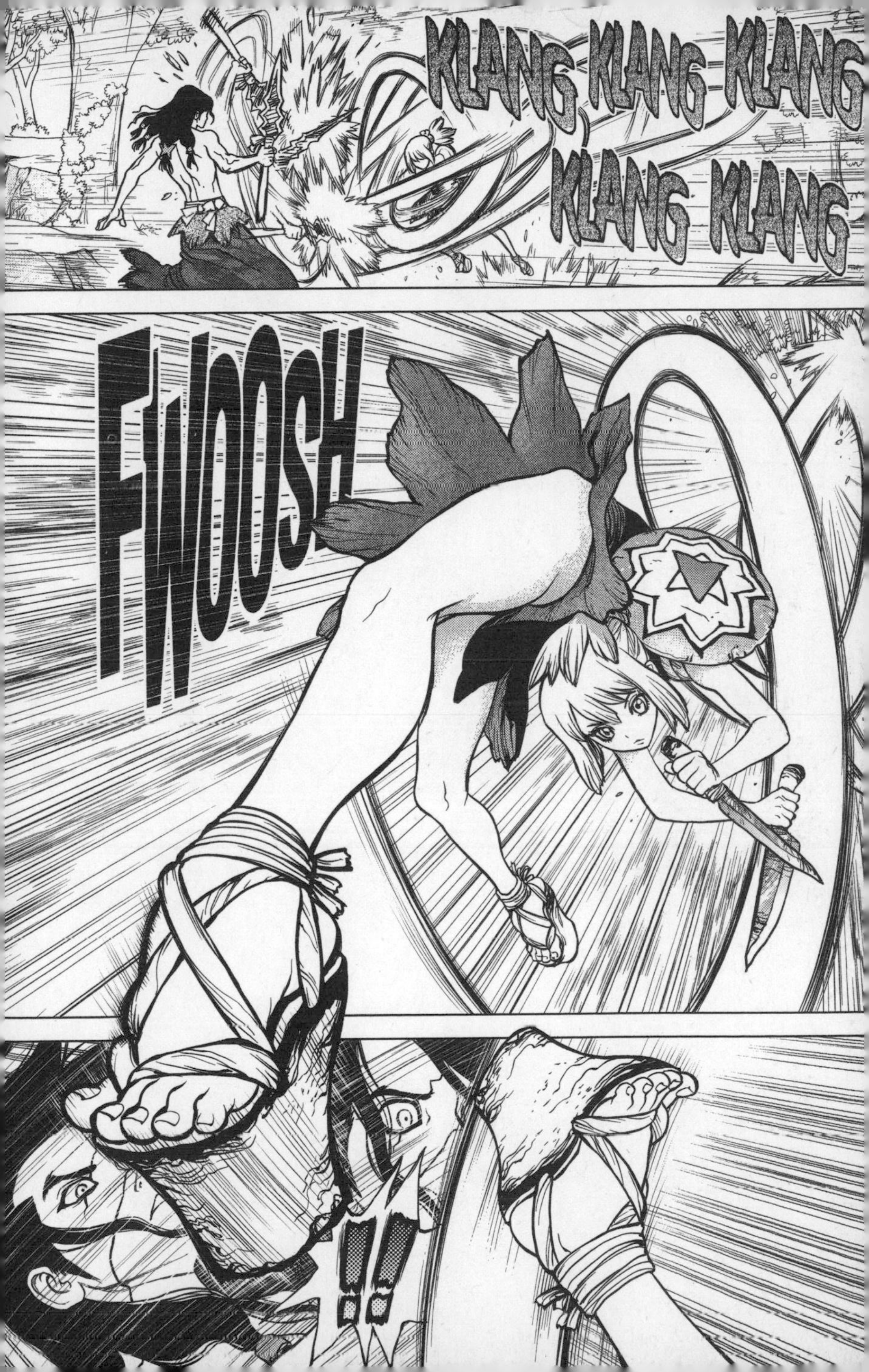
KLANG KLANG KLANG
KLANG KLANG
FWOOSH
!!

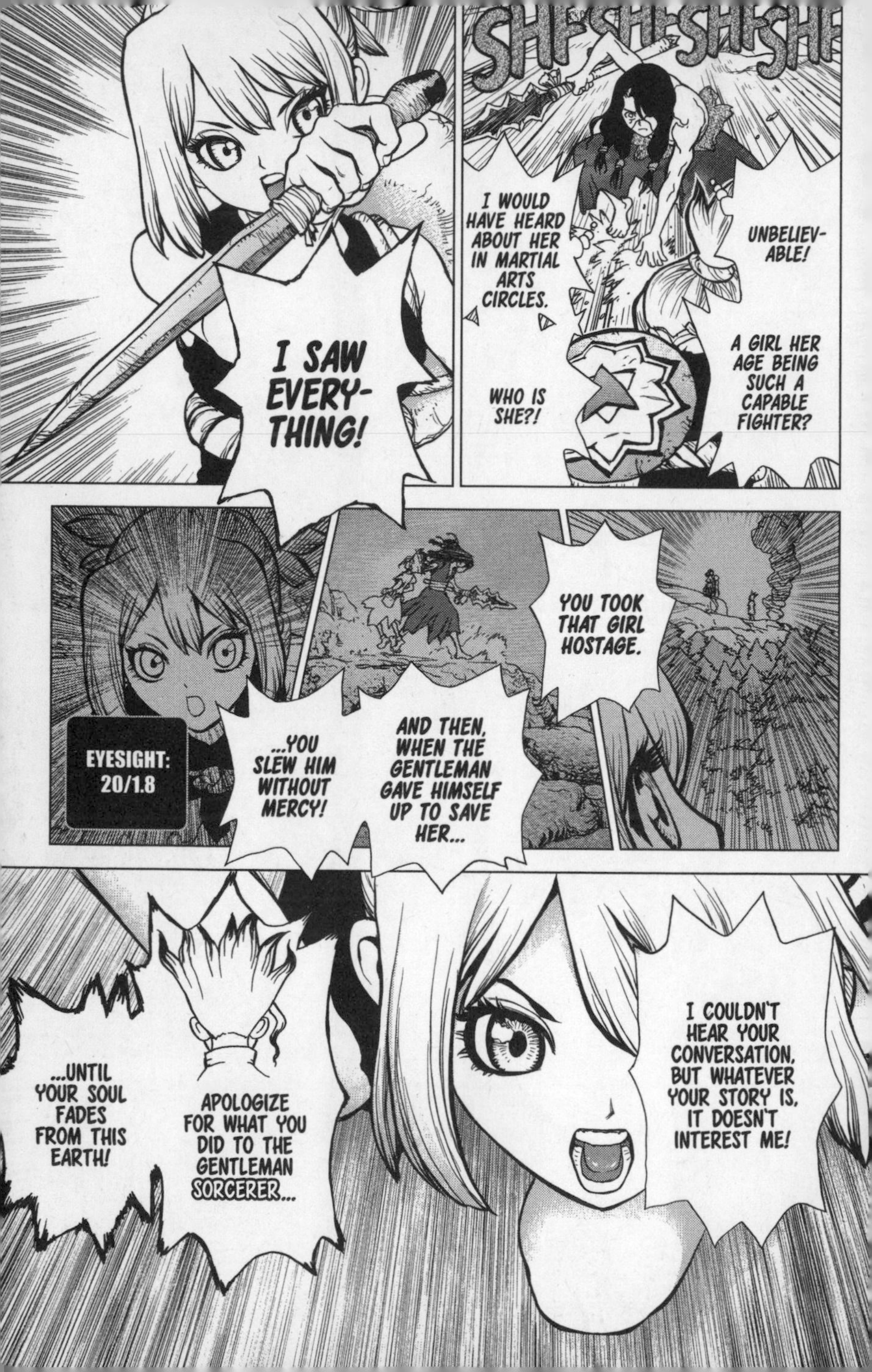
SHFSHFSHFSHF
UNBELIEVABLE!
A GIRL HER AGE BEING SUCH A CAPABLE FIGHTER?
I WOULD HAVE HEARD ABOUT HER IN MARTIAL ARTS CIRCLES.
WHO IS SHE?!
I SAW EVERYTHING!
YOU TOOK THAT GIRL HOSTAGE.
AND THEN, WHEN THE GENTLEMAN GAVE HIMSELF UP TO SAVE HER...
...YOU SLEW HIM WITHOUT MERCY!
EYESIGHT: 20/1.8
I COULDN'T HEAR YOUR CONVERSATION, BUT WHATEVER YOUR STORY IS, IT DOESN'T INTEREST ME!
APOLOGIZE FOR WHAT YOU DID TO THE GENTLEMAN SORCERER...
...UNTIL YOUR SOUL FADES FROM THIS EARTH!

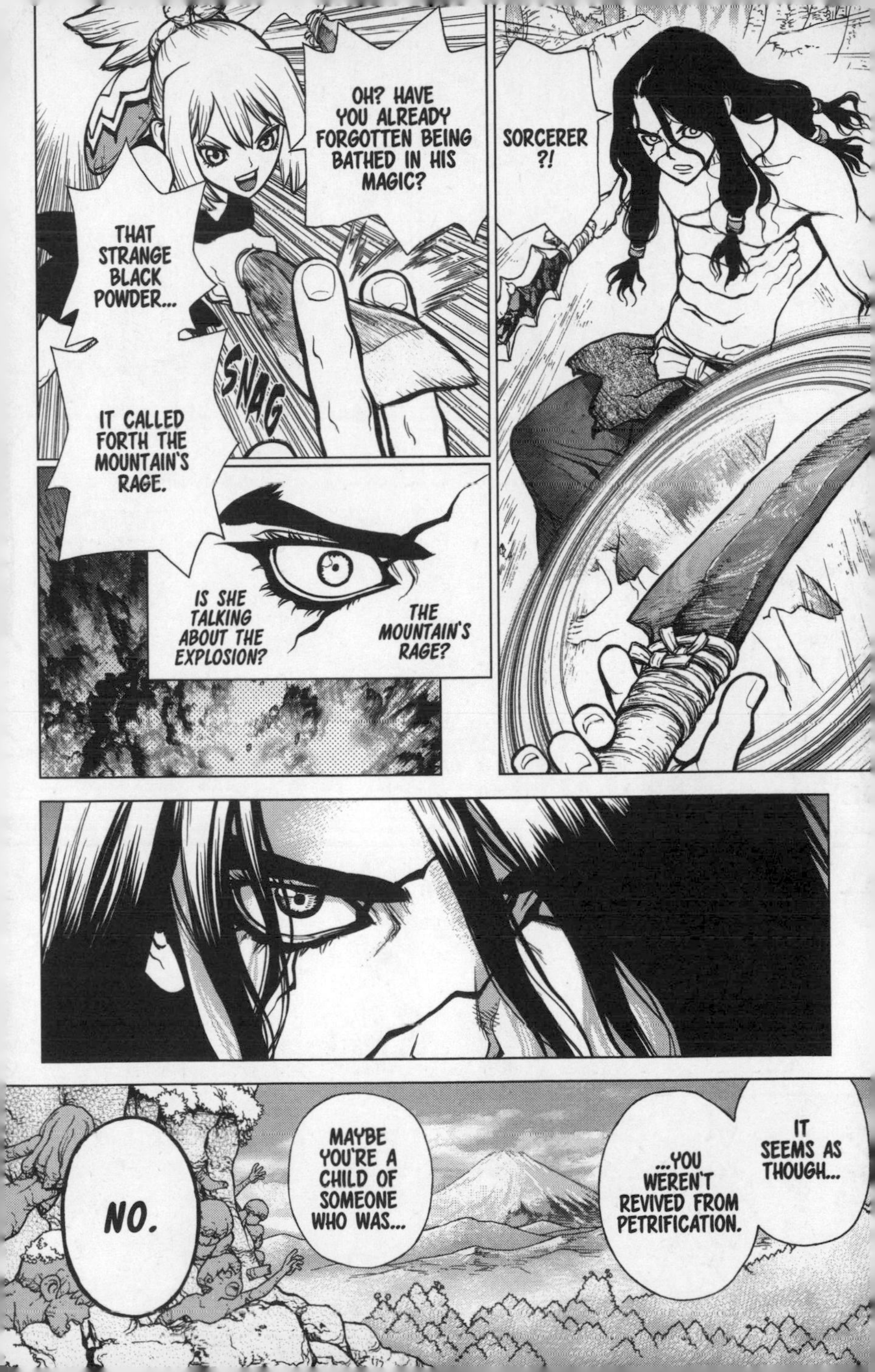
SORCERER ?!
OH? HAVE YOU ALREADY FORGOTTEN BEING BATHED IN HIS MAGIC?
SNAG
THAT STRANGE BLACK POWDER...
IT CALLED FORTH THE MOUNTAIN'S RAGE.
THE MOUNTAIN'S RAGE?
IS SHE TALKING ABOUT THE EXPLOSION?
IT SEEMS AS THOUGH...
...YOU WEREN'T REVIVED FROM PETRIFICATION.
MAYBE YOU'RE A CHILD OF SOMEONE WHO WAS...
NO.

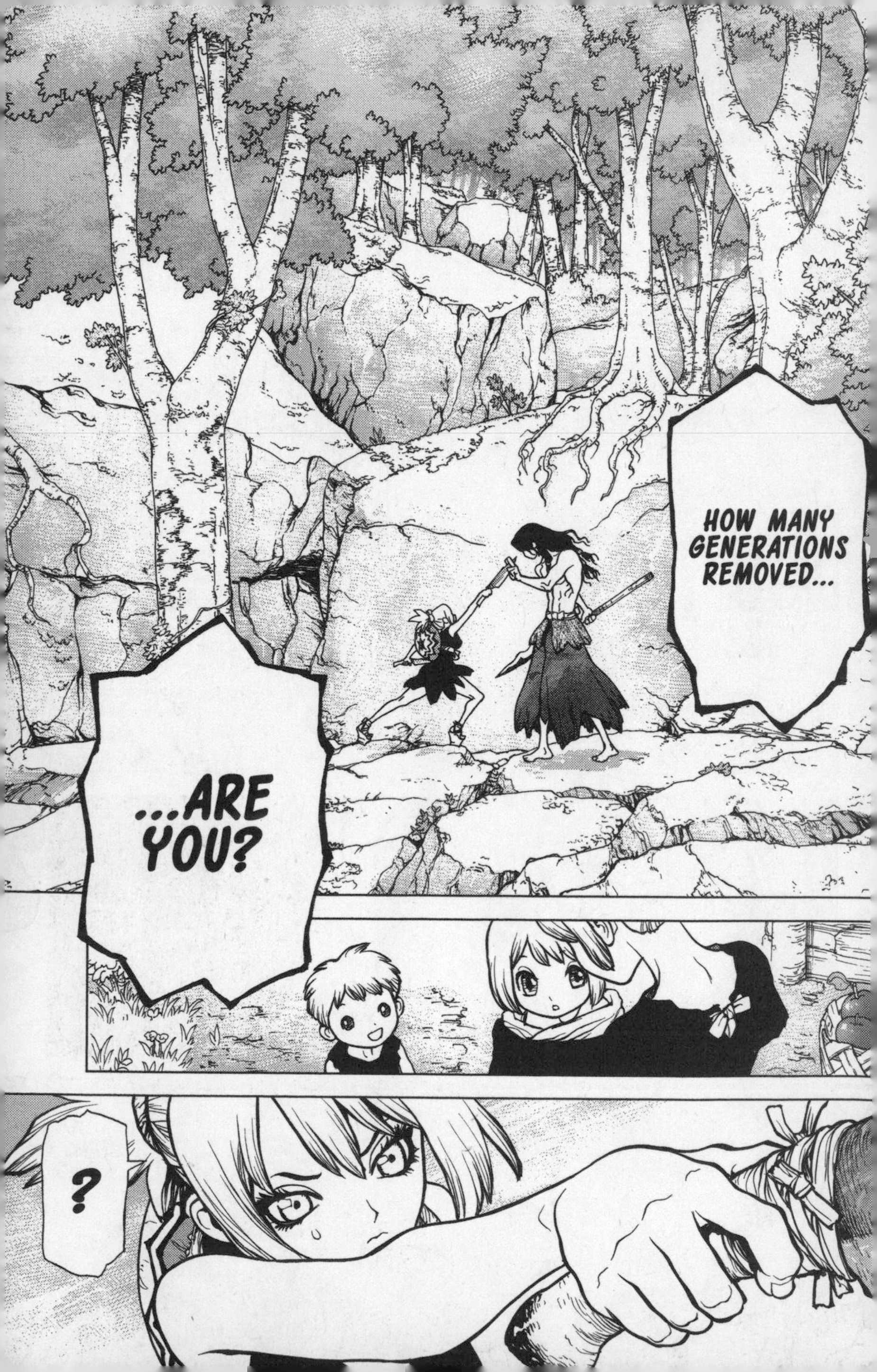
HOW MANY GENERATIONS REMOVED...
...ARE YOU?
?

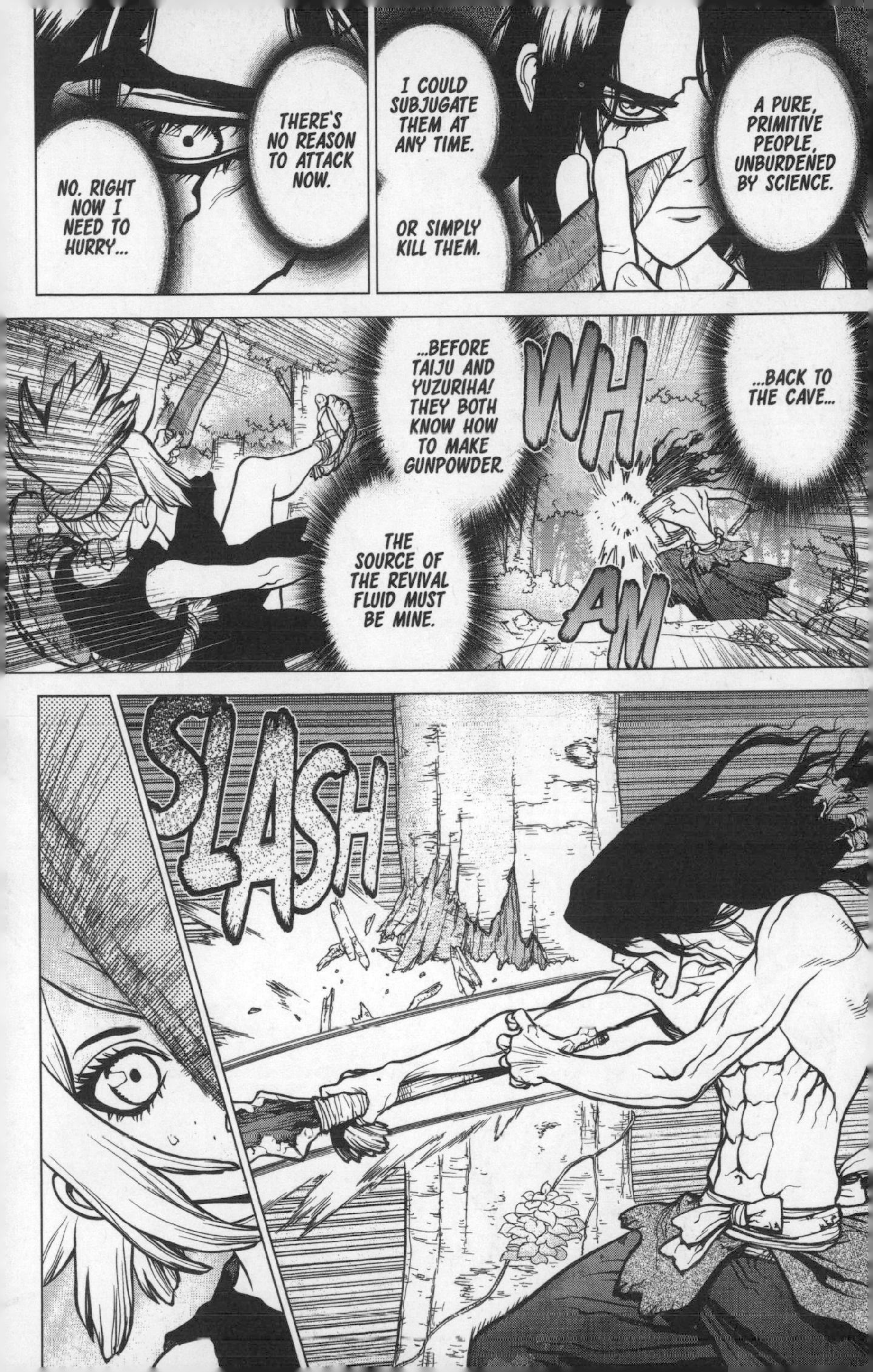
A PURE, PRIMITIVE PEOPLE, UNBURDENED BY SCIENCE.
I COULD SUBJUGATE THEM AT ANY TIME.
OR SIMPLY KILL THEM.
THERE'S NO REASON TO ATTACK NOW.
NO. RIGHT NOW I NEED TO HURRY...
...BACK TO THE CAVE...
WHAM
...BEFORE TAIJU AND YUZURIHA! THEY BOTH KNOW HOW TO MAKE GUNPOWDER.
THE SOURCE OF THE REVIVAL FLUID MUST BE MINE.
SLASH

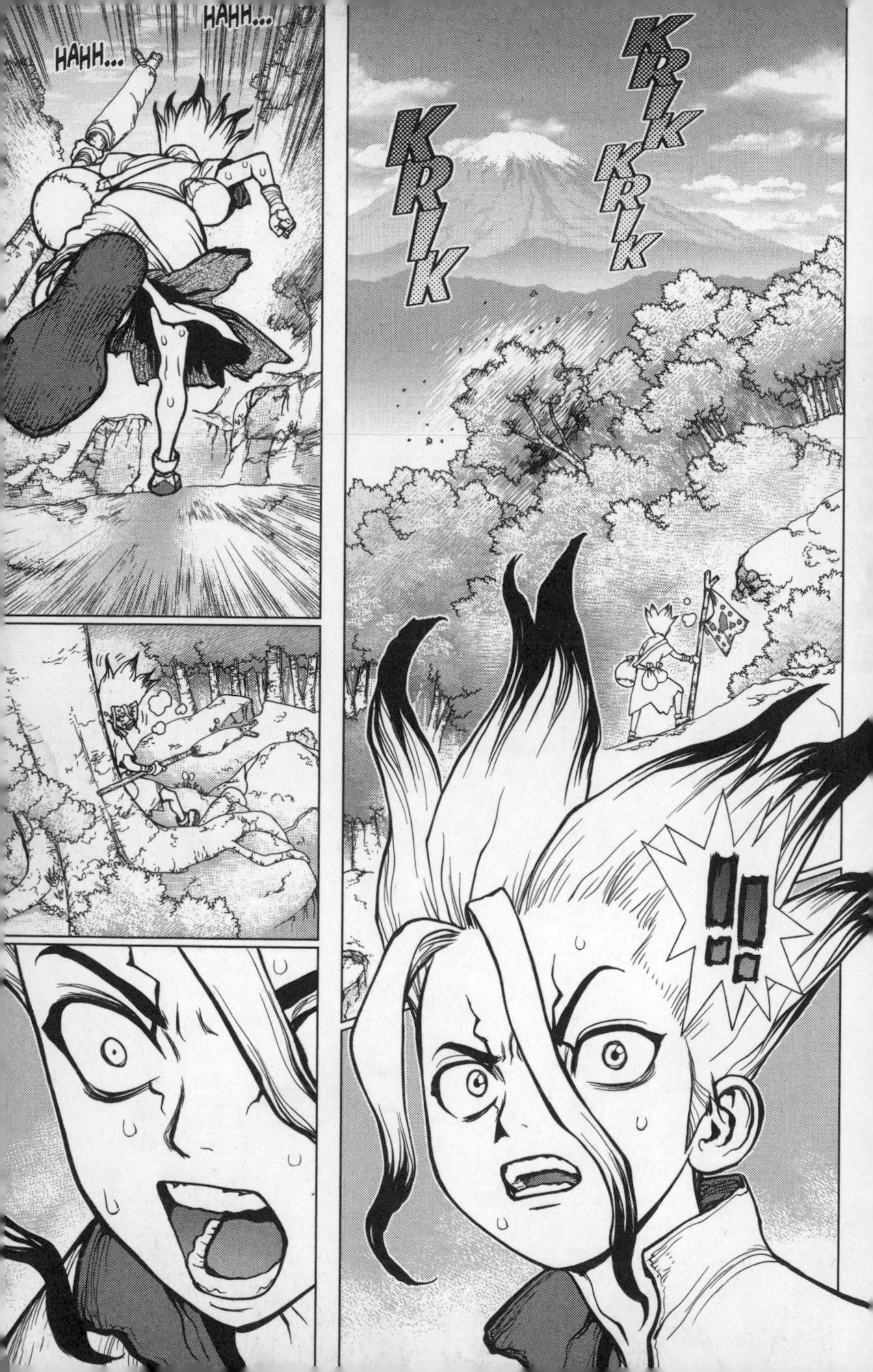
KRIK KRIK
KRIK
!!
HAHH...
HAHH...

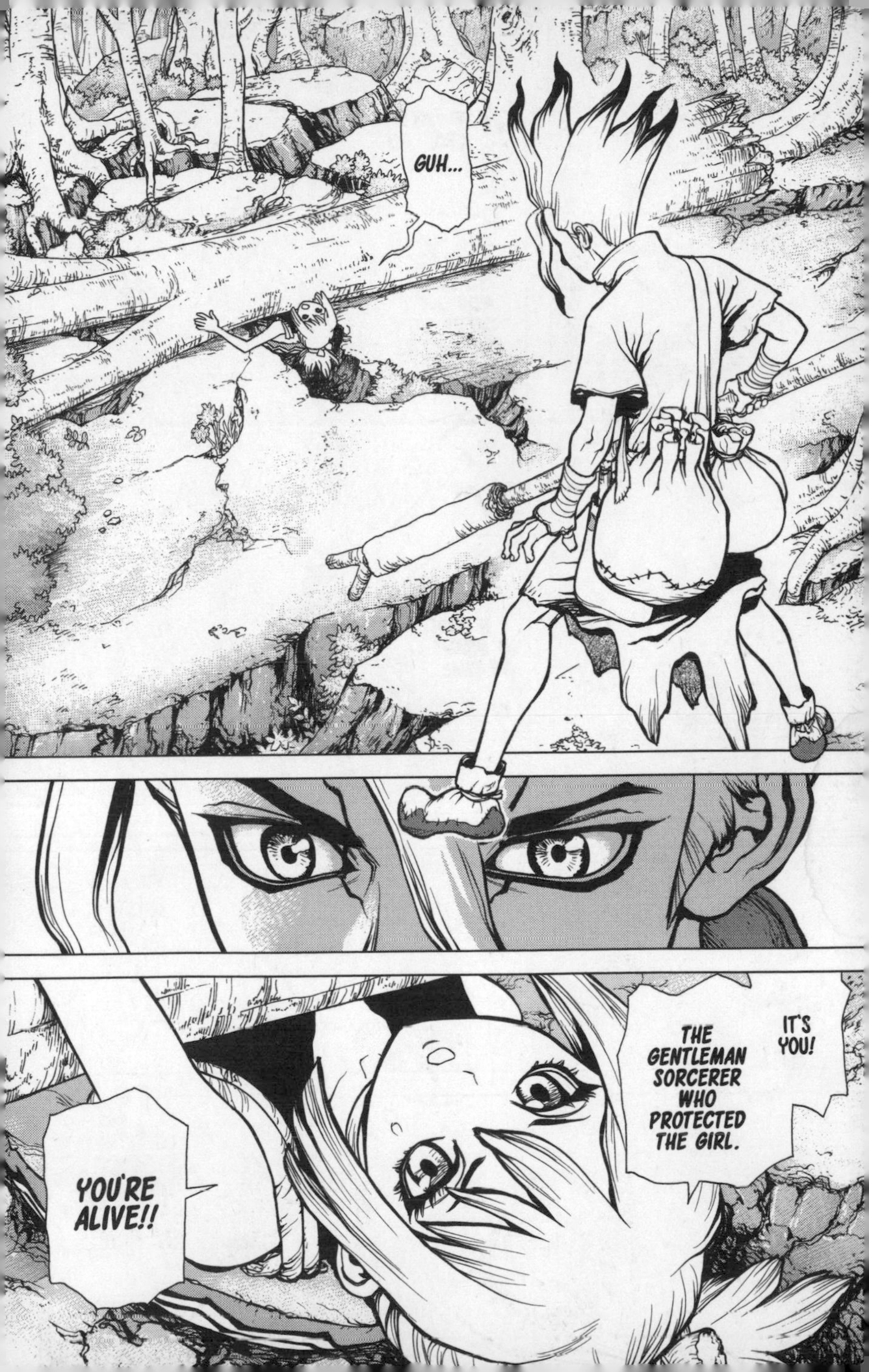
GUH...
IT'S YOU!
THE GENTLEMAN SORCERER WHO PROTECTED THE GIRL.
YOU'RE ALIVE!!

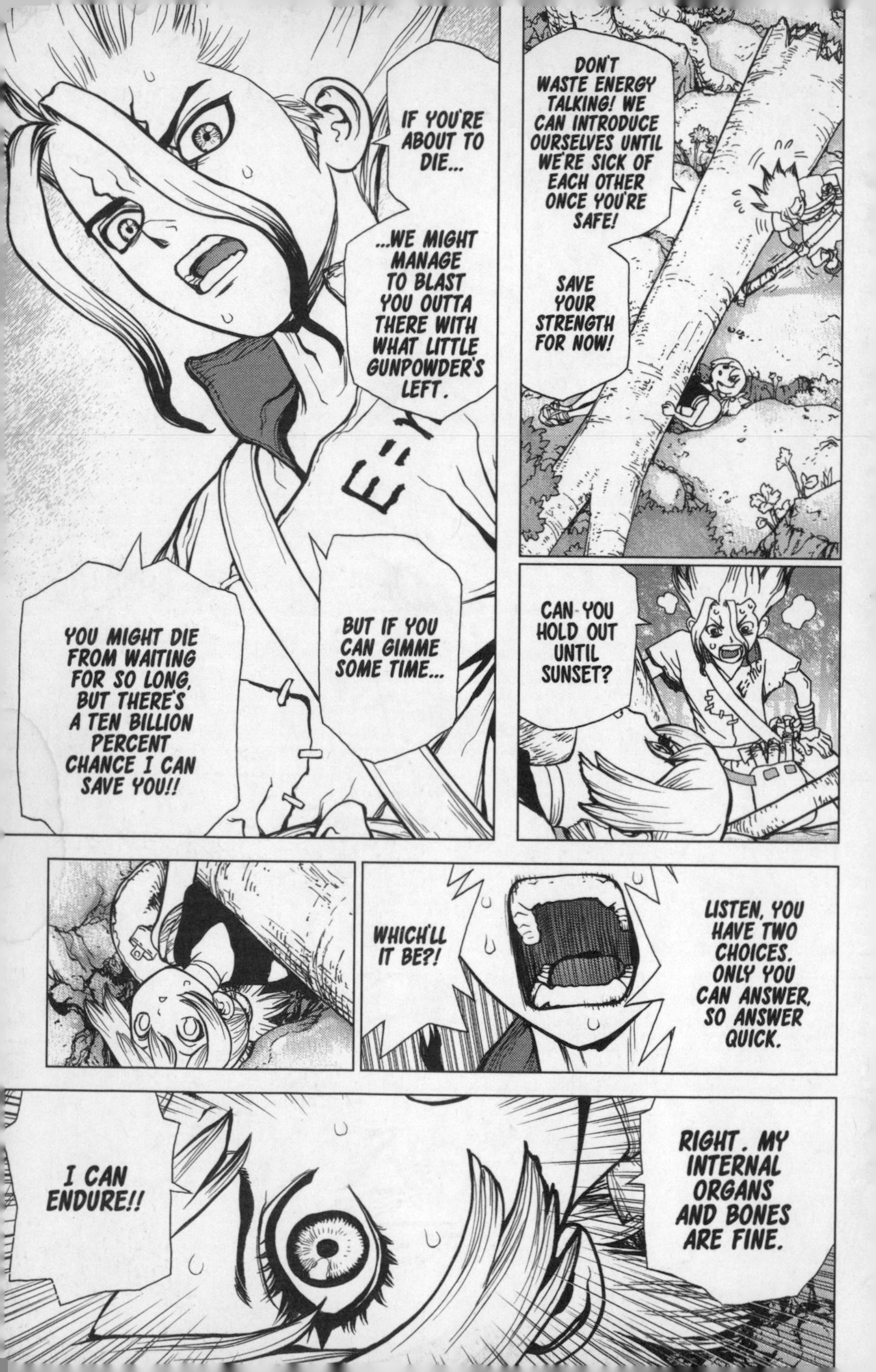
DON'T WASTE ENERGY TALKING! WE CAN INTRODUCE OURSELVES UNTIL WE'RE SICK OF EACH OTHER ONCE YOU'RE SAFE!
SAVE YOUR STRENGTH FOR NOW!
CAN YOU HOLD OUT UNTIL SUNSET?
IF YOU'RE ABOUT TO DIE...
...WE MIGHT MANAGE TO BLAST YOU OUTTA THERE WITH WHAT LITTLE GUNPOWDER'S LEFT.
BUT IF YOU CAN GIMME SOME TIME...
YOU MIGHT DIE FROM WAITING FOR SO LONG, BUT THERE'S A TEN BILLION PERCENT CHANCE I CAN SAVE YOU!!
LISTEN, YOU HAVE TWO CHOICES. ONLY YOU CAN ANSWER, SO ANSWER QUICK.
WHICH'LL IT BE?!
RIGHT. MY INTERNAL ORGANS AND BONES ARE FINE.
I CAN ENDURE!!

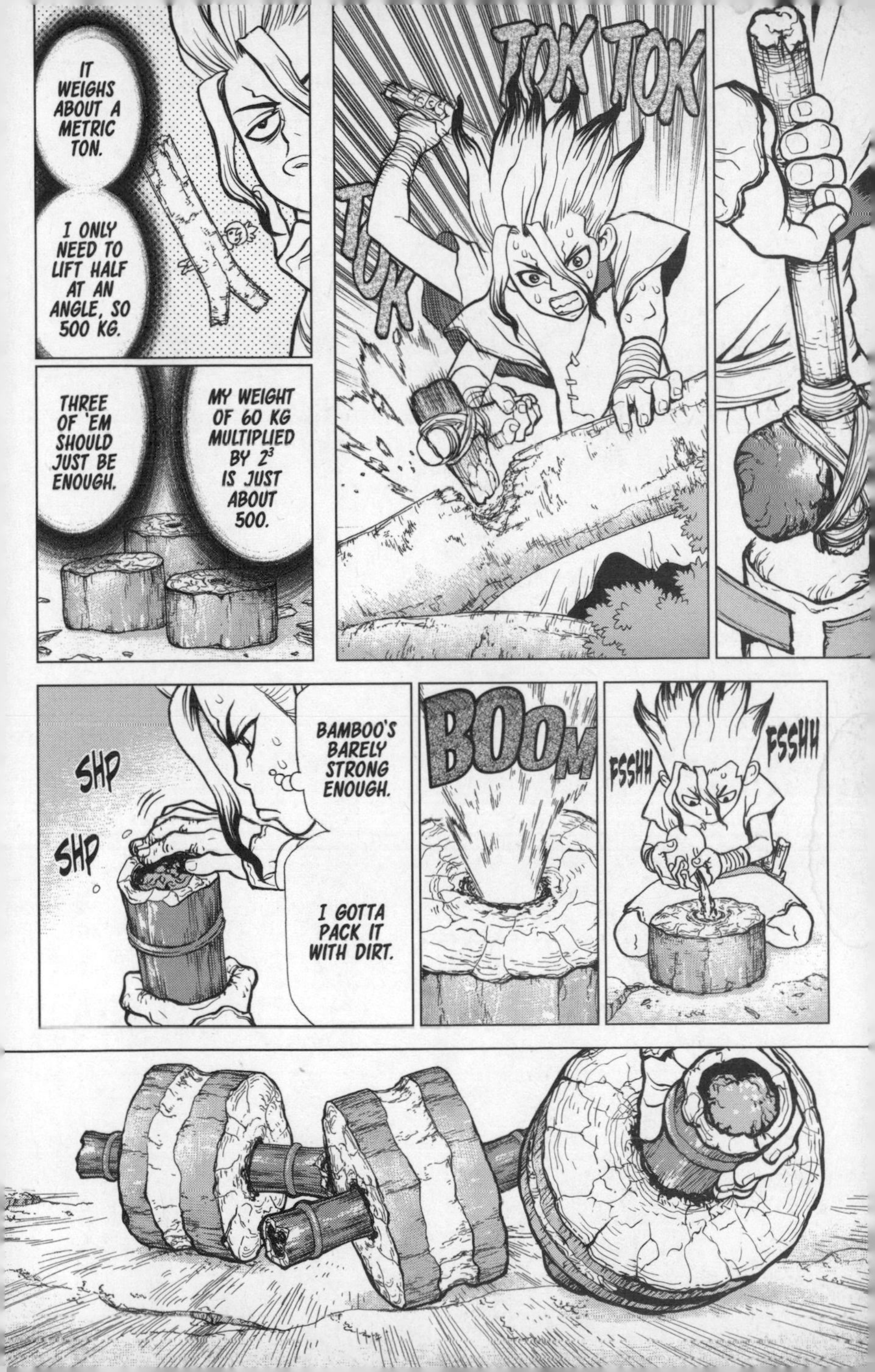
TOK TOK
TOK TOK
IT WEIGHS ABOUT A METRIC TON.
I ONLY NEED TO LIFT HALF AT AN ANGLE, SO 500 KG.
MY WEIGHT OF 60 KG MULTIPLIED BY 2^3 IS JUST ABOUT 500.
THREE OF 'EM SHOULD JUST BE ENOUGH.
FSSHH
FSSHH
BOOM
BAMBOO'S BARELY STRONG ENOUGH.
I GOTTA PACK IT WITH DIRT.
SHP
SHP

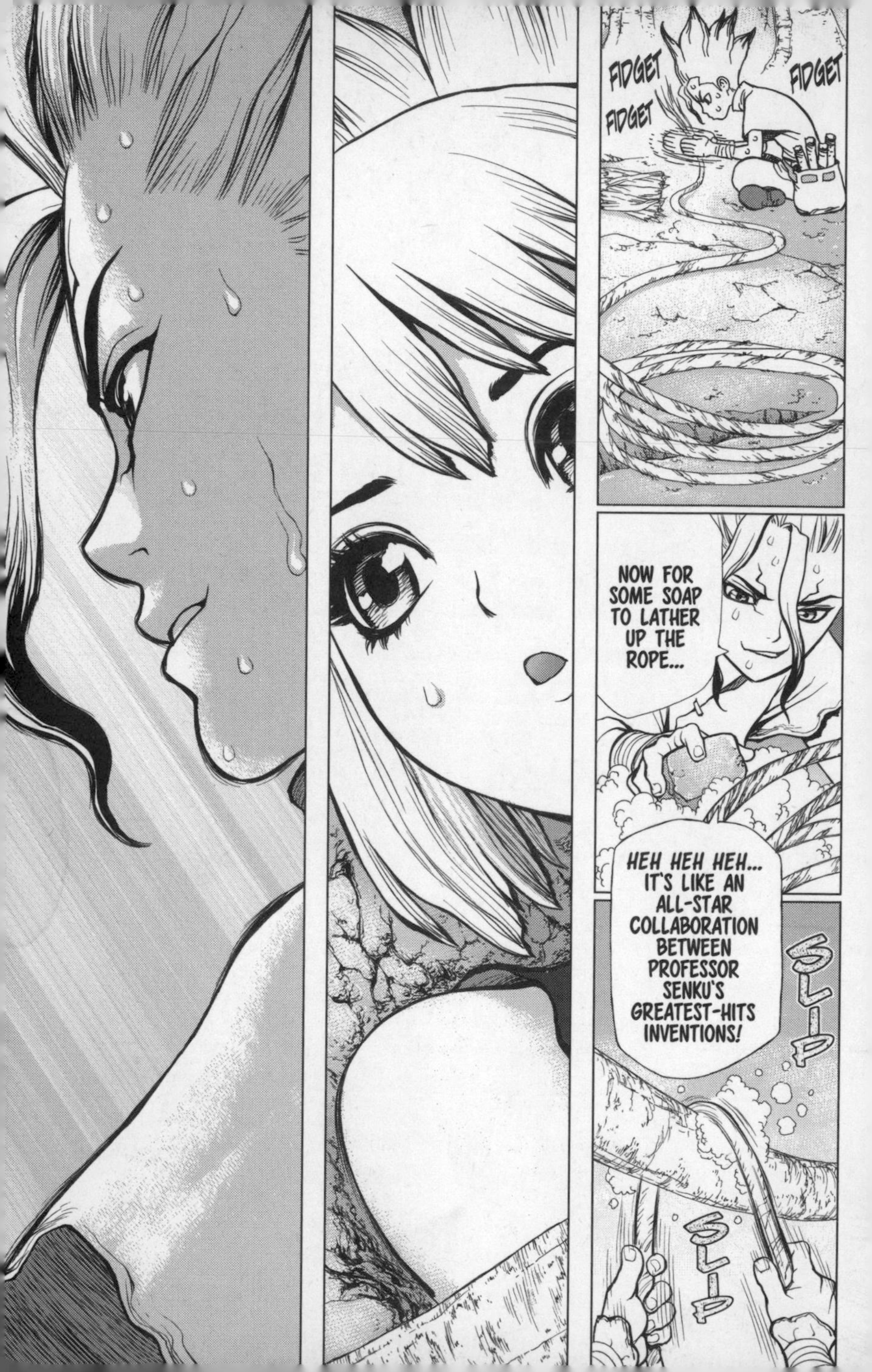
FIDGET
FIDGET
FIDGET
NOW FOR SOME SOAP TO LATHER UP THE ROPE...
HEH HEH HEH... IT'S LIKE AN ALL-STAR COLLABORATION BETWEEN PROFESSOR SENKU'S GREATEST-HITS INVENTIONS!
SLIP
SLIP

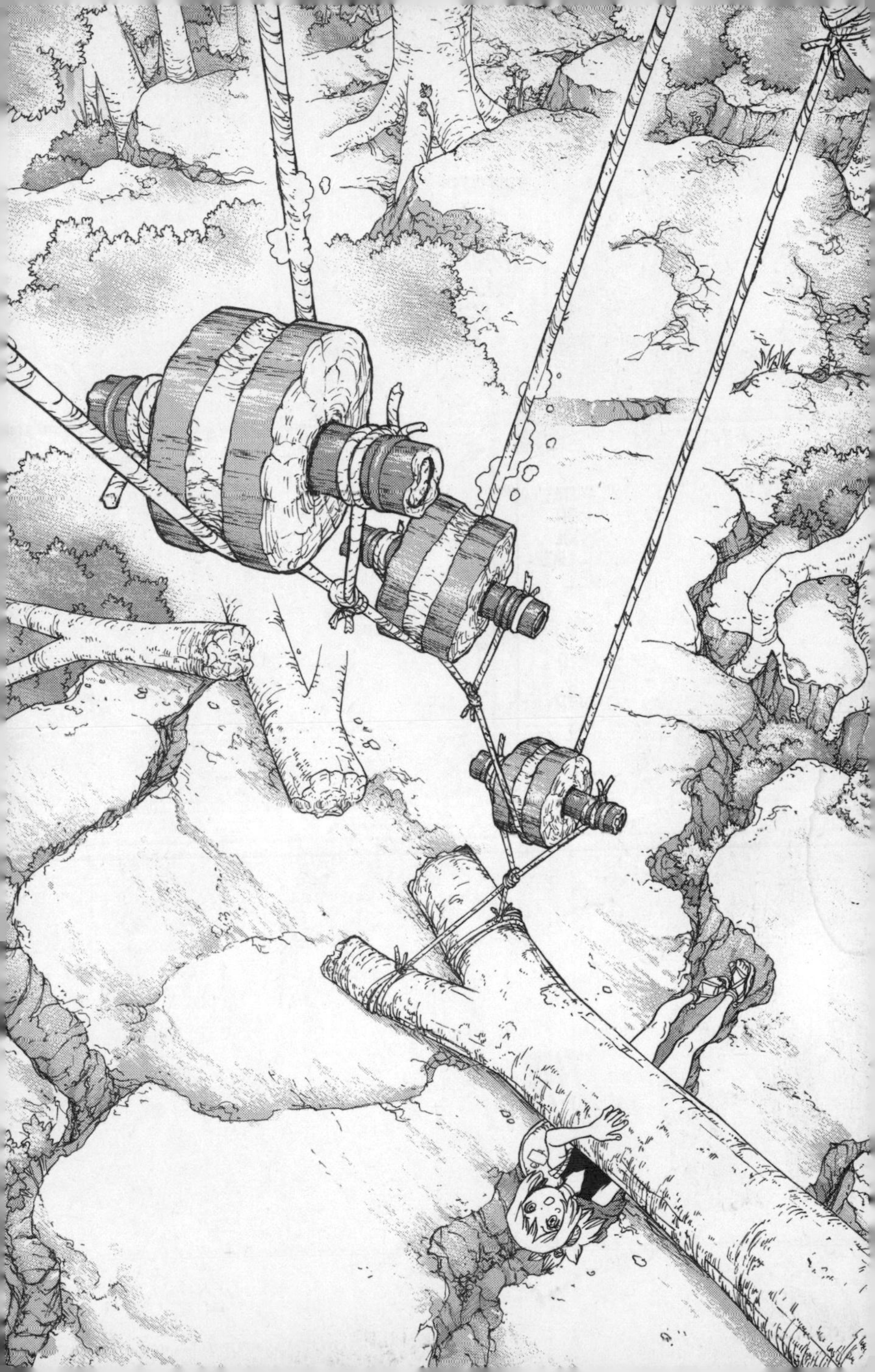

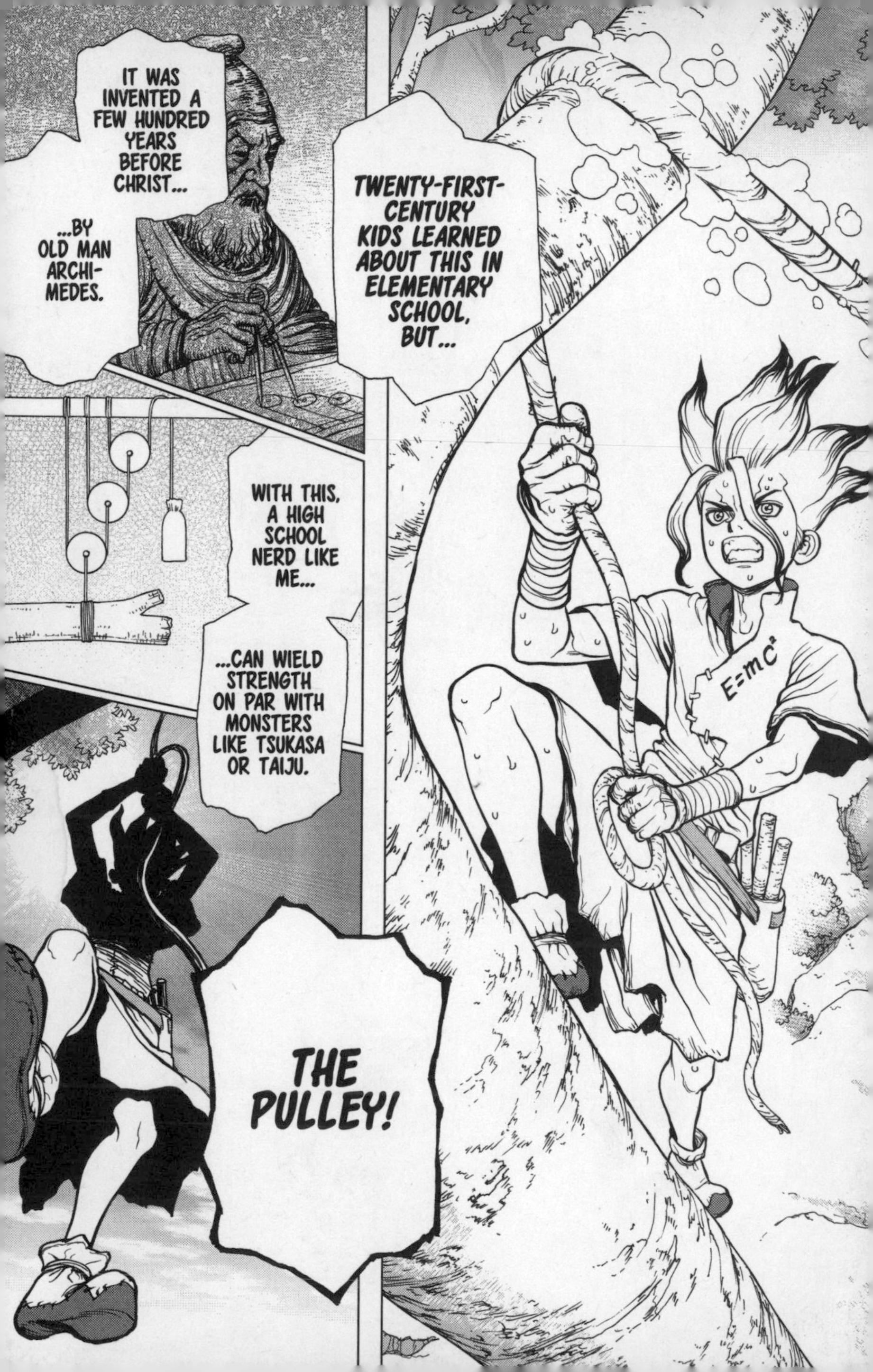
TWENTY-FIRST-CENTURY KIDS LEARNED ABOUT THIS IN ELEMENTARY SCHOOL, BUT...
$E=mc^2$
IT WAS INVENTED A FEW HUNDRED YEARS BEFORE CHRIST...
...BY OLD MAN ARCHIMEDES.
WITH THIS, A HIGH SCHOOL NERD LIKE ME...
...CAN WIELD STRENGTH ON PAR WITH MONSTERS LIKE TSUKASA OR TAIJU.
THE PULLEY!

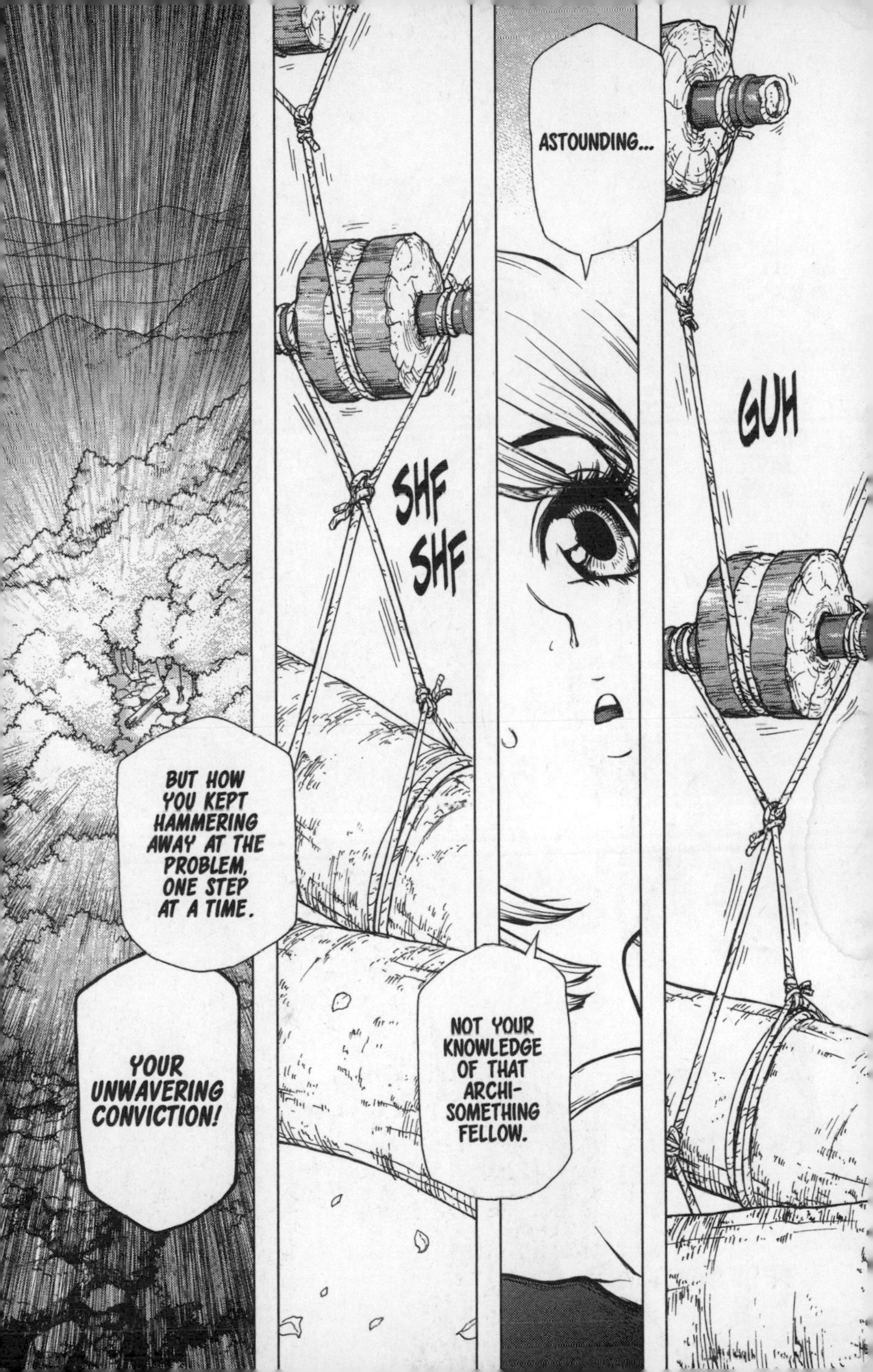
GUH
ASTOUNDING...
NOT YOUR KNOWLEDGE OF THAT ARCHI-SOMETHING FELLOW.
SHF SHF
BUT HOW YOU KEPT HAMMERING AWAY AT THE PROBLEM, ONE STEP AT A TIME.
YOUR UNWAVERING CONVICTION!

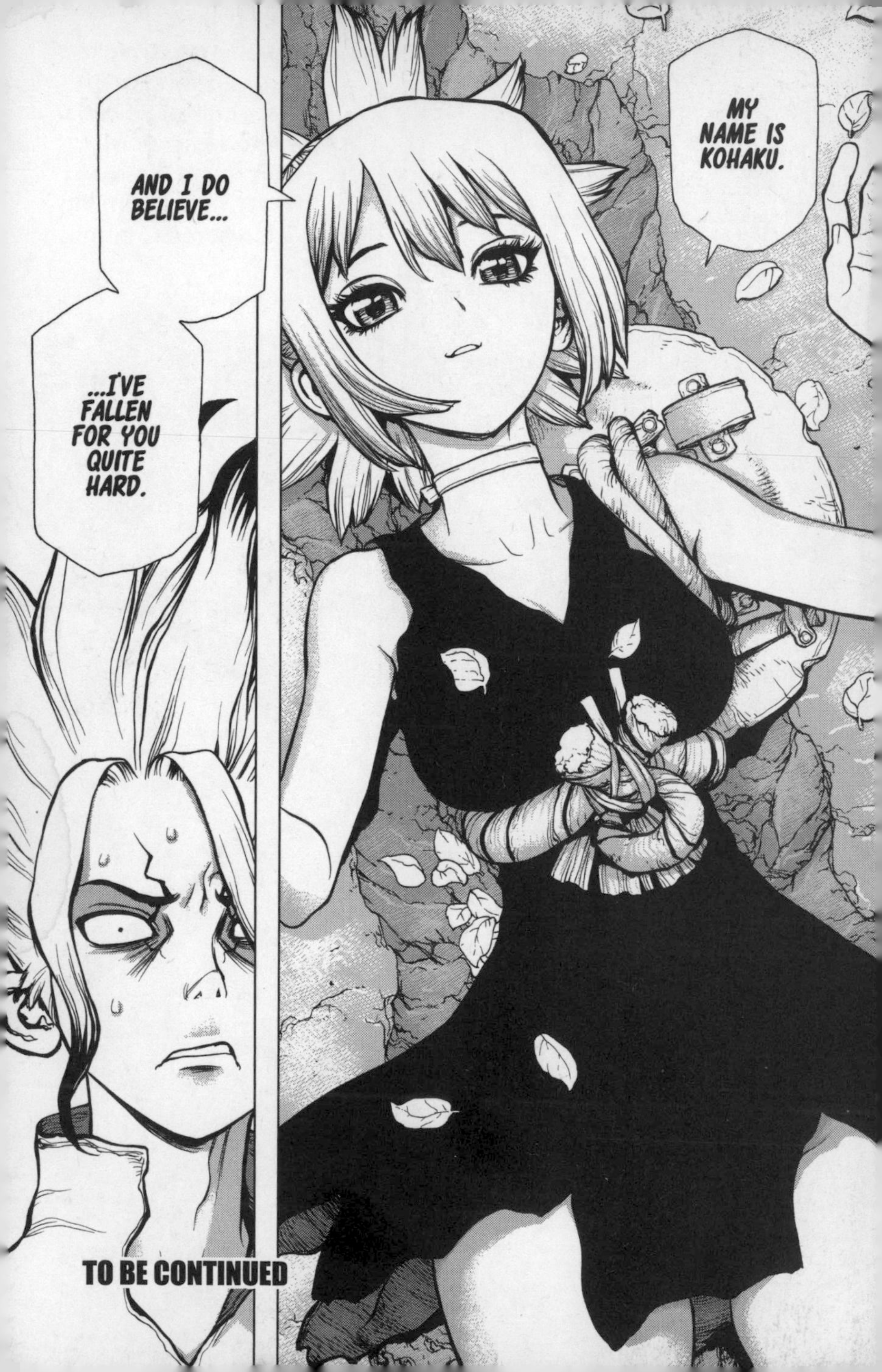
MY NAME IS KOHAKU.
AND I DO BELIEVE...
...I'VE FALLEN FOR YOU QUITE HARD.
TO BE CONTINUED

Ruby, Weiss, Blake and Yang are students at Beacon Academy, learning to protect the world of Remnant from the fearsome Grimm!

RWBY

MANGA BY **Shirow Miwa**
BASED ON THE ROOSTER TEETH SERIES
CREATED BY **Monty Oum**

RATED T TEEN

VIZ
viz.com

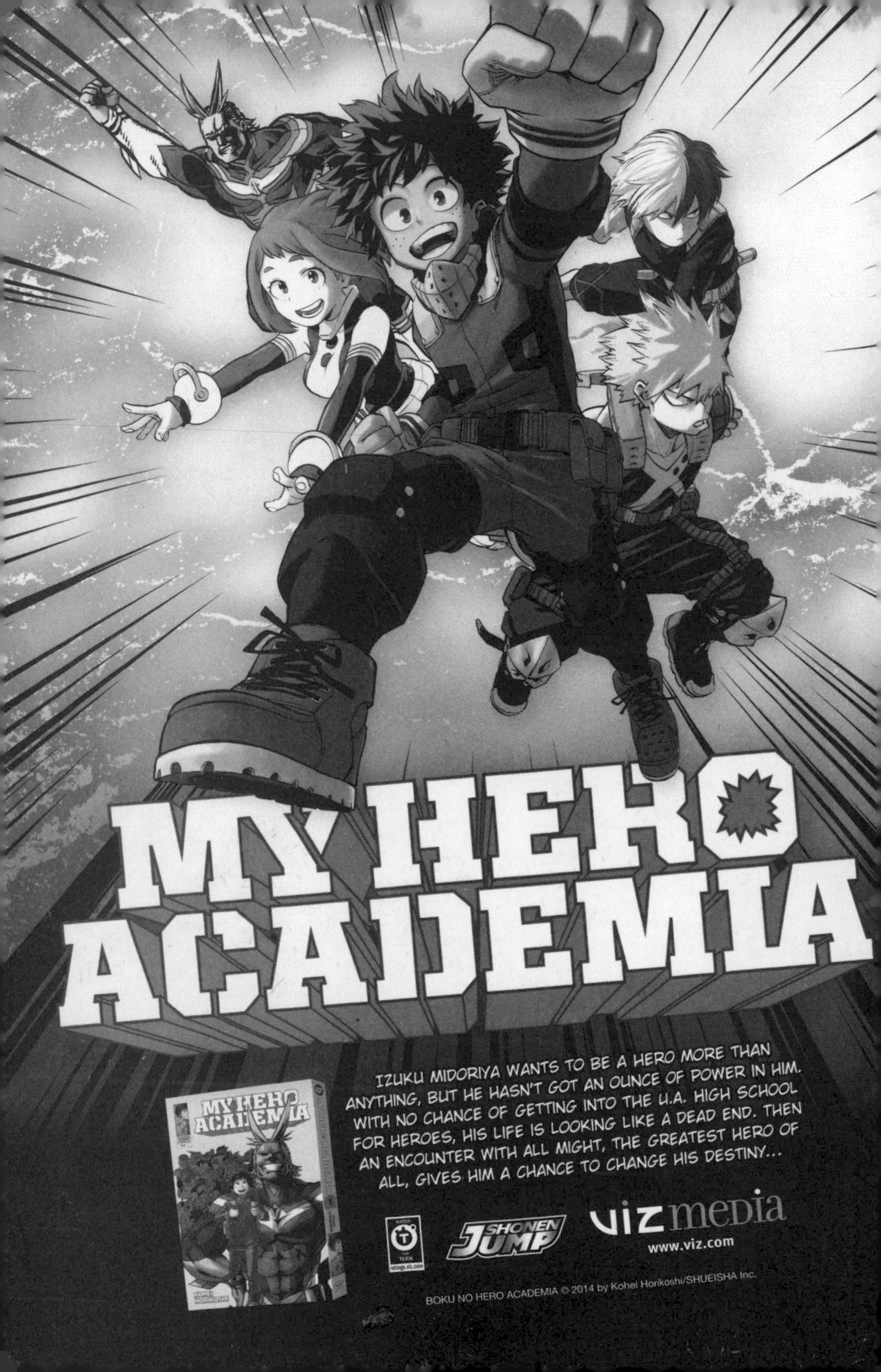
MY HERO ACADEMIA
IZUKU MIDORIYA WANTS TO BE A HERO MORE THAN ANYTHING, BUT HE HASN'T GOT AN OUNCE OF POWER IN HIM. WITH NO CHANCE OF GETTING INTO THE U.A. HIGH SCHOOL FOR HEROES, HIS LIFE IS LOOKING LIKE A DEAD END. THEN AN ENCOUNTER WITH ALL MIGHT, THE GREATEST HERO OF ALL, GIVES HIM A CHANCE TO CHANGE HIS DESTINY...
MY HERO ACADEMIA
KOHEI HORIKOSHI
RATED T TEEN
ratings.viz.com
SHONEN JUMP
VIZ media
www.viz.com
BOKU NO HERO ACADEMIA © 2014 by Kohei Horikoshi/SHUEISHA Inc.

YOU'RE READING THE WRONG WAY

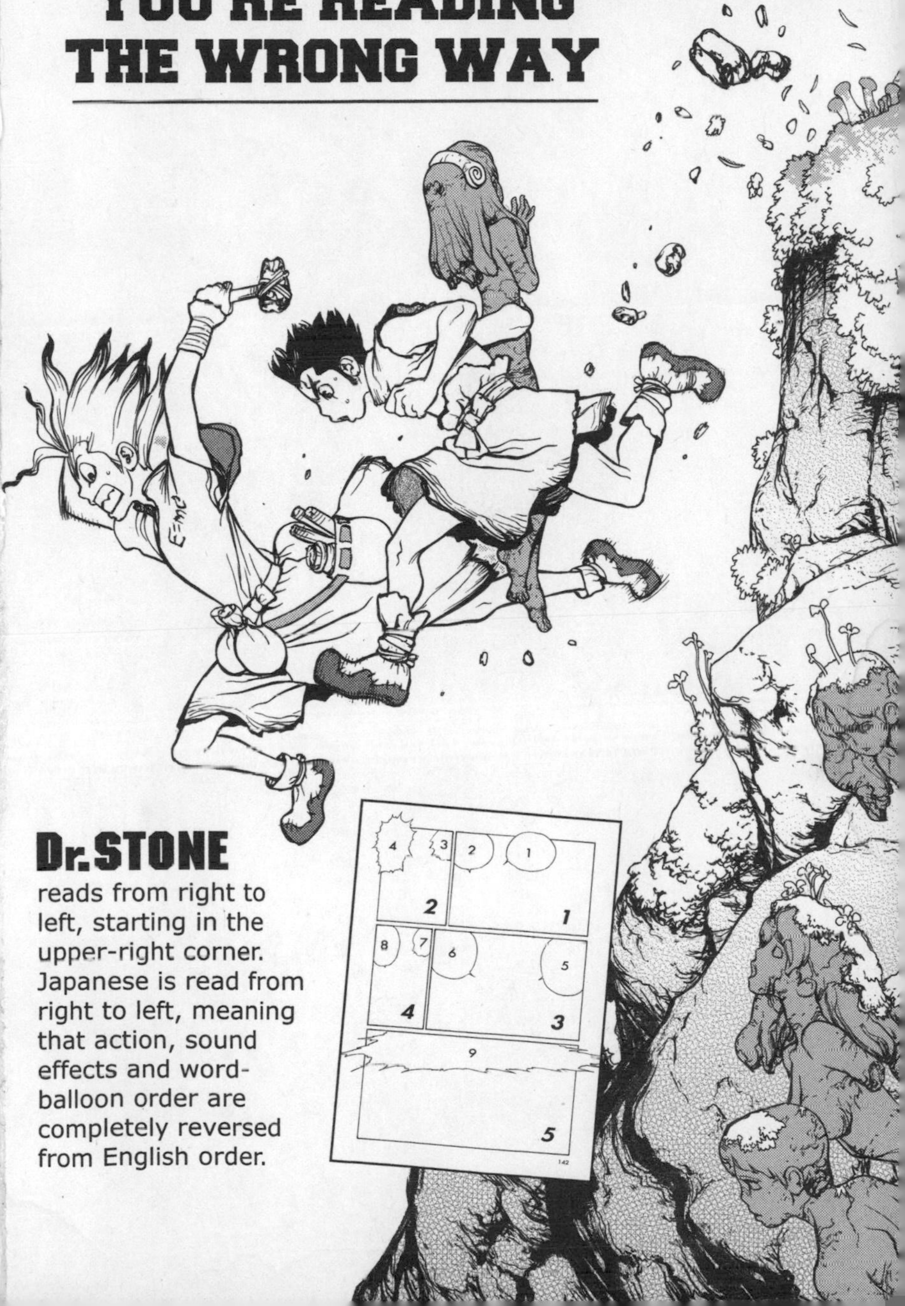

Dr. STONE

reads from right to left, starting in the upper-right corner. Japanese is read from right to left, meaning that action, sound effects and word-balloon order are completely reversed from English order.

1
1
2
2
3
4
3
5
6
4
7
8
5
9
142